EUROPE BY TRAIN

Katharine Wood-de Winne was born in Edinburgh in 1960 of Belgian and English parents. She was educated there, reading communications, then English language and literature after leaving school. Interspersed with working as a public relations consultant she travelled extensively by train in Europe and North Africa, and in 1981 she started full-time research for this guide. In between travelling she lives in the Highlands of Scotland with her husband and young child, and works as a freelance writer.

George McDonald was born in Dumfries, Galloway, in 1955 and was educated at Fettes College and Edinburgh University. He developed a taste for train travel after a journey on the world's highest railway in Peru and a trip through the Soviet Union. Subsequently he has divided his time between working on the family farm and travelling widely in Europe.

KATIE WOOD AND GEORGE McDONALD

EUROPE BY TRAIN
THE COMPLETE GUIDE TO INTER RAILING

FONTANA PAPERBACKS

This revised edition first published in 1985 by
Fontana Paperbacks, 8 Grafton Street, London W1X 3LA
Original edition published by Penguin Books Ltd, 1983

The maps, drawn by Illustra of Reading, are based on
Thomas Cook's Rail Map of Europe.

Set in Linotron Times
Reproduced, printed and bound in Great Britain by
Hazell Watson & Viney Limited,
Member of the BPCC Group,
Aylesbury, Bucks

CONTENTS

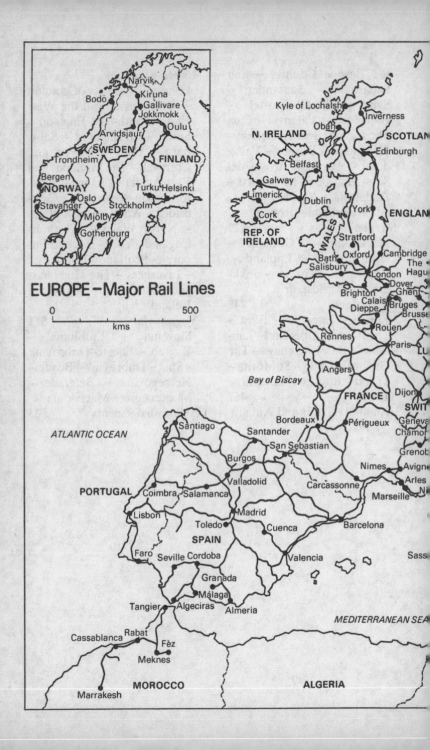

EUROPE – Major Rail Lines

0   500

kms

WHAT THIS GUIDE'S ABOUT

What makes us different from other guidebooks on Europe is that we're train orientated and economy minded. As eurorailers we travelled in every country as extensively and cheaply as possible collecting material for this book. This is the only guide of its kind giving train and station information, as well as accommodation and the sights. It was written because we, like thousands of others, needed a book like this and it didn't exist. Now it's here we hope you'll be able to learn from our mistakes and benefit from our experiences. We tell you of the finds we've made when going round Europe ourselves in recent years and explain the different ways of using the various rail passes which offer an exceptional opportunity to see the sights, meet new people and broaden your horizons – all for an amazingly low price.

• **Prices and exchange rates:** Because these fluctuate, we can only give a rough guide. As a reference this book uses £1 = $1.30, but this rate and all the prices mentioned are subject to change.

INTRODUCTION

For my part, I travel not to go anywhere, but to go. I travel for travel's sake. The great affair is to move; to feel the needs and hitches of our life more nearly; to come down off this feather-bed of civilization, and find the globe granite underfoot and strewn with cutting flints.

ROBERT LOUIS STEVENSON, *Travels with a Donkey in the Cevennes*

Anything is possible on a train, a great meal, a binge, a visit from card players, an intrigue, a good night's sleep, and strange monologues framed like Russian short stories.

PAUL THEROUX, *The Great Railway Bazaar*

We're taking it for granted that the vast majority of eurorailers are looking for the most competitive prices in accommodation and food to get the very most out of their meagre budgets. While this is the main motivation behind this book, it should be borne in mind that you're meant to be enjoying yourself, and if you try to rough it too much or for too long you'll grow disillusioned with the seamy side of Europe that goes along with rough living. If you know where to look, cheap hotels or hostels or campsites can be found, as can good supermarkets and eating places – thus leaving you as much time as possible to see the sights on a full stomach secure in the knowledge that you've somewhere to stay the night. We've met far too many fellow travellers who have spent the best part of their holiday walking round the wrong part of town on an empty stomach and with a heavy rucksack.

Preplanning should not be regarded as a constriction on your flexibility. There's nothing to stop you changing your plans while you're away but, with a little well-structured forethought, you can ensure you see everything you'd ideally like to, and don't waste precious time waiting in the long tourist and train-information queues. It's also a good idea to do a bit of background reading to keep the myriad of sights in perspective. We recommend Lord Clark's *Civilisation*, but most cultural histories will serve the same purpose.

In Part One you'll find information on different aspects of eurorailing which will be of interest to everyone, regardless of your routes. Following this there are individual chapters on the countries of Europe in alphabetical order; these follow the pattern you're best advised to take from the minute you step off the train at your chosen destination. We'll guide you to the accommodation service, the campsites, hostels and hotels, the tourist information office, the eating places, and then the sights themselves. On pages 76–7 you'll find a brief vocabulary section.

We hope you find this book a useful addition to your rucksack and will let us know how it goes. Good eurorailing!

Part One: EURORAILING

The advantages of train travel

Besides the fact that eurorailing is a real bargain, there are many advantages to travelling by train which make your European travels more pleasurable. The train is without doubt the safest, most convenient and interesting means of transport to really uncover some hidden corners of Europe that hitch-hiking can never show you. You can cover a lot of ground in a very short time – you leave from, and arrive at, stations which are invariably in city centres; and you don't lay yourself open to the vagaries of the weather – trains are very rarely cancelled due to fog or rain. You also cut out the inevitable traffic jams you would land in if you van round the roads of Europe in the high season. The advantages of eurorailing over hitching are numerous, but the main one is clear: you can rely on getting to your destination and can thus cram far more into your trip. All in all, there are virtually no tourist centres in Europe that cannot be conveniently reached by rail, and even if there were, there's always buses or bikes at the nearest station.

Believe it or not, the train (assuming you take a high-speed express and not a local shunt-about) can actually travel faster than a plane on a distance of under 400 miles, allowing for the time it takes to commute to and from airports. If you're on a long journey, the train allows you to walk about and stretch your legs, and to go for a meal or a snack when you please. You'll also find trains a wonderful meeting-place to chat to people, both the locals and other euro-railers. It's almost impossible to make a trip on one of the popular routes in a summer month and not end up swapping stories with groups of fellow travellers. On overnight journeys, the intimacy of the train compartment makes it *quite* impossible!

Almost all European trains are diesel- or electric-driven, and most are government-owned (the main exceptions being some lines in Switzerland). A long-distance international train may use rolling stock from several countries along its route, so it pays to discover quickly what each country's carriages look like, and head for the good ones (i.e. the Swiss, German or any of the Scandinavian ones) when the train rolls in.

Every year the main roads of Europe become more and more congested and road improvements move at a slow pace, compared to the investments continually being made on the European rail networks. In northern Europe, second-class seats today are comparable with the first-class ones of twenty years ago. Speeds of 125 m.p.h. and more are common now in France, Britain and Germany; as networks expand, new and simplified routes emerge, allowing you greater choice as to the particular part of the country you'd like to travel through in order to get to your final destination.

Anyone who has travelled by train in North America will notice the difference straight away. European trains are faster, more plentiful and more punctual, serving many more destinations. Historically the European networks have not been maintained on a profit-making basis – few networks actually 'make' any money. They are essentially a public service, and the Inter Rail/Eurail pass is a good measure of this. For example, for the £115 (1984 price) the Inter Rail ticket costs, you end up with an average saving of £200–400 off the fares you'd normally have to pay, and even these are subsidized at source so, economically speaking, you can't really go wrong.

From the environmentalist's point of view, trains are good news when you bear in mind they consume up to seventeen times less energy than aircraft, and five times less than cars, to transport the same volume. Per square foot, a train can carry more people than cars can – and without the same pollution problems.

One of the main beauties of eurorailing – and one of the main pleasures you'll look back on – is the immense feeling of freedom you enjoy. It's entirely up to you where you spend your time, when you move on to somewhere else, and how you choose to get there. It's quite a heady feeling, never really knowing where you'll be this time tomorrow. To preserve this, it's advisable not to book too many hotels, hostels or trains ahead of time – if you bother to book any. However, to counteract the negative side-effects of total flexibility, it's a good idea to arrive in the major cities as early in the morning as possible in order to get yourself a bed for the night. Get to the tourist accommodation office (often on the station premises) before noon if you possibly can, otherwise you might end up having to spend precious sightseeing time searching for a room. Nearly every town has affordable places to stay within a few blocks of the station so don't worry, you will not have to walk far.

Eurorailing: the alternatives

Basically there are three schemes you can choose from: a BIJ (Billet International de Jeunesse) ticket, an individual country pass or an Inter Rail/Eurail, depending on where you live. BIJ operates under the auspices of the continental railways and offers reduced fares to the under 26s. Transalpino and Eurotrain are the two largest companies in this scheme. They offer fares to over 2,000 destinations in Europe and North Africa, with discounts of up to 50 per cent. As they allow you to break your journey anywhere you want on the route you've chosen, you have the flexibility to use your ticket as a sightseeing pass, so it's important to pick the route which takes in the places you most want to see. There are seven or eight routings to some cities, so it's possible to go one way and return another; for example, if your final destination is to be Rome, you could go out via Paris, the south of France and Genoa, and on the return stop off in Florence, Innsbruck, Munich and Belgium. The extra cost in taking two singles is only £5–10 ($7–14), and it lets you see a lot more of Europe. Don't let price be your only consideration when deciding which company to choose – Transalpino offers seven routes to Athens while Eurotrain offers three, and the price difference is minimal. Transalpino and Eurotrain prices can vary by any amount from £1 ($1.30) to £67 ($87), depending on where you want to go. Wherever you're heading for, get both companies' leaflets, just to be on the safe side.

The price of 'add-on' fares (to get you to London from your home town) is considerably cheaper with Transalpino and Transalpino tickets can be issued from any British Rail station. Before committing yourself, however, always check that British Rail aren't offering an even cheaper fare to London – but bear in mind that these concessions are usually only for restricted services, whereas Transalpino's ticket is good for all trains to London. Another tip: don't overlook the coach services to London, especially if you're travelling down from Scotland.

At the end of the day, it all depends on where you want to go and how much distance you intend to cover: an Inter Rail/Eurail would undoubtedly work out better value if you want to do the grand tour of Europe, from Copenhagen to Casablanca. Both Transalpino and

Eurotrain sell Inter Rails through their offices anyway; their staff, who are generally very helpful, will advise you which scheme would work out cheapest. Before you rush out to buy any pass, do your research to find out if it will save you money. Add up the total second-class fares for the major routes you plan to cover (or get a travel agent to do it for you). If the sum comes near the price of the pass, the convenience of the pass is nearly always worth the extra.

• **Group travel:** Ten or more constitute a group, as far as Transalpino and Eurotrain are concerned. This allows you all to travel at still further reductions. Transalpino offers a free ticket to one party member, once you've got more than fifteen travelling. The group leader needn't be under 26, and if you've anyone under 14, he/she gets a further discount. Transalpino has a group brochure available, listing package-type deals for groups, some of which are multi-centre holidays. Further information from Transalpino Group Department (01–828 6440/6421) or Eurotrain (01–730 8111).

INTER RAIL

• **Quick history:** The Inter Rail scheme was thought up by the UIC (the Union of International Railways) in 1972. It was devised to commemorate fifty years of international transport law; its price is decided upon each year at a conference of all participating countries. In 1982, over 270,000 British Inter Rails were sold; since then, dramatic increases in the number of purchasers have taken place and the scheme has become widespread and popular.

• **What is Inter Rail?** It is a ticket anyone living in Europe under the age of 26 can buy; it allows you to travel an unlimited distance for one calendar month on the rail networks of nineteen European countries, and in the country of purchase at half price. The price fluctuates each year, but it's usually round about the £120 ($160) mark.

With an Inter Rail you can travel free in the following countries: Austria, Belgium, France, Denmark, Finland, Greece, Hungary, Italy, Luxembourg, Morocco, the Netherlands, Norway, Portugal, Romania, Spain, Sweden, Switzerland, Ireland, Turkey, the United Kingdom, West Germany and Yugoslavia. As you can see, this allows the Inter Railer to visit the vast majority of European countries, either taking in as much as possible on a whistle-stop tour or concentrating on areas with particular appeal to the individual.

• **Who qualifies?** Anyone under the age of 26 on the first day the pass becomes valid – and it's up to you to decide when it will start and finish. You must hold a passport of a country participating in the scheme or be able to prove residence for over six months.

• **Before you begin:** Once you've bought your ticket, it's a good idea to take an independent note of its number: even though no replacements are issued, it helps for tracing purposes. If you want to travel for more than a month, buy two or more tickets at a time, getting the dates to run consecutively.

• **Rebates:** When you return home, take your Inter Rail pass back to the station where you bought it and you'll get a rebate; it varies from year to year, but it's around £2–2.50. The train authorities use the information (where you travelled on your Inter Rail, etc.) for market research.

• **Reductions:** An Inter Rail pass bought in the UK entitles you to half-price travel on British and Northern Ireland trains and on the ferry services to the continental ports, including Seaspeed hovercraft. Reductions on some of the private European railways are also granted, and these include most of the Swiss mountain railways. For real train buffs, the Inter Rail gets you a reduction on admission into the various transport museums of Europe.
1. *Europabus* have an agreement with the Inter Rail scheme by which they give a 25–50 per cent reduction on many of their runs. These tend to be slow but scenic and the best ones are mainly in France, the south of Italy, Sicily and Switzerland as they often cover areas not on the main rail network and go through small, out-of-the-way places. If you want further information, pick up a Europabus route-planner – but don't forget: they get busy in summer, so reserve ahead.
2. *Ferries:* Half-price concessions are available on Sealink and B & I ships; you can also obtain reduced rates on many continental services (the ones marked by a broken red line on the Inter Rail map). Also, since 1984 the Irish Continental line from Rosslare to Cherbourg or Le Havre offers 50 per cent reductions. See also the individual countries later in this book.

If you need help with travel arrangements you can get in touch with one of the British Rail offices listed below:

AUSTRIA
Weidnerhauptstrasse 5,
Vienna 4.
(Tel. 222 650 336)

BELGIUM
Rue de la Montagne 52,
1000 Brussels.
(Tel. 332-511-6685)

DENMARK
Montergade 5,
DK-1116 Copenhagen K.
(Tel. 12-64-60)

FRANCE
Boulevard de la
Madeleine 12,
F75009 Paris.
(Tel. 266-90-53)
33, Rue de Tournai,
F59043 Lille.
(Tel. 20-06-29-44)

GERMANY
Neue-Mainzer-Strasse 22,
D6000 Frankfurt/Main 1.
(Tel. 23 23 81)
Neuer Wall 86,
2000 Hamburg 36.
Bismarck Strasse 27,
D4000 Düsseldorf.

HOLLAND
(Information)
Leidseplein 5,
1017PR Amsterdam.
(Tel. 23 41 33)
(Reservations)
Harwich Ferry
Agentur BV
Postbus 4 Hoek van
Holland.
(Tel. 01747-4140)

ITALY
Via Pirelli 11,
20124 Milan.
(Tel. 661-683)
Via S. Eufemia 5,
00187 Rome.
(Tel. 678-49-27)

SPAIN
Torre de Madrid 26/3,
Plaza de España,
Madrid 13.
(Tel. 2424141)

SWITZERLAND
Centralbahnplatz 9,
CH4002 Basel.
(Tel. 23-14-04 or
23-14-03)
Limmatquai 78,
CH8001 Zürich.
(Tel. 47-99-38)

N.B. In the UK, Inter Rails can only be bought from British Rail stations or through authorized BR agents. Do not attempt to get one on the black market as the railway authorities do very rigorous checks now, and you'll just end up being packed off home early, not to mention the local repercussions against you.

EURAIL

• **Quick history:** Basically, Eurail came into existence because Europe had a new and expensive network of intercity trains that needed riders. Its purpose was to entice potential passengers from the other side of the Atlantic, by offering two months of unlimited second-class travel on any or all of the member rail systems. The first pass was issued in 1959 when 5,000 tickets were sold. Later developments were one- and three-month passes, 15-day passes, first-class passes and such fringe benefits as free access to many ferry and steamer connections and free or discounted bus transportation. In addition, the 21-day pass was developed in 1966 to complement air excursion fares.

Finally, the Eurail Youthpass was brought into existence for anyone under the age of 26, to capture the market of students who were making use of cheaper transatlantic air fares. Altogether, more than 2.6 million tickets have been sold, 180,000 in 1982 alone.

The value and enjoyment of eurorailing soon became apparent as Europe developed its own Youthpass system (Inter Rail), followed closely by the individual country passes.

• **What is the Eurail Youthpass?** It is an unlimited-mileage pass available to anyone who can prove they are under 26 years old on the first day of travel. The price of one month's travel is £223 ($290), and for two months, £285 ($370). The ticket may be purchased and used only if you reside outside Europe or North Africa.

Eurail Pass and Eurail Youthpass are personal and non-transferable. They are forfeited if presented by anyone other than the person for whom they were issued, or if they bear any evidence of alteration or mutilation. Presentation of a passport to European train personnel is compulsory. Therefore, if the issuing agent has made a mess-up with the spelling of your name, don't use it, but return it to the issuing office and get another. Your pass is valid until midnight of the last day of validity so be sure to take a train scheduled to arrive at your destination before midnight.

A Eurail Youthpass is valid in second class exclusively. This entitles you to unlimited travel on the national railroads (except on special chartered trains) and many private rail lines, steamers and ferry crossings of the following countries: Austria, Belgium, Denmark, Finland, France, Greece, Holland, Ireland (Republic of), Italy, Luxembourg, Norway, Portugal, Spain, Sweden, Switzerland and West Germany. It also entitles you to free or reduced travel on buses run by the railway companies. (For a full list of concessions granted to ticket holders, see Eurail Bonuses in the individual country sections.)

Reservation fees, meals, refreshments, sleeping accommodation and port taxes when using some steamers and ferries are not included in the price of the ticket and will have to be paid extra.

It is sometimes obligatory to have a seat reservation (on Spanish express trains, for instance), so check first with station information. Also, a surcharge is required for travelling on some trains (IC, TGV, Rapidos).

From 1 June to 30 September, Adriatica di Navigazione and Hellenic Mediterranean Lines operating between Brindisi and Patras require payment of about £7.75 ($10) high season surcharge. During July and August advanced reservation, which costs about £3.10 ($4), is recommended.

Having a Eurail Youthpass does not guarantee a seat on a train nor space on ships unless a reservation has been secured in advance.

• **Refunds:** A Eurail Youthpass is not refundable if lost or stolen. It can only be replaced after having been validated, and provided the validation slip can be presented at time of replacement to a Eurail Aid Office. Any refund, if granted, is subject to a deduction of about 15 per cent from the price of the ticket.

• **What is the Eurail Pass?** It's the adult equivalent of the Youthpass, and has no age restrictions placed on it. It's a first-class go-as-you-please pass with prices of $266 for 15 days, $330 for 21 days, $410 for one month, $560 for two months and $680 for three months. These are available from the same outlets as the Youthpass.

• **Where to buy your Eurail:** Eurail Passes must be bought outside Europe. Nearly every travel agent in North America and Canada will be able to supply you with a pass. For more information contact CIEE (Council on International Educational Exchange), 205 East 42nd Street, New York, NY 10017, or CUTS (Canadian Universities Travel Service), 44 St George Street, Toronto, Ontario M5S 2E4.

• **Before you begin:** The pass must be used within six months of purchase, and must be validated before use by a railway official who will enter the first and last dates the pass can be used. It is important to get this done when buying the pass as validating it on board a train costs $5 extra. Rip out the counterfoil card from the pass as soon as you get it, and carry it separately and in a safe place. If you lose the pass you'll need this counterfoil as proof before a replacement can be issued, and if a railway official checks your Eurail during the trip this is considered your confirmation of ownership.

Eurail Aid Offices are there to help you if you have any problems.

They also stock timetables and maps free of charge and can be found at the following stations:

AUSTRIA
ÖBB
Wien Westbahnhof
A–1150 **Vienna**

ÖBB
Salzburg Haptbahnhof
A–5010 **Salzburg**

ÖBB
Innsbruck Hauptbahnhof
A–6010 **Innsbruck**

BELGIUM
Société Nationale des
Chemins de fer
belges
Salon d'Accueil
Service International
Gare de Bruxelles-Midi
Brussels 1070

DENMARK
DSB Travel Agency
Central Station
Banegärdspladsen
DK–1570 **Copenhagen**

FINLAND
Valtionrautatiet
Rautatieasema
VR Lipputoimisto
SF–00100 **Helsinki 10**

FRANCE
Société Nationale des
Chemins de fer
français
Service International
Gare de Paris-St Lazare
F–75008 **Paris**

Société Nationale des
Chemins de fer
français
Bureau Information-
Réservation
Gare de Paris-Nord
F–75010 **Paris**

Société Nationale des
Chemins de fer
français
Bureau SNCF d'Orly
Aéroport
Cedex A 222
F–94396 **Orly-Airport**

Société Nationale des
Chemins de fer
français
Bureau SNCF de Roissy
Aéroport Charles de Gaulle
BP 20215
F–95712 **Roissy Aéroport
Charles de Gaulle**

Société Nationale des
Chemins de fer
français
Guichet 'Billets
Internationaux'
Gare de Marseille St Charles
F–13232 **Marseille**

Société Nationale des
Chemins de fer
français
Gare de Nice-Ville
F–06000 **Nice**

WEST GERMANY
Deutsche Bundesbahn
Fahrkartenausgabe
Hauptbahnhof
D–6 **Frankfurt/Main**

Deutsche Bundesbahn
Fahrkartenausgabe
Hauptbahnhof
D–69 **Heidelberg**

Deutsche Bundesbahn
Fahrkartenausgabe
Hauptbahnhof
D–8 **Munich**

Deutsche Bundesbahn
Fahrkartenausgabe
Hauptbahnhof
D–5 **Cologne**

Deutsche Bundesbahn
Fahrkartenausgabe
Hauptbahnhof
D–7 **Stuttgart**

Deutsche Bundesbahn
Fahrkartenausgabe
Hauptbahnhof
D–2 **Hamburg**

GREAT BRITAIN
French National
Railways
179 Piccadilly
London W1V 0BA

GREECE
Chemins de fer
Hélléniques
Bureau des Voyages et
du Tourisme No.2
1, rue Karolou
Athens 107

Chemins de fer
Hélléniques
Gare Centrale des
Voyageurs
Thessaloniki

IRELAND (Republic of)
Coras Iompair Eireann
International Rail Ticket
Sales Office
35 Lower Abbey Street
Dublin 1

ITALY
Ferrovie Italiane dello
Stato
Stazione Santa Maria
Novella
Officio informazioni
Florence

Ferrovie Italiane dello
Stato
Stazione Centrale
Milan

Ferrovie Italiane dello
Stato
Stazione Santa Lucia
Venice

Ferrovie Italiane dello
Stato
Stazione Termini
Rome

Ferrovie Italiane dello
Stato
Stazione Centrale
Naples

Ferrovie Italiane dello
Stato
Stazione Centrale
Bari

LUXEMBOURG
Société Nationales des
Chemins de fer
Luxembourgeois
Bureau des
renseignements
Gare de Luxembourg
Luxembourg (GD)

NETHERLANDS
N.V. Nederlandse
Spoorwegen
Marketing
Reizigersvervoer
Bureau 13
Kamer 935
Katreinetoren (in the
Hall of Utrecht
Central Station)
Utrecht

NORWAY
NSB Riesebyra
Stortingsgaten 28
Oslo 1

PORTUGAL
Companhia dos
cominhos de
ferro portugueses
Departmento
commercial
Estação de Santa
Apolonia
Lisbon

SPAIN
Red Nacional de los
Ferrocarriles
Españoles
Alcala 44
Madrid

Red Nacional de los
Ferrocarriles
Españoles
Estación central de
Barcelona Sants
Barcelona

Red Nacional de los
Ferrocarriles
Españoles
Martin Villa 5
Sevilla

Red Nacional de los
Ferrocarriles
Españoles
Plaza Alfonso el
Magnanimo 2
Valencia

SWEDEN
Swedish State Railways
Ticket Office
Stockholm Central
Station
S–105-50 **Stockholm**

SWITZERLAND
Schweizerische
Bundesbahnen
Auskunftsbüro
Hauptbahnhof
CH–4051 **Basel**

Schweizerische
Bundesbahnen
Auskunftsbüro
Hauptbahnhof
CH–3000 **Bern**

Chemins de fer
fédéraux suisses
Bureau de
Renseignements CFF
Gare de Genève
CH–1211 **Geneva**

Schweizerische
Bundesbahnen
Auskunftsbüro
Bahnhof
CH–6000 **Lucerne**

Schweizerische   Schweizerische
Bundesbahnen   Bundesbahnen
Auskunftsbüro   Auskunftsbüro
Hauptbahnhof   Zürich Flughafen
CH–8021 **Zürich**   CH–8058 **Zürich**

● **How to get the most out of your pass:** There are three basic ways you can use your Inter Rail/Eurail Youthpass.
1. Cover as many countries as possible on a grand-scale European tour, sampling each country (however sketchily), and deciding which ones you're most keen to return to on a later pass.
2. Head for a specific area or destination (the Greek islands, say, or the south of France or the art towns of Italy). Use the ticket to get you there by planning a route which takes in some of the European highspots, and come back by a different route. Often this can combine the best of both worlds since, if you stop off at three or four places en route and tire yourself out, you can relax, safe in the knowledge that you've still got two weeks' sunbathing on your Greek island before you have to set off, seeing more sights on your way home.
3. Concentrate on one specific country or area and tour it in depth by rail, stopping at every place that catches your eye.
Having carried out and enjoyed trips on all three principles, all we can say is that each is great fun in its own way – the choice is yours.

● **The Britrail Pass:** To travel in Great Britain, which is not covered in the Eurail scheme, it is best to buy a Britrail Pass or Britrail Youthpass. These passes are valid for free travel anywhere by rail in the United Kingdom, excluding the London underground system; they do, however, include a free ferry service to the Isle of Wight and free steamship cruises on Lake Windermere, in the north of England. Below is a table of current prices up to April 1986 in American dollars (Canadian dollars in brackets).

	Youthpass *Ages 16–26*	2nd Class *No age limits*	1st Class *No age limits*
7 days	95 (120)	115 (140)	155 (190)
14 days	150 (185)	175 (210)	230 (280)
21 days	190 (235)	220 (265)	290 (350)
1 month	225 (275)	260 (310)	330 (405)

• **Sea Passes** for ferry crossing between the UK and continental Europe and between the UK and Ireland are sold separately at a flat rate of around $26 (32) single, $52 (64) return for the continent, and $38 (48) single, $76 (96) return for Ireland, irrespective of what type of Britrail Pass you might hold.

A Sea Pass is valid for six months after the date of issue no matter when your Britrail Pass privileges expire. For example, you may tour round the UK for a week with a seven-day Britrail Youthpass then use the Sea Pass to cross over to France to start a two-month Eurail and then use your Sea Pass once more to reach the UK on your return.

Britrail Passes and Sea Passes can be purchased from over 22,000 travel agents throughout North America or by writing direct to Britrail Travel International, 630 Third Avenue, New York, NY 10017. Don't forget that Britrail Passes cannot be purchased in the UK after you arrive.

TRANSALPINO

The largest rail operator for under-26s in Europe, with over 4,000 European agents selling tickets to twenty-five countries, Transalpino have been around for over thirty years and they now offer the most comprehensive deal to over 2,000 destinations on the market. Their prices represent considerable discounts off standard rail fares – in some cases up to 50 per cent. You don't have to be a student to qualify, just under 26 and the holder of a passport. Tickets are valid for two months (six for Turkey and Morocco), and included in the price is a free timetable and seat reservation (where available) for your outward journey. There are over 2,000 Transalpino offices and agents in Britain, so the chances of there being one quite near you are high. Elsewhere they are sold at student travel offices throughout Europe, and in the USA by Campus Holidays, 242 Bellevue Avenue, Upper Montclair, New Jersey 07043 (201 744 8724). Payment can be made by phone by quoting them your Visa, Mastercharge or American Express number. In return they will issue you with a travel voucher for use in Europe.

Transalpino use the scheduled services of British Rail, Sealink and the national railways of Europe – and you can start your journey from literally any BR station – from Aberdeen or Aberystwyth, Liverpool or Luton. There's always at least one departure a day, and often as many as three, to every destination.

Transalpino offer you a choice of up to ten routes to some European destinations. And you can break your journey for as long as you like en route within your ticket validity period. Rather than listing all the route variables here, we suggest you contact your nearest Transalpino office or agent and get the details from them. Recently Transalpino have introduced their cheap fares for travel between the UK and Ireland. This represents a new opportunity for under-26s to enjoy budget travel in a country on their own doorstep. Reduced fares are also available for travel to the Channel Islands. You'll need to book ahead, though, as availability is restricted at peak periods. Tickets are valid for one month. Tickets are available via Hoverspeed Hovercraft services or via the Sealink Jetfoil services on payment of a £2 ($2.60) or £6 ($7.80) supplement respectively.

● **Book-A-Bed-Ahead scheme:** Transalpino have a budget accommodation scheme for London and the continent. The system works like this: you buy a preprinted voucher from their office and you're guaranteed a night's stay at one of their places in London, Paris, Amsterdam or Brussels. This can be quite handy in a busy season, and the dormitory accommodation is both good and cheap.

● **Capital Rail Runners:** This is, without doubt, your best buy if you've set your heart on seeing the big cities of London, Brussels. Paris and Amsterdam. It allows you to stop off anywhere on your specified route and tour around these cities, taking as long as you wish (up to two months) in the place you like best. Budget accommodation in centrally located hotels for an average of £6 ($8) a night can be arranged, and your outward seats are reserved for you. There are three tours: London–Paris–Brussels–London; London–Paris–Brussels–Amsterdam–London; London–Brussels–Amsterdam–London. Check prices with a travel agent.

● **Travel insurance:** Transalpino offer a comprehensive insurance policy, cover for up to 31 days costs £9.90 ($12.90) and for periods up to three months £12.20 ($15.90).

● **Celtic connection:** Why not make the Celtic connection by travelling out and back from Dublin via different routes through England, Wales, Ireland and Scotland? Prices from London start from £48.50 ($63) for the circular tour, using the Holyhead–Dun Laoghaire ferry to Ireland. Alternatively, if you want to take in Wales and the south of Eire it's worth paying the small amount extra to go out via Fishguard to Rosslare. Whichever way you decide to go, this ticket represents a considerable saving on the British Youthpass and the Irish railways Rambler tickets. As with all Transalpino tickets, the Celtic connection is valid for two months and can be extended up to four months if you're prepared to make sure you start the homeward (Dublin–London) leg of your journey up to two months after you set off.

There are many more possibilities for do-it-yourself circular tours within Europe if you do your planning carefully and get the go-ahead from Transalpino.

EUROTRAIN

Eurotrain run an almost identical set-up to Transalpino. They're smaller but their European sales still manage to reach two million tickets per year. Prior to 1977, only students were eligible for their concessionary fares, but since then anyone under 26 qualifies. They also run a group accommodation service for Paris and Amsterdam, so around £7 ($9) will buy you a bed in a multi-bedded room in either of these cities. In Amsterdam, Eurotrain use the Hans Brinker Hotel. Their insurance is handled through the international student insurance service, Endsleigh, and they offer five different policies.

OVER 26s

Those over 26 needn't despair of having to resort to boring package deals from now on; they can still eurorail by travelling according to one of the following two suggestions: take a youth hostel touring holiday or a rail touring card within an individual country. The youth hostel packages are extremely good value, based on rail travel and hostel accommodation, and operate in fifteen different countries, including Iceland, Israel, Japan, Australia and New Zealand. For further details write to YHA Travel, 14 Southampton Street, London WC2E 7HY (01–240 5236). Also, there are the regular Eurail Passes or individual country passes.

PASSES FOR INDIVIDUAL COUNTRIES

Nearly all Western European countries offer their own touring passes which allow you the freedom of their individual rail networks. The disadvantage of these is that it's often more expensive to get to the country where the pass becomes valid than to buy a BIJ ticket or an Inter Rail, which gets you out of Britain as well. Another point: even though you often get the use of ferries and coaches as well as trains, *you are still limited to just the one country*. It can be advantageous, though, if you're only interested in touring one country in depth, and don't want the route restrictions of a BIJ ticket. Many countries have passes with more flexible timescales, with tickets valid from four days to a month. There are no age restrictions on these go-as-you-please schemes so anyone, over or under 26, can still take advantage of them.

The Benelux countries and Denmark offer a realistic alternative to continual touring: they make your ticket valid for travel on any of five or eight days of a holiday lasting 15–17 days, so you can spend a few days in each centre without worrying that you're missing out on the benefits of your rail pass.

The different deals range from 'very good value' to 'not worth your while', depending on currency fluctuations. Before committing yourself, decide how extensive and attractive the rail network of the country is (a quick glance at the Inter Rail map – free from BR stations – will give you a good idea how much track there actually is to cover) and how much it'll cost you to get out there. A cheap flight to Greece, followed by one of their 'tourist cards' for the railways, can be an economical and effective way to see the country; conversely, by the time you've got yourself over to Austria and bought a touring card, you'll have spent well over the price of an Inter Rail.

SNCF, the French railways, introduced a 'youth railcard' called the Carte Jeune in 1983 which offers a 50 per cent reduction on any off-peak rail journeys made in France between 1 June and 30 September. This ticket entitles you to half-price travel, and includes travel on the TGV – the fastest train in the world. There's also a free couchette (worth £10/$13) thrown in on any overnight journey on a French domestic route, so if you're confining your travel to France this could well work out as your best alternative. Also in 1984, SNCF introduced the Carré Jeune which offers a 50 per cent reduction on four single (or two return) journeys made within a period of one year. Both tickets cost £10.50 ($14) and are valid on both first and second class.

Apply in person with your passport and passport photo to SNCF, 179 Piccadilly, London W1V 0BA (01–409 1224), or any other SNCF address.

The following table lists *all* the available European touring passes – the good and the bad. We've starred the ones we thought well worth considering, many of which can be bought in Britain from Transalpino or any BR Travel Centre. For further information, write to the individual country's tourist authority (their addresses appear on pages 51–3).

COUNTRY	NAME OF TICKET	DAYS VALID	APPROXIMATE PRICE PER DAY (2ND CLASS)	$
1–7 Days				
BELGIUM	B-Tourrail*	5 in 16	£3.60	4.70
			(£2.80 if under 26)	3.70
FINLAND	Finnrail Pass	7	£5.50	7.20
GERMANY (WEST)	German Tourist Card	4	£11.00	14.30
LUXEMBOURG	Abonnement	5 in 15	£1.30	1.70
NETHERLANDS	Rail Rover	3	£6.25	8.20
NETHERLANDS	Rail Rover*	7	£3.80	4.90
PORTUGAL	Bilhete Turístico*	7	£3.50 (1st Class)	4.50
SWITZERLAND	Ferienkarte	4	£11.65	15.20
7–14 Days				
AUSTRIA	Austria Ticket	9	£6.35	8.25
BELGIUM	B-Tourrail	8 in 16	£3.10	4.00
			(£2.40 if under 26)	3.10
BENELUX	Benelux-Tourrail*	8 in 16	£5.30	6.90
FINLAND	Finnrail Pass	14	£4.20	5.50
FRANCE	France-Vacances	8 in 30	£11.75	15.30
GERMANY (WEST)	German Tourist Card	9	£7.50	9.75
			(£4.60 if under 26)	6.00
GREECE	Tourist Card*	10	(£1.95 for 1 person)	2.50
			(£3.40 for 2 persons)	4.45
HUNGARY	Runaround	10	£3.50	4.60
ITALY	BTLC*	8	£5.40	7.00
POLAND	Pol Rail Pass	8	£3.60	4.70
PORTUGAL	Bilhete Turístico*	14	£3.00 (1st Class)	3.90
SWITZERLAND	Ferienkarte	8	£6.85	8.90

COUNTRY	NAME OF TICKET	DAYS VALID	APPROXIMATE PRICE PER DAY (2ND CLASS)	$
14–21 Days				
AUSTRIA	Austria Ticket	16	£4.85	6.30
BELGIUM	16-day Season	16	£2.20	2.90
DENMARK	Landresjsekort	16	£6.00	7.80
GERMANY (WEST)	German Tourist Card	16	£5.60	7.30
			(£3.45 if under 26)	4.50
GREECE	Tourist Card*	20	(£1.60 for 1 person)	2.10
			(£2.85 for 2 persons)	3.70
HUNGARY	Runaround	20	£2.50	3.30
ITALY	BTLC	15	£4.20	5.50
ITALY	BTLC	21	£3.60	4.70
POLAND	Pol Rail Pass	15	£2.45	3.20
PORTUGAL	Bilhete Turístico	21	£2.85 (1st Class)	3.70
SCANDINAVIA	Nordic Pass*	21	£5.60	7.30
SWITZERLAND	Ferienkarte	15	£4.40	5.70
22–30 Days				
AUSTRIA	Bundesnetzkarte*	30	£4.10	5.35
FINLAND	Finnrail Pass	22	£3.60	4.70
GREECE	Tourist Card*	30	(£1.45 for 1 person)	1.90
			(£2.60 for 2 persons)	3.40
HUNGARY	Runaround	30	£2.20	2.90
ITALY	BTLC*	30	£2.50	3.30
POLAND	Pol Rail Pass	30	£2.00	2.60
SWITZERLAND	Ferienkarte*	30	£3.05	4.00

• **Spoil yourself:** If you have the opportunity, there are some trains which are a delight to travel on. They connect the major European cities and are called:

RHEINGOLD	Amsterdam–Basel (during summer months, also Mannheim–Stuttgart–Munich)
MEDIOLANUM	Milan–Innsbruck–Munich–Cologne–Dortmund
LIGURE	Marseille–Milan
ETOILE DE NORD	Paris–Brussels–Amsterdam
CATALAN-TALGO	Barcelona–Geneva
ARBALETE	Zürich–Paris
MERKUR	Copenhagen–Karlsruhe

All are accessible with a first-class Eurail Pass (TEEs etc.). The intercity trains carry both first- and second-class passengers and are available to Inter Rail, Eurail Pass and Eurail Youthpass holders, as are TGVs, the world's fastest, linking Paris to Lyon in two hours at 168 m.p.h. TGV trains also link Paris to the south of France, the Alps and Switzerland.

Station information

The average major European city station will have most of the following facilities:

1. *Ticket desk:* At most large stations, tickets for domestic and international travel are purchased at different windows, so make sure you're in the right line.
2. *Train information office:* Marked with a blue letter *i*. Here you can find out the times and availability of trains from multilingual clerks. If the office is packed, see if large timetables are posted up on boards in the station. There are normally separate posters for arrivals (white background) and for departures (yellow background). Fast trains on both are given in red instead of black print, running chronologically from 0 hr to 24 hrs. Next to the time is the name or number of the train, together with its routing, from point of origin to final destination, with the most important stops in between. Finally, the track and platform numbers, at which the train departs or arrives. Major stations provide this information on computerized boards. Train composition boards are always useful to take a glance at: they give you a good idea which part of the platform to position yourself at for the second-class carriages. That way, you don't waste any time running to get your seat when the train rolls up.
3. *Left luggage:* In the big stations, you'll find there'll be a manned depot (usually open until midnight – then it closes down till 5 or 6 a.m.) and automatic lockers. If you're catching a train before the manned depot opens again, get a locker, obviously. Note:

Check that your rucksack will fit into the locker first. There are two sizes of lockers, and if you've a large pack you'll be very lucky if you can cram it in the smaller of the two.

4. *Lost property office:* Usually open 9 a.m.–5 p.m., from Mondays to Fridays only. If it's desperate (say, you've lost your ticket, rucksack, passport or money), go to the station master.

5. *Station master's office:* In theory he's in charge of the trains not the passengers, but as he's the 'king pin' in the station he's your best bet if it's a real emergency.

6. You can always count on there being *telephones* and *post boxes*. Some stations have an international telephone service on the spot, and in some you can even find a full post office operating.

7. Assorted *shops* and *news-stands*.

8. Often a *first-aid post:* In Germany and France there are travellers' aid organizations: 'Bahnhofsmissions' and 'Accueilen-gare'. They'll help if you're ill, lost or generally in distress. If you're ill and there's no first-aid help, again go to the station master.

9. *Toilets:* Vary dramatically in degrees of cleanliness and are not always free.

10. *Waiting rooms:* Again, these range from quite OK to diabolic. Nevertheless, they are useful, obviously, to Eurorailers. Many close at night, so you shouldn't count on them for spending the night in.

11. *Baths/showers:* Most large stations have these facilities where you can buy or rent towels, soap, shampoo, etc. They cost on average £1.50 ($1.95) a bath, £1 ($1.30) a shower.

12. *Foreign-exchange desk:* Unless you're really in need of the local currency, these tend to be a bad idea as their exchange rates are rarely competitive and there are usually long queues.

13. *Tourist information desk:* Extremely useful for eurorailers. Apart from handing out free maps and guides, they invariably run an accommodation service for a small charge, about 50p–£1.50 ($0.70–2). Watch out here as there can be long queues.

Obviously, the larger the station, the more facilities you can expect. If there are any outstanding facts relevant to a particular station, for instance, a cheap and good snack bar downstairs in Stockholm station, we mention that under 'Stockholm'.

PICTOGRAMS

Nearly every station is clearly marked with universal pictograms which overcome the language barrier very efficiently. Most of these are extremely straightforward and don't need explanation. There are some, however, which might cause confusion to first-timers:

Meeting Point

Lost and Found

Luggage and baggage store pictograms can even catch the old hands waiting in the wrong line, for example the self-service luggage-cart sign is:

Self-Service
Luggage-Cart

while that for a porter is:

Call for Porter

In some stations you will have enough trouble fighting the porters off without going out looking for them.

Confusion can also occur between the Luggage Registration Office (for sending luggage through to your next destination):

Luggage Registration
Office

and the left luggage or baggage check room:

Baggage
Check Room

Coin-operated lockers are different again:

Locker

Lockers are
also indicated by: CONSIGNE DES BAGAGES
GEPAECKAUFBEWAHRUNG
CONSIGNA DE EQUIPAJES
DEPOSITO BAGAGLIO

You'll get a ticket which you have to present when you pick your luggage up again.

RESERVATIONS

Unless you don't mind slouching in the corridor for hours on end, a seat reservation can make a lot of sense on a busy route in summer. If you choose not to reserve, at least try to check how busy the train's going to be. For the equivalent of 50p–£1 ($0.70–1.30) a reserved seat is worth it. If you suspect that your departure train's going to be mobbed, check up and reserve before leaving the station on your arrival. In many Western countries, reservations can be made up to two months in advance. Some countries have obligatory reservations, whilst in others you have to make your reservations at least two hours before departure (all this is noted in the chapters on individual countries). When making a reservation try going along at a time when the office should be quiet (generally 9–11 a.m., and 3–5 p.m., Monday to Friday). You'd be amazed how many people roll up at lunchtime and at weekends when all the locals are out in force trying to make their own reservations. In Sweden, if you board a train in which reserved seats are compulsory without having reserved a seat for yourself beforehand, you will be charged an extra fare in addition to the reservation fee on board the train. Trains requiring compulsory seat reservations are marked (R) in timetables.

If you find yourself on a train without having reserved a seat, quickly shoot down the corridors looking for free seats on the reservation notice located outside each compartment or on the actual seats themselves. If the train seems to be completely booked up, try asking the guard whether there are any other carriages being added on, or any cancellations.

When you're making a reservation, tell the clerk exactly what you want – unless you specify, say, a non-smoker, it will be presumed that you want a smoker! In southern Europe especially, you're rarely asked what you want, so make your wishes clearly known when booking. Bear in mind the following:

1. *Class:* Make sure you don't end up unintentionally in first class.

2. *Non-smoker/smoker.*

3. *Which side of the train* you want to sit. On some journeys this can be quite significant; for example, a seat on the south side of the train on a Riviera journey ensures you a good view, but you'd miss most of it by sitting on the north side.

4. *Facing/back* to the engine: Some people have a preference for looking either in the direction of travel or away from it.

5. *Aisle/window seat:* Often the window seat has a pull-out table which is useful for eating or writing, whereas the aisle seat allows more leg room.

SOME TIPS

1. Don't overlook Table 1,000 in Cook's timetable; this lists those places which are not actually on the main railway line but are accessible by suburban trains or buses. The table also shows the nearest main-line station to the resort and gives the distance from that point to the place (useful if you're keen to have a break from other eurorailers and trains for a while).

2. Always check the name of the station if you're dealing with a city with more than one (see below). Don't assume that, as you're travelling north, you'll necessarily be leaving from the city's northernmost station – it doesn't always follow. The following towns and cities have more than one main station:

ANTWERP	COPENHAGEN	LIÈGE	PORTSMOUTH
ATHENS	DOVER	LISBON	PRAGUE
BARCELONA	DUBLIN	LIVERPOOL	ROME
BASEL	DUNKERQUE	LONDON	ROTTERDAM
BELFAST	ESSEN	LYON	SAN SEBASTIÁN
BELGRADE	EXETER	MADRID	SEVILLE
BERLIN	FOLKESTONE	MALMÖ	STOCKHOLM
BILBAO	GENEVA	MANCHESTER	TILBURY
BOULOGNE	GLASGOW	MARSEILLE	TOURS
BRUSSELS	HAMBURG	MILAN	TURIN
BUCHAREST	HARWICH	MUNICH	VENICE
BUDAPEST	HELSINGBORG	NAPLES	VIENNA
CALAIS	HENDAYE	NEWHAVEN	WARSAW
CASABLANCA	IRÚN	OPORTO	WIESBADEN
COLOGNE	ISTANBUL	OSLO	ZÜRICH
COMO	LE HAVRE	PARIS	

Bear in mind the distances between stations in these cities are usually quite substantial (in London, between Paddington and Liverpool Street is about five miles; in Paris, between Gare de Lyon and Gare St Lazare is about four and a half). The moral is: don't count on split-second connections between stations.

Train information

NIGHT TRAVEL

Travelling at night has distinct advantages for the eurorailer who doesn't mind missing the scenery of a particular area or the fact that night trains invariably take longer to get to their destinations. The advantage of night travel is that in effect you add an extra day to your stay by arriving in the morning, ready to start your tour. How exactly you spend the night, and the consequent amount of sleep you manage to get in, depends largely on which of the sleeping arrangements you opt for, and how good a sleeper you are.

Basically there are four ways of travelling at night: sit up in the normal seats; get a seat which pulls down (as on the German trains) and allows you to lie down; buy a couchette; buy a sleeper. Taking each in turn, you can:

1. *Sit up all night* in a seat. It's free, but not guaranteed to find you fresh enough for a full day's sightseeing the next day.
2. *Pull-down seats*. These are great when you can find them, as they're free yet still allow you to stretch out, thus increasing the chances of sleep. Once all six seats are pulled down, they join together to form a massive 'bed'. How much room you end up with depends on how full the compartment was originally; if there are only two or three of you in the compartment, you're home and dry for a free sleep.
3. *Couchettes*. This is a seat by daytime, which at night is converted into a proper full berth. In second class, there are six to a compartment (four in first class). There is no sex segregation but this is not normally a problem even for single girls as the couchettes are nearly always full. For your £8 ($10.50) (average cost, but see under list of individual countries) you get a sheet, blanket and pillow, and there's a bed-light. You can use the washroom next to the toilets for washing. Each couchette has a luggage rack, but it's always wise to take your valuables to bed with you. Standards of couchettes vary enormously as they're run by the individual national rail networks, so that in Switzerland and Germany they're very good, while in Spain and Italy

they're pretty awful. Reservations for couchettes are more or less essential in the summer. You are required to book at least five hours before departure.

4. *Sleepers.* Sleeping cars are a great step up in comfort from couchettes, but they're also a lot more expensive. As in Britain, European sleepers come in two classes and offer: a proper bed with all the trimmings, a sink with soap, towels and warm water, an electrical outlet and occasionally your own WC. Sleepers are operated either by the Wagons-Lits Company (an international concern) or by a subsidiary of the railway. Many of these are developing into combined groups, collectively calling themselves 'Trans Europ Nuit/Nacht/Notte'. The Scandinavian and East European countries operate their own sleepers, as does British Rail. The average two- or three-berth sleeper is £16 ($21) a person, but price often depends on the distance you're covering.

A bit of general advice on travelling at night. Very often, your train gets into the station an hour before departure; if you've had a hard day, this is good to know as you can get yourself bedded down earlier. If you take the train right through to its final destination, you can often lie on for another half-hour or so in the morning, once it arrives, before getting ousted.

If you're reserving a couchette or sleeper, try for the top berths as they're roomier, there's more air and they afford you a slightly greater degree of privacy. Watch out when the train enters for the yellow stripe along the outside of the carriage, just below roof level. This indicates either a couchette or first class.

If you're going by sleeper or couchette on an international trip (or even for some internal ones in Italy, for some strange reason), the attendant will take your passport and ticket from you so that, in theory anyway, you won't need to be woken up at the border in the middle of the night – unless you're entering a communist country, in which case they'll wake you for checks as many times as they choose to.

Once you're all in, lock the door and hope you've not landed yourself – as we have so often in the past – with a collection of snorers!

The best trains for a good night's sleep are those that don't cross international borders (especially into the Eastern Bloc) or stop every couple of hours at stations en route, otherwise you'll have customs officials coming in for a nose-around at 3 a.m., or train announcements blaring out all night long (you can bet it'll be your carriage that stops right beneath the loudspeaker). Our advice to eurorail insomniacs is to have a heavy meal before the journey, take some ear plugs, and don't hold back on the local vino.

Most night trains don't have a bar or eating facilities on board so if you're the type of person who enjoys a midnight feast or gets thirsty in the night, you had better bring your own supplies along or you'll wake up with an empty stomach and a throat like a vacuum cleaner.

● **Good night trains:** Below is a list of just some of the many good night trains in Western Europe. Remember you can save money by sleeping on these night trains and cover more ground during your vacation.

Amsterdam–Copenhagen	Malmö–Stockholm
Amsterdam–Munich	Madrid–Algeciras
Barcelona–Geneva	Madrid–Lisbon
Barcelona–Madrid	Madrid–Santander
Barcelona–Nice	Milan–Paris
Barcelona–Paris	Paris–Amsterdam
Barcelona–Pamplona	Paris–Chamonix
Basel–Hamburg	Paris–Munich
Belgrade–Thessaloniki	Paris–Nice
Brussels–Genoa	Rome–Nice
Brussels–Hamburg	Vienna–Cologne
Hamburg–Munich	Vienna–Frankfurt
Brussels–Munich	Vienna–Lindau
Heidelberg–Lugano	Vienna–Venice
London–Edinburgh	

Don't forget that it's often preferable to sleep in a good compartment than in a crowded youth hostel.

EATING

Few eurorailers can afford to indulge in buffet or restaurant meals on the trains because they're never cheap. The majority of the dining services offered on European trains are run by the Wagons-

Lits Company. However, the quality of the food and service varies from country to country, as it really depends on the staff and hygiene of the host country. Don't be fooled by the mobile mini-bars that wheel temptingly past you – they're a rip-off pricewise, and on top of that the food and drink is of very poor quality. As a general rule all TEEs and most intercity and long-distance express trains have a separate dining car with set-price meals from £5–15 ($6.50–19.50) or a bar/buffet car serving drinks, sandwiches and light snacks. It's a very satisfying experience having a leisurely meal along one of the scenic routes even if you can only afford it once.

Remember: You can't drink the water from the train washrooms anywhere in Europe. Buy in your drink before you get aboard. The best bet is to stock up with food from the supermarkets before you leave and treat yourself to a good picnic on the train.

TRAIN SPLITTING

As the trains of Europe undertake some pretty complicated routes and use one another's rolling stock, trains on long international journeys often split into various sections at certain points, so obviously it's important to check that you get on the relevant part of the train. The best policy is to ask and make sure you're on the right segment before you settle down. If your coach is going to be shunted about on to another train, find out at which station it's due to happen and at what time. It's all made quite easy by the signs posted on the doors and windows at intervals along the train:

CALAIS

PARIS ——————— MILANO

VENEZIA

This shows that the train starts at Calais, stops at Paris and Milan and terminates in Venice. There will also be a '1' or '2' to tell you the class of the carriage. Whatever happens, don't get out of a train which is due to split up, and then get back into another section of it with the intention of walking along to your seat – you could find you're no longer connected to that bit of the train! Just in case you do get separated from your fellow travellers, carry your own money, ticket and passport at all times. This advice is also relevant in case one of you gets mugged – that way you won't lose everything at once. In some stations, mainly termini, you'll find the train reversing and going back in the direction you've just come. This is often the case in Switzerland. Don't worry about it. It's just a standard rerailing procedure. This usually takes place on the last stop before, or first after, an international frontier, and is used to reduce or add on extra carriages. If you're in any doubt about your train splitting, ask the ticket inspector as soon as you are on board. This is particularly necessary in Britain where the trains don't have identification panels on the side.

• **Supplements:** An Inter Rail or BIJ ticket alone is not sufficient to travel on some of the express trains of Europe, or on any of the Trans Europ Express ones. If you want to use these trains, you'll have to pay a supplement, and this is calculated on the distance you're travelling and the type of express you've chosen (unless you have a regular Eurail).

Some countries (notably the Scandinavian ones) don't charge supplements as such, but make seat reservations compulsory on expresses. (Full details of all the supplements and surcharges are to be found below under the individual country chapters.)

It's often worth inquiring how much the additional first-class supplement is, particularly if you're feeling under the weather and the train's packed out. (As two of the survivors of the Spanish Olive Oil Epidemic of '81 trying to get home, we can vouch for it!)

TIMETABLES

One of the best timetables – considered to be the Eurorailer's bible – is Thomas Cook's Continental Timetable. This is published on the first day of each month, though by buying the May or September edition you get one covering both the winter and summer schedules. In this book you'll find most of the trains that run in Europe and most ferry services. You can buy a copy for £4 at Thomas Cook shops or by post at £4.95 from Thomas Cook Ltd, PO Box 36, Peterborough PE3 6SB; or from Forsyth Travel Library, PO Box 2975, 9154 West 57th Street, Shawnee Mission, Kansas 66201 ($15.95 + $1 postage), or Thomas Cook Pty Ltd, PO Box 3590,

Sydney 2001, NSW, Australia (A$10). The timetable explains in simple language how to use the tables; it will take you a few minutes to acquaint yourself with its workings and will save you hours in train info queues. Use it to preplan and then, to be doubly sure, check the times locally at the stations themselves.

Apart from Cook's timetable there's British Rail's equivalent. It only costs £1 ($1.30) (quite a saving on Cook's) and is even easier to follow but it's based on departures from the UK. It fits easily into a rucksack and has the added advantage of giving you a free rail map. The best value is undoubtedly the free UIC international timetable on ABC lines, though copies are like gold in most travel agents. Also very good to have is the Eurail timetable available free from any Eurail issuing office.

Bear in mind the change from winter to summer schedules: all European rail networks start their summer schedules on the last Sunday in May and the winter schedules on the last Sunday in September. Check also the time zone the country's in, and keep an eye out for local and national holidays.

• **Public holidays affecting trains:** At public holiday times, you'll find services reduced or not running at all, and those trains that are operating will be busier than usual and with more reservations. Check with stations for details and turn up earlier for the train. We list all the relevant holidays under the individual country chapters. In many countries the day, or at least the half-day, preceding an official public holiday is also regarded as a holiday. Note also that in the Eastern Bloc countries religious holidays are often locally observed but not nationally recognized. We give below a calendar of moving holidays for the next year:

	1985
Shrove Monday	18 February
Shrove Tuesday	19 February
Maundy Thursday	4 April
Good Friday	5 April
Holy Saturday	6 April
Easter Sunday	7 April
Easter Monday	8 April
Ascension Day	16 May
Whit Monday	27 May
Corpus Christi	6 June

Muslim holidays:

	1985
Ramadan begins	21 May
Id-ul-Fitr	20 June
Id-ul-Adha	27 August
New Year	16 September

● **Hazards:** On those long hot runs in southern Europe, where temperatures are high and trains aren't air-conditioned, the temptation is to stick your head out of the window to cool off. Be warned: you may cool off more than you anticipated. When you feel that unexpected drop of rain upon your face, you may fear the worst . . . someone's been to the loo further up. Moreover, don't be reassured by the notices announcing that it's illegal to throw rubbish out of the window. Expect anything, and be on your guard, especially for cans and bottles. Most importantly of all, always be on your guard for unsecured doors; even the safety-conscious DB (Deutsche Bundesbahn) estimate that nearly 200 people have been wiped out in the last five years by falling from their trains. Always carry your valuables with you when you go to the loo, and be extra careful on night trains as this is when most theft occurs.

TRAINS IN EASTERN EUROPE

To avoid unbelievable anxiety and frustration while travelling in Eastern Europe, it's useful to remember the following:
1. Tickets are often only valid for the specific date and class of the train stated on your ticket. To change your date is more trouble than it's worth, so always be sure of the exact date and time you wish to leave before buying your ticket or making a reservation.
2. Queueing is a fact of life, so try to buy tickets and make reservations at odd hours: one of the best times is late at night, since queues begin long before offices open in the morning. Whenever possible, try to buy your ticket/make your reservation from Western Europe (say, Vienna) at the appropriate student office.
3. For all international journeys, tickets and reservations must be made through the official government travel agents (listed below

under each country). Otherwise use the train stations where queues are slightly shorter.

4. Make sure you're in the right queue. There's often one queue for journeys over 100 kilometres, another for reservations, etc. These are not immediately obvious as often there are no signs and it's quite possible to stand for up to an hour in the wrong line.

5. When you reach the front of the queue try and get everything possible done in one go, so you don't have to queue again later: buy your ticket, make your reservation, ask what platform the train leaves from, etc. Write it all down, in case the assistant doesn't speak English.

6. Try to view the whole exercise as an initiative test, and always be prepared for any eventuality. It's not uncommon to discover that all second-class seats are fully booked so, unless you fancy another hour's wait at the end of the queue, it's best to make your mind up beforehand whether you're prepared to pay the extra.

We found it incredibly difficult to find anyone prepared to divulge details concerning the station facilities in the Eastern Bloc, but it's safe to assume that all the essential services are present in the major stations, though don't expect luxuries like baths/showers.

Before you go

FLYING THE ATLANTIC

The basic rule is the more you pay then the greater your flexibility will be, or conversely the less you pay, the more restrictions you will have to face. As always, forward planning can not only save you money, but also buy you time in Europe. It is a good idea to spend time in countries not covered in the Eurail scheme (Great Britain or the Eastern Bloc, for example), either before your Eurail Pass becomes valid or when it has expired. Don't waste precious days of your pass in countries where you can't use it. Consequently, it's important to choose the right city as your gateway to Europe.

Flying to London with either People Express or Virgin Atlantic is one of the most popular starts and it's easy to see why, with fares at only around £120 ($156) for a one-way ticket. To make a reservation, write or telephone People Express at North Terminal Building, Newark Airport, New Jersey 07114 (201 596 6000), or Gatwick Airport, Crawley, England (0293 38100); Virgin Atlantic, 43 Perry Street, New York, NY 10014 (212 206 7639) or 3 Woodstock Street, London W1 (01–409 2429).

Reservations can normally be cancelled or changed up to three days before departure for a £5.40 ($7) charge, or even after that for about £36 ($47). As we go to press, Virgin Atlantic work out slightly cheaper and offer bonuses included in your ticket cost, such as in-flight snacks, a hot meal with wine, and a low-cost hotel scheme. During the peak season, June to September, both airlines are well booked up and unless you reserve well beforehand you may be forced to travel standby. If this happens, you stand a better chance midweek than at weekends.

There is no shortage of airlines or types of tickets to get you over to Europe, but if money is the prime consideration set yourself the task of getting a really good, reliable travel agent. After briefing him on how much cash you have to spend and where you want to go, leave it to him to come up with a few ideas for you to think about. Do your own homework, too, and plan early as most reduced air fares are payable thirty days in advance. Scan *The New York Times* and talk to as many other eurorailers as you can to pick up tips. Midweek days are usually the quietest for flying, so flexibility is an advantage, particularly if you're flying with People Express or Virgin Atlantic.

If you can't afford the luxury of being flexible, go for a charter flight which gives you a seat reservation but can involve you in backtracking to get back, for the return journey, to the airport you arrived at. If you've a bit more cash, an APEX (Advanced Booking Excursion Fare) allows you greater freedom as you can return from a different airport.

● **APEX:** APEX flights represent one of the most flexible options on the reduced fares market, as they are not so restrictive as charters. With an APEX ticket it's possible to arrive at and depart from different cities (countries) and even on different airlines in some cases. If you decide to fly with a particular airline, ask if they operate a Super-APEX package which can mean an even cheaper deal.

● **Standby:** If you want to keep your options open until the last minute without committing yourself, a standby ticket is your best bet. Not all airlines offer standby, and your choice of both American and European gateways is limited. However, if you are flexible the rewards are high for apart from being the cheapest ticket around, it doesn't commit you to any particular time or place when returning to the US.

There are only a limited number of standby seats on each flight, so it's important to be well organized to improve your chances, particularly in peak season. A few days before you plan on leaving, phone up the airline's reservation desk and check out the seat availability on your optimum flight. Don't mention that you are planning to fly standby, as many officials are cagey about giving information away. Seats are always given out on a first come, first served basis, so be there in good time, and be prepared for a wait, even overnight if necessary. Most sales desks open at around 7 a.m. and it's not unusual for a queue to form before then. As soon as you've bought your ticket don't hang around, go straight to the check-in desk and get your name down on that list.

● **Budget fares:** Pricewise a budget fare is similar to a standby, yet it offers a confirmed seat reserved in advance. The only problem is that you must tell the airline which week you would like to fly out and return (if desired), and they will get back to you at least a week before your flight with the details. In this way, the airline gets to choose the exact day, at a time which is convenient to them, not you. In our opinion, it's only worth considering if you cannot find a suitable APEX flight, and don't want to take the risk of flying standby; even then, it only makes sense if you've got plenty of time on your hands before your rail pass begins.

● **Charter flights:** Charters are back and more competitive than ever. While most charter operators who have survived the last ten years in the hectic US marketplace can be considered reliable, you should still exercise care in booking a charter. Read the charter operator-participant contract to be fully aware of the rules governing a charter flight. Try CIEE or Travac (800 872 8800). CIEE's booklet *Charter Europe* includes year-round low-cost flights to several European cities. Get a free copy from your nearest Council Travel Office or write to CIEE, Charter Europe, 205 East 42nd Street, New York, NY 10017. Finally, try and keep an eye out for good deals in the Sunday papers.

• **Other options:** There are cheap scheduled flights from New York/California offered by People Express, Virgin Atlantic, World, Transamerica Capitol and Icelandic. Check with CIEE for your best option, for apart from being the 'granddaddy' of charter flight operators for students and youths, they also know what else is on offer.

TYPE OF AIR FARE	MIN/MAX STAY REQUIREMENT	ADVANCE PURCHASE REQUIREMENT	CANCELLATION PENALTIES	STOPOVER POSSIBILITIES
STANDBY	None	None	None	None
BUDGET	None	21 days	$50+	None
APEX	Varies from 7–180 days	Varies 21 days round trip only	10% of fare	Sometimes Check with airline
SUPER-APEX	Varies 7–180 days	Varies 21 days round trip only	10% of fare	None

• **Travel agents:** No special licence is required by travel agents in the US so anyone can set themselves up in business regardless of experience. At present, there are about 100,000 to choose from, so be selective. Only a small percentage are members of the American Society of Travel Agents (ASTA) which requires at least three years in business prior to membership. For a list of ASTA members in your area write to the American Society of Travel Agents, PR Dept, 711 Fifth Avenue, New York, NY 10022. They also produce free brochures giving general advice about travel overseas. Alternatively look out for the ASTA globe which is the symbol of membership.

Another good sign is the Institute of Travel Agents certificate which means that the agent must have worked in the industry for at least five years and have passed the relevant exams. For listings of CTAs in your area write to the Institute of Certified Travel Agents, 148 Linden Street, Wellesley, MA 02181 (617 237 0280).

Always go to a travel agent after you've done your own research first to see if they can come up with a better deal than you were able to. Most travel agent services are free, so if it's necessary to make a transatlantic phone call let them make it. Never forget, the cheaper your ticket is, the less their commission will be, so the temptation will be for a travel agent to recommend APEX as opposed to standby unless they see you've done your homework beforehand.

PREPLANNING

This can give great pleasure and add to the fun of the trip, as well as ensuring you get the very most out of your time abroad. After looking at the map of Europe, plan out a rough itinerary in your head and check its feasibility in your timetable (use last summer's one rather than a winter schedule); then write it down and roughly allocate days to it.

When planning a rail itinerary for a complete tour of Europe, there are three main considerations to take into account: the interesting destinations you'd like to go to; how many days you want to spend there; and the most scenic and enjoyable route to get there.

• **Time allocation:** Most cities require a minimum of two or three nights, though obviously you could mix a few 'one-nighters' into your schedule to make your time last out. Time allocation is a more serious consideration for those attempting a 'whistle-stop' tour, whereas those touring only a few countries can be more lax about it.

• **Time differences:** Bear in mind the different time-zones of the countries you'll be travelling in and allow for this when you're making connections. Remember: all these are based on GMT (Greenwich Mean Time).

COUNTRY	SUMMER	WINTER	COUNTRY	SUMMER	WINTER
AUSTRIA	+2(A)	+1	LUXEMBOURG	+2(A)	+1
BELGIUM	+2(A)	+1	MOROCCO	GMT	GMT
BULGARIA	+3(A)	+2	NETHER-		
CZECHO-			LANDS	+2(A)	+1
SLOVAKIA	+2(A)	+1	NORWAY	+2(A)	+1
DENMARK	+2(A)	+2	POLAND	+2(A)	+1
FINLAND	+1(A)	+2	PORTUGAL	+1(A)	GMT
FRANCE	+2(A)	+1	ROMANIA	+3(A)	+2
EAST			SPAIN	+2(A)	+1
GERMANY	+2(A)	+1	SWEDEN	+2(A)	+1
WEST			SWITZER-		
GERMANY	+2(A)	+1	LAND	+2(A)	+1
GREECE	+3(A)	+2	TURKEY	+2	+3
HUNGARY	+2(A)	+1	UNITED		
IRELAND	+1 (B)	GMT	KINGDOM	+1(B)	GMT
ITALY	+2(A)	+1	YUGOSLAVIA	+2(A)	+1

(A) = Summertime runs from about 27 March–24 September.
(B) = Summertime runs from about 27 March–22 October.

• **When to go:** Most eurorailers find themselves on the road (or rail) between June and September – for obvious reasons. Travelling in the high season gives you the advantages of encountering more people, getting better weather and being sure all the museums, hotels and places of interest are going to be open.

However, the counter-argument is obvious: prices are higher, the character of a place tends to get lost beneath the throngs of tourists, accommodation is difficult to find, people involved in the tourist industry have less time for you, and in general there are more hassles on the trains.

For the lucky few able to choose when to go, we'd personally recommend spring to early summer – but whenever you go, you'll find it a fascinating experience.

• **Destination and routes:** Most eurorailers have a few special places in mind before they set off, maybe an urge to see Paris, Rome and Athens, and by using a timetable and the information given later in this guide you'll be able to work out the quickest and best routes between these places. Often there are two or three alternative routes to major cities, and there's bound to be one that appeals to you more than another.

• **Advance tourist information:** If you know all the countries you're going to be visiting before you set off, write to their main Tourist Office in your own country and they'll gladly send you back free booklets and maps to whet your appetite for their country and give an idea as to what you'd like to see and what you can afford to miss out.

Addresses in the UK:
AUSTRIA, 30 St George Street, London W1 (01–629 0461)
BELGIUM, 38 Dover Street, London W1 (01–499 5379)
BULGARIA, 18 Princes Street, London W1 (01–499 6988)
CZECHOSLOVAKIA, Čedok, 17–18 Old Bond Street, London W1 (01–629 6058)
DENMARK, 169–173 Regent Street, London W1 (01–734 2637)
FINLAND, 66 Haymarket, London SW1 (01–839 4048)
FRANCE, 178 Piccadilly, London W1 (01–499 6911)
EAST GERMANY, Berolina Travel Ltd, 20 Conduit Street, London W1 (01–629 1664)
WEST GERMANY, 61 Conduit Street, London W1 (01–734 2600)
GREECE, 195–197 Regent Street, London W1 (01–734 5997)
HUNGARY, 6 Conduit Street, London W1 (01–493 0263)
IRELAND, 150 New Bond Street, London W1 (01–493 3201)
ITALY, 1 Princes Street, London W1 (01–408 1254)
LUXEMBOURG, 36/37 Piccadilly, London W1 (01–434 2800)
MONACO, 34 Sackville Street, London W1 (01–437 3660)
MOROCCO, 174 Regent Street, London W1 (01–437 0073)
NETHERLANDS, 143 New Bond Street, London W1 (01–499 9367)
NORWAY, 20 Pall Mall, London SW1 (01–839 6255)
POLAND, Polorbis, 82 Mortimer Street, London W1 (01–580 8028)
PORTUGAL, 1–5 New Bond Street, London W1 (01–493 3873)
ROMANIA, 77–81 Gloucester Place, London W1 (01–935 8590)
SPAIN, 57–58 St James Street, London SW1 (01–499 0901)
SWEDEN, 3 Cork Street, London W1 (01–437 5816)
SWITZERLAND, 1 New Coventry Street, London W1 (01–734 1921)
TURKEY, 170–173 Piccadilly, London W1 (01–734 8681)
UNITED KINGDOM, 64 St James Street, London SW1 (01–449 9325)
YUGOSLAVIA, 143 Regent Street, London W1 (01–734 5243)

Addresses in the USA:

AUSTRIA, 545 Fifth Avenue, New York, NY 10017 (212 697 0651)

3440 Wilshire Boulevard, Los Angeles, Ca. 90010 (213 380 3309)

BELGIUM, 745 Fifth Avenue, New York, NY 10151 (212 758 8130)

BULGARIA, 161 East 86th Street, New York, NY 10028 (212 722 1110)

CZECHOSLOVAKIA, 10 East 40th Street, Suite 1902, New York, NY 10016 (212 689 9720)

DENMARK, 75 Rockefeller Plaza, New York, NY 10019 (212 582 2802)

3600 Wilshire Boulevard, Los Angeles, Ca. 90010 (213 387 7181)

FINLAND, 75 Rockefeller Plaza, New York, NY 10019 (212 582 2802)

3600 Wilshire Boulevard, Los Angeles, Ca. 90019 (213 387 7181)

FRANCE, 610 Fifth Avenue, New York, NY 10020 (212 757 1125)

645 North Michigan Avenue, Chicago, Ill. 60611 (312 337 6301)

9401 Wilshire Boulevard, Beverly Hills, Ca. 90212 (213 271 6665)

WEST GERMANY, 747 Third Avenue, New York, NY 10017 (212 308 3300)

700 South Flower Street, Los Angeles, Ca. 90017 (213 688 7332)

GREECE, Olympic Tower, Fifth Floor, 645 Fifth Avenue, New York, NY 10022 (212 421 5777)

611 West Sixth Street, Suite 1998, Los Angeles, Ca. 90017 (213 626 6696)

HUNGARY, 500 Fifth Avenue, New York, NY 10110 (212 391 0844)

IRELAND, 590 Fifth Avenue, New York, NY 10036 (212 246 7400)

ITALY, 630 Fifth Avenue, New York, NY 10111 (212 245 4822)

500 North Michigan Avenue, Chicago, Ill. 60611 (312 644 0990)

360 Post Street, San Francisco, Ca. 94108 (415 392 6206)

LUXEMBOURG, 801 Second Avenue, New York, NY 10017 (212 370 9850)

MOROCCO, 20 East 46th Street, New York, NY 10017 (212 557 2520)

NETHERLANDS, 576 Fifth Avenue, New York, NY 10036 (212 245 5320)

681 Market Street, Room 941, San Francisco, Ca. 94105 (415 781 3387)

NORWAY, 75 Rockefeller Plaza, New York, NY 10019 (212 582 2802)

3600 Wilshire Boulevard, Los Angeles, Ca. 90010 (213 387 7181)

POLAND, 630 Fifth Avenue, Rockefeller Center, Suite 520, New York, NY 10020 (212 582 7412)

PORTUGAL, 548 Fifth Avenue, New York, NY 10036 (212 354 4403)

ROMANIA, 573 Third Avenue, New York, NY 10016 (212 697 6971)

SPAIN, 665 Fifth Avenue, New York, NY 10022 (212 759 8822)
845 North Michigan Avenue, Chicago, Ill. 60611 (312 944 0215)
1 Hallidie Plaza, San Francisco, Ca. 94102 (415 346 8100)

SWEDEN, 75 Rockefeller Plaza, New York, NY 10019 (212 582 2802)

SWITZERLAND, 608 Fifth Avenue, New York, NY 10020 (212 757 5944)
250 Stockton Street, San Francisco, Ca. 94108 (415 362 2260)

TURKEY, Suite 821, United Nations Plaza, New York, NY 10017 (212 687 2194)

UNITED KINGDOM, 40 West 57th Street, New York, NY 10019 (212 581 4700)
612 South Flower Street, Los Angeles, Ca. 90017 (213 623 8196)
John Hancock Center, Suite 3320, 875 North Michigan Avenue, Chicago, Ill. 60611 (312 787 0490)
Plaza of the Americas, North Tower Suite 750, Dallas, Texas 75201 (213 623 8196)

YUGOSLAVIA, 630 Fifth Avenue, Suite 210, New York, NY 10111 (212 757 2801)

Remember though, Tourist Offices are in the business of selling their country, so take some of their claims like having the 'most beautiful city in Europe' with a pinch of salt. However, as their brochures are nearly all free and usually very well produced, you've nothing to lose. Make sure you ask for country and city maps; often the tourist authority will send you free the same ones you might otherwise have to buy, once in the country.

• **UK red tape:** A valid passport, with the relevant visas for Hungary, East Germany, Poland, Czechoslovakia, Bulgaria and Romania if you're going there, will get you in without problems. Likewise a British visitor's card is fine for Western Europe but no good for the Eastern Bloc. It costs £7.50 and is valid for twelve months. Apply at a post office in person with two recent passport-type photos and either your National Health Service card or your birth certificate.

For a full ten-year passport, get an application form at a main post office, complete it and send it on to your nearest passport office. This costs £15. Allow a month at least if you're posting off the form and at least three weeks if you take it in person.

• **US red tape:** A valid US passport will get you into the following countries for up to three months without the need for a visa: Austria, Belgium, France, West Germany, Greece, Ireland, Italy, Luxembourg, Morocco, Netherlands, Spain and Switzerland. Portugal allows you 60 days without a visa, and of course, all Eastern Bloc countries, including Yugoslavia, require a visa. Apply to the nearest consulate/embassy of the country concerned (see under US visas).

As far as the Scandinavian countries are concerned (Denmark, Finland, Norway and Sweden), the three-month period without visa is for holidaymakers and can be spent in all or any of the four Scandinavian countries. But a US tourist who has spent three months in, say, Sweden, cannot go on to spend a further period in, say, Denmark. A residence permit would be required in that case.

If you're applying for the first time or your current passport was issued before your eighteenth birthday or if it's more than eight years old, you'll have to go along in person to any US Post Office or Passport Agency, otherwise you can send off a DSP 82 form by mail. Along with your application you should include two recent passport-type photos, signed on the back, plus $35. If you have to go along in person, you'll need your US birth certificate and $42 ($28 if you're under eighteen). Passports are valid for ten years if you're over eighteen, five if you're under. If you've any problems, contact the Passport Office, Department of State, Washington, DC 20520, and ask them for their free booklet 'Your Trip Abroad'. Canadian passports are valid for five years only and can be obtained by mail from the Passport Office, Department of External Affairs, 125 Sussex Drive, Ottawa, Ontario KIA OG3. Allow six to eight weeks' processing time from March to September, and four to six weeks from October to February.

VISAS

Don't be put off from visiting a country because of the visa situation. The procedure is extremely straightforward and is invariably easier than most people imagine, even for a country like Poland.

A visa is required for all East European countries, and where possible it's best arranged in advance, by writing to the relevant embassy for their application form (see below). When you send off your application, don't forget to include two passport-type photos signed on the back, plus the relevant fee, which varies in price from around £6–12 ($8–16) depending on the country. Don't forget that you still need a visa for Hungary and Romania even though free travel is valid on an Inter Rail.

Allow up to four weeks (six for Poland) for the processing of your application form. If you've left it too late, don't worry as it's normally possible to obtain a visa from the relevant embassy in London, Paris or Vienna, if you're prepared to go along in person.

It goes without saying that you must be very careful not to lose your passport or visa; if this should happen, contact your embassy immediately (addresses are given under the individual countries). It is also important to have a recent passport photo; we were once held up for several hours on a Hungarian train merely because George had shaved off his beard since his photo had been taken!

• **UK visas:** For ROMANIA you can only get a visa in advance if you have prepaid accommodation, so it's best to buy your visa at the frontier, where you should have no problems. If you feel more comfortable with things arranged in advance, contact 4 Palace Green, London W8 (01–937 9667).

HUNGARY, on the other hand, requires you to send off for a visa in advance. On receipt of your first letter they'll send you an application form which you'll have to send back, along with three passport photos and the fee, to the Consular Section of the Embassy of the Hungarian People's Republic, 35B Eaton Place, London SW1 (01–235 4048). Allow at least a month for the whole procedure, and don't leave it to luck by hoping to buy a visa at the frontier, as you'll only be disappointed.

For EAST GERMANY, you can buy a transit visa at the frontier in foreign currency, but to avoid delays get it in advance from their embassy at 33 Belgrave Mews South, London SW1 (01–235 9941).

POLAND'S consulate, visa section, is at 47 Portland Place, London W1 (01–580 4324). Apply in advance.

CZECHOSLOVAKIA's rules state that you need to buy a visa in advance. Write to their embassy at 28 Kensington Palace Gardens, London W8 (01–727 3965) for an application form, then send this back with two photos, the fee (in cash or a postal order) and a self-addressed registered envelope to Čedok, 17–18 Old Bond Street, London W1 (01–629 6058).

BULGARIA requires a visa if you're travelling independently or if you're staying at private accommodation. Send for forms to their embassy at 186 Queen's Gate, London SW7 (01–584 9400).

● **US visas:** For CZECHOSLOVAKIA it's necessary to get a visa in advance. For an application form write to the Czechoslovak Embassy, 3900 Linnean Avenue NW, Washington, DC. If you've left things too late, you can always get a visa from the Czech Embassy in Vienna at Renzingstrasse.

A visa must be obtained in advance for BULGARIA. For the relevant forms, write to the Bulgarian Embassy, 2100 16th Street NW, Washington, DC 20009.

A visa for POLAND must be obtained in advance. For the relevant forms, write to Polish People's Republic, 2224 Wyoming Avenue NW, Washington, DC 20008. All visitors to Poland are required to change $15 a day into zlotys ($7 for everyone under 26); the best way to do this is to buy some accommodation vouchers from ORBIS at 500 Fifth Avenue, New York, NY 10036 (212 354 1487).

A 30-day visa for ROMANIA will cost you around $14 at the border, and can be extended for up to 90 days for an extra $10. For further information contact the Romanian Tourist Office at 573 Third Avenue, New York, NY 10016.

The easiest way of seeing EAST GERMANY is to get a day visa in West Berlin (see chapter on East Germany). If you want to stay in East Germany for longer then you must write in advance to GDR Embassy, 1717 Massachusetts Avenue NW, Washington, DC 20036, or get Koch Overseas Travel, 206–208 East 86th Street, New York, NY 10028 (212 513 8600) to arrange it all for you.

Visas for HUNGARY must be obtained in advance when travelling by train. For an application form, write to the Consulate General of the Hungarian People's Republic, 8 East 75th Street, New York, NY 10021, or The Hungarian Embassy, 3910 Shoemaker Street NW, Washington, DC 20008. If you left it too late, it's possible to get one in 48 hours if you go along in person to the Hungarian Embassy in Vienna at Bankgasse 4.

When you cross the border into YUGOSLAVIA, a customs officer will take your passport and return it sometime later with a free 90-day visa. At smaller crossings, you may be asked to get off the train and follow him to the customs office while he does the paper work.

BUDGETING

Exactly how much money you have to spend will affect your 'lifestyle' on eurorail in many ways. We're making the general assumption that the average eurorailer is perennially short of cash and won't ever be keen to spend more than he has to on basics such as accommodation and food. There's no shortage of information for those wishing to spend more – other 'budget' guides to Europe you can buy will list hotels for £30 ($40) a night, or restaurants for £20–25 ($26–33) meals. We're not interested in that. After all, who needs advice on how to *spend* money in Europe?

It's a straight fact that £15 ($20) a day in Norway will just about get you a hostel bed and a cafeteria meal; the same £15 in Spain will give you a hotel bed and a restaurant meal, so take into consideration the countries you want to go to, and budget accordingly. The most expensive countries are: Norway, Sweden, Finland, Denmark, Switzerland and Austria; the intermediate ones are: West Germany, Holland, Belgium, Luxembourg, France and Yugoslavia; and the cheap ones are: Spain, Italy, Greece, Portugal, Eastern Europe and Morocco. The southern part of Europe remains much cheaper than the northern, but to take full advantage of this cheapness you have to be prepared to accept the local standards of hygiene, cuisine, etc. Eastern Europe is cheap for food, drink and entertainment, but hotel accommodation is expensive, so hostel or camp. (Yugoslavia is a tricky one as the food in the local markets is very cheap but the accommodation prices are ridiculously high.) The basic fact of the matter is: camping and hostelling are cheap all over Europe, and if you are prepared to do this and buy your food in the local shops and markets to make your own picnics, you can eurorail for very little money.

On average, for your bed and daily food, you'll need £20 ($26) a day for the expensive countries, £12–15 ($16–20) a day for the intermediate ones, and £10–12 ($13–16) a day for the cheap ones. Remember: if you're travelling on your own and you insist on a single bedroom in a cheap hotel, it can double your costs, so double up with fellow travellers where at all possible.

• **International Student Identity Card:** This saves you money all over Europe – often as much as 75 per cent on museums and art galleries, etc., or even free entry. It also entitles you to 10–15 per cent discount on rail travel (useful if you want to go into a country not covered in the Inter Rail scheme, e.g. Bulgaria or Czechoslovakia), and up to 50 per cent reduction on some air fares. You need a certificate from your college or university. If in doubt, flash your card – you've nothing to lose. More than a million a year are sold. The ID card even provides you with automatic accident/sickness insurance anywhere you travel (outside the US) for the entire validity period of the ID card. Apply to your local Student Travel Office or to one of these addresses:

UK: International Students' Travel Centre, BJC, c/o NUS Marketing, University of London Union, Malet Street, London WC2.

USA: CIEE, New York Student Center, Sloane House YMCA, 356 West 34th Street, New York, NY 10001.

CANADA: AOSC, 44 St George Street, Toronto M5S 2E4, Ontario (416 979 2604).

AUSTRALIA: Australian Student Travel/STA, 220 Faraday Street, Carlton, Victoria 3053 (03 3476911).

SOUTH AFRICA: SASTS, Anreith Corner, Hans Strydom Avenue, Cape Town. Post address: PO Box 1381, Cape Town 8000 (21 6438).

NEW ZEALAND: Student Travel Bureau, Students' Union, University of Auckland, Princes Street, Auckland (375 265).

Ask for a copy of the ID discount guide for 1985.

For the Eastern Bloc countries you should officially have the IUS (International Union of Students) card which is the ISIC's counterpart. It costs about £1 ($1.30) and is available at student travel centres in the Eastern Bloc. From personal experience, we have found that you can often get away with showing your ISIC.

• **Student travel offices:** There are about 60 STOs in the UK. The good thing about them is that they nearly all sell Transalpino, Eurotrain and Inter Rail tickets, and the staff will work out the cheapest alternative for you. They also sell ISICs and are usually found in university or college complexes. Note: They offer their services to anyone under 26, not just students.

• **The Council on International Educational Exchange (CIEE):** The CIEE is a non-profit, membership organization based in the US, and is one of the foremost organizations concerned with student travel.

They are there to help budget travellers with low-cost travel (air, train, etc.) as well as accommodation problems. In fact, they cover every aspect of your trip from your Student ID card to your airline ticket and reservations. Get hold of their 1985 Student Travel catalogue which is a mine of information by writing to CIEE, 205 East 42nd Street, New York, NY 10017 (212 661 1450). They also have offices in Los Angeles, San Francisco, Berkeley, San Diego, Seattle and Boston. Fill in their 1985 travel planner form and they will send you an estimate of the lowest possible air fare they could find, together with details on the Eurail Youthpass and other travel packages that interest you and that fit your budget.

The catalogue also provides further information on Student ID cards, travel, study and work abroad. Use their expertise as much as possible as it's a wonderful service and puts you under no obligation whatsoever to buy your travel tickets from their office.

Getting yourself together

WHAT TO TAKE WITH YOU

Obviously this very much depends on where you're going and at what time of the year: if you're going to Scandinavia in the spring, an extra jumper will certainly come in very useful. However, there are various points to remember, irrespective of where you are going or the time of the year. Unless you're visiting family or friends in Europe and expect to be met at every station, we strongly advise that you use a framed rucksack (preferably with an internal frame). Its advantages are manifold: it gives one the feeling of membership of a eurorail club and this stimulates conversation and communication which otherwise might not take place. Also – and more importantly – both your hands will be left free to use, allowing you to produce your maps, passport, etc., at the right moment.

● **Packing:** Every summer, Europe is full of backpackers wishing they hadn't taken so much, so don't take more than you're prepared to carry with comfort. Before you set out, put out on the bed everything you want to take with you – then halve it. Before you finally make up your mind, try wearing your rucksack with everything you intend to take in it on a good walk. Remember, don't be overgenerous as you'll be returning with more than you left with in the way of presents and souvenirs, so leave room for them. All this is common sense really; however, we all need reminding from time to time, as it can make the difference between a relaxing and an exhausting holiday.

● **Essentials:** The rucksack: without doubt this will be your most important single piece of equipment, so it is essential to ensure that it is both comfortable and light. Beware of back-breakers and spine-grinders. The three most important features you should look out for are: that it sits just above your hips and, if possible, has a support belt for round your waist; that the shoulder-straps are well padded and that the tension can be adjusted; and (most important of all) that your pack is 'high' rather than 'wide', when packed to capacity. I wish we had a pound for every eurorailer we've seen creating havoc along the all-too-narrow train-corridors. If they're not pulling the door shut on someone's leg they're laying out the natives with swinging cameras and boots hanging from the rear.

A small day-pack is also invaluable, especially when sightseeing, as it will hold your maps, guidebook, waterproof, camera, films, food, etc., all conveniently together. However American it may make you feel, it's well worth it as it solves a lot of problems and saves you walking around all the time with a large rucksack. It's a good idea to put your name and address in the inside of your pack, just in case – something which most eurorailers overlook.

• **Valuables:** Keep an independent note of your ticket and passport numbers. If you do lose your passport, notify the police then get a copy of the report the police make out and go along with it to your country's nearest consulate or embassy. A photocopy of your birth certificate is another very useful thing to have with you, as are a couple of passport photos, which can come in handy for impromptu visas, replacement ISICs or passports.

One idea, very popular with the Scandinavians, is to buy a pouch that you hang round your neck with all your tickets and valuables in it. Another good idea is a moneybelt. You can pick up one of these in Greece or Spain quite cheaply – assuming you can get that far without getting ripped off.

• **Sleeping bag:** Unless you plan to spend all your time staying with friends or at cheap hotels you'll need a good bag. Hostels charge for the use of bedding, so you can save by carrying your own. Also at some stage in your travels it's likely you'll be a deck passenger on an overnight ferry somewhere. When you're shopping around for a sleeping bag, price is likely to be your main criterion, as it's not difficult to spend more on your sleeping bag than on your ticket. If you have no bag already, and can't borrow one from a friend, we suggest that you go along to your local camping shop and get the best you can afford. As with the other two basics, rucksack and shoes, the better the quality, the more money you can expect to spend. From personal experience, we would urge you not to make cutbacks in this direction: there are few things worse than a cold sleepless night before a hard day's sightseeing. Buying a cheap sleeping bag is a classic false economy. Shop assistants in camping shops are usually very helpful and only too ready to help you out as best they can.

If you're taking a bag and plan to do a lot of camping or sleeping out on southern beaches, then a foam mattress is also advisable. Try and get one that is long enough but not too wide (remember those train corridors). Lie down on it in the shop to check it out. Print your name on it as you'll find mattresses disappear with remarkable frequency.

• **Comfortable walking shoes** (already broken in) are essential as you can expect to spend as much time walking as you will on trains. Don't go over the top and wear boots that would look better on

Everest rather than strolling round the Vatican. If you're heading south, a pair of sandals is a necessity to give your feet a chance to breathe. If you don't have any, don't worry: they're cheap in southern Europe.

• **Camping gear:** If you're heading for northern Europe and plan to camp a lot, get a strongish tent with a fly-sheet; however, if you'll be mainly in the south, pick a light one, preferably of nylon. A small Calor gas stove can save you a lot of money, especially in places like Norway where buying a cup of tea or coffee can cost £1 ($1.30) or so. Gas refills are widely available so don't bother carrying spares. Unless you're camping non-stop for about a month, don't carry food supplies and a lot of camping equipment with you. Shopping from the local supermarkets makes much more sense. Remember to take a torch for those late-night pitches.

• **Clothes:** Obviously it depends on where you're going and the time of year. Use your common sense, but don't take anything you don't absolutely need and remember: though you may look terrific in your white jeans when they're newly washed and ironed at home, you'll look terrible after you've sat up all night in them on an Italian train.

Take dark comfortable clothes that won't show the battering you're giving them. Laundries are often expensive, so take a little washing powder or liquid detergent and wash your own clothes.

LAST-MINUTE REMINDERS

1. Girls: take a scarf or shawl to cover your head and shoulders as often you'll be refused entry to churches and cathedrals if your arms and shoulders are bare. Shorts are also prohibited in many churches, so go prepared.
2. A travelling alarm clock is a handy thing, especially if you have early trains to catch.
3. Don't forget toilet paper, soap and a small towel. You can never find a place to buy these, just when you need them most.
4. Plastic bags are handy for containing liquids, etc.
5. A Swiss Army penknife, with as many functions as possible (including a corkscrew), comes in handy.

6. A small padlock is often useful when hostelling (for the lockers).
7. A pre-filled water-bottle will save you cash on long thirsty journeys as prices of drinks on trains are high.
8. A good book: take your reading supply from home as English-language books cost a lot abroad.
9. Invaluable are a notepad and a pen. Get shopkeepers to write down prices before saying yes, if you don't have the lingo. This way, you'll know when you're being ripped off.
10. Postcards of your home town are a good ice-breaker and let foreigners see where you're from. It's good public relations and can even boost home town tourism!

MONEY

There's a 'Catch 22' situation with money in Europe. Undoubtedly, with violence and crime the way it is at present in Europe, especially the south, it's a big risk to carry around all your cash in ready notes on you, even in a moneybelt. To be weighed against this is the fact that by taking traveller's cheques you lay yourself open to continual queueing, especially in the summer, not to mention the hassles trying to find a bank or travel agent to cash them. If you decide to play safe and take most of your money in traveller's cheques, then get them from one of the big banks or, even better, from Thomas Cook or American Express. Don't find yourself walking around every bank in town trying to cash an obscure brand of traveller's cheque.

When buying your traveller's cheques, always buy small denominations as this is more economical on a tight budget. Anyone from the USA, Canada, Australia or New Zealand should buy cheques in their own currency – unless you're planning to spend 99 per cent of your time in one country. If you offer a £20 cheque and ask for £14 in French francs and £6 in Italian lire, most banks will charge you first to change into francs, then again into lire. It's better to get traveller's cheques in denominations of £10 ($13). In general, it's a good idea to take some bank notes of the countries you know you'll end up in, especially if there's a chance you will arrive late at night or at weekends. As a rule, we take £25 ($30) cash in four or five different currencies, just to be on the safe side, in case there's no opportunity to change money on arrival and you have to pay for your room in advance. Again, it's best to order the currency you think you'll need from your bank at least two weeks in advance. If you have a credit card, take it along on your trip as it's a good standby.

Remember: take a moneybelt. Sending money on is expensive, so take a realistic amount. Also remember: apart from banks, large stations have exchange facilities, as do some hotels and travel agents.

● **Money in Eastern Europe:** 'Hard' currency from the West helps strengthen the local stuff; as a result, some countries insist on a minimum exchange requirement. This is nearly always more than is strictly necessary, and in some cases you'll have difficulty trying to get rid of it. To discourage black-market dealings, you'll have to declare all your hard currency and any goods that the authorities think you might want to flog off while you're there. This declaration is normally carried out on the train at the border.

If you're thinking of playing the black market (which we strongly advise against) you will have to 'forget' to declare some of your hard currency because if, on departure, you cannot account for the missing money or produce the required receipts, you will be in trouble.

● **Black market:** In recent years the authorities in Eastern Europe have tried to reduce black-market activities by offering good rates of exchange at official tourist offices, and by coming down with a heavy hand on those caught in the act (in some cases this means imprisonment). Hard currency is very much in demand, and many private citizens are prepared to pay far more than the official rate to get it. Some people are still prepared to pay high prices for jeans, pocket calculators, etc., though this is becoming less common. In general, never have any dealings with anyone who approaches you in the street; at best, you're likely to get poor rates and, at worst, they could be plain-clothes police or an informer. A final word: tipping is not general practice here, so hang on to your cash.

● **Banking:** You can cash a personal cheque of up to £50 ($68) in any European bank displaying the EC symbol if you've got a Euro-cheque Encashment Card and appropriate cheque book with you.

Remember that the 24-hour exchange bureaux in general charge a higher commission, so don't always be tempted to cash your cheques at the first place you see in the station. They often have less favourable rates of exchange. In some countries, such as Germany, the post office changes money without taking as large a commission as the banks. In countries where there's a high service charge for cashing traveller's cheques, you're better off cashing your own personal cheques at Eurocheque banks using your banker's card, as only a small charge is made for this. Banks in all countries open in the morning from Monday to Friday, but beware of the siestas in the Mediterranean countries (see the individual countries, for banking hours).

INSURANCE

Whether or not to get insurance cover depends very much on where you're going, and for how long. If you've a lot of expensive new camping gear and photographic equipment then undoubtedly it's worth it. Shop around for the best deal; call in at your local student travel centre and see what they have to offer. It could be you're already insured through your home policy (your parents' or your own), so check up first. Both Transalpino and Eurotrain offer travel insurance schemes (see above, pages 27 and 28). It's worth bearing in mind that train travel is very safe indeed, and it's highly unlikely that you'll end up in hospital because of an accident, but your health and your valuables are a different matter. Still, after food poisoning in Morocco and with a doctor being called out at 2 a.m., the bill for one of us was less than the insurance premium would have been, so think twice if you're really broke.

• **American and Canadian travellers:** If your personal policies don't provide adequate cover abroad, check with your travel agent or CIEE office to see what options are available.

• **Medical:** If you're only travelling in EEC countries and you're British, go along to your local DHSS office and get form E 111. This service is often neglected by eurorailers which is surprising as it provides absolutely free medical cover in EEC countries to the same level that a national of that country enjoys. Doctors in Europe can be very expensive, and often a chemist can give just as good advice – free! To find a 24-hour chemist, either ask at a police station or go to the nearest chemist's shop and look in the window, as there's often a notice saying where one is open.

Watch out, girls: in Eastern Europe it's often impossible to get hold of tampons or sanitary towels, so take a supply along with you. (Also, if you'll need contraceptives, take them from home.)

If you've got to carry drugs or injection needles for medical reasons, take a doctor's note about them as you could otherwise be in for a hard time in Eastern Europe and Turkey.

Unless you've got an iron stomach, it's best to work on the theory that prevention is better than cure: take along some multivitamin pills to keep body and soul together during those long hauls, avoid the tap water in southern Europe, peel all fruit and make sure that meat is always well cooked. You'll be doing enough running for trains . . .

In the event of your having problems with sangria, paella and the like, it's a good idea to keep some Alka-Seltzer and anti-diarrhoea tablets to hand. A mild laxative won't go amiss, in case all that foreign food and drink affects you the other way. The further south you go, the more mosquitoes and other undesirables you're likely to encounter, so if you're a big scratcher take along some soothing cream and a small pack of plasters and, should all else fail, some pain-killers.

When you're there

ACCOMMODATION

As accommodation is the largest potential headache for eurorailers and we're limited for space, we're restricting our suggestions to the main tourist centres. If you plan travelling off the beaten track or arriving late in peak season, we strongly recommend you to splash out £1.50 ($2) on a very worthwhile booklet called 'Low Cost Accommodation Europe 85'. It's published by the International Student Travel Conference and you can buy it from Student Travel Offices throughout the USA, Canada, Australia and New Zealand as well as in Britain and Europe (Student Travel Offices are listed under the main cities in Part Two). The booklet gives over a thousand suggestions covering all Europe, and means you'll never have to wait in long accommodation-finding queues at tourist offices or pay their commission charges again – this booklet itself actually costs less than the equivalent of one placing!

Our suggestions tend to be biased towards hostels, and to places located near stations. Basically there are four types of accommodation open to you: cheap hotels; youth or student hostels; camping and private accommodation. There is, theoretically, a fifth option for those with an open pass – and it will certainly ensure you get round Europe at a phenomenal rate – it is to sleep on the trains themselves, not just in the couchettes or sleepers which vary in price from £5 to £25 ($7–34) for a night's sleep, but for free in the seats. As we've discussed 'night travel' already and we do not really recommend you spending your eurorail doing this, we'll concentrate now on the other four.

• **Cheap hotels/pensions:** If you're travelling with your girlfriend/ boyfriend and don't fancy camping and can't get into private accommodation, this is your only real alternative if you want to spend the night together. The advantages are obvious: relative comfort and convenience. If you're in a city and you haven't long to be there, it's best to try for one located near the centre, to save you bus journeys and hassles. The disadvantages are: it's more expensive than hostelling or camping, and if you're in a really cheap hotel, you often find a sort of 'skid row' atmosphere. The hotels we list under each country are the best compromise we could find between clean, pleasant surroundings and a fair price.

If there are two or more of you room-hunting, it's a good idea for one to wait in the tourist office queue with all the luggage, while the other goes looking for a room in one of the hotels you invariably find close to the stations. The rooms in these places are generally cheap and, of course, very convenient. Alternatively, if you all want to go off to hunt together, leave your heavy packs in left luggage. You won't regret the £1 ($1.50) you spend for the extra comfort and speed you'll get out of it.

Once you've found a suitable place and have been told the prices, ask the receptionist again if she has nothing cheaper. Often this works and you get a cheaper room tucked away near the top. The luxury of taking a room with a private bath or shower is bought at a high price, so you do best to use the communal one. Always ask how much a bath or shower costs. If you're travelling in a group it can be cheaper to have a room with a bath than to pay for four showers. In the vast majority of cheap hotels it's not included in the price, and it can come as a nasty shock when you get the bill.

Unfortunately the wonderful British institution of B&B does not exist in Europe. Breakfast is often extra and rarely does it merit the name or the cost. Anyway, it's far cheaper and more entertaining to find a coffee bar or café where the locals go.

Pensions (guest houses) are often far more attractive and friendly than hotels. A double bed is usually cheaper than two singles. Remember to check all the following before deciding on a room in a hotel: the price of the room, including all taxes; whether breakfast is included; whether a bath/shower is included; whether there is nothing cheaper; whether the hotelier would mind if three or four people used a double room; and finally when you must check out the next day, to avoid paying for another night's accommodation.

● **Hostels:** Hostels run by the International Youth Hostel Federation are good value and an ideal place to meet up with other travellers. They're the next cheapest alternative to camping, ranging from £2 to £8 ($2.60–10.50) a night. You need to be a member of your own country's YHA or that of the country you're in, though often you can buy temporary membership on the spot. If you're already a member of the YHA, attach a photo of yourself to your YHA card to allow you to hostel in Europe.

Youth hostels offer simple basic accommodation for men and women in separate dormitory-style bedrooms, washing and toilet facilities, and a common room. Many hostels have their own communal kitchen, though you need your own utensils. In this way you can buy food at supermarket prices and cater for yourself for next to no cost at all. Economical meals are laid on at many hostels (we list these below, under each country) and hostellers are expected to help with some domestic chores. It is essential to have (or to hire) a sheet sleeping bag to spend the night in a hostel, otherwise they charge you for sheets. The general rule is that you can't stay more than three nights at any one hostel.

If you've never hostelled before, it's a good idea to go round one or two at home so you get to know what it's like. If you're expecting room service or breakfast in bed, forget hostelling. (Actually, if you're strictly the breakfast-in-bed type, forget eurorailing!) Average cost is £6.50 ($8.50) a night and average meal £2–3.50 ($2.60–4.50).

• **Booking ahead:** During July and August it's a good idea to book your hostel bed ahead in the major tourist cities. If you're going to be doing a lot of hostelling in Europe, a useful system is International Multi-Lingual Booking Cards: they cost about 5p each and allow one, two or more people to reserve beds and meals. You post the cards on to the hostel concerned with an International Reply Coupon (on sale at post offices). Beds reserved through this scheme are held until 6 p.m.

Hostels vary a tremendous amount; generally though, the further south you go, the less strict the rules tend to be, and also the more basic the accommodation becomes. Some hostels still insist on midnight curfews and lock you out between 10 a.m. and 4 p.m., while others are far more liberal. If in doubt, it's always a good move to phone ahead from the station and check out if there's space and what rules, if any, apply. Many hostels are open only in the summer.

Beware of the increasing number of unofficial hostels which are springing up, especially in southern Europe. Many call themselves 'Student Youth Hostels' and, though they impose no curfews or sex segregation, the facilities they offer are often very poor and the charges are more than those of official youth hostels.

If you intend staying in youth hostels a lot, it's a good idea to get a full list of all YHA hostels in Europe to complement *Europe by Train*.

If you need more hostelling information, the head office of the YHA is: 14 Southampton Street, London WC2E 7MY (01–836 8541).

• **Student hostels:** Student hostels are similar to youth hostels, but instead of a YHA card you need an International Student ID card. Many student hostels are unused student dorms and are only open during university vacations.

• **YMCA/YWCA Inter Rail Points:** The European Alliance of YMCAs operates a series of twenty-three Inter Rail Points in eleven different countries to provide budget-priced accommodation. They also organize optional events such as sightseeing trips, hill walking, barbecues etc., as well as helping with advice if required. Most of the YMCAs involved in this programme offer hostel facilities throughout the year and reduce their rates during the Eurorailing period from June to September. Unlike the YHA you do not have to be members of the YMCA to use their facilities. Many are near the station and provide showers and cooking facilities. For further details, write with an SAE to: YMCA Special Programmes, Crown House, 550 Mauldeth Road West, Manchester M21 2RX.

• **Camping:** If you're keen on the 'great outdoors', then camping in conjunction with a eurorail is ideal for you. There's no shortage of scenic sites, and even the major cities of Europe have campgrounds on their outskirts. But as a general rule we advise against it for big cities. The advantages of camping are obvious: it's cheap, if you're on a campsite you have all necessary facilities to hand, and it adds a dash of 'pioneering spirit' to your holiday. Prices on official campsites range from £1 to £4 ($1.30–5.20) a tent, and £1 to £6 ($1.30–7.80) per person.

The International Camping Carnet is useful if you're doing a lot of camping, as many European campgrounds insist on it, particularly those in the state forests of France and Denmark. You can buy the Carnet at most sites.

The disadvantages of official camping that spring to mind are: other people, cars, radios, tents all around, queueing for showers, etc. Unofficial camping, however, removes all these problems and can be a memorable experience. Remember to check with the farmer or landowner before pitching tent for the night, and observe strict hygiene.

It's quite feasible to camp throughout your entire eurorail. A tent, gas stove, utensils, sleeping bag and foam mattress will solve all your accommodation problems at once. Don't skimp too much on equipment, however; a good tent is far and away the most important thing.

• **Private accommodation:** This is an interesting and, in many ways, preferable alternative to hotels. Pricewise, it's slightly cheaper than hotels, but more expensive than hostels or camping. Individuals arrange through local tourist authorities for tourists to come and stay at their houses for any period of time from a night to the whole summer. It's a good way to meet the locals and get a home-from-home atmosphere. Ask at the tourist office and they will arrange the details for you. The only problem is that you may find all the places full in the high season as in many cities there are more prospective guests than recipient hosts.

• **Accommodation – Eastern Europe:** Nearly all hotels are owned and run by the state tourist company of the country. They cater mainly for large parties who tend to book *en masse* months ahead, making it difficult, but not impossible, to find a room. They also tend to work out expensive, as they charge higher prices for Western tourists. Go for private accommodation where you can. It's cheaper, gives you a better idea of Eastern Bloc life, and can either be arranged through the state tourist authority or negotiated in the street. You often find women meeting the trains to offer their rooms out; don't be afraid, it's perfectly legal and acceptable. Camping is another option, but always check first how far out of town the sites are, and how good the bus services are. During the summer, students with ID cards can sleep in university dormitories: book these through the national student organizations.

The East European tourist authorities will find a room for you for a commission, and will give you a list of campsites. Be prepared for long queues in summer and for their commissions to be higher than their Western equivalents. East European authorities work under the assumption that all young people travel in large groups, not in ones and twos. As a result, you will often be told that hostels are only run for groups; however, don't give in, but insist.

EATING

Whenever possible it's a good thing to sample the local cuisine, for quite apart from being an extremely enjoyable way of learning about another culture, it's often a lot cheaper and more appetizing than eating the type of food one's accustomed to at home. If all the restaurants are expensive, don't despair; you'll find that nearly every supermarket has a section devoted to regional specialities where with a little bit of imagination you can prepare yourself a veritable feast. Like everything else, a little background knowledge can add greatly to one's enjoyment. Try collecting articles on regional food from travel magazines, cook books, Sunday supplements and the like; or, even better, check out your local library. Time-Life books do a good series called *Foods of the World* and it's well worth reading the European section on the countries you plan to visit.

Here are the basic rules, accumulated over years of good and bad eating out:

1. Avoid expensive, pretentious-looking restaurants and cafés which display no prices.
2. Read the menu first, then add up the cost of your choices and all the taxes and service charges before ordering.
3. Go for 'menus of the day' or tourist menus with fixed prices wherever you can.
4. Serve yourself whenever you can.
5. Don't buy food or drink from vendors on the trains or from stalls in the stations. Buy in advance at supermarkets.
6. If you've an addiction to something like coffee in the morning, take your supplies with you in the form of a camping stove, a small pan and some instant coffee.
7. When it comes to cheeses, wines, meats, biscuits, etc., buy the local stuff. Imports are always more expensive and, anyway, it's good to sample the local produce.
8. Use fast-food chains if nothing else is available for cheap, reliable snacks. They're often far better and cheaper than local snack bars, especially in southern Europe where hygiene is often suspect.
9. Be adventurous, try something new. Ask for house wine: it's always cheaper than listed wine and there's a good chance it's the popular wine of the region.

10. Eat breakfast out when it's optional at your hotel as it's nearly always cheaper at a local cafe.
11. Make lunch your main meal of the day. Prepare yourself a big picnic whenever possible. Even when you eat at restaurants, it's at least 15 per cent cheaper than in the evening. Avoid tourist areas, where prices are nearly always higher. In large towns search out the university areas, where prices are generally more reasonable.

CITY TRANSPORT SYSTEMS

If you're going to stay in one place for more than a day or two, find out about the cheap travel passes on offer. Some cities offer day passes, others weekly ones and, if your accommodation is out of town, they can save you quite a bit. Before rushing off to buy one, however, check on a map for the location of the main sights you're interested in, as in many towns these are all within easy walking distance of one another and you won't need a bus pass. If you're not in a rush, using the buses as opposed to the underground lets you see a bit more of the city – which is worth bearing in mind. Tickets for the buses and underground can often be bought at tobacco kiosks. Thomas Cook's *European Cities* guidebook is particularly good on local transport.

TELEPHONE AND TELEGRAM

You will usually find both these facilities at the general post office. Some countries also offer special telephone kiosks for international calls. Find out the international dialling code (44 for Britain; 0101 for the USA) before you start.

Always try to dial direct as it's much cheaper. Never telephone via the switchboard at hotels or hostels as they invariably add on a whack – sometimes as much as the call itself – for themselves. Throughout Europe it's pretty standard that calls out of business hours (7 p.m.–8 a.m.) are charged at a cheaper rate. In nearly every country, either dialling instructions in English or pictograms are to be found inside telephone boxes.

Telegrams are expensive, and in almost every case you'll find it cheaper making a quick phone call; but if that's impossible, write out your message and hand it to the clerk to avoid spelling mistakes.

MAIL

Airmail letters from major West European cities to the USA and Britain arrive within a week or so. Letters from southern or Eastern Europe take anything from two weeks to a month, so if you're on a eurorail lasting a month, it's hardly worthwhile writing. Postcards tend to be even worse. Use surface mail (by ship) for posting home any books or clothes you don't fancy carrying around. It's usually very cheap – but very slow too.

Trying to collect mail in Europe is more often than not a nerve-racking business. If you've no fixed address, the best method to use (and it's free or costs very little) is poste restante. This means your mail is sent to you c/o the main post office of any city or town. Depending on the vagaries of the country's domestic postal system, your mail should be at the poste restante office filed under your surname. Produce your passport or equivalent proof of identity and pick it up. If the clerk says there's nothing for you, get him to check under your first name too. Use AMEX if you have their traveller's cheques and kill two birds with one stone.

In Eastern Europe, get the sender to put a '1' after the city's name to ensure it goes to the main post office. American Express card holders can get mail sent on to AMEX offices to await collection (but we haven't met too many American Express eurorailers yet!).

SHOPPING

Unlike many other guidebooks, we don't include details on shopping. We are taking it for granted that most people won't have spare cash to blow in the shops, and if you do, you'll have enough common sense to head for the centre and find the main shopping areas for yourselves. In general, the studenty part of a city is cheaper, and for food the large supermarkets are your best bet.

Shopping hours vary from country to country but they're all based round the 8–6 routine, though lunch hours can range from none at all to three hours. As a basic rule, the further south you go, the longer the 'siesta', and you can only count on a half day on Saturday.

TOURIST INFORMATION

At most stations you'll find a *Tourist Information Office*. When this isn't the case we give directions below on how to get there. These tourist offices are easily your best source of maps and detailed information. There seemed little point to us in reproducing their maps and rewriting the minuscule details of the sights for you here. Our main aim in this book has been to direct you to the main things of interest, give you the basics, and let you fill in the rest from what you're given at tourist offices. Finally, so far as opening times are concerned, we've generally only listed irregular ones; take the rest as following the local norm.

Good eurorailing!

Please feel free to write in your comments and suggestions to us. Let us know whether, in your opinion, any of the items deserve more detailed treatment. Obviously, in a book containing the amount of information that this does, facts and figures get out of date easily, and though we try to update as thoroughly as possible we would appreciate your help. All correspondence should be addressed to: Katie Wood and George McDonald, 'Europe by Train', Fontana Paperbacks, 8 Grafton Street, London W1X 3LA.

VOCABULARY

We've listed some common words and expressions you're bound to encounter while away. We've kept it pretty simple as there's no point in getting too involved in a language you don't know the basics of; and we've stuck to the big four: French, German, Italian and Spanish. If you encounter linguistic problems in the Eastern Bloc, try German as an alternative.

ENGLISH	FRENCH	GERMAN	ITALIAN	SPANISH
please	s'il vous plaît	bitte	per piacere	por favor
thank you	merci	danke schön	grazie	gracias
yes	oui	ja	si	si
no	non	nein	no	no
where is . . .	où est . . .	wo ist . . .	dov'è . . .	dónde está . . .
the station	la gare	der Bahnhof	la stazione	la estación
the youth hostel	l'auberge de jeunesse	die Jugendherberge	l'albergo per giovani	el albergue juvenil
the toilet	le lavabo	die Toilette	il gabinetto	el retrete
how much?	combien?	wieviel?	quanto?	¿cuánto?
I would like . . .	je voudrais . . .	ich möchte . . .	vorrei . . .	querria . . .
a room	une chambre	ein Zimmer	una camera	una habitación
seat reservation	réservation	Bestellung	prenotazione	reservación
couchette	couchette	Liegeplatz	cuccetta	litera
sleeping car	wagon-lit	Schlafwagen	carrozza letti	coche cama
arrival	arrivée	Ankunft/Ankommen	arrivo	llegada
departure	départ	Abfahrt	partenza	salida
left-luggage locker	consigne automatique	Schliessfach	custodia automatica	consigna automática
left-luggage store	consigne	Gepäckaufbewahrung	deposito bagagli	deposito

information	renseignements	Auskunft	informazioni	información
platform	quai	Bahnsteig	binario	andén
smoker	fumeur	Raucher	fumatori	fumar
supplement	supplément	Zuschlag	supplemento	supplemento
is this a through train for . . . ?	est-ce un train direct pour . . . ?	ist das der direkte Zug nach . . . ?	c'è un treno diretto per . . . ?	¿Es un tren directo a . . . ?
where do I change for . . . ?	où change-t-on de train pour . . . ?	wo steigt man nach . . . . um?	si cambia treno per . . . ?	¿Dónde se cambia de tren para . . . ?
currency exchange	bureau de change	Wechselstube	cambio	officina de cambio

SOME INTERNATIONAL TIMETABLE SYMBOLS

Reservations compulsory

Couchette

Sleeping Car

Restaurant Car

Buffet/Cafeteria

Drinks service and snacks

Except Sundays and public holidays

Sundays and public holidays only

Trains running on certain days only

Trains subject to special regulations stated in the information notes of the relevant timetable

Frontier border station; customs and passport checks

Connection by bus

Connection by boat

Part Two: THE COUNTRIES

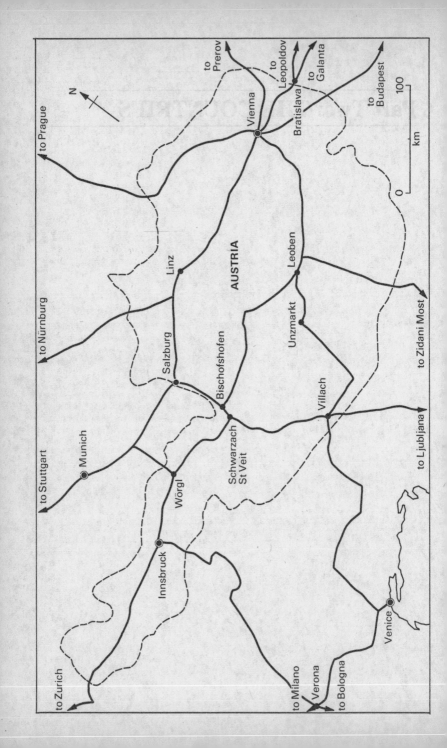

AUSTRIA

Entry requirements	Passport
Population	7,600,000
Capital	Vienna (pop.: 1,900,000)
Currency	Austrian Schilling
	£1 = approx. AS 26
Political system	Federal Republic
Religion	Roman Catholic
Language	German (English spoken)
Public holidays	1, 6 Jan.; Good Friday; Easter Monday; 1 May;
	Ascension Day; Whit Monday; Corpus Christi; 15
	Aug.; 26 Oct.; 1 Nov.; 8, 25, 26 Dec.

Austria would have been no place for eurorailing during its early history, certainly not for sleeping out at the station, as one power struggle followed another until the Habsburgs emerged at the end of the thirteenth century. As good Catholics and Holy Roman Emperors for four centuries, they spent most of their time fighting the Turks as well as keeping everyone at home in order. As a result of this, they provided a strong monarchy, but it was no fun to be in the army as Austria continued to be involved in political struggles till the eighteenth century. By then, Vienna had become the home of Europe's finest musicians such as Mozart, Beethoven and, of course, later on, Strauss. With the First World War the monarchy came to an end and her empire folded up. She had a hard time in the Second World War as she was forcibly joined on to Germany, and suffered heavily from Allied bombing. In 1955, Austria became a neutral country and has since made a spectacular economic recovery. This is particularly so with Vienna, which has been lovingly restored and once again fulfils its ancient role as a stopover place where eurorailers can enjoy their last few days of Western comfort before heading east to Yugoslavia. The alpine scenery and Tyrolean villages make Austria one of Europe's most attractive countries and a perfect destination for those seeking the great outdoors.

AUSTRIAN FEDERAL RAILWAYS
(Österreichische Bundesbahnen, ÖBB)

As you might expect, trains run on time. They are clean and

comfortable, as are the stations. However, there's generally a lot of queueing in summer, thanks to over-bureaucracy (a hangover from the Habsburg days, we suspect). Most intercities run two hours apart.

Train types are: international expresses (Expresszüge), long-distance expresses (Schnellzüge), semi-fast services (Eilzüge), and TEE trains. Apart from on the TEE trains, you can get by without supplements. Avoid local trains unless you have plenty of time as they tend to be slow, especially if you're on a mountainous route.

• **Inter Rail bonuses:** Half price is offered on the following services:

COMPANY	FROM	TO
	(*or vice versa*)	
Puchberg am Schneeberg–Hochschneeberg Mountain Railway	All	
St Wolfgang Schafbergbahnhof–Schafbergspitze Mountain Railway	All	
ÖBB Wolfgangseeschiffahrt	All	
Vereinigte Schiffahrtsverwaltungen für den Bodensee und Rhein	All	
Erste Donau–Dampfschiffahrts–Gesellschaft	Passau	Wien
Steiermarkische Landesbahnen	Feldbach	Bad Gleichenberg
	Gleisdorf	Weiz
	Peggau–Deutschfeistritz	Übelbach
	Unzmarkt	Tamsweg

Free entry to Railway Museum, 212 Mariahilferstrasse, Wien.

• **Eurail bonuses:** The following services are free:
—Puchberg am Schneeberg–Hochschneeberg rack railway.
—St Wolfgang–Schafbergspitze rack railway.
—Steamers on Lake Wolfgang.
—Steamers operated by the Erste Donau–Dampfschiffahrts–Gesellschaft between Passau and Vienna.

Reduced fares:
—50 per cent reduction on steamers operated by steamship companies on Lake Constance.

TRAIN INFORMATION

Information officers are multilingual, other rail staff less so. You can easily tell the information officers: they wear yellow cap bands. Luggage lockers use five-schilling pieces.

• **Reservations:** Are not necessary. If you want to make one, it can be done until two hours before your train leaves (cost: approximately AS 60).

• **Night travel:** Austria's too small for an extensive service. Sleepers and couchettes are clean and comfortable. Reserve at least five hours beforehand. Couchettes cost around AS 250. There are also compartments with pull-down seats which cost nothing.

• **Eating on trains:** For those with money, there are dining cars on all intercity trains. Mini-bars are to be found on all trains except locals. As always, we advise picnics, but if you don't have time to go to a supermarket before the train leaves, there are kiosks at most stations. Vienna's stations, in particular, have well-stocked delicatessens which are open long hours, including Sundays.

• **Scenic tips:** The main Innsbruck–Zell am See–Salzburg line is one of the most scenic in the country. If you're going from Innsbruck to Italy, take the train to Brennero for beautiful mountainous scenery. If you're heading towards Yugoslavia, try Vienna–Trieste – this goes via Klagenfurt and Udine. If you're travelling from Innsbruck to Munich or vice versa, try the route via Garmisch – again the mountain scenery is beautiful. Bregenz, situated on the Bodensee in the west of Austria, is a good point of departure to sail through to Germany. From here you can go to Konstanz over the border (ask about reductions for train pass holders). Also at Bregenz you can take the Pfanderbahn up to the top for a wonderful view of the Alps and over the Bodensee. Go to the Vorarlberg Tourist Office in Bregenz on Jahnstrasse for information on Alpine villages and excursions. You can sail from the German–Austrian border (Passau) to Vienna or from Vienna to Passau. The trip lasts a day and a half, stopping overnight at Linz. Alternatively, there's the Linz–Vienna trip or vice versa. The prettiest part of the trip is from Kerens to Melk. The train runs from both Melk and Krems. Further information from DDSG, Reisedienst 2, Handelskai 265. In Passau, go to DDSG-Schiffsstation, Im Ort 14A, Dreiflunseck. Get off the boat and take a look around as often as possible, as many of the stopping-off places are well-preserved medieval or baroque towns. If you're leaving Vienna for Salzburg, stop off at the village of Mariazell. It's beautiful. Surrounded by hills, it was a religious pilgrimage site. Take the cable for the view. From Wien take the train tò St Pölten from the Westbahnhof, then change there to a train for Mariazell.

• **Bikes:** You can rent out a bike in nearly every important station in Austria, thirty-seven in all – 'Fahrrad Am Bahnhof'. Take a quick look at the traffic situation before committing yourself.

TOURIST INFORMATION

There's a local tourist office (Verkehrsverein) in every large town which will give you the addresses of the provincial tourist boards if required.

• **ISIC bonuses:** 50 per cent reductions on most art galleries and museums. For further information, contact Fuhrichngasse 10, Wien.

• **Money matters:** 1 Austrian schilling (AS) = 100 groschen (gr). Banking hours are Mon.–Wed., Fri.: 8.30 a.m.–12.30 p.m., 1.30 p.m.–3.30 p.m., Thurs.: 8 a.m.–12.30 p.m., 1.30 p.m.–5.30 p.m. It's best to cash your traveller's cheques in large denominations as commission charges are high.

• **Post offices:** Open Mon.–Fri.: 8 a.m.–12 noon, 2 p.m.–6 p.m., Sat.: 8 a.m.–10 a.m. Stamps can also be bought from Tabak-Trafik shops.

• **Shops:** Keep to the same hours as the post office, closing on Saturday afternoons.

• **Museums:** Tend to close on Mondays.

SLEEPING

• **Hostels:** To stay at any Austrian youth hostel, you need an International Youth Hostel Association membership card. In general, they're open from about 6 a.m. till 10 p.m. and charge about AS 80–150 for a bed, and about AS 60–100 for a meal, adding on an extra charge where cooking facilities are available. At many hostels breakfast is compulsory; check first. Provided space is available, you can stay more than three nights at most hostels unless you're travelling in a large group. If you are, write in advance to the warden and book your space.

• **Hotels:** Hotels are nearly always clean but wildly expensive, particularly in Vienna and Salzburg. If you travel off-season, prices are 20–40 per cent cheaper; also in May, June and September they're 15–25 per cent cheaper than in July and August. You can expect to pay at least AS 350 for a double. Bear this in mind if you're approached by an Austrian hotelier trying to fill his hotel – he may be offering you a bargain. Don't be put off by this approach as it's a buyer's market; ask the price and location and what's included. You're under no obligation.

• **Camping:** The International Camping Carnet is not obligatory, but it'll get you preferential treatment on most sites. Generally, the sites are very good: clean, efficient and well laid out. Austrians are keen campers themselves, so in peak season you might find it advisable to get to the site and pitch as early in the day as you can.

EATING AND NIGHTLIFE

Austrian food is wholesome stuff and great if you've a soft spot for pastries. In general, the pork (schwein) and fish dishes are better value than lamb and beef. Tafelspitz (boiled beef) is good and cheap, and this with a noodle or dumpling soup is a filling, inexpensive meal. The coffee-and-cakes scene is good news all round, except for the price. Strudel is excellent, as is Sachertorte.

Having said all this, you may well end up eating from fast-food chains most of the time, owing to high restaurant prices. If so, try and eat the local dishes at least once, you won't regret it.

The nightlife is centred round coffee houses and the opera, rather than heavy-metal gigs and bars. You have to remember that discos and bars cost money in Austria and anyway they tend to be a bit smooth. The best advice is to head towards a wine tavern or beer cellar in the studenty areas where possible, as prices tend to be more realistic there. However, if you're into opera, Vienna's the place. The season runs from September to June, but prices are high.

Vienna (Wien)

Gateway between the East and West for over two thousand years, Vienna's middle-European flavour makes it unique among all capital cities. Its position as ruler of half of Europe for over six centuries has left behind a legacy of impressive buildings and an atmosphere of solid institutionalism. This is probably helped by the fact that over a third of Vienna's nearly two million population are pensioners.

The city is divided into twenty-three districts, with the 'Ring' in the city centre as No. 1. Vienna's not actually on the Danube – the river only runs through its suburbs – but the Danube Canal is part of the city.

Use this book, and do your sums carefully in Vienna to avoid its high costs during your stay. It's a great place, but at a price.

STATION FACILITIES

Vienna has two main stations: the West and the South, with trains leaving daily from the West station at Europaplatz to France, Switzerland and Germany. Trains for the Eastern Bloc countries and Italy leave from either the South Station, or the smaller East Station.

	SÜDBAHNHOF (South Station)	WESTBAHNHOF (West Station)
Train information	6.30 a.m.–9.30 p.m.	7 a.m.–8.30 p.m.
Reservations	7 a.m.–8.30 p.m.	7 a.m.–8.30 p.m.
Tourist information	6.30 a.m.–10 p.m.	6.15 a.m.–11 p.m.
Foreign exchange	6.30 a.m.–10 p.m.	6.30 a.m.–11.15 p.m.
Bar, Buffet	6 a.m.–9.30 p.m.	6 a.m.–10.30 p.m.
Snack bar	6 a.m.–7 p.m.	6.30 a.m.–11 p.m.
Bath, Shower	6 a.m.–7 p.m.	Mon.–Sat.: 6 a.m.–10 p.m. Sun.: 8 a.m.–noon
Left-luggage lockers	Shut midnight	Shut 12.30 a.m.–3.30 a.m.
Left-luggage store	4.30 a.m.–11.45 p.m.	Always open
Shops	6 a.m.–10 p.m.	6 a.m.–11 p.m.
Waiting room	Always open	Always open
Station shuts	Midnight–4 a.m.	12.30 a.m.–3.30 a.m.

There are post office facilities at both stations. Tram 18 connects the South and West stations. N.B. The West Station is not on the underground system.

TOURIST INFORMATION

The main office is at the Opernpassage in the underground station at the Opera (Tel. 431–608). Open 9 a.m.–7 p.m. The station offices can also help out and provide an accommodation-finding service. Pick up the city map, transport map and the students' leaflet 'Wien Live'. Tourist information for all of Austria is available at Margaretenstrasse 1.

● **Addresses:**
POST OFFICE: Fleischmarkt 19. Poste restante. Open Mon.–Sat.: 7 a.m.–10 p.m., Sun.: 8 a.m.–9 p.m.
POSTE RESTANTE: 11 Dominikaner bastei, open 6 a.m.–10 p.m.
AMEX: 21–23 Kärtnerstrasse, Mon.–Fri.: 9 a.m.–5.30 p.m., Sat.: 9 a.m.–noon (Tel. 520544).
UK EMBASSY: Reisnerstrasse 40 (Tel. 731575).
US EMBASSY: Boltzmanngasse 16 (Tel. 346611).
CANADIAN EMBASSY: 10 Karl-Lueger-Ring (Tel. 633691).
AUSTRALIAN EMBASSY: 2–4 Mattiellistrasse (Tel. 528580).
POLICE EMERGENCY: Tel. 133.

MEDICAL EMERGENCY: Tel. 144.

ÖKISTA (Student Travel): 4–6 Turkenstrasse, Mon.–Fri.: 9.30 a.m.–5 p.m. (Tel. 3475260). They help out with any accommodation problems you may have.

TRANSALPINO: Opernring 1, open Mon.–Fri.: 9.30 a.m.–4 p.m.

● **Getting about:** Information on city transport is available at Karlsplatz U-Bahn Station. There are various passes on offer, ranging from one day to a week, but remember you can see most of Vienna on foot. Pick up a map of the city transport's system at the tourist office. The S-Bahn is free on Inter Rail. Forget the city tours, taxis, and 'Fiakers' (two-horse coaches at AS 300 a go) as they'll cripple your budget.

SEEING

Pick up leaflets from tourist information offices. These will give you all the history, details, opening times, etc.

At the heart of Vienna is St Stephan's Cathedral and its square, Ştephansplatz, at the intersection of Graben and Kärtnerstrasse – it's a good place to sit and watch Viennese life go by. Rather than suggest a walking tour with everyone tramping round exactly the same treadmill like guinea pigs, we list the major sights and you can devise your own route by using the map.

ST STEPHAN'S CATHEDRAL: Built in the thirteenth and fourteenth centuries, it's the most important Gothic building in Vienna. Climb the 458 steps of the south steeple (or take the lift) for a good view of Vienna, or descend to the catacombs and look at the Habsburgs' innards in the 'Old Prince's Vault'.

THE HOFBURG: The old imperial winter palace sprawling all over the heart of the city and encompassing every architectural style from the thirteenth to the twentieth century; it includes the Spanish Riding School and the Hofburgkapelle where the Vienna Boys' Choir perform – though, crazily, the latter close down in summer. Entry to the Hofburg is reduced for ISIC holders.

SCHÖNBRUNN PALACE: This was the Habsburgs' summer palace. Situated at Schönbrunner Schloss-Strasse in the outskirts, southwest from Westbahnhof. There's an English tour for AS 40 (less for students) which is worth it.

THE BELVEDERE: Includes the Austrian gallery of modern art and a museum of medieval art.

THE KUNSTHISTORISCHES MUSEUM, Maria-Theresien Platz: One of the great art collections and the fourth largest gallery in the world. All the treasures the Habsburgs could get their imperial hands on are here. The Breughel room contains over half the artist's remaining pictures. Go at weekends if you can as it's free then. It's also free to ISIC holders.

The above are the main sights but, if you've any time left, take in the FREUD MUSEUM. Followers of the master can visit his house at Berggasse 19.

Of interest to musicians will be: HAYDN MUSEUM at Haydngasse 19; MOZART ERINNERUNGSRAUM, Domgasse 5; BEETHOVEN ERIN-NERUNGSRAUM, Morkerbastel 8; SCHUBERT MUSEUM, Nussdorfer-strasse 54; and SCHUBERT STERBEZIMMER, Kettenbrückengasse 6; JOHANN STRAUSS MUSEUM, Praterstrasse 54. At most of these addresses, the composers' original houses are still standing.

If museums are one of your passions, consider buying a seven-day museum ticket (AS 70) for entry to all fifty of Vienna's museums as often as you like. Alternatively, as a break take a walk and a picnic in the Vienna woods which border the city on its southern and western sides. Take tram 38 to its terminus at Grinzing, then bus 38 to Kahlenberg.

SLEEPING

Write in advance if at all possible as cheap beds are few and far between in the summer. This is mainly due to the fact that they don't open their student hostels till July (making late June a particularly bad time); hotels are ridiculously expensive and the cheap pensions get full quickly. Use the ISTC accommodation booklet as it lists all the best places.

There are two main accommodation-finding services in Vienna: the tourist office (at the stations), and the student organization Ökista. If you want to save the commission charge, try phoning yourself. Most hoteliers speak English, or you can try out your phrase-book German.

• **Student hostels:** Try the Internationales Studenthaus at Seiler-stätte 30 (Tel. 528463). The location is very central, and they give

10 per cent reduction to ISIC holders. If they are full try Asylverein der Wiener Universität at Porzellangasse 30 (Tel. 347282), with doubles at around AS 120 per person.

• **Youth hostels:** Ruthensteiner, Robert Hanerlinggasse 24 (Tel. 834693 and 8308265). 77 beds with all facilities.

Hütteldorf, Schlossbergasse 8 (Tel. 821501). 300 beds and all facilities. Must be IYHF member. Take the underground to Hütteldorf, then a ten-minute walk.

• **Pensions:** Pension Columbia, Kochgasse 9 (Tel. 426757), quiet with doubles from AS 450, including breakfast.

Pension Schweitzer, Heinrichsgasse 2 (Tel. 638156). Clean and comfortable. English spoken.

• **Camping:** All grounds are located well out of the city with an average price of AS 35 per person and AS 35 per tent.

Wien West II, Hüttelbergstrasse 80 (Tel. 942314). Take tram 49 to terminus. Open April–Oct.

Wien West I (just up the same street) (Tel. 941449). Open mid-May–mid-Sept. If desperate, sleep out at the Prater Park.

EATING AND NIGHTLIFE

There's no shortage of places to eat in Vienna – the only problem's the prices. As usual, though, if you know where to look you'll be OK. The Hungarian and Turkish restaurants are usually good value.

The Schnell Imbiss counters (quick snacks) dotted all over the city serve cheap filling snacks (AS 30–70), and of course there's always McDonalds.

Cafés are a Viennese institution, serving up their delicious pastries and cakes, but they're expensive, so make your café visit on a wet afternoon when you can hang around reading the papers, playing cards and generally getting your money's worth.

For picnics, use the self-service supermarkets. There's no shortage of good breads, sausages, cheeses, fruits and wines, so picnicking is easy. Vienna's largest market, the NASCHMARKT, lying from the fourth to the sixth districts, has a few food bargains and plenty more besides. Get to it by the underground to Kettenbrück-engasse.

• **Suggestions:** The cheapest lunch to be found in Vienna is at Naschmarkt (AS 50–80). They have places all over the city. The central ones are at Schottengasse 1 or 7, and Mariahilferstrasse 85. Open Mon.–Fri.: 7.30 a.m.–7 p.m., Sat.: 9 a.m.–5 p.m., Sun.: 11 a.m.–5 p.m. The student restaurant Mensa is at Universitätsstrasse 7. It's open for lunch and dinner, Mon.–Sat., but you need an ISIC to get in.

The Viennese are happier at the opera or the theatre than engaged in active nightlife. Young people tend to congregate in the Kaffeekonditorei rather than in pubs or discos, but Vienna still has a few surprises up its sleeve. A good night out can be had at the Prater – Vienna's large amusement park on the outskirts of the city (free). It's open from Easter to October with rides averaging AS 25 – not bad by Austrian standards.

Bars and nightclubs are sleazy and expensive so, unless you're desperate, don't bother. If you are, try Atrium Studentenbude, Schwarzenbergplatz 10. This is a student disco and has the best prices and largest choice of bars. In general, though, you're better off heading for a wine tavern or beer cellar. These represent best value by far. Try: Esterhazykeller, Haarhof, good studenty crowd with the best prices in town; or Zwölf-Apostelkeller, Sonnenfels-gasse 3, near St Stephan's, so low down from street level, the walls are covered with straw to diminish the dampness. Go down to the lowest level – it's liveliest. Open Sundays, but closed all July. There's a good atmosphere here. And for the connoisseur, Melker-keller, Schottengasse 3, run by Benedictine monks, has excellent wine.

For enthusiasts, Europe's largest bowling alley is in Vienna. It's the Bowling-Brunswick at Hauptallee 124 and costs around AS 20 a line. Plenty of students congregate here.

If you're keen on opera and classical music, check with tourist information, but when buying tickets don't use an agency as they charge a 20 per cent commission.

Southern Austria

If you're travelling south on to Italy or Yugoslavia, you'll pass through the southern regions of BURGENLAND, STEIERMARK and KÄRNTEN.

Burgenland is the province next to the Hungarian border and is famous for its wines. EISENSTADT is its capital and between late August and early September this turns into a pretty lively place, thanks to its Weinwoche (wine week). Steiermark is in the south-eastern area of Austria, along the Yugoslavian border which the 'Weinstrasse' (wine road) runs through.

Kärnten (Carinthia) has as its capital KLAGENFURT. This is an attractive region with lakes, wildlife parks and rolling hills. Klagenfurt itself has two campsites, and a youth hostel in its centre, and is a good place to base yourself to explore the surrounding Naturpark Kreuzbergl.

Central Austria

South of the Linz–Salzburg line lies a region of Austria that the tourist hordes haven't as yet discovered or spoilt. It consists mainly of mountains, lakes and tiny old villages – the sort of Austria you'd optimistically imagined. Not being commercialized, prices are low, so it's really got everything going for it.

From Vienna or Salzburg catch a train to ATTNANG PUCHHEIM, then take a local train going in the direction of Stainach Irdning, passing through Gmunden, Hallstatt and Obertraun.

GMUNDEN, a town at the northernmost end of the Traunsee by the largest lake of the region, is particularly lovely. Tourist information is at Am Graben 2. Traunsteinstrasse is one of the best streets in which to look for accommodation.

HALLSTATT is the stop after Bad Goisern. It is a particularly beautiful village with lakes, cliffs and a waterfall as the backdrop to your views. The youth hostel on Salzburgstrasse (Tel. 06134 279) is open from May to September, and there's camping at Campingplatz

Höll (Tel. 06134 329). Tourist information is in the Prehistorisches Museum just off Seestrasse; they'll advise on accommodation. The oldest salt mines in the world (they claim) are here and can be visited. This area is rich in walks and sails; you can rent a small boat for around AS 80 an hour.

OBERTRAUN, the next stop along, has some interesting ice caves, but the admission cost is quite high. Their youth hostel is at Winkl 26 (Tel. 06134 360) and opens at 5 p.m.

Salzburg

Extremely expensive, touristy, but beautiful. The prince-arch-bishops who ruled over the town built many fine churches, palaces, mansions and gardens until it became known as the 'Rome of the North'. The town is famous for its festival (from late July to end of August), which attracts all the big international names in music and fills every hotel, hostel and campsite with the thousands who flock to this event.

Luckily, Salzburg is a university town, so this slightly eases some of the financial problems eurorailers may encounter. There are some student hostels and restaurants which are less than half the price of their commercial counterparts, but basically Salzburg is a town which caters for the middle-aged and middle-class.

STATION FACILITIES

Train information	Daily 6.30 a.m.–8.45 p.m.
	(Tel. 71400 or 72400)
Reservations	Daily 8 a.m.–7 p.m. in train office
Tourist information	Daily 8 a.m.–8 p.m.
Foreign exchange	Daily 7 a.m.–9 p.m.
Bar, Buffet	Mon.–Fri.: 6.30 a.m.–9.00 p.m.
Restaurant	Mon.–Fri.: 6 a.m.–11.45 p.m.
Left-luggage lockers	Always open
Waiting room	Always open
Food shops (or head towards centre for supermarkets)	Mon.–Sat.: 8 a.m.–6 p.m.

Salzburg is 3½ hours from Vienna, 2 hours from Munich in West Germany, 2½ hours from Innsbruck and 5 hours from Zürich; there are daily trains to Cologne, Hamburg and Copenhagen. The tourist information office at the station gives out free maps and will help you find a room for AS 5.

TOURIST INFORMATION AND ADDRESSES

The city's tourist information offices are next to American Express, at Mozartplatz 5 (Tel. 71511) (open July and August 8 a.m.–7 p.m.) and at the station. There's also an office at Auerspergstrasse 7 (Tel. 74620) which operates an accommodation-finding service. Also pick up a copy of 'Salzburg für die Jugend' – very useful. City transport information and free maps are obtained from the bus drivers.

POST OFFICE: Residenzplatz 9, Mon.–Fri.: 7 a.m.–7 p.m., Sat. 8 a.m.–10 a.m.
AMEX: Mozartplatz 5 (Tel. 42501).
STUDENT TRAVEL SERVICE: Hildmannplatz 1, Mon.–Fri.: 9.30 a.m.–5.30 p.m.
ÖKISTA: Hildmannplatz (Tel. 46769) and Young Austria, 108a Alpenstrasse (Tel. 25758), Mon.–Fri.: 8 a.m.–6 p.m. Both help out with travel problems.

SEEING

Gone are the days when Salzburg depended on its salt; tourists now come in their thousands to see the impressive baroque legacy of the powerful archbishops. They weren't all good, though; they did their fair share of expelling the Jews, pillaging and persecuting the local Protestants – all the usual stuff. The HOHENSALZBURG FORTRESS (their main residence) shouldn't be missed. Take the cable car up 1,780 feet and kill two birds with one stone, as the view from the top over the city is tremendous. If you're getting fed up with your travelling companion, check out the MUSEUM OF TORTURE there. Don't bother with the conducted tour, wander round yourself.

The other four main sites are the RESIDENZ (seventeenth-century archbishops' palace), SCHLOSS MIRABELL, the CATHEDRAL and MOZART'S HOUSE at Getreidegasse 9. Slightly outside Salzburg is SCHLOSS HELLBRUNN, the castle built by a bishop for his mistress, surrounded by an Alpine zoo (take the local train from Salzburg). If you've had enough of tourists, there are several escape routes: a train and bus will take you to Hitler's retreat, the 'EAGLE'S NEST' (details from the station), or take the cable car up to the top of the UNTERSBERG (5,800 feet). Alternatively, go down the salt mines at BERCHTESGADEN over in Bavaria. Take the train from Salzburg over the border, then a bus from the station to the mines. Once you've been suitably decked out, they'll take you down the mine shafts for around 20 DM.

SLEEPING

Your best bet here is to go for private accommodation: ask at tourist information for their list of private rooms. Forget hotels and try one of the hostels or campsites. If you've no luck here, go to the tourist office at Auerspergstrasse and tell them the most you can afford, then wait and see what they can come up with. If all else fails, consider going out to one of the villages on the outskirts.

• **Youth hostels:** The hostel at Josef-Preis Allee 18 (Tel. 42670) has 360 beds and all facilities. Take bus 3 or 5 to Justizgebäude. The International Hostel at Paracelsusstrasse 9, is only a few blocks from the station and gives you a bed from only AS 90 (open mid-June–mid-Aug.) (Tel. 74649/73460). Showers and breakfast are extra.

• **Pensions:** Zum Junger Fuchs, Linzer Gasse 54 (Tel. 75496). Doubles AS 300. Very good.

• **Camping:** There are several campsites including Gersbergalm at Gersbergweg and City Camping at Bayerhamerstrasse. Most are open from 1 May to 30 September, and prices vary from AS 30–50 per person and tent.

EATING AND NIGHTLIFE

There are plenty of flash restaurants in Salzburg and no shortage of ways to blow your money if you have any. Try Zwettler Stiftskeller, Kaigasse 3, in Mozartplatz. They do an excellent three-courser for AS 80. Alternatively, any of the Mensa restaurants will stand you in good stead.

For picnic food, there's a good open-air market on Thursdays by St Andrew's Church, and there's one every weekday on Franz-Josef Strasse.

Beer Gardens: Salzburg is a bit more orientated towards beer than to wine, probably due to its proximity to the German border. The beer cellars invariably offer good value in eating, drinking and entertainment. Try Pitterkeller, Rainerstrasse 6 (meals AS 90–140), open Sundays, or Augustiner Bräustuble, Augustinergasse 4 – there are several small stalls in this building where you can treat yourself.

If it's just a drink you're after, try Sternbräu Beer Garden, Getreidegasse 23, with dancing every Friday night, or Students' Centre, Gstattengasse 16, 4 p.m.–9 p.m.

Western Austria

From Lichtenstein to the Arlberg Tunnel, the Vorarlberg Alps are particularly scenic: mountains, chalets, green fields, etc. The best towns to base yourself in to explore this region are FELDKIRCH and BREGENZ.

Feldkirch is an old town with many reminders of its Gothic heyday. The tourist offices are at Schlossergasse and Herrengasse (Mon.–Fri.: 8.30 a.m.–12 noon, 2 p.m.–6 p.m., Sat.: 9 a.m.–noon). They'll suggest walking tours. There's a youth hostel (Tel. 23181) at Noflerstrasse, or use Pension Grete at Mutterstrasse 12.

Bregenz is a medieval city on the Bodensee. The information office is at Inselstrasse. There's a youth hostel at Belruptstrasse 16A (Tel. 22867) and three campsites.

Innsbruck

As capital of the Tyrol and the Austrian ski scene, Innsbruck is busy all the year round. It is beautifully situated and well worth a day or two of your time.

STATION FACILITIES

Train information office	Daily 8.30 a.m.–7 p.m.
	(Tel. 25275)
Reservations	Daily 8 a.m.–12 noon
Restaurant	Daily 6.30 a.m.–midnight
Bar, Buffet	Daily 7 a.m.–8 p.m.
Left-luggage lockers	Always open
Waiting room	Always open

For food and provisions, head towards the Maria-Theresienstrasse area, two streets straight ahead from the station.

There are daily trains from Innsbruck to Cologne, Hamburg, Munich (2¼ hours), Salzburg (2¼ hours), Vienna (5½ hours), Milan, Rome, Venice and Zürich (4 hours).

There's a centre for young travellers at the station. It's wonderful. Seize this opportunity to be treated like a human being and use it.

TOURIST INFORMATION AND ADDRESSES

At the station, open daily 9 a.m.–10 p.m. They'll find you a room, change your cash (10 a.m.–10 p.m.) and fill you in on what's happening. There's another office at Burggraben 3, in the city centre. The post office is at Maximilianstrasse 2 (one block away from the Triumphal Arch). The AMEX office is at Brixnerstrasse 3, and the student travel service with Transalpino tickets is at Josef-Hirnstrasse 7/2 and Erlerstrasse 19–25.

• **Alpine information:** As you're in one of the best Alpine centres in Europe, you may feel inclined to head for the hills. Check up on conditions before setting off at Wilhelm-Greillstrasse 15 (Tel. 23171) or, if you prefer to take an organized hike, contact Verkehrsverein at Burggraben 3 (Tel. 25715).

• **Mountain hut scheme:** There are over 700 huts up in the mountains surrounding Innsbruck. They belong to various local and national Alpine associations, and doing a tour of them, or even just staying the night in one, is very rewarding, cheap and provides a good memory of Austria. All the huts have some cooking facilities and some even serve up hot food. Prices range from about AS 100 to AS 200 for a night.

Before setting out, make sure you have emergency food supplies, a waterproof and are wearing good climbing boots. The distress call in this neck of the woods is six visible or audible signals spaced evenly over one minute, followed by a minute's break, then the six signals again.

SEEING

The Nordkette mountains dominate the main shopping street – Maria-Theresienstrasse. At one end is the TRIUMPHAL ARCH and at the other the old Gothic town. The GOLDEN ROOF is the symbol of Innsbruck; it's an ornate Gothic balcony built in 1500 from 2,657 gilded copper tiles. The HOFBURG (Imperial Palace) is the other big sight, and the FOLK-ART MUSEUM at Universitätsstrasse 2 is a good bet for a rainy afternoon.

For an all-round perspective, take the cable car up to HAFELE-KAR. At 7,500 feet, the view is quite spectacular. The 1964 Winter Olympics were held at IGLS near Innsbruck, and if you're in the ski set you can still go and see the set-up (bus J from Innsbruck Station or tram 6). Enjoy the view but stay out of the cafés there. If you want to see a pretty Alpine village and travel on an open-sectioned train (highly recommended), go to the village of FULPMES, in good picnic country (tram 1 to Stubaitalbahnhof where the mountain train leaves).

SLEEPING

Avoid hotels and ask at tourist information if you get stuck for ideas. The youth hostel at Reichenauerstrasse 147 is popular despite the 10.30 p.m. curfew. Take bus O or R to Campingplatz. Pension Paula at Weiherburggasse 15 (Tel. 37795) is an attractive mountain chalet overlooking the old town of Innsbruck. Take bus K from the city centre. The nearest campsite is Reichenau at Reichenauerstrasse (Tel. 46252), 20 minutes' walk from the station or take buses R, O, or OA.

EATING AND NIGHTLIFE

Head towards the university area. Try Gasthaus Gruber, Innrain 24 (between University and Old Town). Also, the Mensa (off Innrain) at Josef-Hirnstrasse offers cheap meals for ISIC holders.

There's a free Tyrolean evening in front of the Golden Roof every Thursday evening at 8.30 p.m. Or try the St Nikolaus Kellerei, Innstrasse, open 8 a.m.–12 noon, 2 p.m.–8 p.m. Good wine, but no English spoken.

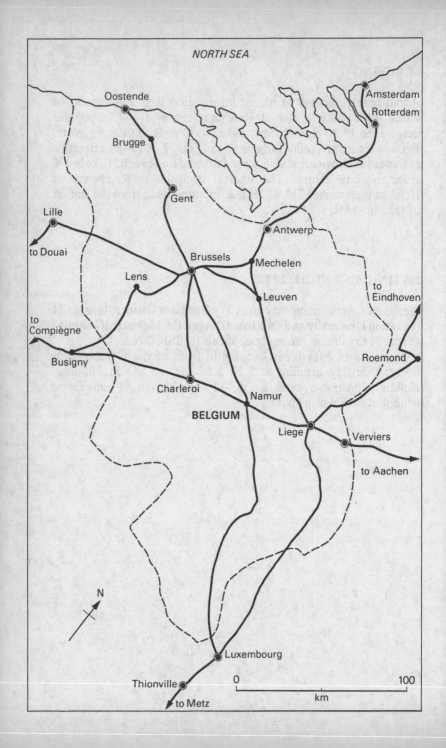

BELGIUM

Entry requirements	Passport
Population	10,000,000
Capital	Brussels (pop.: 1,200,000)
Currency	Belgian Franc
	£1 = approx. 76 BF
Political system	Constitutional Monarchy
Religion	Roman Catholic
Languages	French and Flemish (English widely spoken)
Public holidays	1 Jan.; Easter Monday; 1 May; Ascension Day;
	Whit Monday; 21 July; 15 Aug.; 1, 11 Nov.;
	25, 26 Dec.

To confuse the Flemish with the Walloons is like calling the Scots English; it is a mistake to be avoided in a country where the two major ethnic groups each speak their own language and are equally proud of their historical and cultural differences. The Flemish speak their own language closely akin to Dutch, live in the north and west, and still carry the hard-working characteristics of their Germanic forebears. The Walloons, on the other hand, speak French, often in the 'old French' dialect and are in every way more like their French neighbours.

During the early Middle Ages, trade and commerce created a rich town life unrivalled in northern Europe. All this was to change, however, as Belgium got caught up in the crossfire of European affairs through marriage and alliance. The French, Spanish and Austrians all fought to secure her strategic ports and the fertile lands of Flanders, until she gained independence in 1830.

The four main centres of interest are: Bruges, Brussels, Antwerp and Ghent, and although Belgium is the second most densely populated country in Europe, it's still possible to find solitude among the forests and hills of the Ardennes in the south.

BELGIAN NATIONAL RAILWAYS
(Nationale Maatschappij der Belgische Spoorwegen, NMBS)
(Société Nationale des Chemins de Fer Belges, SNCB)

Belgium's train network is one of the most reliable and extensive in Europe. The trains are frequent and go just about everywhere. To cross the country takes only 3½ hours, and trains leave for most internal destinations within every hour. Eurorailers get a good deal here as normal train fares are expensive. Inter Railers and Eurail pass holders have an extra bonus as it's possible – and often advisable – to use one city as a base and tour the rest of the country from it (it only takes 1 hour from Bruges to Brussels).

● **Inter Rail bonuses:** RTM–BR (Sealink) ferries give half-price reductions from Dover to Ostend.

● **Eurail bonuses:** The following half-price reductions are granted by Europabus on transportation costs only and by local offices in Europe.
—Antwerp–Brussels–Menton
—Antwerp–Brussels–Barcelona
—Ostend–Brussels–Frankfurt (M.)
—Ostend–Lille
—Antwerp–Brussels–Le Havre–Lisieux

TRAIN INFORMATION

Information officers speak good English, other rail staff speak both Flemish and French. If you're spending any time in Belgium, ask for a copy of the official SNCB timetable ('indicateur'/'spoorboekje') from any station. It has an introduction in English and explains all you need to know about schedules and supplements. If you don't get one, don't worry as there are large posters everywhere, giving departure and arrival information. Lockers take 5 BF coins.

● **Reservations:** Are not necessary, or even possible on inland routes. International reservations cost about 100 BF and can be made up to two months in advance, if you're that highly organized. If you are, you'd probably also like to know that you can reserve seats on trains leaving from Austria, Denmark, Germany, Italy, Luxembourg, the Netherlands and Switzerland, at Brussels North or South stations, as the SNCB's computer is linked up with these countries.

• **Night travel:** Belgium is too small to warrant inland services, but SNCB have couchettes and wagon-lit sleepers on international routes. (Look out for the German rolling stock with pull-down seats, to save a bit of money.)

• **Eating on trains:** There are not many services on inland trains; some have a mini-bar and a few have a buffet. Don't let that worry you, though, as Belgium's supermarkets are renowned for their food. International trains have all the usual expensive facilities, so either way prepare a picnic in advance, and don't count on station shops to supply it as there aren't any.

• **Bikes:** SNCB run a scheme called 'Train et Vélo' which allows you to take advantage of Belgium's perfect cycling conditions. You can rent a bike for around 200 BF per day from over 30 stations and hand it back at over 100. Most roads have cycle tracks and it's flat going all the way to explore the surrounding countryside. (Don't forget to ask for a free tour map.)

TOURIST INFORMATION

Local tourist offices are to be found in every large town. For any extra information on the provinces and the country, ask at the main office in Brussels. If you've any problems tourist information can't help out with, try the Info-Jeunes (Info-Jeugd) office. There are branches in most large towns.

• **ISIC bonuses:** 50 per cent off most museums. For further information, contact TEJ, 61 rue Belliard, Brussels.

• **Money matters:** 1 Belgian franc (BF) = 100 centimes.
Banking hours are Mon.–Fri.: 9 a.m.–1 p.m., 2.30 p.m.–3.30 p.m. Late opening, Friday till 4.30 p.m. AMEX are the only bank that won't charge a ridiculous commission of around 90 BF on each transaction involving traveller's cheques. The station exchanges take no commission, but their rate of exchange is about 10 per cent below the official one. The ferries give a good rate and their commission is considerably less.

• **Post offices:** Open Mon.–Fri.: 9 a.m.–4 p.m.

• **Shops and museums:** There are no hard-and-fast rules here, but museums tend to shut either on Mondays or Fridays, and some in the afternoons. Shops open from 9 a.m. to 6 p.m., Monday–Saturday, with lunch 12 noon–2 p.m. Bakers and newsagents open early in the morning, and you can also find a grocer open on Sunday somewhere. In Brussels, many shops stay open till 8 p.m. Late night Friday.

SLEEPING

Apart from tourist information, the Info-Jeunes offices also give help with accommodation. Unmarried couples wanting to sleep together might find problems if they are under 21 as hoteliers can be imprisoned for up to three years under Belgian law for allowing this.

Hostels are your best bet – either the IYHF ones or those run by an organization called 'Amis de la Nature'. There are a few unofficial ones as well as student hostels which offer a more relaxed atmosphere. All of these are given in the Budget Holiday booklet which you can pick up at any tourist information office.

Hotels tend to be expensive (minimum 500 BF single, 900 BF double) but clean, and offer an inclusive continental breakfast.

EATING AND NIGHTLIFE

The Belgians love their food and take eating very seriously, a fact which is borne out by the well-stocked supermarkets you will find even in the small towns. Always be prepared for an impromptu picnic. If you're eating out, go for your main meal at lunchtime as the fixed menu is not available at night, so making dinner a more expensive affair. Belgian cuisine is similar to French, both in quality and in price. If possible, try some local specialities: carbonnades flamandes (beef stewed in beer) and waterzooi (chicken and vegetables stewed in mustard sauce). Don't miss the Belgian waffles served with fruit or cream, or the excellent pastry and cakes, and if you think the Swiss are the only Europeans who know how to make delicious chocolates, try the Belgian pralines (especially the fresh-cream-filled white chocolates, available from any branch of Leonidas). Apologies for making your mouth water if you're really broke, but there are always Belgian chips, which are small, thin and delicious and are served with mayonnaise. In fact, the 'friterie/frituur' is the cheapest and most prolific source of fast food in Belgium. There's always one near a station, and they serve kebabs, sausages, etc., too.

Belgium's selection of bars would satisfy the most demanding drinker. While wine is good and cheaper than at home, you'll do best to try what they're famous for: beer. In the cities, it's quite common to find pubs serving up to fifty varieties (La Houblonnière in Brussels boasts a hundred). Try one of the Trappist brews, a good nightcap.

There is no shortage of theatres, cinemas or discos, and the set-up is very similar to at home. Don't waste your time looking for cheap seats or student discounts, as there aren't any.

Bruges
(Brugge – Flemish, Bruges – French)

This beautifully preserved medieval town is more like an open-air museum than a twentieth-century city. If you're going to stop off anywhere in Belgium, make sure it's Bruges, as this is definitely one of the most attractive towns in Europe. For over 200 years, Bruges was one of the most important commercial centres in Western Europe, and the Counts of Flanders spent their money making the town's guildhalls, palaces and churches as impressive as they could. All this glory came to an end when their harbour silted up and made trade impossible. Bruges is known as the 'Venice of the North', and its network of canals, bridges (Brugge means bridges) and tall Gothic buildings reminds you very much of its Italian counterpart.

STATION FACILITIES

The station is on the southern edge of the town, one mile from the city centre. If you don't feel like a walk, get bus No. 1 to the Markt. The station's quite small but has the basic facilities. There's a left-luggage depot (open till midnight), and it's possible to hire bikes.

TOURIST INFORMATION AND ADDRESSES

The tourist office is at the Markt (Tel. 330711) and is open 9 a.m.–7 p.m. weekdays and 9.30 a.m.–12.30 p.m., 2 p.m.–7 p.m. at weekends. They'll hand you free maps and leaflets, fix up a bed for you, and change your currency at weekends. The post office is also on the Markt and the Flanders Youth Hostel Centre is at Predikheren Straat 15 (open 1.30 p.m.–6 p.m.). They're a helpful crowd and will give you general information on Bruges as well as filling you in on the hostel position.

SEEING

The main things to see are: THE BELFRY on the Markt, built from the thirteenth to the fifteenth century. Climb up for a good view of the layout of the old town and listen out for the CARILLON (bell concert). Two museums right next door to each other on the Dyver are GRUUTHUSE and GROENINGE (closed at lunchtime, and on Tuesdays in winter). Gruuthuse is a museum of applied arts, housed in a particularly beautiful fifteenth-century mansion, while Groeninge is devoted to Flemish Renaissance painting. Joined on to Gruuthuse is the thirteenth-century CHURCH OF OUR LADY, containing Michelangelo's 'Madonna and Child'. The BEGIJNHOF (a Belgian type of convent) is in a peaceful location off the Wijngaardplein. You can wander around the interior and the grounds for a few francs. The canal boat trips may seem a rip-off at around 100 BF a go, but they're actually quite good value as you get an added perspective on the town and they don't rush.

SLEEPING

Try and stay central as all the sights in Bruges are close together; bear in mind too that the town gets its fair share of visitors in summer, so get there early. The youth hostel is at Baron Ruzettlelaan 143 (Tel. 352679). It's not too central but it's OK. There's an 11 p.m. curfew and you'll need an IYHF card and about 300 BF for B&B. Closed 10 a.m.–5 p.m. and all through October and November. Bus 2 to Steenbrugge.

Camping St Michael is at Tillegemstraat 55, St Michaels (Tel. 313819), 95 BF per person, 75 BF per tent. Quite a way out: take bus 7 from the station or Markt.

The Snuffel Sleep-In is good value. It's at Ezelstraat 49 (Tel. 333133). Though not exactly luxurious, it is central and friendly; they have only thirty-eight beds, so get there early. Elckerlye House, Hauwersstraat 23 (Tel. 336226) averages 700 BF a double.

EATING AND NIGHTLIFE

As Bruges is not a university town, there's no specific cheap studenty area, but you can get by. The Lotus at Wapenmakers Straat do a good 'plat du jour', and the Ganzespel at Ganzestraat 37 do a 'menu du jour' for about 200 BF. There are late-night cafés dotted around the old town; Vlissinge on Blekerstraat claims to be the oldest in Europe.

Brussels
(Flemish – Brussel, French – Bruxelles)

Brussels is a real patchwork of old and new: a city of extreme contrasts, from the fifteenth-century GRAND' PLACE to the modern skyscrapers of the multinationals, and the new EEC headquarters. The main part of this capital which is worth seeing is enclosed in quite a small area of the old town; don't waste your time on the new 'cement heap', as predictably there's nothing unique or particularly Belgian about it. The city revolves round 'the most beautiful square in Europe' – the Grand' Place. Try to view it in daytime, and then again when it's floodlit at night.

STATION FACILITIES

Brussels has three main stations: the Gare du Nord, Gare du Midi and Gare Centrale. Though Centrale handles few international trains, it is conveniently located for the Grand' Place area, and there are interconnecting trains between the three stations every 15–20 minutes. Trains leave daily for Holland, Denmark, Germany, Switzerland, Italy and France. It takes less than 2½ hours to get to Paris or Amsterdam from Brussels.

	NORTH (Nord/Noord) STATION	SOUTH (Midi/Zuid) STATION	CENTRAL (Centrale/Centraal) STATION
Train information	Mon.–Sat. (& Sun. May–Sept.): 8 a.m.–8 p.m.	6 a.m.–11 p.m.	7 a.m.–9 p.m.
Reservations	8 a.m.–7 p.m.	Mon.–Fri.: 8 a.m.–8 p.m. Sat., Sun.: 9 a.m.–7 p.m.	No service
Foreign exchange	7 a.m.– 12 midnight	7 a.m.– 12 midnight	Mon.–Fri.: 8.45 a.m.–5.20 p.m. Sat.: 9 a.m.–4.30 p.m.
Bar, Buffet	7 a.m.–11 p.m.	Mon.–Fri.: 9.30 a.m.–11 p.m.	No service
Restaurant	7.30 a.m.–10 p.m.	8.30 a.m.–11 p.m.	11 a.m.–9 p.m.
Bath, Shower	–	–	Mon.–Sat.: 9 a.m.–6.30 p.m.
Left-luggage lockers	Always open	Always open	Closed 1.20 a.m.– 3.50 a.m.
Left-luggage store	Always open	Always open	Always open
Waiting room	Always open	Always open	5 a.m.–1 a.m.
Duty officer (Sous-Chef de Gare)	Always open	Always open	Always open
Station shuts	1.30 a.m.– 2.30 a.m.	Always open	1.20 a.m.– 3.50 a.m.

There are some booths near the South station selling food, and friteries in the nearby rue de France. For tourist information go to Gare Centrale and walk across Place de l'Europe for three blocks. There's a post office at Gare du Midi (open 24 hours) and at Centrale. You'll find social segregation at the Midi station in the form of the TEE Club, which provides a snack bar, shower, bath, etc. Officially these are only for the use of TEE passengers, but in practice you can gain admission if you're reasonably dressed. For information on city transport, head down to the metro station at Gare du Midi. Finally, if you arrive late at night when the tourist office is shut, head for the Gard du Nord as there are several student hostels in this area.

TOURIST INFORMATION

The main office is at rue Marché-aux-Herbes 61 (Tel. 513 9090) – just behind the Grand' Place. Open 9 a.m.–8 p.m., weekend till 7 p.m. They'll fix you up with accommodation and give you maps and all the usual handouts. Other organizations providing help with accommodation and what to see are: ACOTRA, rue de la Montagne 38 (Tel. 513 4480). This youth organization provides a *free room-finding service*.

They're open Mon.–Fri.: 9.30 a.m.–12.30 p.m., 2 p.m.–5 p.m. Also Saturday mornings in summer. INFO-JEUGD/JEUNES, in rue Marché-aux-Herbes 27 (Tel. 218 1180) is near the Grand' Place and is open Mon.–Fri.: 10 a.m.–6 p.m., Sat.: noon–6 p.m.; during July and August it's open Tues.–Fri.: 10 a.m.–3 p.m.

• **Addresses:**
POST OFFICE: Second floor of tall building at Place de la Monnaie, poste restante here.
AMEX: 2 Place Louise (Tel. 512 1740), open Mon.–Fri.: 9 a.m.–5 p.m., Sat.: 9 a.m.–noon.
UK EMBASSY: Britannia House, 28 rue Joseph II (Tel. 219 1165).
US EMBASSY: 27 Boulevard du Régent (Tel. 513 3830).
CANADIAN EMBASSY: 6 rue de Loxum (Tel. 513 7940).
AUSTRALIAN EMBASSY: 52 Avenue des Arts (Tel. 511 3997).
24-HOUR CHEMIST: Tel. 479 1818.
TRANSALPINO: 1a Square du Bastion, Porte de Namur (Tel. 511 1980).

For information on city transport, there's an office under the Place Rogier.

• **Getting about:** Basically, there's a flat rate of around 30 BF within the city which is valid for transfers between metro, bus and tram. There's also a tourist pass which gives unlimited travel for one day, as well as a ten-day pass.

SEEING

If you've only a single day, the city bus tours are not too bad for the amount of ground they cover. If you've a bit more time or like to be independent, head for the GRAND' PLACE which is *the* sight of Brussels – a well-preserved collection of Gothic guildhalls and public buildings from the fifteenth century. In the mornings a flower market is held there and at night it's floodlit. Opposite the MAISON DU ROI (the city museum) is the TOWN HALL, considered Brussels' most elegant building. MANNEKEN-PIS (a small statue of a boy having a pee) is the symbol of Brussels and is situated behind the Town Hall on rue l'Etuve. There are several stories as to his origin, the main one being that he saved the city by damping down some dynamite – in a natural and effective fashion.

The MUSÉE DES BEAUX ARTS has a good collection of early Flemish masters (free on Sundays, Wednesdays and Saturday afternoons). In contrast, next door is the modern art gallery: the MUSEUM OF ART AND HISTORY, one of the largest in Europe, covering absolutely everything (closed Monday). The MUSICAL INSTRUMENT MUSEUM has the largest collection in the world (over 4,000).

The FLEA MARKET at Place du Jeu de Balle is at its best on Saturday and Sunday mornings. If you've any time left, try and see the PALAIS DE JUSTICE (there's a good view from its cupola), ST MICHAEL'S CATHEDRAL and ERASMUS' LIBRARY.

A few interesting day-trips from Brussels are: LEUVEN, a medieval university town (20 minutes by train); WATERLOO, site of the battle, now with museums; and BOKRIJK, the largest open-air museum in Europe with over a hundred reconstructions of medieval buildings (April–October). Trains from any Brussels station (9 minutes).

SLEEPING

Unless you're prepared to go a long way out of town, your choice is limited to hostelling or hotelling (the campsites are miles out).

There's not much difficulty getting a bed in Brussels, even in summer. The best area to concentrate your efforts on is round the Gare du Nord.

• **Student hostels:** Sleep Well at rue de la Blanchisserie 27 (Tel. 218 5050) is the best value in the city. It's clean, central, cheap and has a good atmosphere. Dormitory beds are around 250 BF, doubles 700 BF and singles 400 BF. Closes 10 a.m.–5 p.m. Try to reserve ahead as it's popular. In summer, the hostel even arranges free city tours by local students.

• **Youth hostels:** There's a hostel at Heilig Geeststraat 2, near the Kappelle Kerk/Église de la Chapelle. Also try Maison Internationale, Chaussée de Wavre 205 (Tel. 648 8529), metro to Porte de Namur or Luxembourg. Open June–Sept.

• **Pensions/hotels:** There are a few at Avenue Fonsny (opposite Gare du Midi): the Merlo and Hôtel le Petit Coq are both OK and reasonably priced by Brussels standards. Hôtel Pacific at rue Antoine Dansaert 57 (Tel. 511 8459) is only five minutes from Grand' Place (two blocks from the Bourse metro). It's good, but take your breakfast and shower elsewhere, to save on the bill.

• **Camping:** Try Beerzel, Ukkelseweg 75 (Tel. 376 2561), 9 km south.

EATING AND NIGHTLIFE

It's easy to eat cheaply and well in Brussels. Use the stalls on the main shopping streets for waffles. There are plenty of fast-food chains and no shortage of cheap restaurants with fixed-price meals. For a splash out, go along the rue des Bouchers, trying the varieties of moules marinières (350–400 BF). The department stores offer good food at reasonable prices and the shopping centre, City 2, located off Place Rogier (5 minutes from Gare du Nord), has several cafés; the one on the top floor does soup and as much salad as you can get on your plate for around 85 BF. Open 9 a.m.–8.30 p.m. The Vietnamese and African restaurants are also good value and Le Breton, 59 rue des Drapiers, offers authentic Belgian food, beer and wines in a studenty atmosphere.

Head for the Gare du Midi – the student quarter – for pubs, clubs, etc. Discos are expensive, so make do with a lively pub: Le El Poncho, rue de la Fourche 21 (South American food and music); Florio, rue Marché-aux-Fromages 20; Bierdrome, Place Fernand Cocq 21. Films are good value (usually 160 BF for students), and the Styx, 72 rue de l'Arbre Bénit, shows revival films with midnight meals, which usually attract an interesting crowd.

Southern Belgium

The main line to Luxembourg passes through Namur and the Ardennes. To explore the area, it's best to base yourself at NAMUR; the regional tourist office is at rue Nôtre Dame 3 (Tel. 22 29 98). For information on the city, go to the pavilion next to the station or the Info-Jeunes at the belfry in the town. Namur has one of the friendliest youth hostels in Europe at Avenue Felicien Rops 8 (Tel. 22 36 88, bus 1 or 4 from the station).

Antwerp
(Antwerpen – Flemish, Anvers – French)

Belgium's second city is famous for its flourishing diamond trade, its shipping and fine art. There are two stations: Berchem and Central. International trains stop only at Berchem, except for those coming from Paris and Amsterdam. Opposite Central Station is the information pavilion (open 8.30 a.m.–8 p.m. weekdays, 9 a.m.–7 p.m. Saturdays, and 9 a.m.–5 p.m. Sundays). They'll give you maps and brochures on what to see, and city transport information. The main tourist office is at Suikerrui 19. Most sights are concentrated in the old town: OUR LADY'S CATHEDRAL, PETER PAUL RUBENS HOUSE, the ROYAL MUSEUM OF FINE ART with over 2,500 paintings and an excellent exhibition of eight centuries of northern painting, the GROTE MARKT, ST CHARLES BORROMEO'S CHURCH, the PLANTIN-

MORETUS MUSEUM of sixteenth-century printing, and CASTLE STEEN – a maritime museum. Three-quarters of the museums are shut on Mondays. There are free diamond-cutting exhibitions and tours of diamond works – ask at tourist information.

The youth hostel at Volkstraat 58 (Tel. 384782) is centrally located and reasonably priced. Take tram 12 or 24 from Gemeentestraat (across the square from the station). Hôtel Florida, at De Keyserlei 59, is right in front of Central Station. Don't be taken in by the 'rooms for tourists' advertised in cafés around the station – they're brothels. The campsite is at Jan Van Rijswijklaan Straat, and is cheap. For food, the Prinsstraat area (round the university) has several cafés doing fixed-price menus. The docks area is lively in the evenings and round the Grote Markt there are bars and restaurants – but they're expensive.

Ghent
(Gent – Flemish, Gand – French)

Renowned for its art and flowers and a glut of historic buildings. Day-trippers from Antwerp should get off at Dampoort Station which is nearer the centre, but from all other destinations you go on to St Pieter's Station which has all the basic facilities: left luggage, reservations, etc. Tram 4 will take you to the centre, Koornmarkt. Tourist information is at Belfortstraat 9 near the Town Hall (open 8.30 a.m.–7 p.m. weekdays, 10 a.m.–7 p.m. Saturdays, 10 a.m.–4 p.m. Sundays).

All the sights are central and within easy walking distance of one another. The main sights are: the CATHEDRAL OF ST BAAF, containing Van Eycks; next door is the BELFRY, 'S'GRAVENKASTEEL' – the twelfth-century FLEMISH COUNTS' CASTLE – and the guildhouses by the KOORNMARKT. Use the university halls of residence at Stalhof 6, just off Overpoortstraat, or the youth hostel at St Pietersplein, or one of the pensions near the station for a place to sleep. Het Postje at Prinses Clementinalaan 136 (Tel. 225406) is OK. The university at Overpoortstraat is also your best bet for eats and nightlife.

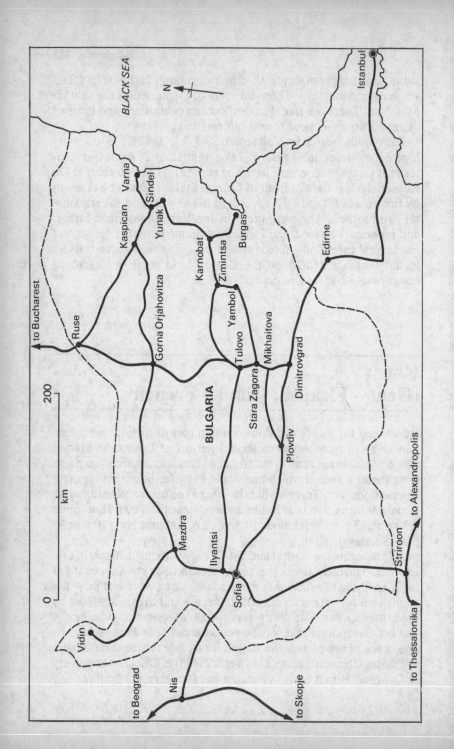

BULGARIA

Entry requirements	Passport and visa
Population	9,000,000
Capital	Sofia (pop.: 1,000,000+)
Currency	Leva
	£1 = approx. 1.34 leva
Political system	Socialist People's Republic
Religion	Eastern Orthodox
Language	Bulgarian (Russian widely spoken; some German, French and English understood)
Public holidays	1, 2 Jan.; 1, 2, 24 May; 9, 10 Sept.; 7 Nov.

Every year, swarms of tourists from East and West alike flock to the Black Sea coast for the sun. Few venture far from their hotels, leaving much of the country's interior unspoilt. The original Bulgars were an Asiatic tribe who were eventually conquered by Slavs from the north. By the tenth century, Bulgaria had her own empire in which literature and the arts flourished. This process continued till the fourteenth century, when trade helped Bulgaria to become the leader in south-eastern Europe. In 1396, the Turks became worried at what was going on and moved in. For the next 500 years they hung about to keep a check on things, and only left after the Russo-Turkish war of 1877 obliged them to do so. Fortunately during this long period the Bulgarians managed to preserve their native culture by giving refuge to writers and artists in their monasteries, many of which survive. The Bulgarians backed the losing side in the First World War, and supported the Allies in the Second. Today, they're right in there with their Russian comrades, as they have been since their liberation from the Turks in 1877.

BULGARIAN STATE RAILWAYS (BDZ)

Trains tend to be overcrowded and slow in Bulgaria. Occasionally things come together and they run on time, but this is the exception rather than the rule. There are three types of trains: express (Ekspresen), fast (Brzi), and slow (Putnichki). Avoid the latter at all costs. Unfortunately, Transalpino (and Eurotrain) only run as far as Sofia. In theory, it should be quite easy to cross the country to the Black Sea coast and return again the same day – trains leave Sofia every morning, arriving at Burgas in the early afternoon. In practice, there are often delays at intermediate stations. Whenever possible, buy your ticket at least a day before setting off, or arrive early at the station to be sure of a seat. Fortunately for railers, Sofia is not too far across the Yugoslavian border: take the 'Marmara' Express from Belgrade to Dimitrovgrad, then the normal fare to Sofia.

TRAIN INFORMATION

Few of the staff speak English, so you might find German and French more helpful. Timetables are given in the Cyrillic alphabet, so if you're stuck, try: 'Ot koi peron zaminava vlakuh za . . . ?' (From which platform does the train to . . . leave?) Depend on your Thomas Cook Continental Timetable for most of the time. (Remember: a nod in Bulgaria means 'No' and a horizontal shake of the head means 'Yes'.)

• **Reservations:** To be sure of a seat you'll have to reserve at least one day in advance. Reservations are obligatory on international expresses and can be made through a Balkantourist office.

• **Night travel:** All couchettes and sleepers are operated by the state railways and fall well short of Western standards.

• **Eating on trains:** There's either a buffet car or mini-bar on all fast trains.

TOURIST INFORMATION

There are Balkantourist offices in nearly every large town. They answer all your travel and accommodation problems as well as giving out tourist information.

• **ISIC bonuses:** With an IUS card (obtainable from Orbita Youth Travel Bureau, 45a Boulevard Stambolijski, Sofia), you can get reductions for international train travel within the Eastern Bloc, and cheaper entrance charges to many museums and galleries.

• **Money matters:** 1 leva = 100 stotinki.
Banking hours are 8 a.m.–11.45 a.m. It's best to exchange your money at Balkantourist offices as they give an 80 per cent bonus on the official rate. In theory, you're supposed to have prepaid for two nights' accommodation, but in practice they don't worry you.

• **Shops:** Open 9 a.m.–8 p.m. with a siesta from 1 p.m.–4 p.m. Look out for Corecom which sell Bulgarian goods at favourable prices.

• **Museums:** Tend to shut on Mondays, but there's no fixed pattern.

SLEEPING

When dealing with Balkantourist offices, bear in mind that they always try to fill up their own hotels first. Ask for a room in a private home whenever possible, as they're always a lot cheaper and more interesting. If you decide to bypass the tourist office and take up a local on the offer of a room, you're supposed to register this with the police. There's no real need to do this if you've already got a couple of official stamps on the card you were given at the border, for the mention of the police will bring many a host out in a sweat. Be careful here, for if you cannot account for several nights, you could face a 220 leva fine. Orbita (the student travel service) will find you a bed for about 6–7 leva in one of their hostels any time between mid-July and mid-September. For advance bookings write to International Tourist Relations, Orbita Youth Travel Office, 45a Boulevard Stambolijski, Sofia. Camping costs about 1.50 leva per tent and 2 leva per person on any of the hundred or so official campsites.

EATING AND NIGHTLIFE

Eat as much as you can in Bulgaria as food is tasty and cheap. National dishes have a strong Turkish influence, with lamb and pork as the most common meats. Try haiduchki kebab (lamb cooked with onions, white wine and pepper) or one of their wonderful vegetable dishes such as gyuvech. You can't go wrong with any charcoal-roasted meat and fresh salad. Yoghurt originated here and the Bulgarians are addicted to it. For drinks, try any slivova – a spirit made from plums. If you're really broke, try a kebabche (strongly spiced and grilled mince rolls) with mustard from any kebabche bar. For other nightlife, you'll have to turn to the local Balkantourist office; they often lay on folklore performances for foreign tourists.

Sofia

The 5,000-year-old city of Sofia lies in the middle of the Balkan peninsula. It's got a lot going for it: it's the 'greenest city in Europe', has skiing (from December to April) less than half an hour away, and has some fascinating buildings – mosques, museums and churches which range from Byzantine to Roman, Turkish and Greek architecture.

TOURIST INFORMATION

The Balkantourist office at the station will change money but does little else. It's open 7 a.m.–10 p.m. The main office is on Dondukov Ulica 37 (open 7 a.m.–10 p.m. daily); they will find you a private room and give you a map and general information. Take tram 1, 7 or 9 and look out for the large Balkantourist sign.

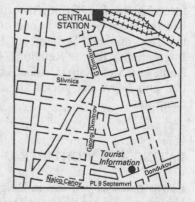

• **Addresses:**

CENTRAL POST OFFICE: Gurko Ulica 2, open daily 7 a.m.–8.30 p.m. Also poste restante here.

ORBITA – STUDENT TRAVEL OFFICE: Will find you a room in a student hostel. 45a Boulevard Stambolijski (Tel. 510739). Open daily 8 a.m.–5 p.m.

RILA: International Railway Bureau, Gurko Ulica 5 (Tel. 870777). All tickets for international journeys, except those wanted for today's date, are to be bought here. Open daily 8 a.m.–11.30 a.m., 12 noon–4 p.m.
UK EMBASSY: 18 Boulevard Tolbuhin.
US EMBASSY: 1a Boulevard Stambolijski.
24-HOUR CHEMIST: 152 Boulevard Stambolijski.

• **Getting about:** The city buses and trams are fair enough. Buy your tickets in advance from the special kiosks, and also grocery stalls. The main area worth seeing, however, is easily walked around.

SEEING

The two main churches of Sofia are the ALEXANDER NEVSKY – a twentieth-century neo-Byzantine church with a fascinating crypt stuffed full of beautiful icons from all over Bulgaria, and the sixth-century ST SOPHIA on Nevski Square. Also worth seeing are the BOYANA CHURCH on the outskirts, and ST GEORGE ROTUNDA – a fourth-century Roman church now in the courtyard of the Balkan Hotel. The ARCHAEOLOGICAL MUSEUM, 2 Boulevard Stambolijski (closed Monday), is in one of the city's mosques and has a collection of Bulgarian finds from various digs and discoveries.

The MUSEUM OF THE REVOLUTIONARY MOVEMENT IN BULGARIA is their version of the take-over and a monument to party members long gone. It's at 14 Boulevard Ruski, and on the other side on September 9th Square is the MAUSOLEUM of Georgi Dimitrov, Bulgaria's deceased prime minister, and the former royal palace which now houses the NATIONAL GALLERY OF PAINTING AND SCULPTURE. Continuing back along Boulevard Ruski, you come to the FREEDOM PARK which has an open-air theatre, sports complex, zoo and swimming pool. Newly opened and well worth visiting is the NATIONAL HISTORY MUSEUM at Boulevard Vitosha.

SLEEPING

Use either Balkantourist or Orbita for private accommodation and expect to pay 15–17 leva for a double through Balkantourist, and less through Orbita. If you're arriving late and these offices are shut, stay in the station and 'look lost'. You'll find locals coming up to you and offering a place in their house for about 8 leva a person. People do halve this price by *discreetly* paying them in hard currency (sterling, dollars, marks, francs).

Orbita Student Hostel, Anton Ivanov 76 (Tel. 652952). This official students' residence (you'll need ISIC) is OK and not too far out from the centre.

Hotel Preclav, Trijadica Ulica 5 (Tel. 876586) is one of the cheapest available. Singles cost 12 leva, doubles 18 including breakfast. Also worth a try is Hotel Bulgaria at 4 Boulevard Ruski (Tel. 871977).

If things look desperate, make your way to the university (trams 1, 2, 7, 9, 14, and 18, then change to 4 or 10) and ask around for a student to let you share. Camping Vrana (Tel. 781213) is on Boulevard Lenin and offers campsites and bungalows. Bus 13 or 213 from station.

EATING AND NIGHTLIFE

Food's cheap and good, and eating out in Sofia can cost far less than picnicking in Western Europe. Count on 9 to 12 leva for a full and excellent meal. For Bulgarian specialities, try Koprivshtitsa, on 3 Boulevard Vitosha; for Russian food, try Krim, 2 Dobroudja St; and for German food, Berlin on 4 Boulevard V. Zaimor. If you're really cutting corners, there are plenty of self-service places and an open-air market on Georgi Kirkov Ulica near the station.

Balkantourist fill you in on what shows and concerts are on. These tend to be more classical than popular, but the National Folk Ensemble put on some good things.

● **Excursions:** If your long journey to Sofia has filled your lungs with smoke, hike up to the VITOSHA MOUNTAINS NATIONAL PARK, five miles from Sofia. The mountain air will do you good, and if you're feeling energetic ZLATNIY MOSTOVE, the glacial moraine, should provide the necessary challenge. Ask at Balkantourist or the bus station for the services.

PLOVDIV is only three hours away from Sofia by train and is Bulgaria's second city. When you arrive at the station, take trolley bus 2 to the tourist office at Boulevard Moskva (Tel. 52807). Equipped with a map of the city, head straight for the old town which has been a commercial centre for over 2,000 years. See the ROMAN REMAINS, and the ARCHAEOLOGICAL MUSEUM with its excellent collection of Thracian gold, and the ETHNOGRAPHICAL MUSEUM.

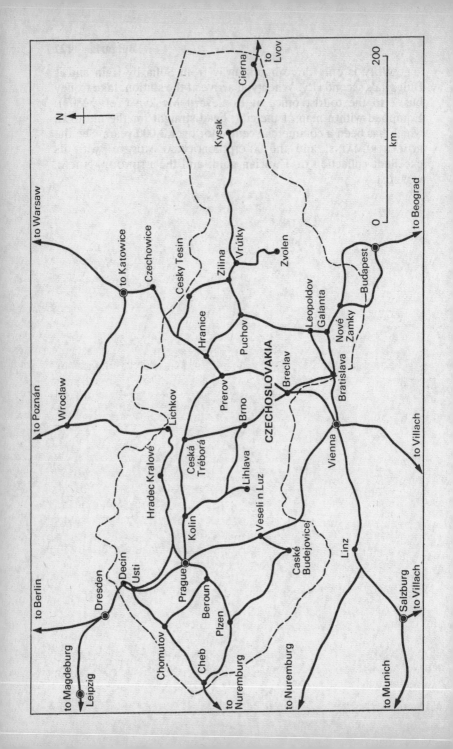

CZECHOSLOVAKIA

Entry requirements	Passport and advance visa
Population	15,500,000
Capital	Prague (pop.: 1,500,000)
Currency	Koruna
	£1 = 15.51 Kčs.
Political system	Socialist Federal Republic
Religions	Catholic and Protestant
Languages	Czech and Slovak (some German
	and English understood)
Public holidays	1 Jan.; Easter Monday;
	1, 9 May; 28 Oct.; 25, 26 Dec.

Czechoslovakia came into being in 1918 with the political union of Bohemia, Moravia and Slovakia, all former provinces of the Austro-Hungarian empire. Geographically, Czechoslovakia is at the very heart of Europe – not a good place to be at the best of times, but before the Second World War it was positively disastrous. Hitler was chafing at the bit, demanding the return of German-speaking land. France, Britain and Italy agreed to let him have it in 1939, and before long Poland and Hungary got in on the act and divided up the rest. After the war, Czechoslovakia was restored to its original boundaries, except for Ruthenia which the Russians decided to hang on to.

Dubček's ill-fated attempt to combine Communist ideology with democracy in 1968 brought Soviet disapproval and occupation. Today, there is little evidence of the open protests of the 1960s. In 1970, a twenty-year friendship agreement was signed with the Russians, a fact of life which most Czechs seem to accept. Fortunately for eurorailers, great efforts have been taken to preserve the past. It's just a pity that this is not reinforced by the authorities to make one feel more welcome.

CZECHOSLOVAK STATE RAILWAYS
(Československé Státní Dráhy, CSD)

The service is a hot contender for the slowest trains in Europe. Like Britain, they have their own 125 – the only trouble is it's 12.5 m.p.h.

Whenever possible, try to fix up your travel arrangements outside Czechoslovakia, as it's quite possible on a day-trip to Prague to spend all day queueing for a seat reservation (záznam) for the journey back. Trains are frequent and tickets are sold according to the speed of the train. Don't cut corners here as it's generally recognized that even buses are faster than the expresses. Go for the fastest possible (Expresní or Rychlík). Unfortunately, these sometimes require seat reservations and that may mean enormous queues, either at the station or at the Čedok office for international trains.

The best way of travelling to Czechoslovakia is by Transalpino. It's possible to buy an ordinary ticket in Vienna if you're on an Inter Rail. If you're travelling to Czechoslovakia from any of the other Eastern Bloc countries, you can get a 25 per cent reduction with an IUS card. At the border the train might stop for an hour or so while the police and other officials check things out. They are very thorough: on our first visit they even took down the panelling on the roof and had a good look round with mirrors, so take no chances and declare all your personal possessions: cameras, films, etc., as they enjoy 'great discretionary powers'. Also at the border you are obliged to change £10 ($13) a day into koruna. This is done on the train, and it's only after you've done this that your visa becomes valid.

TRAIN INFORMATION

Take it for granted that they won't speak English at information offices so have the German vocabulary at the ready. If you still have no success, try: 'Zlkterého nástupiště odjízdi vlak do . . . ?' (From which platform does the train to . . . leave?) A lot of the left-luggage lockers are vandalized – it's not that you've got the combination wrong.

• **Reservations:** Try to reserve well ahead of time to be sure of a seat, as trains are always busy. This is obligatory on some expresses. Check with Čedok.

• **Night travel:** Sleepers and couchettes are operated by the state railways and run on all long journeys. Avoid sleepers as they tend to be expensive.

• **Eating on trains:** There's either a restaurant car or buffet on all fast trains.

TOURIST INFORMATION

This is mostly handled by Čedok. They suggest tours and supply local information. The student travel offices (CKM) are staffed by students and issue IUS and IYHF cards. They are normally very good, except in Prague where they have become almost as bureaucratic as Čedok.

• **IUS bonuses:** 25 per cent off East European train fares.

• **Money matters:** 1 koruna (Kčs) = 100 hellers.
Banking hours are Mon.–Fri.: 8 a.m.–3 or 4 p.m. The £10 ($13) per day you were obliged to change on the train should be plenty to keep you going, as prices are low. Spend *all* your koruna, because it's not possible to change them back when you leave. Instead, you are given a voucher for your next visit (regardless of whether or not you intend to return). If you think you're going to need more than your daily £10 worth, then it's best to change it at Čedok, as they give an extra 36 per cent bonus over the official rate of 15.51 Kčs to the £. It's not worth the risk for the little extra you might get on street transactions.

• **Post offices:** Open from 8 a.m. to 4 p.m.

• **Shops:** Follow the usual pattern, opening at 9 a.m. and shutting at 6 p.m. on weekdays and at noon on Saturdays. Tuzex is the name of the government hard-currency chain.

• **Museums:** Open Tues.–Sun.: 10 a.m.–5 p.m. Closed Mondays.

SLEEPING

Whenever possible, try to arrange for prepaid accommodation through Čedok offices outside Czechoslovakia. In Vienna, their office is at Parkring 12 (Tel. 528 699). Hotels are graded from 2 to 5 stars. A 3-star double will cost about 200 Kčs per night. Camping is very cheap: 15 Kčs per person. Ask Čedok for their map with lists of all campsites.

Staying at a private home also works out a lot cheaper than hotels.

Apart from Čedok offices, where queues are normally large, it's also possible to find accommodation through the student travel offices (CKM) during July and August.

Dormitories are converted into youth hostels (juni strèdiska), many of which have good two-bedded rooms for only 50 Kčs per person on an IYHF card, or about 65 Kčs without.

Wherever you stay, remember to have your visa stamped every night; if you're staying at a private home, register with the police within 48 hours of arrival.

EATING AND NIGHTLIFE

Don't worry about picnics as food is incredibly cheap and good in Czechoslovakia. Just to make sure you don't get a raw deal, the government has graded restaurants into four price categories. Specialities include zeleninová (a vegetable and cream soup) and any dish made from pork (vepřové). For really cheap meals, try any of the self-service stand-up restaurants (samoobsluha). You'll never get it as good again, so eat as much as you can. A lot of the grade-one and -two restaurants have dancing, but apart from this things are very quiet by Western standards. Čedok should be able to help out on what open-air concerts, etc., there might be. The best way to find out what's happening is to ask any young Czechs. They will probably advise you to head towards a wine bar or beer hall where most young people meet. Try Budvar or any other beer you're recommended, for not only is Czech beer among the best in Europe, it's also the cheapest.

Bratislava

The third largest city and capital of Slovakia was also the former capital of Hungary. Today it is essentially a modern city, though it still has over 400 historically interesting buildings. See the thirteenth-century BRATISLAVA CASTLE, the OLD TOWN HALL, ST MICHAEL'S CATHEDRAL, the PRIMATIAL PALACE, the PHARMACY MUSEUM and the SLOVAK NATIONAL MUSEUM.

Brno

The capital of Moravia and Czechoslovakia's second city has quite a lot to offer. See ŠPILBERK CASTLE (1287) with its display of torture instruments, FREEDOM SQUARE with its Renaissance and baroque buildings, the CATHEDRAL OF ST PETER AND PAUL, and the colourful outdoor 'CABBAGE MARKET'.

Pilsen (Plzeň)

Basically, this is an ugly, uninspiring place situated in western Bohemia, but if you're a beer-fan it's pilgrimage country, for this is the birthplace of Pilsner Urquell beer. See the BURGHER'S BREWERY, the BREWING MUSEUM on Roosevelt St. The ABBEY OF THE VIRGIN MARY and ST BARTHOLOMEW'S CHURCH are the town's other saving graces.

Prague (Praha)

Prague, the fourteenth-century capital of the Holy Roman Empire, is where to go if you want to step back into medieval life and have all your preconceptions of an Eastern Bloc city shattered. As far as sights are concerned, many consider Prague to be on a par with Paris, London or Rome. We feel it is too, and a good deal of the reason lies in the fact that there are only a tenth of the tourists there to spoil it. It lies in western Bohemia and is a riot of bridges, parks, hills and a fascinating array of architectural styles. Despite the hassles of getting there, we're sure you'll think it was worth it.

STATION FACILITIES

There are actually three stations in Prague, but you'll only ever use two of them: Praha–Hlavní Nádraží on Vítězného února (which has good showers for 8 Kčs and a left-luggage store), and Praha–Střed on Hybernská. International trains leave from both, so always check.

TOURIST INFORMATION

From the main station (Praha–Hlavní Nádraží) or the alternative station of Praha–Střed, walk up Hybernská to the centre. The Prague Information Service is at Na Příkopě 20. They'll give you maps, what's on and general information (open Mon.–Fri.: 8 a.m.–8 p.m., Sat.: 8 a.m.–noon). Čedok, the Czechoslovak national travel organization, are on Na Pří-

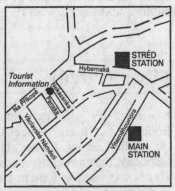

kopě 18 (Tel. 224251). They change money, arrange rail tickets (but get there before 8.30 a.m. for this, and expect delays) and operate a room-finding service round the corner on Panská 5 (open Mon.–Fri.: 8 a.m.–10 p.m., Sat.: 8 a.m.–8 p.m., Sun.: 8 a.m.–5 p.m.), Tel. 227004.

● Addresses:

POST OFFICE: Jindřišská 14, 24-hour service. Also poste restante here.

CKM (the student agency): Junior Hotel Praha, Žitná 9. Open Mon.–Fri.: 8 a.m.–10 a.m., 1 p.m.–5 p.m. (Tel. 298589).

FIRST AID: Jungmannova 14 (Tel. 247771).

24-HOUR CHEMIST: Na Příkopě 7 (Tel. 220081).

UK EMBASSY: Thunovská Ulice 14, Malá Strana.

US EMBASSY: Tržiště 15, Malá Strana (Tel. 536641).

CANADIAN EMBASSY: Hradčany Mickiewuzova (Tel. 326941).

PRAGOTUR: U Obecniho domu 2; also operate a room-finding service. Open Mon.–Fri.: 8 a.m.–9.30 p.m., Sat.: 8 a.m.–8 p.m., Sun.: 8.30 a.m.–3 p.m. (Tel. 2317281).

INFORMATION SERVICES: Na Příkopě 20 (Tel. 544444); Panská 4 (Tel. 223411).

• **Getting about:** The new underground is efficient and cheap, and the bus and tram network covers every corner of the city. The buses with green badges are for the suburbs. Buy tickets in advance from news-stands and hotels and stamp them on the buses. Forget taxis altogether.

SEEING

Don't judge the city by its station. We nearly boarded the first train out again on our first visit, but had we done so, we'd have missed a city with as much to see and do in as Paris. Prague started off as five separate towns, and each one of them merits a visit: the New Town (Nové Město), the nineteenth-century commercial centre; the Old Town (Staré Město), medieval buildings and fascinating Jewish Quarter; the Lesser Town (Malá Strana), the baroque area of palaces and churches; Hradčany, the area round Prague Castle; and Vyšehrad, the ninth-century fortress-town opposite the castle.

• **Nové Město:** The main sights are WENCESLAS SQUARE, the main boulevard, the NATIONAL MUSEUM and CHARLES SQUARE, the largest square in Prague with a park in its centre and the NEW TOWN HALL on its north side. Also DVOŘÁK'S MUSEUM, Ke Karlovu 20, is in this vicinity.

• **Staré Město:** The Old Town dates back to 1120 – and you can feel it. The POWDER TOWER, used to store gunpowder in the fifteenth century, gives a good view from the top, while the OLD TOWN SQUARE was at the centre of medieval Prague. Here is to be found the 1490 Astronomical Clock of the OLD TOWN HALL which performs every hour. Tour round the Town Hall, and then see the TÝN CHURCH on the east side of the square. This twin-Gothic-spired church has a baroque interior and dates from 1365.

The JEWISH QUARTER houses the oldest synagogue in Europe (1270) and the fifteenth-century JEWISH CEMETERY with its 12,000 tombstones piled on top of one another. The museum in KLAUS SYNAGOGUE tells of the extermination of Jews in the Second World War.

Bordering the New Town is the BETHLEHEM CHAPEL where the Czech hero John Hus preached, and the baroque CHARLES BRIDGE has superb views of the castle, the island of Kampa and the River Vltava.

● **Malá Strana:** The rich seventeenth- and eighteenth-century merchants spent their money on this town. The LESSER TOWN SQUARE and NERUDA ST are testament to that. ST NICHOLAS' CHURCH is the finest baroque building in Prague, and just north of it is the palace of the Habsburg general, Albrecht Wallenstein.

● **Hradčany:** PRAGUE CASTLE today houses the Czech government, but it used to be the palace of the kings of Bohemia. Try to get on a tour round it. Also in this 'royal city' is ST VITUS' CATHEDRAL which is quite incredible, and is certainly the most detailed Gothic church in central Europe. The National Gallery is in the ŠTERNBERK PALACE in the castle square.

A charming walk can be taken down the GOLDEN LANE where the alchemists tried to turn their lead into gold. The STRAHOV MONASTERY, west of the castle, houses the Museum of Czech Literature and offers a good view over the whole of Prague.

● **Vyšehrad:** The VYŠEHRAD FORTRESS has in its grounds the eleventh-century Rotunda of St Martin, and in its cemetery Dvořák, Smetana, and other Czech 'greats' are buried.

SLEEPING

This is your main headache in Prague. If it's at all possible, book ahead, particularly in the summer; but if you've only decided to go on the spur of the moment, don't panic. You'll get something. Čedok or Pragotur are your best bets for finding a room (see above). Prepare yourself for the inevitable long queues and insist on somewhere central and cheap. They charge a small commission, but it's well worth it, with their cheapest double around 180 Kčs. Private accommodation is cheaper, so always ask for this or, better still, the CKM student hostels. You do best contacting the campsites yourself, as the officials will tell you they're full when they're not.

You should register with the police within 48 hours, if you've handled your own accommodation. At weekends you'll find them hard to trace as their offices close. They're at Olšanká 2 (Tel. 242960, ext. 2211).

• **Hostels:** CKM student hostels charge about 60 Kčs a night. Go in person as the CKM office only books for groups and tends to be less than helpful on the phone. Čedok's hostels are booked through Panská 5. They don't make waves about unmarried couples, but cost more than CKM.

Strahov, Spartakiádní Station. Reception opens at 10 a.m. (be there at about 8.30 a.m.).

Hotel Jarov, Kověvova 196 (Tel. 824641) is not terribly central (next to the Economics Institute), but pleasant. Tram 9 or 21.

• **1-star hotels:** Every year they get thinner on the ground, and those which are left all charge about the same rate. Expect to pay about 200 Kčs for a double and 120 Kčs for a single. Hotel Balkan, Svornosti 28 (Tel. 540777): a good place with a good pub for grub. Národní dum, Bořivojova 53 (Tel. 275365): multi-bed rooms for around 120 Kčs each.

EATING AND NIGHTLIFE

Beer halls (pivnice) and wine cellars (vinárny) are dotted all over the city. These are safe bets for cheap food and drink, as are the stand-up snack places. Don't expect a huge menu, but what there is is usually OK. Take advantage of the Czech beer while you can. Specially recommended are: U Prince, Old Town Square, opposite the Town Hall: good and cheap in a wonderful setting; closed Thursdays. Berjozka Bistro, Na Příkopě: a good Russian restaurant next to the Prague information service.

The Prague Spring Festival (12 May–4 June) is a big draw for music- and drama-lovers. The monthly 'What's On' can be had from PIS, Na Příkopě 20. The Laterna Magika, Národní 40, is a review of films, ballet and drama which deserves a mention, but you usually need reservations of up to a month.

Beer halls or wine cellars are the most likely places to meet East European students. Try: U Malvaze, Karlova 10, big student dive; U Zelené Žáby, U Radnice 8, good wine and a friendly crowd (closed Fridays and Saturdays); Ve staré radnice, Loretánská, open till 8 p.m.

• **Excursions from Prague:** Half an hour in the train is all it takes to get to the amazing fourteenth-century castle of KARLŠTEJN – Bohemia's finest example. The famous spa of KARLOVY VARY (Carlsbad) also makes an interesting trip. Trains to get there are dead cheap.

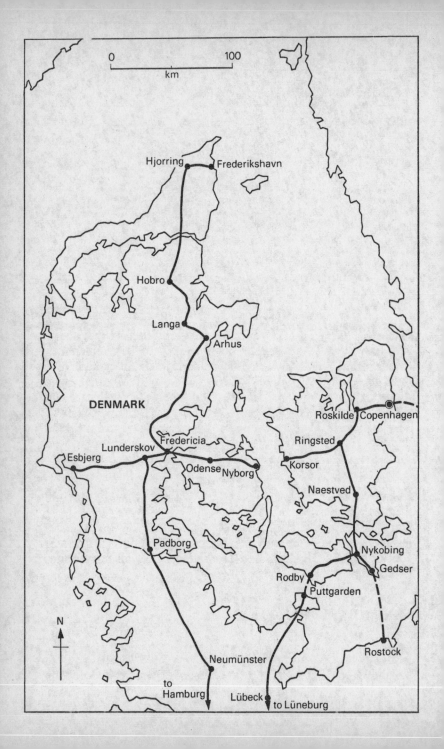

DENMARK

Entry requirements	Passport
Population	5,200,000
Capital	Copenhagen (pop.: 1,400,000 +)
Currency	Kroner
	£1 = approx. 13.58 kr.
Political system	Constitutional Monarchy
Religion	Lutheran
Language	Danish (English widely spoken)
Public holidays	1 Jan.; Good Friday;
	Easter Monday; Common Prayer Day;
	29 Apr.; Ascension Day; 12 May; 23 May;
	Whit Monday; Constitution Day; 25, 26 Dec.

Over a hundred of Denmark's islands are inhabited, the largest of these being Zealand where Copenhagen was founded in the twelfth century. During the Middle Ages the economy prospered, and in 1397 Sweden and Norway came under Danish rule. The union with Sweden lasted till 1523, while Norway remained united until 1814. The acceptance of Luther's Reformation was followed by a flowering of the arts and sciences and culturally the nineteenth century was Denmark's 'Golden Age'. Today Denmark enjoys a very high standard of living; from a Eurorailer's point of view, the high degree of social planning and the number of public facilities available make travelling here a pleasure, whether you head for Copenhagen or one of the smaller, picturesque islands.

• **Getting there:** From Britain the cheapest way is to take the train from London to Copenhagen (26 hours). There are ferries from Harwich to Esbjerg (20 hours), Newcastle to Esbjerg (19 hours, summertime only). There's a 50 per cent reduction with an Inter Rail on the DFDS ships, and Transalpino offer all ferry routes except the last.

DANISH STATE RAILWAYS
(Danske Statsbaner, DSB)

In Denmark you'll spend almost as much time on water as you will on land, as entire trains clamp down on ferries which connect up the islands as well as with mainland Sweden and Germany. With hourly intercity trains, they've had plenty of practice and have got the whole operation down to a fine art. There's a great feeling of camaraderie once you're on board. Passengers are free to get out and wander about. This is particularly the case on the Kalundborg–Århus crossing (3 hours); a more leisurely affair than the Great Belt (Storebaelt) crossing (1 hour). The whole system runs efficiently with trains rarely running late.

The rail network is divided into four categories:

1. Lyntog–Lightning trains L. Almost as luxurious as TEEs and used on long hauls, such as Copenhagen to Frederikshavn.
2. Intercity IC. Equally fast, serving the shorter distances between large towns.
3. Regionaltoget. Slower regional trains, connecting up the smaller towns with the main network.
4. S-tog. Copenhagen's underground, connecting up the city with the suburbs.

There are supplements to pay in Denmark – about 12 kr.

• **Inter Rail bonuses:**

	FROM	TO	REDUCTION %
Det forenede Dampskibs-	Esbjerg	Harwich PQ	50 (1st)
selskab (DFDS)	Esbjerg	Newcastle	50 (1st)
	Copenhagen	Oslo	50 (2nd)
Hjørring Privatbaner (HP)	Hjørring	Hirtshals	50
Flyvebadene	Copenhagen	Malmö	50

Inter Rails are also valid on the S-tog in Copenhagen as well as on island ferries.

• **Eurail bonuses:** The following services are free:
—Ferry crossings Aarhus to Kalundborg, Knudshoved to Halskov, Nyborg to Korsør, Fynshavn to Bøjden.
—Ferry crossings Rødby Faerge to Puttgarden (Federal Republic of Germany).
—Ferry crossings operated by the Danish and Swedish State Railways between Helsingør and Helsingborg (Sweden).
—Ferry crossings operated by Stena Sessan Line between Frederikshavn and Gothenburg (Sweden).

Reduced fares:
—50 per cent reduction on the Danish Navigation Company, 'Øresund', on the hydrofoil between Copenhagen and Malmö.
—20 per cent reduction on the normal fares of the Steamship Company DFDS between Esbjerg–Harwich, Esbjerg–Newcastle, Esbjerg–Far Oer Islands, Copenhagen–Oslo.

TRAIN INFORMATION

Timetables are dotted everywhere around the stations, and all the staff seem to speak fluent English. If you're spending some time in Denmark ask for the Koreplan, a timetable for all the ferries, trains and buses.

• **Reservations:** Are only compulsory when crossing the Great Belt between Sjaelland and Fyn (that is, from Korsør to Nyborg or Kalundborg to Århus). Also all L and IC trains can be reserved if required.

• **Night travel:** Couchettes/sleepers cost *relatively* less in Scandinavia than elsewhere in Europe. A bed in a six-berther costs approximately 120 kr. Within Denmark, they operate between Copenhagen and Esbjerg as well as to Struer and Frederikshavn and cost less than on international journeys.

• **Eating on trains:** There are no dining cars, even if you could afford them, though on L and IC trains there are buffets and trolleys selling snacks, etc. If you're starving, try to survive till you get aboard the ferries as they have self-service cafeterias.

If you're on an international crossing, don't forget to check out the duty-free shops. They have good prices for cheese, wine, cigarettes and chocolates. Don't forget that in Scandinavia, and especially in Norway, normal prices are high.

• **Scenic tips:** There's good coastline scenery if you're on your way to Frederikshavn from Copenhagen or vice versa. Take the route which goes via Odense and Fredericia. If you're heading for Stockholm from Copenhagen, your best route is to train it to Helsingør (1 hour) then take the ferry to Helsingborg (free on Inter Rail).

• **Bikes:** You can rent out a bike in the summer at most of the larger stations, with the exception of Copenhagen, for about 25–30 kr. per day.

TOURIST INFORMATION

In Denmark the tourist offices are the best in Europe, particularly for the under 26s. They are both friendly and efficient, and if every tourist board was like them we would be out of a job.

• **ISIC bonsues:** 50 per cent reductions on films, theatres and museums. For further information, contact DIS Skindergade 28, Copenhagen.

• **Money matters:** 1 kroner (kr.) = 100 øre.
Banking hours are Mon., Tues., Wed., Fri.: 9.30 a.m.–4 p.m., Thurs.: 9.30 a.m.–6 p.m. It's best to change money with American Express if you have the opportunity as Danish banks sometimes charge a ridiculous 20 kr. commission. For late-night service there are facilities at Central Station and Tivoli Park in Copenhagen. Tourist offices exchange money out of banking hours.

• **Post office:** Opens Mon.–Fri.: 9 a.m.–5 p.m., Sat.: 9 a.m.–12 noon.

• **Shops:** Hours vary from town to town; in general: Mon.–Thurs.: 9 a.m.–5.30 p.m., Friday to 7 or 8 p.m., Saturday to 1 p.m.

SLEEPING

Youth hostels require you to register before 9 p.m. and have IYHF membership. An average charge is 35–45 kr. per night and outside Copenhagen an 11 p.m. curfew is the norm. A free booklet listing all of Denmark's hostels and many campsites is available from the tourist office. There are over 500 campsites and the International Camping Carnet is required. An average overnight stay will cost 30 kr. Town mission hostels are excellent, clean and cheap. If you can't get into a hostel and don't want to be bothered with camping stay in a private home (anything but a hotel, as these really are very expensive). Tourist information will put you in touch with a Danish family who'll put you up.

EATING AND NIGHTLIFE

Danish food is expensive, but don't despair: shop at the well-stocked supermarkets and prepare your own smørrebrød (open sandwiches). Pølser (hot dog) stands are on most street corners, and the famous Danish brews round off picnics in style. Look out for cafés with signs 'Madkurve kan Medbringes' (literally, 'bring your own food'), so just buy a coffee.

ISIC gives you 50 per cent off films, theatres, etc., and there's no shortage of pubs in Denmark. For Copenhagen, 'Use It' have a useful magazine called 'Playtime' which gives you a rundown on what's on, and if that's not enough they also have special information sheets on entertainment.

Copenhagen (Købnhavn)

The largest city in Scandinavia, situated on the north-eastern shore of Zealand, Copenhagen is a well-run, exciting place with lots going for it and an almost Parisian *joie de vivre*. The Danes are known to be a socially-minded lot, and this shows particularly in their capital where they operate two free services for young travellers which are almost too good to be true. The YMCA and YWCA get together and open a centre for eurorailers in the summer where you can go for advice on what to see and where to go, and for help with problems. They're at St Kannikestraede 19. Open 8 a.m.–11.30 p.m.; 1 July–15 August.

The second organization, called 'Use It', is much larger, is open all year, and is sponsored by the city youth organization. It offers countless free or non-profit-making services: free maps, tourist information and advice, a series of leaflets on cheap restaurants and hostels, free luggage storage, and at its centre at Magstraede 14 (not far from Central Station) there is a restaurant, jazz club, rock/folk club and cinema where you can meet fellow travellers and young Danes. Pick up their magazine, 'Playtime'. 'Use It' will also find you a bed you can afford, or help you out if you've an emergency or crisis. They're open in summer from 10 a.m.–8 p.m. and off-season

Mon. and Wed. from 11 a.m.–5 p.m., 7 p.m. on Tues. and Thurs. (Tel. 156518).

Bear in mind: the YMCA/YWCA set-up is a Christian organization and can be quite strict – even in Copenhagen – so if you're after advice on the hottest places for evening entertainment, etc., go to 'Use It'.

These sort of facilities are unique in Europe, so make the most of them whilst you're there, and don't expect anything remotely like it in southern Europe.

STATION FACILITIES

Train information	7 a.m.–9 p.m.
	(Tel. 141701)
Reservations	8 a.m.–9 p.m.
Left-luggage lockers	Shut 1.30 a.m.–4.30 a.m.
Left-luggage store	6.30 a.m.–0.15 a.m.
Duty officer 'Inspektion'	All hours
Chemist	7 a.m.–11 p.m.
Waiting room (in cafeteria)	6.30 a.m.–11.45 p.m.
Restaurant	7 a.m.–10 p.m. (bistro)
	11.30 a.m.–11 p.m. (grill)
Cafeteria	6.30 a.m.–11.45 p.m.
Bar, Buffet	7 a.m.–11 p.m.
Snack bar	7 a.m.–11.45 p.m.
Shopping	Grocery stores open late
Foreign exchange	7 a.m.–10 p.m.
Station shuts	1.30 a.m.–4.30 a.m.

There are post office, banking and telephoning facilities.
Copenhagen–Malmö 40 minutes, to Gothenburg 4½ hours, to Hamburg 5 hours.

Copenhagen's 'Hovedbanegård' is the terminus for all main-line trains. It's a particularly fine station with many facilities. The platforms are below ground level. The 'S' trains (suburban electrics) also use the station.

Note: These S-togs are free to Inter Rail or Eurail card holders. Kiosk P (9 a.m.–midnight in summer) is the room-finding service in the station. As their commission is quite considerable, best to go to 'Use It' who offer this service free.

• **Inter Rail Centre:** DSB's Inter Rail Centre was opened on 1 July 1984 and is the first of its kind in the world. Anyone with an Inter Rail, Eurail Youthpass or BIJ ticket can use its excellent facilities from June through till the end of September. (Open 7 a.m.–1 a.m.). These facilities include a common room and a dining room where everyone meets up, as well as toilets and washing facilities. Throughout the day, there are news bulletins in English, German and French, and tape-recorded tourist information in the same languages. There are also vending machines with hot and cold beverages and sandwiches, music and a large collection of folders.

TOURIST INFORMATION

At the Town Hall Square is Danmarks Turistråd – tourist information, H. C. Andersens Boulevard 22 (Tel. 111415). Open May–Sept.: 9 a.m.–7 p.m. (9 a.m.–9 p.m. July and Aug.), Sun.: 9 a.m.–1 p.m. Off season: Mon.–Fri.: 9 a.m.–5 p.m., Sat.: 9 a.m.–noon. Their service is excellent and there are leaflets on everything you could possibly need to know. Be specific and ask for everything you might need, for instance camping, walking, other parts of Denmark, etc. Don't forget to pick up their free map and a copy of 'Copenhagen This Week'.

• **Addresses:**
USE IT: Magstraede 14 (Tel. 156518). They help out eurorailers with everything and will even hold your mail and find you a bed for the night.
POST OFFICE: Tietgensgade 37 (behind Central Station). Poste restante here too.
AMEX: Amagertor 18 (Tel. 122301).
UK EMBASSY: Kastelsvej 36–40 (Tel. 264600).
US EMBASSY: Dag Hammarskjölds Allé 24 (Tel. 423144).
CANADIAN EMBASSY: Kristen Bernikowsgade 1 (Tel. 122299).
AUSTRALIAN EMBASSY: Kristianiagade 21 (Tel. 262244).
24-HOUR CHEMIST: Steno Apotek, Vesterbrogade 6c (Tel. 148266).
TRANSALPINO: Skoubogade 6 (Tel. 144633), Mon.–Fri.: 9 a.m.–5 p.m., Sat.: 10 a.m.–1 p.m.

• **Getting about:** The S-tog is free with any rail pass. If you haven't got one, the buses are a better bet but at 5 kr. a ride you're better off buying a card from the driver for eleven rides at around 55 kr. All tickets are interchangeable between buses and trains providing they are used within an hour.

SEEING

Copenhagen is a great walking city and most of the sights can easily be negotiated on foot. There are six well-planned city walking tours which last about 2 hours (ask tourist information).

TIVOLI (the famous amusement park) is in the centre and has, over the years, become rather too commercial for our liking. Avoid eating there. Open May–mid-September, 10 a.m.–midnight. The CARLSBERG and TUBORG breweries run a good deal (a classic favourite for thirsty eurorailers): tours of the breweries with free samples afterwards. (Tourist information will give you times, etc.) At the commune 'Christiana' on PRINCESSEGADE you'll see the 'anything goes' Danish attitude lived out, in the form of the pot-smoking, drinking, often nude-bathing 'hippies' who occupied the area in 1971. Unfortunately there was some difficulty with bikers last year and the area has become a bit sordid.

Of all the museums in Copenhagen, the one to choose if time is short is the NATIONAL MUSEUM OF DENMARK, though you may find THORVALDSEN'S MUSEUM OF SCULPTURE or the RESISTANCE MUSEUM interesting. The Bellevue is a beach between Copenhagen and Helsingør, known locally as 'Fluepapiret' (fly-paper) for its ability to draw the bikini-clad blondes and the local likely lads.

The walk to the little mermaid, along the LANGELINIE, is the best part of the trip, as the statue's nothing special. Final note: avoid the boat trips.

SLEEPING

As hotels can start at a crippling 180 kr. (single) a night, investigate the city hostels, private houses scheme and campsites.

• **Hostels:** These are busy in summer, so don't waste time touring round them yourself. 'Use It' will help you find a bed (when their office is shut, they post up the latest bed situation outside their office). The main youth hostel (you'll need an IYHF card) is Bellahøj Vandrerhjêm at Herbergvejen 8 (Tel. 289715), 20 minutes from the centre (approximately 50 kr. per night). The Copenhagen Hostel (IYHF) at Sjaellandsbroen 55 is very clean, modern and is open 24 hours (Tel. 522908). Vesterbro Ungdoms-gaard, Absalomsgade 8 (Tel. 312070) is more expensive than the other hostels, due to its good location. Finally, there's 'Sleep In' which is now permanently based at Per Henrik Lings Alte 6 (Tel. 265059). Very few restrictions; IYHF cards are not required; co-ed dorms; bring your own sleeping bag.

• **Private accommodation:** Use Kiosk P (in the station) to find yourself a room in a private house, and expect to pay up to 200 kr. for a single, 300 kr. a double. They also take about 10 kr. commission per person.

• **Hotels:** If you've no alternative, one of the cheapest (if not the poshest) areas is behind Central Station where you will find places on Helgolandsgade and Colbjørnsensgade. Try the Savoy Hotel (Tel. 314073) across from the station.

• **Camping:** There are seven sites costing around 20 kr. per person (check admission fees). The all-year site is at Absalon Camping, 132 Korsdalsvej (Tel. 410600).

EATING AND NIGHTLIFE

This is varied, interesting and there is no shortage of places to choose from. For meals, you can't do much better than the set menus at Chinese restaurants. To keep you going there are pølser (hot dog) stalls, fast-food chains, daily specials (dagens ret) and smørrebrød.

Universitelpoppen (university refectory), 52 Kobmagergade, charge 40–50 kr. for huge meals. You'll need an ISIC, but they are closed July and August.

Spisehuset, 14 Magstraede (part of 'Use It'). All you can eat reasonably cheaply (noon–3 p.m.). In the evenings it's a pub (serving food).

There are hundreds of pubs, clubs and discos in Copenhagen. NYHAVN (the dock district) makes an interesting nocturnal wander – but not advisable for girls to go there alone. The 'Use It' house is as good and cheap a place for a drink, etc., as any, and Frederiksberg-gade comes alive at night. Basically, in Copenhagen you don't need to look hard for nightlife.

Your best day trip from Copenhagen is 40 km north to Frederiks-borg Castle at Hillerød (35 minutes by S-tog).

Århus

Denmark's second city is a busy industrial and commercial centre. See the old town (den gamle by) OPEN AIR MUSEUM, a reconstructed sixteenth-century village, the CITY PREHISTORIC MUSEUM with the amazing red-headed mummy of the Grauballe man, the twelfth-century CATHEDRAL and the VIKING MUSEUM.

Tourist information is in the Town Hall, one block from the station, and is open 9 a.m.–9 p.m. (Tel. 167298). It's a university town and the student centre is at 84 Niels Juelsgade. The youth hostel is Pavillonen Østre Skovvej (Tel. 167298); closed 1 p.m.–4 p.m. It's good and well situated in a forest, near beaches. Hotel Århus Sommandshjêm at 20 Havnegade, near the port (Tel. 121599), has single and double rooms which are quite cheap. The campsite is 7 km out at Blommehavn (bus 6).

Your cheapest lunch is at the Matematiske Fag (University) off Langelandsgade; closed after 1 p.m. and all July. Even better is the Youth Centre at 15 Vesteralle. They also give free concerts and plays. Tagskaegget at Klostergade 34 is a good jazz club.

Odense

En route from Copenhagen to Jutland, Odense is one of Denmark's oldest towns. It's the home town of Hans Christian Andersen; you can visit his house at Jensenstraede 39–43 (2 kr. on IYHF card).

Tourist information is in the Town Hall, south of the station (Tel. 127520). Open in summer 9 a.m.–8 p.m., Sundays 10 a.m.–12 noon,

6 p.m.–8 p.m. ST CANUTE'S thirteenth-century cathedral and the OPEN AIR FOLK MUSEUM and operating farm at Fyn are interesting. At Ladby (20 km north-east of Odense) is the coffin ship of a tenth-century Viking chief.

The youth hostel is at 121 Kragsbjergvej (Tel. 130425). It has 300 beds and is on bus route 6 from the station.

Aalborg

The 1,000-year-old centre of north Jutland. The main sights include the remains of a Viking village and mass grave (at Nørresundby, just outside Aalborg), the well-preserved OLD TOWN, the fifteenth-century MONASTERY OF THE HOLY GHOST, ALBORGHUS CASTLE, ST BOTOLPH'S CATHEDRAL and the baby brother of Tivoli, TIVOLILAND. All Americans in Aalborg on 4 July should make their way to the Rebild National Park, 30 km south of the city, for the most extensive Independence Day celebrations in Scandinavia.

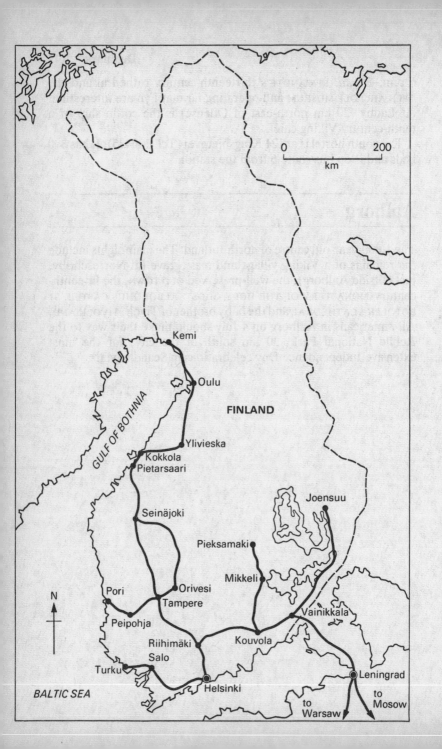

FINLAND (Suomi)

Entry requirements	Passport
Population	4,800,000
Capital	Helsinki (pop.: 500,000 +)
Currency	Finnish Markka
	£1 = approx. 7.79 mk.
Political system	Republic
Religions	Lutheran and Orthodox ministry
Languages	Finnish and Swedish (some English spoken)
Public holidays	1 Jan.; Epiphany; Good Friday; Easter Monday;
	1 May; Ascension Day; Whit Sunday;
	Midsummer Eve and Day; All Saints Day;
	3 Nov; 6, 24, 25, 26 Dec.

Finland is an interesting mixture of both east and west, and once you reach there you really do feel a long way from home. In summer, darkness hardly ever comes and in winter daylight lasts only a few hours. Geographically, Finland is very beautiful: 70 per cent of her land is covered by lush pine forests and over 60,000 lakes; added to this is clear air and an environmentally conscious people.

For centuries, her neighbours, Sweden and Russia, played political chess with Finland as the pawn. (Finland was linked with Sweden for 650 years and with Russia for 100 before proclaiming independence in 1917.) As a result, you won't find the Finns too keen on either the Swedes or the Russians. Conflict with Russia in the Second World War lost her valuable territories and landed her with large war reparations to pay off. Today, prices are lower in Finland than in the rest of Scandinavia, as is the standard of living – though it's still a wealthy country.

• **Getting there:** Unless you're going by train round the north of Sweden, your most direct route is to take a ferry from Stockholm to either Turku or Helsinki. It's a beautiful cruise (10–11 hours and 14–16 hours respectively). The main shipping lines are Silja and Viking. An Inter Rail gets you a 50 per cent reduction on both lines, while Eurail holders travel free with Silja. Facilities on both lines are excellent. Cabins are expensive, so get your sleeping bag down on deck somewhere. They run three ferries to Turku daily at 8.30

a.m., 7.30 p.m. and 9.30 p.m. Prices vary from 80 mk. to 140 mk. depending on the crossing. The Helsinki ferries leave at 6 p.m. and cost between 130 mk. and 200 mk.

FINNISH STATE RAILWAYS
(Valtionrautatiet, VR)

Reliable and comfortable with wide carriages owing to their broad five-foot Russian gauge. The majority of their rolling stock is new. There are three types of trains: special expresses (Erikoispikajuna), regular expresses (Pikajuna) and locals (Henkilöjuna). Their service extends as far north as Lapland and includes over 6,000 km of track.

● **Inter Rail bonuses:** 50 per cent reductions are offered on Oy Finnlines Ltd from Helsinki to Lübeck–Travemünde, and on Oy Vaasa–Umeå Ab lines from Vaasa to Umeå. On the crossing over to Stockholm, there are also 50 per cent reductions.

● **Eurail bonuses:** Free services:
—Steamer service of the Silja Line between Helsinki and Stockholm and between Turku–Aland Islands–Stockholm. Full fare is charged for cabin space.

TRAIN INFORMATION

At the major stations you'll find the staff speak English. Contact the 'Neuvonta' at the station if you've problems.

● **Reservations:** Obligatory on the special expresses; optional on other trains.

● **Night travel:** There are no couchettes, only sleepers which are reasonably priced. During the peak periods (Easter and July/August) try and reserve sleepers as far ahead as possible.

TOURIST INFORMATION

City offices, Matkailutoimistot, provide excellent maps and leaflets on their locality. For Finland as a whole the national tourist board, 'MEK', has its base in Helsinki.

• **ISIC bonuses:** Student discounts on museums, art galleries and theatres.

• **Money matters:** 1 Finnish markka (mk.) = 100 penni (p).
Banking hours are: Mon.–Fri.: 9.30 a.m.–4 p.m. Banks give the best rate of exchange.

• **Post offices and shops:** Keep to the 9 to 5 routine, Monday to Friday. During the summer some stay open till 8 p.m. on Monday and Friday. Stamps are also sold at bookshops, newsagents and stations.

SLEEPING

Youth hostels and campsites are graded on a star basis from one to four. There's no age limit to Finland's 150 hostels and you don't need IYHF membership, except in the most expensive category. Prices range from 25–60 mk., though most cost around 40 mk. For further information about youth hostels in Finland contact Suomen Retkeilymajajärjestö, Yriönkatu 38 B 16, 00100 Helsinki 10 (Tel. 906 940 377). There are something like 350 campsites, varying in price from 20–40 mk. per tent. For more details on hostelling and camping, ask at tourist information for the leaflet 'Finland Camping 84'.

Private accommodation and small boarding houses are also available. Summer hotels are often made out of student dorms, and they're usually clean, modern and reasonably priced. The cheapest you'll get for a hotel room (double) with breakfast is 70–100 mk.

EATING AND NIGHTLIFE

The baaris, grillis, krouvis or kahvilas are a mixture of cafés and fast-food chains. They're OK but vary dramatically in quality. The student-run cafés are your best bet. Finnish specialities include salted Baltic herring, rye bread, crayfish and fruit-filled pancakes.

Nearly all restaurants have set lunch and dinner menus but you're better advised to starve yourself all day, then go to a Voileipä-pöytä (Scandinavian cold table) for a set price. This often includes hot dishes as well, and you work on the basis of eating as much as you like for a set price.

Finns are keen on dancing and there's plenty of that going on on Vappu Night (30 April). This is the students' spring festival which is a good excuse for Helsinki's 20,000 students to let rip and have a knees-up after the long winter. Whether you've been sleeping on deck or going by train round the north, there's nothing like a real Finnish sauna to relax you. Most hotels welcome non-residents. (Rub birch-leaves with the Finns – it's cheaper to take a sauna in a group.)

Helsinki

A clean, bright, modern capital city. Your first impression will probably be of the colourful harbourside market, a daily event in front of the City Hall and President's Palace. Helsinki particularly reminds one visually of its geographical location: the solid eastern-looking buildings contrast with the modern department stores selling endless well-designed consumer goods. In some ways, you feel closer to Russia in Helsinki than you do in Budapest.

STATION FACILITIES

There are daily trains from Helsinki to Leningrad, Turku, Tampere, Kontiomäki, Oulu, Kemi and Rovaniemi (10–13 hours). Helsinki Central is one of the world's few architecturally famous stations. It's a classic example of *art nouveau*, designed by Eliel Saarinen.

Train information	Mon.–Fri.: 7.30 a.m.–8 p.m., Sat.: 7.30 a.m.–5 p.m. Sun.: 9 a.m.–7 p.m. (Tel. 659 411)
Reservations	Daily 7 a.m.–9 p.m.
Tourist information	Mon.–Sat.: 9 a.m.–9 p.m., Sun.: 12 noon–7 p.m.
Foreign exchange	Mon.–Sat.: 8.30 a.m.–8 p.m., Sun.: 12.30 p.m.–7 p.m.
Cafeteria	Mon.–Fri.: 6.30 a.m.–10 p.m., Sat., Sun.: 7 a.m.–10 p.m.
Restaurant	Daily 9 a.m.–1 a.m.
Left-luggage lockers	Shut Mon.–Sat.: 1.30 a.m.–2.40 a.m. (Sun.: 5.25 a.m.)
Left-luggage store	Open 6.15 a.m.–11.25 p.m.
Shops	Mon.–Sat.: 10 a.m.–10 p.m., Sun.: 12 noon–10 p.m. Shopping gallery in underground passage
Post office	9 a.m.–5 p.m.
Station shuts	Weekdays 1.30 a.m.–2.40 a.m. Sun.: 1.35 a.m.–5.25 a.m.

'Hotellikeskus' is the accommodation-finding service downstairs in the station. They take 10 mk. commission per find. Summer hours: weekdays open 9 a.m.–9 p.m., Sat.: 9 a.m.–7 p.m., Sun.: 12 noon–7 p.m.; off-season Mon.–Fri.: 9 a.m.–6 p.m. They also have a list of all the IYHF youth hostels in Finland.

TOURIST INFORMATION

The main city tourist office is west of the market at Pohjois Esplanadi 19 (Tel. 169 3757). Open weekdays 8.30 a.m.–6 p.m., Sat. till 1 p.m., closed Sundays. They produce very comprehensive leaflets and are incredibly helpful. Pick up 'Helsinki This Week', 'Helsinki Guide', 'Helsinki Today', a tourist map and the four self-guiding walking-tour brochures. They have a free phone here which you can use to

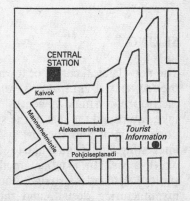

ring up your accommodation. If you're staying for a while, ask them about the city transport passes. Another possibility is the Helsinki Card which is valid for either two or three days (50–65 mk.). Not only does it allow you free travel on all public transport, but it also entitles you to free entry of various museums.

If it's a wet day or you're fed up with walking, tram 3T does an excellent round trip from the station. It takes about an hour and all the main sights are pointed out. (Weekdays 10 a.m.–3 p.m. and 6 p.m.–8 p.m., weekends 9 a.m.–8 p.m.)

● **Addresses:**

FINNISH TOURIST BOARD: Kluvrikatu 8 (Tel. 650 155) for information on all of Finland. Open Mon.–Fri.: 8 a.m.–4.15 p.m.

POST OFFICE: Mannerheimintie 11, open Mon.–Sat.: 9 a.m.–5 p.m. Poste restante is here.

AMEX: Travek, Eteläranta 16, open Mon.–Fri.: 8 a.m.–12 noon, 1 p.m.–4.30 p.m.

UK EMBASSY: Uudenmaankatu 16–20 (Tel. 647 922).

US EMBASSY: Itäinen Puistotie 14a (Tel. 171 931).

CANADIAN EMBASSY: Pohjois Esplanadi 25B (Tel. 171 141).

24-HOUR CHEMIST: Yliopiston Apteekki, Mannerheimintie 5.

TRANSALPINO: Travela, Mannerheimintie 5 (Tel. 624 101).

STUDENT TRAVEL AGENCY: Travela, Mannerheimintie 5 (Tel. 624 101).

HELSINKI TODAY: Tel. 058 for information and events in English.

SEEING

The neo-classical centre of town makes a good starting point with the TOWN HALL, PRESIDENT'S PALACE, UNIVERSITY, CATHEDRAL, and ORTHODOX CATHEDRAL nearby. The tourist board's walking tours take you round the rest of the sights. The NATIONAL MUSEUM, the ROCK CHURCH and the OPEN-AIR MUSEUM of Seurasaari are all interesting, and if you'd like to see town planning at its best it's well worth a visit to TAPIOLA on the outskirts (bus from main bus station). Finland is also rightly acclaimed for being a world leader in manufacturing design, and the Helsinki Design Centre at 19 Kasarmikatu brings together all the best the country has to offer.

SLEEPING

Hotels are expensive in Helsinki and often fully booked in summer. The hostelling news is good and there are always Matkustajakoti (rooms for travellers) advertised round the station if you're desperate.

Youth Hostel Stadion, Pohjoinen Stadiontie 3B (Tel. 496 071), 60 mk. on IYHF card. In Olympic Stadium complex. Tram 3T from Mannerheimintie (right of station). Youth Hostel Dipoli, Otaniemi, Espoo (Tel. 460 211). Open in summer. Hotelli Satakuntatalo: ask for the dormitory here. Lapinrinne 1 (Tel. 694 0311). Fifteen minutes from station. Open in summer.

EATING AND NIGHTLIFE

There are plenty of stalls, takeaways and cafés, as well as the excellent markets, so eating is no problem. If you're really down on your luck, wait till the end of the markets and fight for the pickings of the stall-holders' leftovers. Stockman's department store have a good food hall, and if you're going for a restaurant meal you've the usual choice of Chinese, Indian, etc., or Russian.

Vanhan Kellari, Mannerheimintie 3. Good self-service, popular with students. Open till 1 a.m. Vanha Manala, Töölönkatu 3. Good Finnish specialities. Open for weekday lunches and weekend dinners. Troikka, Caloniuksenkatu 3. Russian food.

Finns really come to life in the pub, of which Helsinki has no shortage. You don't have to look far for them. Tavastia on Kampinkatu 4–6 is the best dance hall in town (free on ISIC, Sunday to Tuesday). Club Ostrobotnia, Museokatu 10, has a disco, dance hall and bars (free Monday to Wednesday; student ID required). St Urho's Pub, next door, is lively and open till 1 a.m.

If you're in Helsinki on 12 June (Helsinki Day) or Midsummer's Eve, prepare yourself for a late night as they stay up all night dancing and drinking.

Turku (Åbo)

The old capital and main seaport of the nineteenth century.

TOURIST INFORMATION

Käsityöläiskatu 4. Also at Silja and Viking line terminals and at Marketplace. Open weekdays 9 a.m.–8 p.m., Sat.: 9 a.m.–6 p.m.

There are boat excursions through the archipelago to the village of Nauvo and the church of Seili: 6½ hours for about 40 mk.

The main sights are the twelfth-century CASTLE, originally a Swedish stronghold (2 mk. admission), TURKU CATHEDRAL, the SIBELIUS MUSEUM containing his instruments and personal possessions, and the LUOSTARINMÄKI MUSEUM where craftsmen put on live demonstrations of their skills.

SLEEPING

• **Hostel:** Kaupungin Retkeilymaja at Linnankatu 39 (Tel. 16578). 15 dormitory beds. Bus 3B from station. Reception open 1 p.m. to midnight.

Turisti-Aula (Tel. 28141). Central and very good. One block north of city tourist office on Käsityöläiskatu, 100 single, 140 double.

• **Camp:** Island of Ruissalo (Tel. 306649), bus 8 from market.

EATING

Go to MARKETPLACE (8 a.m.–2 p.m.) where the food's good, as cheap as you can expect to find, and is a sight in itself.

Just up the road is the KAUPPAHALLI (covered market). It's open 8 a.m.–5 p.m. and Saturday morning, and is full of delights.

There are several pizza places and the department stores have good cafés. Restaurant Kåren, at Hämeenkatu 22, do good meals at reasonable prices.

Northern Finland

If you want to sail in the midnight sun and walk in the forests of Europe's remotest northern land, prepare yourself for a minimum of twenty hours' train travel from Helsinki and buses and ferries which don't always connect up as smoothly as one would like.

The end goal is a unique experience, but to be honest it's easier to get up to the Arctic tundra through Norway or Sweden. OULU is the most attractive of the northern towns. The trip from Helsinki to Rovaniemi isn't too bad – a direct 12-hour train journey – and this takes you to a convenient starting point for your Lapland excursions. The tourist offices at Oulu and Rovaniemi will supply you with all you need to know and suggest accommodation.

Southern Finland

The lakes and woods of the south make this area an outdoor recreation paradise and one of Europe's last wildernesses. SAVONLINNA is a good centre to base yourself at. In this neck of the woods you really ought to camp to get the feel of Finland. The tourist office can arrange canoes and bikes for you.

Savonlinna, near the Russian border, 6 hours from Helsinki, has more charm than the other towns in the Lake Region.

Don't wait on the train for the main station at Savonlinna, get off at the stop near the centre as you're nearer the tourist office there. It's at Olavinkatu 35 and is open 7.15 a.m.–10 p.m. every day in summer.

At the heart of the town is Olavinlinna, the medieval castle with the old wooden houses of Linnankatu surrounding it. Take the English guided tour of the castle.

From 5–28 July, the Opera Festival takes place, and it fills up beds at an incredible rate and is expensive to participate in. Use the open-air markets to picnic from, and try to stay at the excellent Malakius Youth Hostel at Pihlajavedenkuja 6 (Tel. 23283), 35 mk., or camp at Kyrönniemi (Tel. 21507) in summer for 24 mk.

FRANCE

Entry requirements	Passport
Population	53,500,000
Capital	Paris (pop.: 10,825,000)
Currency	Franc
	£1 = approx. 11.55 F
Political system	Republic
Religion	Mainly Roman Catholic
Language	French (English spoken in cities)
Public holidays	1 Jan.; Easter Monday; 1 May; 8 May; Ascension Day; Whit Monday; 14 July; 15 Aug.; 1, 11 Nov.; 25 Dec.

France is a country of great diversity whose long and eventful history has left behind a wealth of attractions and pleasures to experience. Because of the efficient rail network, you can make as much or as little of France as you want: it's just as possible to explore each region in depth as it is to take an overnight express straight to the Riviera, if time and tanning are of the essence.

France (Gaul) was part of the Roman Empire till the Germanic Franks moved in during the fifth century. Charlemagne was crowned by the Pope on Christmas Day 800, but after his death the French nobles tried to go it alone. More successful than most were the Dukes of Burgundy and Normandy. In 987 the Capetian dynasty began to centralize power which led to a period of prosperity and trade, and the eventual growth of Paris as the intellectual centre of Europe in the thirteenth century. England's Norman kings held vast estates in France till the Hundred Years War sent them packing. This further strengthened the French monarchy; a process which continued under the Valois and Bourbon kings, till Louis XIV said it all – 'L'état, c'est moi' ('I am the state').

Under the 'Sun King' (Louis XIV), literature and the arts flourished and all the stylish people in Europe wanted to speak French. From this high point things gradually turned sour, and heads began to roll with the revolution in 1789. The First Republic didn't last long; then out of the chaos emerged Napoleon and dictatorship. During the nineteenth century the French Empire continued to grow, with power constantly changing hands between democracy and dictatorship. The revolution of 1848 brought about the Second Republic, which was followed by a coup d'état and the dictatorship of Napoleon III (nephew of the first). The Third Republic of 1870 survived until the German occupation of France in 1940. After Liberation the Fourth was created, and de Gaulle got the Fifth off the ground in 1958.

FRENCH NATIONAL RAILWAYS
(Société Nationale des Chemins de Fer Français, SNCF)

Arguably, Europe's best railway with the most luxurious carriages travelling at the fastest speeds on the most extensive rail network. Until recently one had to pay hefty TEE or smaller TGV (train à grande vitesse) supplements in order to experience the speeds of 168 m.p.h. of which SNCF justifiably are proud. Fortunately things are changing as TEEs are rapidly decreasing in number and Corail trains are taking over. On some routes the TGVs offer the only convenient services (Paris–Lyon–Marseille–Toulon), and in these cases are well worth the extra 35 francs. In general, though, supplements are only required on about 40 per cent of the journeys. In recent years SNCF's policy has been to spread both speed and comfort more equitably between its passengers. As a result Bordeaux and Strasbourg are now less than four hours away from Paris, while the non-supplement Corail trains are almost indistinguishable from the TEEs in comfort and in many cases run at the same speed. The network serves over 4,000 destinations using five different types of trains: TGV; TEE; Corail; Intercité; and Turbo-train.

There's a special overnight train which runs between Calais and the French Riviera which is the only one that saves you having to cross Paris to change stations. As with most other aspects of French life, the train network is centred round Paris, so if your route is via Paris, generally you're OK, but if you're crossing France from east to west, your impression of SNCF will be somewhat less glowing. Everyone under 26 gets a good deal from French Railways – up to 50 per cent reduction with a 'Carré Jeune' railcard valid for a year or with a 'Carte Jeune' valid for the summer months.

• **Carte Jeune** (on sale from 1 May 1985): The Carte Jeune offers you a 50 per cent reduction on any journey made within France between 1 June and 30 September, provided it starts in a 'blue' (off-peak) period (see below). Off-peak dates account for approximately 80 per cent of the total number of days during the period in question.

Valid in both first and second class, the Carte Jeune costs just 120 F and even includes a special bonus in the form of a free couchette for an overnight journey on any French domestic route. In 1983, over 400,000 Cartes Jeune were sold, helping French Railways to increase their share of the under-26 market.

It is a good investment, as the initial cost is recouped after travelling just 135 miles in second class, if you take advantage of the free couchette offer.

• **Carré Jeune:** Travel anywhere on the French Railways network, except on Paris suburban lines, and you will get the following discounts on 4 single (or 2 return) journeys in first or second class made within a period of one year:

—50 per cent on journeys started during a 'blue' (off-peak) period.
—20 per cent on journeys started during a 'white' (standard) period.

See below for details.

If you do a lot of travelling you can, of course, buy two or more Carré Jeune railcards during the year – you'll save yourself a lot of money because you get the reduction on all French domestic train services including the 168 m.p.h. TGV, the fastest train in the world. Only seat reservations (compulsory on TGV) and supplements for travel on certain trains and sleeping accommodation have to be paid for in the normal way.

The Carré Jeune will cost you just 120 F which you recoup after 199 miles of second class travel started during a 'blue' period or 510 miles of travel started during a 'white' period.

• **The 'blue, white and red' tariff calendar:** The French Railways tariff calendar is colour coded as follows:

'Blue' (off-peak) period: generally from 12 noon Monday to 3 p.m. Friday and from 12 noon Saturday to 3 p.m. Sunday.

'White' (standard) period: generally from 3 p.m. Friday to 12 noon Saturday and from 3 p.m. Sunday to 12 noon Monday plus some French public holidays.

'Red' (peak) period: approximately 20 days in the year when no reduction is available.

To help you plan your trip(s), you are supplied with a copy of the tariff calendar when you buy your Carré Jeune or Carte Jeune.

• **Where to buy your railcard:** You can buy your Carré Jeune or Carte Jeune at French Railways, 179 Piccadilly, London W1, upon presentation of your passport, as proof of your age, accompanied by a passport-size photograph in the case of the Carte Jeune.

• **Who qualifies?** Anyone under 26, regardless of nationality. For further information telephone 01–409 1224.

• **French 'Holiday Trains':** On 10 railway routes throughout France, you don't have to worry about long, boring train journeys any more. Leave your newspapers and magazines behind and take a Holiday Train. The Holiday Train is much more than a means of getting from A to B – it can be as enjoyable and relaxing as any other part of your holiday. On board, you will receive a detailed map of the route with information on landmarks along the way. A presenter or hostess will give a live commentary on historical, cultural and natural aspects of the region coupled with amusing anecdotes. Depending on the train, you will be invited to listen to live music or mini-theatre, talks or readings by local writers or poets and watch audio-visual presentations. When it comes to mealtime, you will have a chance to sample regional specialities.

Holiday Trains run from now until the end of the holiday season on the most picturesque routes in France (see list below) and are available to everyone at no extra charge, whether travelling with a first or second class ordinary rail ticket or a France-Vacances Rail Rover. They are also valid to anyone holding an Inter Rail or Eurail Youthpass at no extra cost.

1985 HOLIDAY TRAINS

L'ALPAZUR from Lyon to Marseille (via Grenoble) or from Lyon to Nice and vice versa (v.v.) with part of this journey on the famous Chemins de Fer de Provence.

L'AUBRAC from Clermont-Ferrand to Béziers and v.v. through Auvergne, famous for its volcanic landscapes, and the Causses.

LE BOCAGE from Paris to Granville through the Normandy countryside and v.v.

LE CEVENOL from Paris to Marseille (through Clermont-Ferrand and Nîmes) and v.v. through the Auvergne and the Cevennes.

LE ROUGET DE L'ISLE from Strasbourg to Nice and v.v. through Alsace, Franche-Comté, Bresse and Dombes.

LE THERMAL from Paris to Clermont-Ferrand and v.v. through the ancient province of Bourbonnais.

LE TROUVÈRE from Paris to Calais and v.v.

LE VALENTRE from Paris to Toulouse and v.v. crossing the Paris Basin, Berry, Marche, Limousin, Quercy and the Midi-Pyrénées.

LE VENTADOUR from Bordeaux to Lyon and v.v. through the Périgord and the Auvergne with its volcanoes.

LE VERT GALANT from Toulouse to Bayonne and v.v. through the Pyrénées, Lourdes, Comminges, Bigorre, Béarn and the Basque country.

You can, of course, stop off at intermediate stations and hire a bike or a car from French Railways for a day or two, or even go on a walking tour before rejoining the train to continue your journey.

Reduced bike hire is all part of the deal, when you buy your ticket. Holiday Trains are a novel innovation by SNCF and make a good way of discovering little-known areas of rural France which have a lot to offer the eurorailer.

For further information, phone 01–409 1224.

● **Inter Rail bonuses:**

FROM	TO	REDUCTION %
Chemins de Fer de la Corse	All	50
Société Nationale Maritime Corse-Méditerranée	All routes	30 (in 2nd class)
Services d'Autocars de Tourisme Portant Label SNCF	France–Corsica	

Also free entry to French Railway Museum, 2 rue Alfred de Glehn, Mulhouse.

- **Eurail bonuses:** Free:
—Digne–Nice or vice versa on the Chemins de Fer de la Provence.
—Ferry crossing on the Irish Continental Line between Le Havre
(France) and Rosslare (Ireland) 21 hours, or Cork (Ireland) 21½
hours, and between Cherbourg (France) and Rosslare (Ireland)
17 hours. If cabin accommodation is requested, an extra charge
will be made. Port taxes are extra and payable in French francs.
During July and August advance reservation is recommended. It
is compulsory if cabin accommodation is requested. Check the
sailing schedule always.

The following half-price reductions are granted by Europabus on
transportation costs only and by local offices in Europe.
253 Besançon–Lausanne
254 Grenoble–Chamonix–Evian–Geneva
255 Geneva–Nice
256 Grenoble–Nice
257 Grenoble–Briançon
258 Thonon–Evian–Stresa
446 Best of Brittany

- **Transalpino:** If you're going with Transalpino it's a small saving to
go via Dieppe, but the sailings are few. Think twice if it's not better
to pay a bit extra and have the Dunkirk/Calais/Boulogne choice.

TRAIN INFORMATION

English is spoken by rail staff at the major stations. Agents d'accueil
('welcome officers') wear orange caps and armbands and are in the
stations to help with travel queries and any problems you've
encountered on your journey, i.e. if you've had your rucksack
stolen. These guys tour round as opposed to sitting in the
information offices. At the ticket barriers in all French stations
you'll see a bright orange machine. Use this to validate your ticket
only if you've bought it in France. Otherwise ignore it.

- **Reservations:** Obligatory on all TEEs and TGVs as well as a few of
the Rapide trains, but if you are taking one you'll find the
reservation charge is included in the supplement you'll have to pay.

Other optional reservations cost about 10 F. Reservations must be made by noon for trains leaving that day between 5 p.m. and midnight, and by 8 p.m. for trains leaving between midnight and 5 p.m. the next day. TEEs are reservable up to three hours before departure from the station where they start out. Generally, it's a good idea to reserve on international trains and on days before public holidays.

• **Night travel:** A sleeper or couchette in France will cost you more than anywhere else in Europe. Granted the service is good, but at a price. SNCF offer both first- and second-class couchettes with four and six berths respectively. You have to reserve your couchette (cost about 70 F) at least two hours before departure, and not later than 8 p.m. Unless you're loaded with cash, avoid the TEN (Trans Euro Nuit) sleepers. Second-class sleepers are either (T3) three beds or (T2) two beds.

• **Eating on trains:** Surprisingly, the stations have no tempting delicatessen selling fresh croissants, pâtés and cheeses, so you must come prepared if you want to picnic. There are restaurants and bars at stations which are good but pricey. If you're going to have a blow out, you'd do far better going for a meal which you can at least be sure will be good, rather than for a snack from the ridiculously priced mini-bar trolleys.

• **Scenic tips:** Take a train anywhere in southern France and you won't be disappointed. Not surprisingly the Alps provide a spectacular backdrop on any run. If you just want to breeze through, consider the Paris to Turin route (10 hours) which goes via the Mont Cenis tunnel (8½ miles long). For those who aren't happy with anything but the best, change at Culoz or Aix-les-Bains, for Chamonix. If you want to head down to the coast, we recommend the run from Grenoble to Marseille (5 hours), then Marseille–Genoa (be sure to sit on the right-hand side of the train on the Riviera stretch). All this journey along the Côte d'Azur is beautiful.

On the other side of the country: the lines between Clermont-Ferrand and Béziers, and Limoges and Toulouse, provide fine upland scenery. The Perpignan to La Tour de Carol is another favourite, as is Valence to Briançon.

- **Bikes:** The scheme's called 'Train et Vélo', and bikes can be hired at any of 250 stations.

TOURIST INFORMATION

There are over 5,000 tourist information offices in France. They're called Syndicats d'Initiative and will help you out with your travel and accommodation problems, as well as booking a bed for you for a small fee. The French tourist literature is good and mostly free. Always ask for a map. If you're touring a whole region in depth and require further information, look up the address and phone number of the Comité Régional de Tourisme, and contact them.

For further information on Andorra the tourist office is: 63 Westover Rd, London SW18 (Tel. 01–874 4806).

- **ISIC bonuses:** Up to 40 per cent reduction on long-distance coach journeys. 50 per cent off all state museums and galleries, museums and theatres.

- **Money matters:** 1 franc (F) = 100 centimes.
Banking hours are 9 a.m.–12 noon, 2 p.m.–4 p.m. weekdays. Closed Saturdays (main towns) or Mondays. Shop around before exchanging currency, as banks vary with their commission charges. The best we could find was the Crédit Agricole. Not every bank now changes currency, so if you're arriving on a Sunday night you won't be able to get any anywhere except the main station in the larger cities, where commission charges average 10 F and credit cards and some traveller's cheques are not accepted. French traveller's cheques are much more useful than those in sterling or dollars.

- **Post offices:** Open 8 a.m.–7 p.m. weekdays, and 8 a.m.–12 noon on Saturday. The larger railway stations have post offices which keep these, or longer, hours.

- **Shops:** Tend to shut from around noon to 2 p.m., and even longer in the south. They generally stay open till 7.30 p.m.

- **Museums:** Follow the same pattern as shops; you'll find many of the state-owned ones closed on Tuesdays.

SLEEPING

Your best bet is to use the facilities offered in the various Foyers des Jeunes Travailleurs which are in all major centres. These studenty hostels are usually more central and less strictly run than youth hostels (they don't make a fuss about unmarried couples, etc.).

France is well supplied with official youth hostels (auberges de jeunesse) which charge around 30 F per person. They do ask for IYHF cards, so membership is obligatory. You can join up in France: their head office is 6 rue Mesnil, Paris.

Hotels run on a one- to four-star system with the government fixing prices; these are posted on the back of hotel room doors. So always check you've been quoted the right price. One stars start at about 70 F and are perfectly adequate so long as you don't expect the luxury of a bath. In France a shower or bath (and often breakfast, too) will almost always cost extra. Try to reduce your costs if you're travelling in a group by getting a third bed put in the room – this'll cost an extra 30 per cent or so and is cheaper than another room.

Camping should present no problems in France as nearly every major town has at least one site. They also operate on a star system. The International Camping Carnet is obligatory at most sites – you can buy it at site offices on the spot.

EATING AND NIGHTLIFE

Eating and drinking are about the only things in France not centred on Paris. Each region has its own specialities based on the local produce. There's no such thing as a hurried snack – the midday lunch break is at least a 12-to-2 affair. The French take their food very seriously and like to think themselves connoisseurs. Cafés are for sitting and watching the world go by, not for cheap eating. If you're desperate for a coffee, make it last and drink in the atmosphere as long as possible. It's far better, though, to get a baguette under your arm and head for the corner charcuterie and crémerie, where you can choose from a huge selection of cheeses (watch out: chèvre is goat). Fortunately, supermarkets are reasonable and still maintain a high standard. Look out for branches of Prisunic, Monoprix, Uniprix, or Codec.

The wines are cheap and the parks free. Unless you're really broke, it's well worth eating out in the evenings with the fixed-price menus always a safe bet. Try where possible to sample the local dishes, as they give an added interest to touring.

Normandy

If you're arriving at Dieppe, you can't do much better than to make your first stop ROUEN, capital of the region. The OLD TOWN dates from the twelfth century and boasts many fine churches as well as a Gothic CATHEDRAL. The MUSÉE DES ANTIQUES has a splendid collection of artefacts documenting the age when this area was at its zenith.

When you arrive, head straight for tourist information at 25 Place de la Cathédrale (Tel. 71 41 77), open Mon.–Sat.: 8 a.m.–12.30 p.m., 1 p.m.–7 p.m., Sun.: 10 a.m.–12 noon, 2 p.m.–6 p.m. They'll find you a cheap room and hand out useful leaflets. The youth hostel is at 17 rue Diderot (Tel. 72 06 45). Take bus 6 or 12 from the rail station. There's also a youth information centre at 12 Quai Corneille.

Brittany

You'll curse the rail network if you want to visit this region in depth. Local trains all connect up to the main Paris–Brest line rather than other nearby towns. For accommodation and general information on the area, visit the Centre Information Jeunesse Bretagne in the Maison du Champ de Mars at 6 Cours des Alliés, Rennes.

From RENNES it's possible to make a day trip to the impressive walled port of ST MALO, formerly a pirates' stronghold, and preserved almost intact. Pushing south, NANTES has a majestic fifteenth-century ducal palace, as well as a very good museum devoted to Breton folklore.

The Loire Valley

This pastoral region contains many of France's most elegant and impressive buildings. To do justice to the area would take at least a week. Fortunately for the eurorailer, most of the châteaux and palaces lie between Angers and Blois, a distance of about 80 miles. Where to base yourself depends on your style. There are campsites everywhere, and youth hostels at Saumur, Tours, and Blois.

BLOIS is typical of the Loire: THE BISHOPS' PALACE, the CHÂTEAU, the OLD QUARTER – all set in a picturesque location among fine churches and gardens. For those who prefer a cheap hotel, it's best to base yourself at TOURS, where rooms are plentiful around the station. Try the Olympic opposite the station at 74 rue Palissy (Tel. 05 10 17), or Hôtel Comte behind the station, at 51 rue Auguste Comte (Tel. 15 53 16). If you're out of luck, the tourist office is just in front of the station at Place Maréchal Leclerc (Tel. 05 58 08) (open Mon.–Sat.: 9 a.m.–12.30 p.m., 2 p.m.–9 p.m., Sun.: 10 a.m.–12.30 p.m., 4 p.m.–9 p.m.). For a fee of 3 F they will fix you up with a room and give free advice on bus tours, etc., to the châteaux. If you can't afford the bus, don't worry as they rent out bikes at the station for around 30 F a day and most of the châteaux are easily accessible. The town itself, like Blois, has a charming OLD QUARTER and a former BISHOPS' PALACE which now hosts the MUSÉE DES BEAUX ARTS. Further down the line, SAUMUR and ANGERS both have very impressive castles perched on high, overlooking the Loire and Maine respectively. If you prefer to stay at this end of château country, the Syndicat d'Initiative, opposite the station at Angers, will find you a room for a small charge.

Wherever you end up, it's a good idea to go along to any train information desk in the area and pick up one of the local timetables giving all the smaller stops.

Paris

Everyone has his or her own impressions and expectations of Paris – so much has been said and written about it, and it all seems a cliché, yet Paris is everything you've probably ever heard, and more.

Paris has twenty 'arrondissements' (districts) with the Louvre as No. 1. The city is divided into the Left Bank (Rive Gauche) and Right Bank (Rive Droite), with the River Seine dividing them. Generally speaking, the Left Bank is the trendy, studenty and less expensive area, and the Right Bank is more classy.

STATION FACILITIES

		AUSTERLITZ	EST
Train information	Mon.–Sun.:	All hours (Tel. 584 1616)	All hours (Tel. 208 4990)
Reservations	Mon.–Sun.:	8 a.m.–8 p.m. (Tel. 584 1520)	8 a.m.–8 p.m. (Tel. 240 1122)
Tourist information	Mon.–Fri.:	9 a.m.–12.30 p.m. 2 p.m.–6.15 p.m.	Mon.–Sat.: 7 a.m.–1 p.m.
	Sat.:	9 a.m.–12 noon	5 p.m.–8 p.m.
Foreign exchange	Mon.–Fri.:	8.45 a.m.–5 p.m.	7.30 a.m.–8 p.m.
Bar, Snacks	Daily	6 a.m.–12 midnight	7 a.m.–11 p.m.
Bath, Shower	Daily	5.30 a.m.–8.30 p.m.	6.15 a.m.–10 p.m.
Left-luggage lockers	No access:	0.30 a.m.–5.30 a.m.	1.15 a.m.–5.45 a.m.
Left-luggage store	Daily	6 a.m.–0.30 a.m.	6 a.m.–12 midnight
Shops		7 a.m.–11 p.m. Lower level and at Blvd de l'Hôpital	Mon.–Sat.: 8 a.m.–12.45 p.m. 2.30 p.m.–7.30 p.m. Sun.: 8 a.m.– 12.45 p.m. Rue du 8 Mai and Faubourg St Denis
Waiting room		All hours	All hours
Toilets		All hours	All hours
Station shuts		0.30 a.m.–5.30 a.m.	1.15 a.m.–5.45 a.m.

There are post office facilities at both these stations (8 a.m.–7 p.m., half day Saturdays). SNCF run buses for 8 F which connect most of the stations, or metro line 5 connects Paris Est and Paris Nord and Austerlitz. Paris Lyon is reached by buses 61 and 69 from Austerlitz, and bus 65 from Est. SNCF have recently introduced a train information telephone service in English. The number is 380 50 50.

	PARIS LYON	PARIS NORD
Train information	All hours (Tel. 345 9292)	All hours (Tel. 280 0303)
Reservations	8 a.m.–8 p.m. (Tel. 345 9333)	8 a.m.–8 p.m. (Tel. 873 8754)
Tourist information	8.30 a.m.–12.30 p.m. 5 p.m.–10 p.m.	Mon.–Sat.: 8.30 a.m.–10 p.m.
Foreign exchange	6.30 a.m.–10 p.m.	6.30 a.m.–10.25 p.m.
Bar, Buffet	5.40 a.m.–11.30 p.m.	5.45 a.m.–11 p.m.
Restaurant	5.40 a.m.–11.30 p.m. (ground level) 11 a.m.–2 p.m. 6 p.m.–9.15 p.m. (upstairs)	11.30 a.m.–2 p.m. 6.30 p.m.–9.45 p.m.
Bath, Showers	6 a.m.–8.30 p.m.	6 a.m.–8.30 p.m.
Left-luggage lockers	No access 1 a.m.–4 a.m.	No access 0.15 a.m.–5.45 a.m.
Left-luggage store	All hours	6 a.m.–12 midnight
Shops	Rue Hector Malot	Mon.–Sat.: 8 a.m.–12.45 p.m. 2.30 p.m.–7.30 p.m. Sun.: 8 a.m.–12.45 p.m.
Waiting room	All hours	All hours
Toilets	All hours	All hours
Station shuts	1 a.m.–4 a.m.	0.15 a.m.–5.45 a.m.

Post office facilities at both stations, Mon.–Fri.: 8 a.m.–7 p.m., Sat.: 8 a.m.–12 noon (rue Diderot for Paris Lyon). SNCF buses will get you from one station to another, or from Paris Lyon you can get to all the other stations by metro line 1 to Bastille then change to line 5. From Paris Nord, line 5 takes you to Austerlitz, Est and Lyon (change on to line 1 at Bastille). An additional route from Nord to Lyon is to take line B to Châtelet les Halles, then line A to Lyon (much faster). With six stations in Paris it's important to get the right one.

	ST LAZARE	MONTPARNASSE
Information	Tel. 538 5229	Tel. 538 5229
Reservations	Tel. 387 9170	Tel. 538 5239

FROM	TRAINS GO TO:
Gare de l'Est	Eastern France
	Germany
	Switzerland
	Eastern Europe
Gare de Lyon	Riviera
	South-east France
Gare d'Austerlitz	Central France
	Southern Atlantic coast
	Spain
Gare Montparnasse	Western France
	(Chartres, Loire Valley and Brittany)
Gare St Lazare	Normandy
Gare du Nord	North coast
	Belgium
	Holland
	Germany (Hamburg)
	Britain

Daily trains to: Amsterdam, Hamburg, Brussels (Nord); Strasbourg, Frankfurt, Munich, Zürich, Luxembourg and Basel (Est); Lyon, Milan, Genoa, Nice (Lyon); and Bordeaux, Barcelona, Madrid, Lisbon (Austerlitz).

TOURIST INFORMATION

The main office of 'Accueil de France' is at 127 Avenue des Champs Elysées (Tel. 723 6172) (metro to Etoile). Open Mon.–Sat.: 9 a.m.–10 p.m., Sun.: 9 a.m.–8 p.m. They'll give you information on Paris and the rest of France. They also run an accommodation-finding service on a commission basis.

• **Accueil des Jeunes en France (AJF):** This non-profit-making tourist office for the young is at 119 rue St Martin (Tel. 277 8780), across from the Beaubourg. Open Mon.–Sat.: 9.30 a.m.–7 p.m. They'll find you a bed or a place in a Foyer for 45 F. They also have offices at Gare du Nord and 16 rue du Pont Louis-Philippe. The policy these days seems to be to pay the full accommodation price over to AJF when booking, so remember to change money before joining the queue.

● **Addresses:**

ALL-NIGHT POST OFFICE AND POSTE RESTANTE: 52 rue du Louvre (Tel. 233 7160).

AMEX: 11 rue Scribe, Mon.–Fri.: 9 a.m.–5 p.m., Sat.: 9 a.m.–12 noon (Tel. 073 4290).

CIEE: 51 rue Dauphine 6e (Tel. 326 7965), Mon.–Sat.: 10 a.m.–1 p.m., 2 p.m.–6.30 p.m. They will help out in all your travel needs and fix you up with an ISIC.

UK EMBASSY: 35 rue du Faubourg St Honoré.

US EMBASSY: 2 Avenue Gabriel, Mon.–Fri.: 9 a.m.–4 p.m. (metro Concorde).

CANADIAN EMBASSY: 35 Avenue Montaigne 8e (Tel. 723 0101).

AUSTRALIAN EMBASSY: 4 rue Jean Rey 15e (Tel. 575 6200).

24-HOUR CHEMIST: Pharmacie Dhéry, 84 Avenue des Champs-Elysées (metro George V).

SOS HELP LINE: English speakers to help you with personal problems, etc. 3 p.m.–11 p.m. (Tel. 723 8080).

TRANSALPINO: 14, 16 and 48 rue Lafayette (Tel. 247 1240); 36 bis, rue de Dunkerque; 137 rue de Rennes.

● **Getting about:** the metro in Paris is one of the world's best underground systems and you're bound to use it at some point to get you quickly round this incredibly large and sprawling city. It's a cheap as well as efficient way of getting about. Buy tickets in 'carnets' of 10 for 25 F, and hold on to them till the end of your journey. Ask tourist information about the different passes if you're staying for a while.

SEEING

● **The Champs Elysées:** The ÉTOILE is the great circle at the western end of the Champs Elysées with twelve avenues radiating out from it, literally a 'star'. In its centre is the massive ARC DE TRIOMPHE, Napoleon's thank-you to his army; note the sculpture of 'the Marseillaise' by Rude. At the other end of the long and elegant Champs Elysées is the PLACE DE LA CONCORDE, regarded as the most beautiful square in the world. This is where Louis XVI, Marie-Antoinette and some 1,300 others met their death in the French Revolution.

• **The Left Bank:** ST GERMAIN-DES-PRÉS, the oldest church in Paris, is surrounded by open-air restaurants and cafés and quiet little streets like PLACE FURSTEMBERG which make a pleasant stroll.

BOULEVARD ST MICHEL, the centre of Bohemian student life of the 1960s, still makes an interesting excursion. Sitting in one of the cafés along the 'Boul Mich' in the Latin Quarter (so called because the Sorbonne students were lectured to in Latin in the Middle Ages), you're bound to make new friends. The tallest building in Europe, TOUR MAINE-MONTPARNASSE (690 feet), gives you a great view over the city. (The lift up is supposed to be the fastest one in Europe.)

Also on the Rive Gauche is the beautiful church of LES INVALIDES with its golden dome and the mortal remains of Napoleon. A good view of NOTRE DAME CATHEDRAL can be seen from SQUARE RENÉ VIVIANI.

• **The Right Bank:** Opposite the LOUVRE is Richelieu's PALAIS ROYAL where the Comédie Française is based, and not far from here is the oldest square in Paris – PLACE DES VOSGES – the beautiful Renaissance square built by Henry IV early in the seventeenth century; VICTOR HUGO'S HOUSE at No. 6 is now a museum. The GEORGES POMPIDOU CENTRE (known as the Beaubourg) is a good place to meet trendy young Parisians and see interesting exhibitions. Closed Tuesdays, it's open till 10 p.m. at weekends.

The SACRÉ-COEUR is the white dome that dominates all of Paris, built on the hill at MONTMARTRE, the artists' quarter that flourished in the late nineteenth century when many of the Impressionist painters lived and worked there. A climb to the dome of the Sacré-Coeur gives you a thirty-mile view over Paris.

• **Île de la Cité and Île St-Louis:** The tiny island where Paris began in pre-Roman times is the Île de la Cité. The oldest bridge in Paris, the PONT NEUF, leads you to the statue of Henry IV and on to the PALAIS DE JUSTICE (law courts). The SAINTE CHAPELLE is the Gothic church which houses many holy relics and dates from 1248.

NOTRE DAME is only a short walk from here; this thirteenth-century cathedral is the first church of Paris, where Napoleon was crowned and all national celebrations are staged.

The other main sights are the OPÉRA (1875) and, of course, the EIFFEL TOWER, which looks its best floodlit at night. If you want to tour the famous PARIS SEWERS, call in at 93 Quai d'Orsay.

There are various city tours: Parisvision buses with prerecorded commentary, and Cityrama tours, or the famous bateaux-mouches which sail down the Seine (go for the evening one when the illuminations are on). Shop about, as they vary from reasonably priced to extortionate. Still, if you've only a day or two, the three-hour Parisvision tour gives you a pretty comprehensive idea of the city.

• **Museums:** All state-owned museums in Paris are shut on Tuesdays and those owned by the city close on Mondays. An ISIC will get you into most places for half price. The Louvre and the Pompidou Centre are free on Sundays (and packed). There are over 100 interesting museums in the city; pick up a leaflet on them from tourist information. We list the few it would be a shame to miss.

THE LOUVRE: Porte Denon, Place du Carrousel (in the Tuileries Gardens). Treasures include the Venus de Milo, and the Mona Lisa. Open 9.45 a.m.–8 p.m. (though many departments close at 5 or 5.30 p.m.).

JEU DE PAUME: Tuileries Gardens. Open 9.45 a.m.–5.15 p.m. Famous collection of Impressionists. Tours, Saturdays at 3 p.m.

MUSÉE DE CLUNY: 6 Place Paul-Painlevé (corner of Boulevard St Michel and Boulevard St Germain). Open 9.45 a.m.–12.30 p.m., 2 p.m.–5 p.m. Medieval art housed in a fifteenth-century mansion next to the Roman baths of Paris.

MUSÉE DE L'HOMME: Palais de Chaillot, Place du Trocadéro. Open 10 a.m.–6 p.m. (5 p.m. in winter). Very good anthropological museum – documentary films are shown daily.

• **Parks:** There is no shortage of attractive parks and gardens in Paris, and they make good picnic venues or places to sleep if you're running out of money.

The BOIS DE BOULOGNE is the wood at the western edge of the city with seven lakes, a waterfall, various sports facilities and a campsite. The BOIS DE VINCENNES is the wood on the south-eastern edge which tends to be a better bet to sleep rough in, but is a bit rougher (not recommended for girls alone). There's a zoo, a racetrack and a couple of museums out here too. The two most central picnic parks are the JARDIN DES TUILERIES and the JARDIN DES CHAMPS ELYSÉES; the LUXEMBOURG, off Boulevard St Michel, is a very picturesque, formally laid-out garden in French style.

SLEEPING

Campsites are not at all central, and with so much to see in Paris the commuting seems a waste of valuable time. Private accommodation is hardly heard of in Paris and sleeping rough gets riskier each year, so if you're wise you'll choose between a cheap hotel, a student hostel or a Foyer. Your choice will be dictated not just by your pocket but also by how many you are. Paris really is a city for lovers – it's often virtually the same price for a single or a double bed so couples are on to a good deal, but singles are better off in a Foyer.

The average night in a hotel double room is 85–100 F and a single Foyer stay will be about 65 F. Always ask hoteliers if there's nothing cheaper and get as many as possible into a room to bring the cost down. The four youth hostels aren't very good or central, though the one at Avenue de Villeneuve–St Georges isn't too far out. The best districts to concentrate your attention on for cheap hotels and basic B&B-type accommodation are around the Place de la Bastille, Nation, St Paul, Gare de Lyon, Place de Clichy and Pigalle.

● **Hotels:** Try: Eugénie, 31 rue St André-des-Arts (Tel. 326 2903); Hôtel Notre Dame, 1 Quai St Michel; Hôtel des Vosges, 5 passage de la Petite Boucherie (Tel. 354 7907); Hôtel de Flandres, 16 rue Cujas (Tel. 354 6730), or Hôtel Cujas at No. 18 (take metro to Luxembourg). Also worth a try are Hôtel des Médicis, 214 rue St Jacques (Tel. 329 1466), and Hôtel Henri IV at 9 rue St Jacques (Tel. 354 5143).

● **Foyers and student hostels:** Centre International de Séjour de Paris (CISP), 6 Avenue Maurice-Ravel (Tel. 343 1901) offers the best value in Paris (metro to Porte de Vincennes); Maison des Clubs Unesco, 43 rue de la Glacière 13e (Tel. 336 0063) and 13 rue de Vaugirard (Tel. 326 5078); Hôtel des Jeunes (AJF), 11 rue du Fauconnier, 6 rue François-Miron, 6 rue de Fourcy (Tel. 274 2345), 12 rue des Barres (Tel. 272 7209); Centre International de Paris (BVJ), 20 rue Jean-Jacques Rousseau (Tel. 261 6643); Foyer International d'Accueil de Paris, 30 rue Cabanis (Tel. 589 8915).

EATING AND NIGHTLIFE

Both are a great pleasure in Paris and can be afforded, in one category or another, by everyone. The French seem to have invented the picnic and you'd have to be completely blind or stupid not to be able to make yourself a delicious picnic of baguette, pâté, cheese, wine and fruits. There are several open-air markets and boulangeries (bakers) in every district while the épiceries (grocers) stay open till 7.30 p.m.

If you want a change from French food, there are plenty of alternatives provided by the numerous immigrants from France's ex-colonies. The centre of the North African (Algerian, Tunisian, Moroccan, etc.) restaurant area is between rue St Jacques and Boulevard St Michel.

There are fast-food chains and self-service cafés too in Paris, but you're better – and it's often just as cheap – to look for a French restaurant which offers a 'menu du jour', and eat real French cuisine – for once at a price you can afford. The areas round rue de la Huchette, rue de la Harpe and Place de la Contrescarpe in the Latin Quarter will prove fruitful for reasonably priced restaurants.

For those wanting to eat at student restaurants on their ISIC, call at CROUS, rue Mabillon (metro Mabillon) for a list of all the places you can eat for under 20 F in this scheme.

A few suggestions: Piccolo–Théatro, 6 rue des Ecouffes – vegetarian restaurant; Chartier, 7 rue du Faubourg Montmartre; La Petite Source, 130 Boulevard St Germain; Pergola du Bonheur, 12 rue Gambey – cheap Chinese restaurant; Restaurant des Beaux Arts, 11 rue Bonaparte – good cheap set menus; and Crêperie de la Houff, 9 rue Mouffetard.

For current events in Paris, pick up a copy of *Pariscope* from tourist information.

If you were thinking of the stereotyped trip to the Moulin Rouge, Lido or Folies Bergère, you might as well forget the rest of your European itinerary, as a night out in one of these places will cost you about 275 F minimum. It's actually more of a spectacle walking round the Blanche and Pigalle areas, just down from Montmartre, or Montparnasse, but watch out for drug-pushers and pickpockets around here. For the serious red-light seekers, the place is rue St Denis.

Slightly more sedate a time can be had watching the fountains at the Trocadéro and admiring the view of the Eiffel Tower, or wandering down by the Seine; often there are buskers in the area round Place du Vert Galant.

There's an active theatre and cinema scene in Paris – for details of what's on, see *Pariscope*. The area along the Seine on the Left Bank is best for affordable jazz and rock clubs. Le Caveau de la Huchette, 5 rue de la Huchette, is known to all Parisian students as their informal club, but they ask 30 F on nights when there's jazz or dancing. The cafés at Montparnasse remain a typically Parisian vantage point from which to watch life go by, but watch out for the prices. In August, when many French restaurants are closed, these are often the only places open.

EXCURSIONS FROM PARIS

VERSAILLES, the elaborate palace of Louis XIV, is the main attraction near to Paris. Take a train from Montparnasse or Invalides out to it. The palace is open Tues.–Sun.: 10 a.m.–5 p.m. (free under 18, half price on ISIC). Also within striking distance is the palace of FONTAINEBLEAU with its beautiful park-forest. Take the train from Gare de Lyon. Open 10 a.m.–12.30 p.m., 2 p.m.–6 p.m., except Tues. CHANTILLY is an attractive small château, reached by train from Gare du Nord, but it's open only on Sundays and holidays. CHARTRES, home of the world's most famous Gothic cathedral, is an hour away from Gare Montparnasse, and RHEIMS at the heart of Champagne country makes an interesting trip; it's two hours from Gare de l'Est. Don't miss the cathedral here or the free samples of bubbly from 'Mumm', 34 rue du Champ de Mars. If you really want to make a day of it, take the short train ride to Epernay where Moët et Chandon, on Avenue de Champagne, play hosts for another enjoyable tour with free samples.

Alsace and Lorraine

After many years of occupation, the German influence is strongly felt in this region, especially in the cuisine: choucroute (sauerkraut with ham and sausage) and backaoffe (casserole with lamb, pork, beef and potatoes) are our favourites; swallowed down with some pression (local draught lager), they make a meal you won't forget.

Strasbourg

Apart from being the seat of the European parliament and the capital of Alsace, it is one of France's most attractive cities. The tourist office is at the station when you arrive. They will supply you with a map and information on the city, as well as provide a room-finding service. Alternatively there is another office at 10 Place Gutenberg (Tel. 325707). The youth hostel is quite far away so it's best to try somewhere more central like Hôtel du Cycliste, 8 rue des Bateliers (Tel. 362001).

STATION FACILITIES

	STRASBOURG GARE
Train information	Mon.–Sat.: 7.30 a.m.–8 p.m.
	Sun.: 8 a.m.–8 p.m. (Tel. 22 50 50)
Reservations	Mon.–Sat.: 7.30 a.m.–8 p.m.
	Sun.: 9 a.m.–5.30 p.m.
Tourist information	Mon.–Fri.: 9 a.m.–12 noon, 2 p.m.–6 p.m.
	Sat.: 9 a.m.–12 noon
	Outside in front of station
Foreign exchange	8 a.m.–8 p.m.
Left-luggage lockers	All hours
Left-luggage store	All hours
Showers	6 a.m.–10 p.m.
Cafeteria	4 a.m.–2 a.m.
Restaurant	11 a.m.–10 p.m.
Waiting room	All hours
Post office	Mon.–Fri.: 8 a.m.–7.30 p.m.
	Sat.: 8 a.m.–12 noon

Daily trains to: Luxembourg (2 hours), Brussels (4 hours), Munich, Stuttgart (2½ hours), Basel (1½ hours), Zürich (2½ hours), Milan, Lyon, Paris (4 hours). (The main tourist office is at 10 Place Gutenberg, open till 7.30 p.m. in summer.)

From the station, walk down to LITTLE FRANCE (well-preserved old houses bordering the canal) and wind your way through the covered bridges and narrow medieval streets to the Gothic CATHEDRAL. Try and arrive at noon when the astronomical clock comes into action.

Opposite the cathedral, the CHÂTEAU DES ROHANS contains a fine museum of archaeology, ceramics and paintings. For eating, try the areas around Place du Marché aux Cochons de Lait and Place du Corbeau. The student restaurant FEC is at Place St Etienne. For cheap and well-prepared Alsacian specialities, go to 9 Porte de Kehl. If you like to eat in a crowd try Au Pont St Martin at 13–15 rue des Moulins (Tel. 324513) overlooking the river. In early June there is an International Music Festival.

The Alps

In our opinion, CHAMONIX is one of the best places to visit in the Alps by train. The mountain railway which winds its way through picture-book villages is an unforgettable experience; sit on the right-hand side for the best view. When you're there, the tourist office at Place de l'Eglise (open till 8 p.m.) will help you out on accommodation, etc. Prices are expensive; the cheapest bed we found was at Le Weekend, 193 Bois du Buchet (Tel. 531916), or you could try camping.

If you have only a day and want to head for the hills, ask tourist information for the list of 'Promenades à Pied' (walking tours), state how long you want to walk and ask what their suggestions are, as the possibilities are endless. If you take your walking seriously, contact the *Club Alpin Français* on Avenue Michel Croz (Tel. 531603) for information on mountain refuges and conditions.

Even if you don't make it up the mountains, go and rub shoulders with the climbing set and have a beer with them in the Nationale, rue Paccard. Local Alpine food specialities include smoked sausage, various cheeses and, of course, fondue.

Burgundy

If wine is what takes you to Burgundy, be sure to visit the MUSÉE DU VIN in the Hôtel des Ducs de Bourgogne at BEAUNE and take the tour at MAISON PATRIARCHE, rue du Collège, where they even give you a little bottle for the train. Apart from wine, Burgundy possesses some of the finest abbeys in France, the most spectacular one being at VÉZELAY, and though this isn't on the rail, there's a bus from AVALLON which is. From Paris or Dijon, change at Laroche-Migennes.

Dijon

Capital of Burgundy and an important centre in the fourteenth and fifteenth centuries, Dijon went into a decline for about 400 years until the railway brought commerce and industry back in the 1850s. Now it is known for its edible specialities such as mustard, cassis (blackcurrant liqueur) and snails, and is a thriving commercial and industrial centre.

STATION FACILITIES

	DIJON GARE DE VILLE
Train information	Mon.–Sat.: 8 a.m.–7.30 p.m.
	Sun.: 9 a.m.–12 noon, 2 p.m.–6.30 p.m.
	(Tel. 41 50 50)
Reservations	As above
Tourist information	Mon.–Sat.: 9 a.m.–12 noon, 2 p.m.–8 p.m.
	In Place Darcy, three blocks away
Foreign exchange	As 'train information'
Bar, Buffet	7.30 a.m.–10 p.m.
Left-luggage lockers	No access 1 a.m.–4 a.m.
Left-luggage store	All hours
Shops	Regular hours. In Place Darcy
Station shut	1 a.m.–4 a.m.

Daily trains to: Paris (2½ hours), Strasbourg (4 hours), Venice, Genoa, Lyon (1½ hours) and Marseille – Nice.

TOURIST INFORMATION AND ADDRESSES

Place Darcy (Tel. 434 212), near city centre; open daily 9 a.m.–12 noon, 2 p.m.–9 p.m. Room-finding service.

● **Addresses:**

POST OFFICE: Place Grangier, Mon.–Fri.: 8 a.m.–7 p.m., Sat. and Sun.: 8 a.m.–12 noon.

24-HOUR CHEMIST: Tel. 412 828.

CENTRE INFORMATION JEUNESSE DE BOURGOGNE: 22 rue Audra (Tel. 322 500).

SEEING

The best way to see Dijon's well-preserved past is on foot; the tourist office gives out a free brochure on walking tours.

The former ducal palace, which houses an art museum, deserves a visit, as do the streets of the old town surrounding it. The archaeological museum has artefacts dating back to the ninth century BC (closed Tuesdays).

The youth hostel at 1 Boulevard Champollion (Tel. 713 212) is good but a long way from the station. The Foyer International d'Etudiants at Avenue Maréchal Leclerc (Tel. 715 101) requires an ISIC and is also quite far out of town. Hôtel du Miroir, 7 rue Bossuet (Tel. 305 481) has rooms for 70 F, as does Hôtel Monge, 20 rue Monge (Tel. 305 541). The campsite is at Avenue Albert (Tel. 435 472), overlooking the lake. It's clean, and in the summer it fills up early, so phone first.

Restaurants can be an expensive luxury in Dijon, so buy from the market stalls along rue de la Liberté. One of the least expensive restaurants is Moulin à Vent at 8 Place Françoise-Fude. For a jar of the famous mustard, go to 'Maille' on rue de la Liberté.

The Riviera (Côte d'Azur)

EXCURSIONS

You'd be crazy to try and base yourself anywhere but Nice on the Côte d'Azur, but that doesn't mean you shouldn't visit the swanky resorts such as Cannes, Monte Carlo, Juan-les-Pins and St Tropez. A day's sunbathing will cost you nothing and it's always nice to see how the other half live. The beautiful people of St Trop have not permitted such vulgar inventions as public trains to spoil their paradise, so you'll have to bus it from St Raphael to get there. Still, if you want an all-over tan – or to scrutinize other people's – it's the only place to be.

If you hit a cloudy day, go through to Monaco and put on your best bib and tucker and brave it out in the famous casino at Monte Carlo: the main gambling room is free, but you must be able to prove you're 21 or over. If you're staying overnight, try and get into the Relais International de Jeunesse in Cap d'Ail (Tel. 781 858) just outside Monte Carlo. It's a beautiful villa on the beach.

The island of CORSICA can be reached from either Nice or Marseille. The cheapest fare is on a night ferry travelling fourth class (sleeping on deck) from Nice, Marseille or Toulon, one way. Corsica is very beautiful and very unspoilt. Bonifacio, Ajaccio (Napoleon's hometown) and Calvi are the three most attractive centres on the island. Basically though, you'll need to be really keen to go to Corsica to make it worth while as rail fares are expensive and rail passes aren't valid here, though Inter Railers get a reduction.

Nice

This is without doubt your best base for a spell on the Riviera; it's cheaper than the more pretentious resorts along the Côte d'Azur and has more facilities suited to the eurorailer's lifestyle. It gets very busy, especially in August, and you might have to fight hard for your space on the pebbly beach, but at least there's the reassurance that you're only a few minutes by train from other small Riviera resorts with less crowded beaches like Villefranche, Beaulieu and Menton.

STATION FACILITIES

	NICE GARE DE VILLE
Train information	Daily 6 a.m.–10 p.m. (Tel. 875 050)
Reservations	Mon.–Sat.: 8 a.m.–7 p.m. Sun.: 8 a.m.–12 noon, 2 p.m.–7 p.m.
Tourist information	Mon.–Sat.: 8 a.m.–12 noon, 2 p.m.–6 p.m. In summer, daily 7 a.m.–10 p.m.
Foreign exchange	Tues.–Sat.: 8.30 a.m.–12 noon, 2 p.m.–6 p.m.
Café	7.30 a.m.–10 p.m.
Left-luggage lockers	No access 1.15 a.m.–5.30 a.m.
Left-luggage store	6 a.m.–10 p.m.
Bath, Shower	8 a.m.–9 p.m.
Station shuts	1.15 a.m.–5.30 a.m.

Daily trains to: Paris, Strasbourg, Genoa, Milan, Rome, Marseille.

TOURIST INFORMATION AND ADDRESSES

The main office to the right of the station, at Avenue Thiers (Tel. 870 707).

• **Addresses:**
POST OFFICE: 23 Avenue Thiers. Daily 6 a.m.–10 p.m.
AMEX: 11 Promenade des Anglais, Mon.–Fri.: 9 a.m.–12 noon, 2 p.m.–5.30 p.m., Sat.: 9 a.m.–12 noon.
TRANSALPINO: Vovac France, 6 bis, rue de Russie (Tel. 889 595).
NIGHT CHEMIST: 7 rue Masséna. 7.30 p.m.–8.30 a.m.
DOCTOR AND AMBULANCE: SOS Médecins (Tel. 830 101).
CRISIS LINE: Tel. 874 874.
SNCM: 3 Avenue Gustave V, for boats to Corsica.

SEEING

The old town of Nice with its street markets and Italian atmosphere has some typically Mediterranean walks through narrow winding alleys, which come as a sharp contrast to the commercial, touristy feeling on the main streets of Nice. To get a view over Nice and the Mediterranean, climb the 300 feet up to the château. If you've only an hour or two in Nice, spend it walking the length of the Promenade des Anglais. Eating in the cafés is prohibitive but the manwatching scope is great.

Among the main things to see are: the PALAIS LASCARIS at 15 rue Droite (former residence of the Count of Ventimiglia), the RUSSIAN ORTHODOX CATHEDRAL, the old PORT of Nice where the beautiful people keep their beautiful yachts, the MATISSE MUSEUM at Avenue des Arènes with some of the artist's works and personal possessions, and the MUSÉE NATIONAL MARC CHAGALL, Avenue du Dr Ménard.

SLEEPING

During the Jazz Parade each July beds become very scarce, and at any other time beds are still hard to find, so come early and phone around. Most of the cheap hotels are located round the station. The youth hostel is 4 km away at route Forestière du Mont Alban (Tel. 892 364). The Relais International de Jeunesse, Avenue Seuderi, is badly run and not worth bothering with unless you're desperate. However, hotels in the following streets are central, clean(ish) and affordable: rue d'Angleterre, Avenue Durante, rue Alsace-Lorraine, rue de Belgique, Avenue Thiers. If you're really stuck, the beaches are OK to sleep on, but guard your valuables carefully.

EATING AND NIGHTLIFE

Food in Nice is among the best in France; the proximity of Italy (30 minutes away) is clear in the cuisine, so the pizzas in Nice are better than many you'll find in Italy, and there's plenty of fresh seafood from the Mediterranean. Sitting in an outside restaurant in one of the pedestrianized streets watching life go by is one of life's great pleasures, and Nice abounds with good set menus at prices from 40–65 F.

Discos and clubs are expensive, and anyway a walk down the Promenade des Anglais is just as entertaining.

Marseille

Marseille lacks the charm and finesse of the Riviera resorts but it does have character. It's France's oldest city (dating back to 600 BC) and one of the world's major ports, but it tends to cater more for businessmen than tourists.

STATION FACILITIES

	MARSEILLE ST CHARLES
Train information	5 a.m.–1 a.m.
	(Tel. 085 050)
Reservations	8 a.m.–7 p.m.
Tourist information	June–Aug.: Mon.–Sat.:
	7.30 a.m.–9 a.m., 3 p.m.–8.30 p.m.
	Otherwise main office
Foreign exchange	6 a.m.–8 p.m.
Bar, Buffet	5 a.m.–12 midnight
Restaurant	11 a.m.–2 p.m., 6 p.m.–9.30 p.m.
Left-luggage lockers	No access 1.30 a.m.–4 a.m.
Left-luggage store	All hours
Shower	4 a.m.–12 midnight
Station shuts	1.30 a.m.–4 a.m.

Daily trains to: Paris, Strasbourg, Lyon (4 hours), Nice (2¼ hours), Milan, Bordeaux, Nantes.

TOURIST INFORMATION AND ADDRESSES

To be found only at the station in summer, otherwise at 4 La Canebière (near the Old Port) (Tel. 549 111). They have an accommodation-finding service.

● **Addresses:**
POST OFFICE: Place de l'Hôtel-des-Postes (metro Colbert).
TRANSALPINO: Vovac France, 8 rue du Bailly du Sufresne (Tel. 336 223).
24-HOUR CHEMIST AND DOCTOR: Tel. 528 485.

SEEING

Marseille's most famous street is the Canebière (can-of-beer to generations of British sailors) which leads up from the Old Port to the Quai des Belges. This gets quite lively at night (the Bar du Téléphone was the scene of the biggest gangland massacre ever), but you're safer walking round here than in the slums of the North African quarter round the Porte d'Aix and rue Ste-Barbe.

The MUSÉE DES BEAUX ARTS in the Palais de Longchamp is the city's art gallery and the MUSÉE DES DOCKS ROMAINS (Roman docks) was the unexpected result of a 1943 German bomb.

The other 'sights' are the old town, ST VICTOR'S BASILICA and CATACOMBS, Le Corbusier's 17-storey CITÉ RADIEUSE, the CATHEDRAL and the park and CHÂTEAU BORLEY.

SLEEPING

The two youth hostels are a long way from the centre but are all right once you get there: Avenue de Bois-Luzy (Tel. 490 618) and Auberge de Bonneveine at 47 Avenue J. Vidal (Tel. 732 181). Beware when looking round for a cheap hotel, especially near the docks – many of them are 'multi-purpose' establishments. Foyer des Jeunes St Charles at 3 rue Palestro (Tel. 500 178) has dormitory beds for 50 F. There's also camping at Les Vagues (Tel. 730 488) and at Mazarques (Tel. 400 980).

EATING AND NIGHTLIFE

Bouillabaisse, the famous French fish stew, comes from Marseille, and is at its best here. There's no shortage of restaurants-cafés and fixed-price menus can be found. The Tunisian and Moroccan restaurants are cheap, though not always good – but it's not wise for unaccompanied girls to head into the North African quarter at night.

Nightlife more or less finds you in Marseille. Just watch out you don't go into too low a dive as, if things get nasty, we've heard the police don't lose too much sleep over the odd mugged eurorailer.

Provence

Renowned for its cloudless skies and Roman remains, Provence's rich countryside has acted like a magnet to artists and Eurorailers alike for years. The best time to go is May or September as Aix-en-Provence and Avignon have Arts festivals in July and August, and rooms are hard to find.

Avignon

If you're coming from Lyon, consider getting off the train half an hour before Avignon at ORANGE to see one of the finest Roman theatres in the world.

After a fracas between the Vatican and Philip IV of France, Boniface VII moved to Avignon. The inner walled city is still dominated by his palace, the PALAIS DES PAPES, which is most impressive from the outside; they are restoring it and English tours are available. Be sure to visit the park above the palace for a superb view of the River Rhône.

Sleeping will be your greatest problem in Avignon, but there is an accommodation service opposite the station, which you're advised to use to save yourself hassle. If you don't mind large dormitories, try Camping Bagatelle (Tel. 83 30 39). Prices are good and there is a superb view of the palace. Also try the YMCA foyer, 7 bis, Chemin de la Justice (Tel. 254 620). The tourist information office is at rue de la République and in front of the station.

Arles

An important centre in Roman and medieval times with an impressive amphitheatre which today has reverted to its function as a blood bath, imported Spanish bulls having replaced the gladiators. The MUSEUM OF CHRISTIAN ART is well worth a visit, as is the ROMAN THEATRE from the first century BC and the ROMAN CEMETERY.

Tourist information is on Boulevard des Lices (Tel. 96 29 35): they'll supply a ticket for 20 F (14 F on ISIC) for entry to all the museums and monuments as well as help you out with accommodation if necessary. The youth hostel is on rue Foch (Tel. 96 18 25), a block behind the tourist office. Try Hôtel Mistral, 16 rue du Docteur Fanton, or Hôtel Moderne at 12 Place du Forum (Tel. 96 08 21) for a cheap bed. If you want to venture into the Camargue, Arles is about the nearest you'll get by rail (they rent out bikes at the station and the going is flat).

Nîmes

Some of the best Roman remains in France are here, with the MAISON CARRÉE and the AMPHITHEATRE stealing the show. Tourist information is at 6 rue Auguste, and they run a similar system to Arles: ticket for the monuments, ISIC reduction. They'll also give you the best route to the PONT DU GARD, a 2,000-year-old Roman aqueduct which is almost intact, and the old Crusaders' port of AIGUES-MORTES, now well inland through silting up. Both are well worth visiting.

Aix-en-Provence

Birthplace of Cézanne and intellectual and cultural centre of the region, Aix fancies itself somewhat and gives off an air of sophistication that is lacking elsewhere. Sit in any café and you'll feel a strange air of self-importance. The MUSEUM OF TAPESTRIES is particularly interesting. Avoid their festival, as prices and crowds increase dramatically. Tourist information is at Place du Général de Gaulle (Tel. 260 293). Try Hôtel du Casino, 38 rue Victor Leydet (Tel. 260 688), or the Auberge de Jeunesse on Avenue Marcel Pagnol (Tel. 201 599) – take bus number 7 or 8 from the Place de Gaulle as it's 2 km from the station. Transalpino's agent is Vovac France, 3 rue Lieutand (Tel. 279 383).

Central/South-west France

The Auvergne, Dordogne and Languedoc regions are sparsely populated and consequently trains are few and far between; however, if you have the time and patience for the local trains, the rewards are great.

CARCASSONNE, the medieval gem of the Languedoc region, is on the main line and services are good. This is arguably Europe's best-preserved relic of the Middle Ages, and certainly the most interesting walled city in France. After centuries of building and fortifying the town, it was left to rot in the sixteenth century and it wasn't till the nineteenth that restoration began. The tourist office is on Boulevard Camille Pelleton; they find rooms and are generally helpful. Arrive early as Carcassonne is not a well-kept secret and in summer rooms get scarce.

CLERMONT-FERRAND and PÉRIGUEUX are not particularly interesting towns in themselves but they make excellent bases for touring the Auvergne and Dordogne. The tourist board at Clermont is at 69 Boulevard Gergovia, and Périgueux's is in Avenue de l'Aquitaine. They'll provide you with details on the surrounding area and how best to reach the places of interest. Accommodation should be no problem in either town: most of the cheap hotels surround the stations.

LES EYZIES DE TAYAC (the prehistoric capital of Europe) is about 40 minutes south-east of Périgueux by train and its cave paintings are within easy walking distance of the station, as is the tourist information office (Tel. 069705). There are plenty of hotels to choose from in the village and there's camping on the other side of the river.

Bordeaux

Famed for the many quality wines it produces, Bordeaux is a good place to head for if your money's running out and you fancy a week or two working on the grape harvest. A short stay here will give you a totally different perspective on French life from your few days in Paris: whilst Paris is very Parisian, Bordeaux is terribly French.

STATION FACILITIES

	ST JEAN STATION
Train information	Daily 5.30 a.m.–9 p.m. (Tel. 92 50 50)
Reservations	Daily 7 a.m.–8 p.m.
Tourist information	Bureau de tourisme SNCF, otherwise in centre
Foreign exchange	5 a.m.–8 p.m. At ticket windows
Bar, Buffet	All hours
Restaurant	Daily 7 a.m.–9.30 p.m.
Shower	5 a.m.–11 p.m.
Left-luggage lockers	No access 12 midnight–5 a.m.
Left-luggage store	All hours
Shops	Regular hours. In Cours de la Marne
Waiting room	All hours
Post office	Mon.–Fri.: 8 a.m.–7 p.m. Sat.: 8 a.m.–12 noon
Station shuts	12 midnight–5 a.m.

Daily trains to: Paris, Lyon, Nantes, Toulouse, Marseille, Nice, Biarritz, Madrid and Lisbon.

TOURIST INFORMATION AND ADDRESSES

The tourist information office is at 12 Cours du 30 Juillet (Tel. 442 841). The post office is at 52 rue Georges Bonnac. For a 24-hour chemist, doctor, dentist or ambulance telephone 91 91 91.

SEEING

Explore Bordeaux on foot, starting your tour at the GRAND THÉÂTRE on the Place de la Comédie. From here you can work out the best route on the map to take you to the other sights: the ESPLANADE DE QUINCONCES, the largest square in France, the PLACE DE LA BOURSE with its eighteenth-century façades, the CATHÉDRALE ST ANDRÉ, the MUSÉE DES BEAUX ARTS and the smart shopping streets round RUE BOUFFARD.

To get the feel of things, take a 'wine tour'; the Syndicat d'Initiative (in the tourist office) arrange these daily.

SLEEPING

A bed is no problem in Bordeaux, even though many places close down in August. The youth hostel is close to the station at 22 Cours Barbey (Tel. 915 951), and there are several cheap hotels in the area: Hôtel de la Poste, 66 rue Porte-Dijeaux (Tel. 481 418) and Hôtel St François, 22 rue du Mirail (Tel. 955 641), with beds for 60 F.

EATING AND NIGHTLIFE

Predictably enough, the local cuisine makes good use of the regional wines and there are all sorts of dishes using the delicious Bordelaise sauce. Set menus at affordable prices can be found in restaurants on rue des Augustins, Place Général Carvail, and rue du Maréchal-Joffre.

Ask tourist information for a 'What's On' and try sampling the regional wines at bistros.

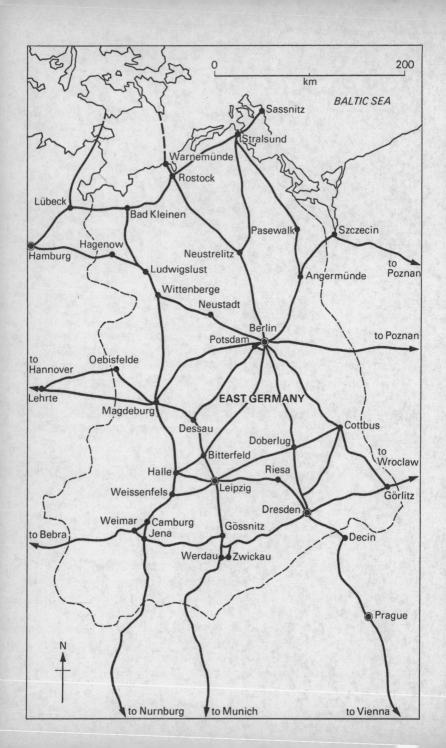

EAST GERMANY
(German Democratic Republic, GDR)

Entry requirements	Passport and advance visa
Population	17,000,000
Capital	Berlin (pop.: 1,200,000)
Currency	Mark
	£1 = approx. 3.75 M
Political system	Socialist Republic
Religions	Protestant and Catholic
Language	German
Public holidays	1 Jan.; Good Friday; 1 May;
	Whit Monday; 7 Oct.; 7, 25, 26 Dec.

East Germany is not as grey and uninviting as it's made out to be, but if you like the bright lights you might find it a bit grim. Its economic recovery since the war is just as remarkable as its Western neighbour's. Without US aid, and despite the departure of nearly three million of its best qualified personnel, East Germany is among the top ten industrial nations in the world and enjoys a standard of living unrivalled in Eastern Europe.

Officially, industry is seen as the key to economic development, and much of the countryside is spoilt because of this. Unfortunately, tourists are not encouraged, especially eurorailers (Inter Rail is not valid here). If you don't mind getting organized well beforehand and are not easily put off by excessive bureaucracy, the rewards are numerous. The centres you're most likely to want to visit in East Germany are quite easily defined: East Berlin, Potsdam, Weimar, Dresden and Leipzig. The rural areas worth exploring are the Harz Mountains to the west, the Thuringian forest to the south-west and the Erzgebirge Mountains to the south.

The two main towns of the Harz Mountains are QUEDLINEBURG with its perfectly kept half-timbered houses, Renaissance town hall, castle and cathedral, and WERNIGERODE, another picturesque 'old German' town and terminal for the mountain steam railway.

Weimar is the main town of the Thuringian forest, with Eisenach and Erfurt the other two centres of the region. At EISENACH, birthplace of Bach, see his house which is now a museum, and the fifteenth-century castle. ERFURT suffered hardly any damage in the

Second World War, so there are more genuinely old buildings here than elsewhere. The KRÄMERBRÜCKE is a collection of fourteenth-century houses on a bridge and there are two fifteenth-century CATHEDRALS side by side on Domberg.

EAST GERMAN STATE RAILWAYS
(Deutsche Reichsbahn, DR)

By Eastern European standards, DR runs an efficient and frequent service but, compared to the West, trains are slow and crowded. In order to travel at reasonable speeds you'll have to pay extra for the supplements on special diesel expresses (Ex), expresses (D) and semi-fast (E) trains. Avoid at all costs the local (Personen) trains as they stop at nearly every station. If you find the queues unbearable when you go to purchase a ticket, it makes sense to pay the 1 M fine and get it on the train.

TRAIN INFORMATION

Don't always count on English being spoken, especially in smaller towns.

• **Reservations:** Whenever possible, try and reserve a seat as trains are always full during summer. This costs about 2 M.

• **Night travel:** It makes sense to travel at night as couchettes are cheap and it cuts out the hassle of finding somewhere to stay.

• **Eating on trains:** Prices are high by East German standards, so you're better off with a picnic.

TOURIST INFORMATION

Every large town has its own tourist information office dealing with local attractions, in addition to the official government offices (Reisebüros) which handle the whole of East Germany. If you speak German, it's well worth finding out as much as you can from West Germany beforehand. Contact BMB, Kölnerstrasse 140, 5300 Bonn, Bad Godesberg.

● **ISIC bonuses:** With an IUS card there's a 25 per cent reduction on international trains within the Eastern Bloc, as well as at some state museums. For further information, contact Jugendtourist, Alexanderplatz 5, 1026 Berlin.

● **Money matters:** 1 Mark (M) = 100 Pfennig (pf).
Banking hours are 8 a.m.–12 noon, Mon.–Fri., though times vary locally. In our opinion, it's not worth the risk changing money on the black market. The rewards are high, but the penalties are higher.

● **Shops:** Open 9 a.m.–6 p.m. except in Berlin where they open 9.30 a.m.–7 p.m.

● **Post offices and museums:** Vary depending on locality. Check with tourist information.

SLEEPING

This is a big problem in East Germany. If you want to stay for any time, it's best to fix things up beforehand as the authorities won't issue a visa unless you have somewhere to stay. If you've not already done this, then there are always the Inter hotels (specifically for foreign tourists) but at £15–20 ($20–30) a night minimum these are expensive. Try asking at any Reisebüro der DDR about the Verband Christlicher Hospize which has hostels in Berlin, Leipzig and Weimar. The only other alternative is to camp at about 20 M a night. If you decide to camp or stay at Inter hotels, it's best to write to Reisebüro der DDR, Generaldirektion, Postschliessfach 77, DDR – 1026 Berlin, at least two months in advance. The only problem is, you have to be well enough organized to give the exact dates you expect to be at a certain town. When they have all the relevant information (and of course your money), they will send on a voucher which, when shown at the DDR border, entitles you to your visa for camping or Inter hotels. If you're not sure whether East Germany's for you, it's possible to take out a day visa for East Berlin and pay for vouchers there, but be prepared for a lot of queueing. The visa is also available from Berolina Travel in London, and from Koch Overseas Travel, 206–208 East 208th Street, New York (Tel. 212 513 8600).

EATING AND NIGHTLIFE

Food in the DDR is not particularly wonderful, but it's filling and usually fresh and hygienically prepared. You can get a meal for about 10 M in most East German cities. 'High culture' is plentiful and of high quality. For the student set, it's basically back to pubs and dancing, and that's about it.

Weimar

Homeland of Bach, Liszt, Goethe and Nietzsche, and the Buchenwald concentration camp, this town was also the site of the first German Republic (the Weimar Republic) which fell in the 1930s, just before Nazism rose to power.

TOURIST INFORMATION

Weimar Informationszentrum, Marktstrasse 4 (Tel. 21 73), open Mon.: 10 a.m.–5 p.m., Tues.–Fri.: 9 a.m.–5 p.m., Sat.: 8.30 a.m.–12.45 p.m., 1.30 p.m.–4.30 p.m. Take bus 1 or 6 from the station to Goetheplatz and walk along Dimitroffstrasse to the Marktplatz. They'll direct you to the Zentralkasse where you can buy a museum pass for about 5 M and tickets for concerts and theatrical events, as well as bus tickets.

SEEING, EATING AND NIGHTLIFE

The LUCAS-CRANACH-HAUS is the richly decorated Renaissance building in the Marktplatz. Close by is the SCHLOSSMUSEUM (closed Mondays) with a collection of German Renaissance works, and the Gothic church HERDERKIRCHE. The KIRMS-KRACHOW-HAUS MIT HERDER-MUSEUM looks at Goethe and Schiller among others. The museum devoted to Schiller is nearby, and the GOETHE-NATIONAL MUSEUM and his house (closed Tuesdays) completes your visit to Weimar's 'musts'.

Two very different excursions from Weimar are to SCHLOSS BELVEDERE (open Wed.–Sun.), a rococo palace, and BUCHENWALD, the camp where 56,000 people were killed in 1937–45.

People eat early in Weimar and you'll find places closed round 8 p.m. and all weekend, so get some supplies in. Try Alt Weimar, Steubenstrasse 27, or the Elephantkeller on the Markt. For a drink and a look at the local students, try Zum Pilsner, Friedrichstrasse 18.

East Berlin

Though it hardly rivals West Berlin, East Berlin can hold its own and, as it's the showpiece of the Eastern Bloc, a visit here cannot be taken as representative of the rest of the country. The grey skyscrapers are in stark contrast to the old Prussian buildings and this new mini-Moscow seems very out of place, lying as it does in old Berlin. There are sufficient incentives to merit a trip: the excellent museums and baroque palaces are unequalled elsewhere.

THE DAY VISA

• **Getting in:** It's quite simple now to go in for a day: either go through as a pedestrian at Bahnhof Friedrichstrasse (S-Bahn or U-Bahn line 6 connects) or through Checkpoint Charlie (take U-Bahn to Kochstrasse). You need 35 DM to change and your passport. It'll take between one and three hours to get through, and you can go from 7 a.m.–8 p.m.; you must be back by midnight.

Bureaucracy has run riot so, if they take it into their heads, you'll be asked to fill in customs declaration forms, etc., and you can count on anything up to half an hour to exit. Make sure to get stamped confirmation (Bestätigung) for any Western currency you have paid out in East Berlin, as this keeps the police happy if you're stopped. If your appetite for this country has been whetted and you want to stay longer, go to the travel agents Reisebüro der DDR, Alexanderplatz 5, for information on the procedure.

TOURIST INFORMATION AND ADDRESSES

TOURIST INFORMATION: Informationszentrum am Fernsehturm (Tel. 212 4675) under the TV tower. Open Mon.: 1 p.m.–6 p.m. Also information booth on Friedrichstrasse near station.
REISEBÜRO DER DDR: Alexanderplatz 5 (Tel. 2150). Tickets for trains and cultural events.
CURRENCY EXCHANGE: Reisebüro, Alexanderplatz or Bahnhof Friedrichstrasse or Ostbahnhof.
'WHAT'S ON': 'Wohin in Berlin' (3 M) bi-weekly booklet on events.
UK EMBASSY: Unter den Linden 32–34 (Tel. 220 2431).
US EMBASSY: 108 Berlin-Mitte, Neustädtische Kirchstrasse 4/5 (Tel. 220 2741).
CITY TRANSPORT: Tram, bus or U-Bahn costs very little and is very efficient.

SEEING

UNTER DEN LINDEN is the most impressive street of East Berlin and is at its very centre. From here you can see the Brandenburg Gate and the new city centre. Not far from here is MUSEUM ISLAND where the main museums are located. East Berlin definitely got the best of the deal in the carve-up of the museums. The Reisebüro at Alexander-platz sell a three-day museum ticket for about 2 M. MARIENKIRCHE is Berlin's oldest church dating from the thirteenth century. This, predictably, stands next to a huge, very twentieth-century television tower which offers a good view, if nothing else.

For signs of the past, try a walk to the SYNAGOGUE on Oranienburgerstrasse. This was burnt on the infamous Kristall-nacht 1938, and hasn't been renovated since. The MONUMENT TO THE VICTIMS OF FASCISM AND MILITARISM on Unter den Linden and the SOVIET WAR MEMORIAL in Treptower Park will set you thinking.

The main museums are: the PERGAMON (stunning collections of Eastern and Roman artefacts), the BODEMUSEUM with its Egyptian works; the twentieth-century art gallery, the ALTES MUSEUM and the NATIONAL GALERIE of nineteenth-century art. The MUSEUM FÜR DEUTSCHE GESCHICHTE in the Arsenal (Zeughaus), the oldest building on Unter den Linden, is the Communist viewpoint on eighteenth- to twentieth-century German history, and the MÄRKIS-CHES MUSEUM traces Berlin's history.

The Spree River flows through the city and it's possible to take a boat ride on one of the white excursion boats (Weisse Flotte) from April to September. You can get off at various points; the best is the MECKLENBURGER DORF – a reconstruction of a nineteenth-century German village. Boats leave eight times a day from Treptower Park S-Bahn Station. (The commentary is usually given in German only.)

SLEEPING

If you're here for more than a day and want a bed, go to desk 13 of the Reisebüro on Alexanderplatz 5. They'll arrange for you to stay in an Inter hotel or camp (there are cheaper hotels than those in the Inter hotel chain, but it's up to the officials whether or not they'll recommend one to you).

EATING AND NIGHTLIFE

Food isn't as good as it is 'over the Wall', but you can get by on the Schnell Imbiss and the supermarkets. Try Zum Thuringer, Klement-Gottwald Allee, which serves East German specialities.

Classical music and drama are of a high calibre here. Tickets for most events can be had from Zentralbesucherdienst at the Palast Hotel, Karl-Liebknechtstrasse, or desk 1 of the Reisebüro, Alexanderplatz 5. The Haus der Jungen Talente, Klosterstrasse, have young musicians' concerts with cheap tickets.

Many of the city's bars are to the north, over the river from the Friedrichstrasse station. Try the 'Kleine Melodie', Friedrichstrasse 127, for a disco.

Potsdam

In 1744, Frederick the Great chose this town as his permanent seat, and from then on Potsdam flourished, to become one of the main imperial centres of Europe. There are four castles and many elaborate pavilions in the impressive SANS SOUCI PARK. NEUES

PALAIS is another rococo castle to see, as is the ORANGERIE set above the SICILIAN GARDENS which house sixty-seven very good fake Raphaels. See also the gold-plated Chinese Tea House in the grounds of the Orangerie.

While in Potsdam, eat out at a Schnell Imbiss and have a beer at the Schwarzer Adler on Gutenbergstrasse.

Dresden

Two hours from Berlin, Dresden is the cultural centre of the DDR and, though the city was virtually wiped off the map in a bomb attack in February 1945, what was left was carefully restored. There are two stations – Bahnhof Neustadt, for east-bound trains, and the Hauptbahnhof.

TOURIST INFORMATION

Dresden information centre is at Pragerstrasse 10/11 (Tel. 44031) (five minutes from station, past Inter hotel Newa). Open Mon.–Sat.: 9 a.m.–8 p.m., Sun.: 9 a.m.–2 p.m. Change money here or in the Hauptbahnhof. 'What's On' leaflet from here: 'Dresden-Information'. Bus and tram tickets have to be bought in advance.

SEEING

The ZWINGER PALACE contains half of Dresden's impressive museums: the magnificent GEMÄLDEGALERIE ALTE MEISTER (closed Mondays); the HISTORISCHES MUSEUM of weapons (closed Wednesdays); the MATHEMATISCH PHYSIKALISCHER SALON (maths and physics); and both the ZINNSAMMLUNG and the PORZELLANSAMMLUNG display the famous Dresden porcelain and pewter (closed Fridays).

On the other side of the street is what's left of the palace of Saxony's electors and kings. The ALBERTINUM is Dresden's other museum complex. It is near the remains of the bombed-out FRAUENKIRCHE behind Bruhlische Terrasse.

The 'old' nineteenth-century part of the town is across the Elbe, with its Markt.

SLEEPING

The campsites are all quite far flung; tourist information will direct you to them. Alternatively, there's the youth hostel (Rudi Arndt) at 11 Hubnerstrasse (Tel. 470667) which is near the station. Also worth a try is the brand new youth hostel (Schloss Eckberg) at Bautznerstrasse 134.

EATING

Places on Pernaisches Tor are cheap, as are the restaurants in the 'Am Zwinger' complex on Thälmanstrasse.

Leipzig

The second city of East Germany is only 1½ hours from Dresden, and though it is more a commercial and industrial centre, there are still enough points of interest to make it worth a stop-off. The Hauptbahnhof here is Europe's largest. Tourist information is at Katharinenstrasse 1/3, Alte Wagge.

SEEING, EATING AND NIGHTLIFE

Bach spent twenty-seven of his creative years working as the choirmaster in ST THOMAS' CATHEDRAL here. This church, dating from 1482, has been beautifully restored, as has the old sixteenth-century TOWN HALL. AUERBACHS KELLER in Madlerpassage is the cellar where Goethe set his scene between Faust and the Devil.

Leipzig has plenty of reasonably priced restaurants and pubs, and for free entertainment go to St Thomas' church, where Bach is buried, on Friday nights or Sunday mornings to hear the boys' choir, once conducted by Bach.

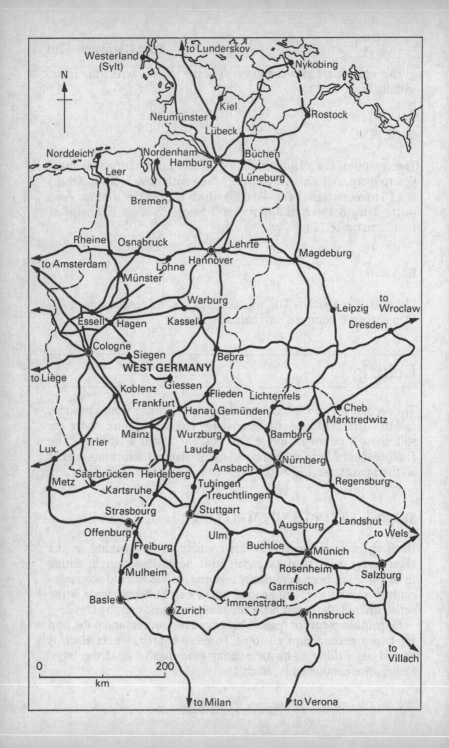

WEST GERMANY
(Federal Republic of Germany, FDR)

Entry requirements	Passport
Population	63,000,000 +
Capital	Bonn (pop.: 300,000)
Currency	Deutsche Mark
	£1 = approx. 3.75 DM
Political system	Federal Republic
Religions	Protestant and Catholic
Language	German (English spoken in major cities)
Public holidays	1 Jan.; Good Friday; Easter Monday;
	1 May; Ascension Day; Whit Monday;
	17 June; Corpus Christi; 15 Aug.;
	1, 17, 21 Nov.; 25, 26 Dec.

The Germans are a restless lot. Wherever you go in Europe, there they are. It's always been like this from the days of the Franks and Saxons. Most people have heard of the Holy Roman Empire, created by Otto I in 962, which survived till 1806, but few realize that the local German regimes were often much more powerful. The Hanseatic League of merchants, associated with the towns of Lübeck and Hamburg, controlled much of northern Europe's wealth in the medieval period.

Long after the rest of Europe had formed itself into single nation-states, 'Germany' was still divided, a fact not helped by the incredible number of feuding princedoms and the country's lack of natural boundaries. These divisions came to a head in the Thirty Years War of 1618–48 when the Catholic south defending the Habsburg emperors and Protestant north, inspired by men such as Luther and the Reformation movement, fought it out between themselves. In 1871 Bismarck got everyone organized and the German nation came into being. The autocratic rule, feeble attempts to conquer an empire, and rapid industrialization led to discontent, and with Kaiser Bill's blunderings, this ended up as the First World War. After the failure of the liberal Weimar Republic, Hitler started stirring things up again, and we all know what Nazism led to . . . Today Germany is again divided and, though it's possible to get beyond 'the Wall', it stands as a lasting reminder of the political polarities under which the East and West of Germany live.

GERMAN FEDERAL RAILWAYS
(Deutsche Bundesbahn, DB)

As far as we're concerned, DB offer one of the best deals in Europe. French trains travel faster, but at a price only businessmen can afford. If you're in a hurry, you'll find German trains travel fast enough for a much smaller supplement. Unlike Britain and France where all the main lines radiate out from the capital, the Germans have an excellent series of interconnecting cross-country lines which serve all the principal cities and the smaller towns throughout the country.

There are four types of train, apart from TEEs: fast intercity trains (IC) which require a 50 DM supplement; international expresses and fast long-distance inland trains, Schnellzüge (D) which require a supplement for short journeys; the Eilzüge (E) serving the regional areas; Personenzüge or Nahverkehrszüge, which are slow local trains. The DB Tourist card (see page 30) is becoming more popular each year at 275 DM for 9 days' unlimited travel and 16 days for 360 DM. This includes a reduced round-trip ticket to West Berlin. Cards are available at the German Railway Office, 10 Old Bond Street, London W1, and at their office in New York at 630 Fifth Avenue, Suite 1418, NY 10020. When in Germany anyone under 23 (students, 27) can buy a one-month go-as-you-please Tramper-Monat ticket for around 240 DM at any of the larger stations. If you plan on spending a long time in Germany, look out for the Youth Pass available to anyone under 22 (students, 27). It's valid for a year and gets you 50 per cent reduction on all rail tickets. Transalpino have offices all over Germany offering their usual 25–60 per cent discount on domestic or international routes.

● **Inter Rail bonuses:**

	SECTION		REDUCTION
	FROM	TO	%
Schauinslandbahn GmbH, Freiburg (Breisgau)	All		50
Vorwohle-Emmerthaler Verkehrs-betriebe GmbH, Bodenwerder	All		50
Kahlgrund-Verkehrs-GmbH, Schöllkrippen	All		50

	SECTION		REDUCTION
	FROM	TO	%
Oberrheinische Eisenbahn-Gesellschaft AG, Mannheim	Rail sections only		50
Regentalbahn AG, Viechtach	All		50
Lokalbahn Lam-Kötzting, Lam			50
Tegernsee-Bahn AG, Tegernsee			50
Verkehrsbetriebe Peine-Salzgitter GmbH, Salzgitter-Hallendorf			50
Kreisbahn Aurich GmbH, Aurich			50
Eisenbahn-Gesellschaft Altona-Kaltenkirchen-Neumünster, Hamburg	Kaltenkirchen-Neumünster		50
Regionalverkehr Munsterland GmbH	All coach lines		50
Regionalverkehr Ruhr-Lippe GmbH	All coach lines		50
Verkehrsbetriebe Kreis Tecklenburg – Techlenburger Nordbahn – AG	All coach lines		50
Verkehrsgesellschaft Kreis Unna GmbH	All		50
Köln-Düsseldorfer Deutsche Rheinschiffahrt AG, Köln	Day service only		50
Vereinigte Schiffahrtsunternehmen für den Bodensee und Rhein, Frankfurt (M)	All		50
Postal and Railway buses (1)	All		50

- **Eurail bonuses:** Free:
—Ferry crossings from Puttgarden to Rødby (Denmark).
—Steamers operated by the Köln-Düsseldorfer Deutsche Rheinschiffahrt (KD) making regular runs on the Rhine between Cologne and Frankfurt (Main) and on the Moselle between Trier and Koblenz (except on ships making cruises of several days between Basel and Rotterdam and vice versa). For the use of Express-steamers, an extra charge will have to be paid by Eurail Youthpass holders, and for the use of hydrofoils by Eurail Pass as well as by Eurail Youthpass holders.

—Most of the bus lines of the integrated bus transport Post/Railway bus union.

—Europabus line 189 – Burgenstrasse (Castle Road) from Mannheim–Heidelberg–Heilbronn–Rothenburg ob der Tauber–Ansbach–Nürmberg.

—Europabus line 190 – Romantische Strasse (Romantic Road) from Wiesbaden–Frankfurt (Main)–Rothenburg ob der Tauber–Füssen/Munich.

Reduced fares:

—50 per cent reduction on hydrofoil service between Cologne and Mainz.

—50 per cent reduction to Eurail Pass and Eurail Youthpass holders on the normal fares of the ferry crossing operated by TT-Saga-Line between Lübeck–Travemünde and Malmö (Sweden).

—50 per cent reduction on regular steamer services operated by the German Federal Railways on Lake Constance.

—Eurail Pass and Eurail Youthpass are not valid on private railways in the Federal Republic of Germany. However, the following mountain railways grant reduced fares:

1. Garmisch-Partenkirchen–Grainau–Zugspitze (Schneefernerhaus).

2. Freiburg (Breisgau)–Schauinsland: 50 per cent on ordinary tickets, for Eurail Pass and Eurail Youthpass.

—25 per cent reduction for students producing a valid student ID card on the round-trip bus fare Braunschweig–Berlin or vice versa operated by Bayern Express and P. Kuhn Berlin GmbH.

—20 per cent reduction on some half-day or full-day excursions out of Munich operated by the Oberbayern GmbH.

—10 per cent on Munich city sightseeing tours operated by the Oberbayern GmbH.

TRAIN INFORMATION

Information officers wear yellow capbands and speak good English. Left-luggage lockers take 1 DM and 50 Pfennig pieces.

• **Reservations:** Can be made up to two hours before departing, but not after 10 p.m. They are included in the price of the supplement on ICs and TEEs. On all other trains, it's optional and costs about 4 DM. Rail pass holders are exempt from the IC supplement.

• **Night travel:** Most German compartments have pull-down seats which make excellent free beds. Couchettes have six berths and cost about 22 DM. Tourist-class sleepers (three-berth) are more expensive at around 45 DM, but it's often possible to get one between two out of season, as they're usually underbooked. During the summer of 1984, DB introduced a special couchette between Dortmund and Munich. 54 persons up to the age of 26 now have the possibility to sleep for only 4 DM. This arrangement is called 'Rollende Jugendherberge' (Rolling Youth Hostel) and all you need is a sleeping bag (or blankets). If you haven't already got one you can buy a paper blanket on board for around 6 DM. It's also possible to pay the 4 DM to the conductor during the journey, so you don't have to worry about reservations. This service was extended in mid-June until September to include the route between Hamburg and Munich and Aachen to Copenhagen. Hopefully DB will see it as a success and extend it even further in the future.

• **Eating on trains:** Prices are lower than British Rail, while the quality is higher. So if you've the money, it's worth considering a meal on the ICs. Other trains have mini-bars which are pricey for what you get.

• **Scenic routes:** The Rhine valley, Black Forest, Romantic and Castle roads, as well as the Alps, all provide scenic routes within Germany. If you've always wanted to go cruising down the Rhine, it's best to do it between Koblenz and Rüdesheim or Mainz as this gives you magnificent views of both sides of the valley. If you're coming from the opposite direction and want to stay with rivers, then head to Giessen from Koblenz. To see the Black Forest, there are a variety of options. The Romantic and Castle roads are arguably best seen by Europabus, which are nearly always busy and require advance reservations. The Munich–Nürnberg, Heilbronn–Heidelberg train follows more or less the same route as the bus at no extra cost. For the Alps, try the line to Salzburg or Innsbruck from Munich – both are equally attractive. If you're going to Switzerland, try Freiburg–Basel or Würzburg–Zürich.

● **Bikes:** Can be hired from over 200 stations throughout Germany at half the normal rate (5 DM) to anyone with a valid ticket or rail pass.

TOURIST INFORMATION

Tourist offices are usually called Verkehrsamt or Verkehrsverein. Many cities have free pamphlets specially prepared for the under 26s.

● **ISIC bonuses:** 75 per cent museum discount, with varying reductions at some sports centres. For further information, contact Europa Sprach Club, Amalienstrasse 67, Munich 40. There are branches in all main cities.

● **Money matters:** 1 Deutsche Mark (DM) = 100 Pfennig.
Banking hours are Mon.–Fri.: 9 a.m.–12 noon, 2 p.m.–4 p.m. It's also possible to change money at some post offices; they often give a better rate, because they make mistakes.

● **Post offices:** Open Mon.–Fri.: 8 a.m.–6 p.m., Sat.: 8 a.m.–12 noon.

● **Shops:** Open Mon.–Fri.: 8.30 a.m.–6/6.30 p.m. In smaller towns they shut for lunch, 12 noon–3 p.m. On Sat. they open till midday, and until 6 p.m. on the first Sat. of each month.

SLEEPING

Youth hostels cost 15–25 DM a night and there are over 600 scattered throughout Germany. Tourist information have a free map and brochure showing their locations. Youth guest houses (Jugendgasthäuser) are in nearly all the large towns, but they tend to be stuffed with groups, so always phone first. There's no uniform system of classification for Germany's hostels and hotels, so you'll find they vary dramatically. The accommodation side of tourist information, however, is usually very obliging and you need never feel really stuck as in the end they'll fix you up with something in your price range. As in many other countries, the towns are ideally laid out for eurorailers and many of the cheap hotels are near the stations. In smaller places, look out for signs hanging up saying

'Zimmer frei' (room to let) or 'Gasthof' (inn), and for private accommodation turn to tourist information for lists. With over 2,000 campsites in Germany, you shouldn't find any problems. Again, tourist information have a free map and brochure showing where they are. Facilities are generally very good and prices usually fair.

EATING AND NIGHTLIFE

German cuisine is as varied as French – the only difference is that the former like to eat more of it. There are countless types of beer and Würste (sausages), but it's unfair to think that's all there is, as so many do. The food halls of the large department stores (e.g. Hertie, Kaufhaus) are real show-pieces, and the quality and quantity of the produce means there's no excuse for not living off picnics and saving your Marks that way. Fast food's also available in the major cities, and Schnell Imbiss stalls with Würste and beer also crop up. Drinks can be very expensive in Germany.

As far as regional specialities go, try some of the following: Grünkohl mit Pinkel (green cabbage with bacon sausage) from the north, Sauerbraten (braised beef in sour sauce) from the west, and for your picnics sample Westphalian Pumpernickel (black bread) or Vollkornbrot (bread made of whole unground grains of wheat). Many of the Würste look revolting, but don't let that put you off.

The Germans are keen on large-scale celebrations: some of their festivals resemble Wagnerian opera sets, and no expense is spared. If you get a chance to join in, do. As far as music goes, the classics are always well represented and there's an active jazz and disco scene in all the major cities.

Northern Germany

Northern Germany – the area between Schleswig and Bremen – is comparatively unspoilt by tourism. The main centres of interest are: Bremen, Hamburg, and Lübeck, and also you could take in the little towns of Hameln (of Pied Piper fame) and Celle, if you've enough time left.

Bremen

Bremen with its port, Bremerhaven, is the oldest seaport in Germany. The tourist information office is right in front of the station. Tackle Bremen on foot and take in the old medieval section round the MARKTPLATZ, the RATHAUS, the FOCKE MUSEUM and ST PETER'S eleventh-century CATHEDRAL with its cellar full of mummified bodies. The old section of the town called the SCHNOOR is particularly attractive, with its narrow winding streets dating back to the 1400s and its half-timbered houses. Take a stroll down the WALLANLAGEN (Rampart Walk) with its windmill, and have a look in the craft shops round there.

Hamburg

Germany's second largest city, after Berlin, and largest seaport. Unlike many of Germany's cities, Hamburg does not lack character or things to see.

STATION FACILITIES

	HAUPTBAHNHOF
Train information	All hours
	(Tel. 339 911)
Reservations	7 a.m.–8 p.m.
Tourist information	7 a.m.–11 p.m.
Foreign exchange	7.30 a.m.–10 p.m.
Left-luggage lockers	No access 2 a.m.–5 a.m.
Left-luggage store	6 a.m.–11.30 p.m.
Bar, Buffet	All hours
Restaurant	6 a.m.–12 midnight (intercity)
Waiting room	All hours
Post office	All hours

Daily trains to: Copenhagen (5 hours), Hanover (1½ hours), Frankfurt (5 hours), Vienna, Munich, Basel, Zürich, Milan, Bremen, Düsseldorf (4 hours), Cologne (4½ hours), Brussels, Paris.

TOURIST INFORMATION AND ADDRESSES

The main tourist information office is outside the station at Hachmannplatz. They'll supply you with maps, a fortnightly programme of local events 'Where to go in Hamburg', and the 'Hamburg Guide'.

There's a separate information office (Hotelnachweis) also at the station and they'll find you a bed for a fee.

Rail pass holders go free on Hamburg's S-Bahn.

TRANSALPINO: SSR, Rothenbaumchaussee 61 (Tel. 410 2081), Mon.–Fri.: 9 a.m.–6 p.m., Sat.: 9 a.m.–12 noon.

US CONSULATE: Alsterufer 28 (Tel. 441 061).

POST OFFICE: Münzstrasse 1, near the station. Poste restante and 24-hour telephone service is here also.

SEEING

The PORT dominates the city and is difficult to ignore. It's also quite interesting to watch what goes on and there are tours of it available. ST MICHAEL'S, the eighteenth-century baroque brick church, affords a good view from its tower. Of the many museums in Hamburg the best are: the HAMBURG ART GALLERY; the DECORATIVE ARTS AND CRAFTS MUSEUM; and the MILLERS VETERAN CAR MUSEUM. Take a day trip to the nearby open-air museums: the VIERLANDE MUSEUM (S-Bahn to Bergedorf) and the MUSEUM VILLAGE in Volksdorf (U-Bahn).

SLEEPING

There are plenty of cheap pensions north of the station along Steindamm and Bremer Reihe so you shouldn't have any problems. Consider spending ½ DM for the Hotelführer list available from the tourist office. Try Pension Nord at 22 Bremer Reihe (Tel. 244 693).

The two youth hostels are at Alfred-Wegener-Weg 5 (Tel. 313 488) and Rennbahnstrasse 100 (Tel. 651 1671). The best of the campsites is at Kielerstrasse 650 (Tel. 570 4498), closed 9 a.m.–4.30 p.m.

For cheap hotels – and there are plenty – head for the commercial area or, if you don't mind the noise of squeaking bedsprings, the red-light district.

EATING AND NIGHTLIFE

The university Mensa is at Schlüterstrasse 7 and is open for lunches. Being a port, seafood and fish restaurants are plentiful and good in Hamburg. Try the ones along Landungsbrücken or the Fischerhaus at the St Pauli fish market.

One thing Hamburg's not short of is nightlife. The famous Reeperbahn area is one of the liveliest in Europe with clubs, bars, legalized sex shops, discos and porno movie-houses abounding. Try to avoid getting ripped off as thousands of other tourists do, and don't wander into the Palais d'Amour or Eros Centre looking for a room, as these blocks of flats offer more than a bed for the night . . .

Lübeck

Only 40 minutes away from Hamburg is the attractive old town of Lübeck, former headquarters of the medieval trading group, the Hanseatic League. You'll see as many Scandinavians as Germans here as this is one of their favourite holiday destinations. Tourist information is in the station. Open Mon.–Sat.: 9 a.m.–1 p.m., 3 p.m.–8 p.m., Sun.: 10 a.m.–noon, at Speicher, Bechergrube 95.

Lübeck is renowned for its brickwork, so take a close look at the gabled houses, particularly BUDDENBROOKHAUS – the house Thomas Mann (a Lübecker) used as the background to his novel *Buddenbrooks*. The actual city centre is quite small and it's possible to walk round all the sights there: the thirteenth-century RATHAUS with its original black glazed tiles, the Romanesque ST MARIEN DOM, the HOLSTEYN GATE and the old city walls and MUSEUM.

The youth hostel is at Am Gertrudenkirchhof 4 (Tel. 3 34 33) and tourist information will find rooms for you.

The Central Belt and the Harz Mountains

Frankfurt, Düsseldorf and Bonn are all fairly modern industrial centres which have little to offer that is worth breaking your journey for. You do far better to head for centres like Marburg, Göttingen, Hannoversch-Münden, Karlshafen, Goslar or the resorts round Münster: Attendorn, Alt-Astenburg and Berleburg. These have far more of the aspects of German life you're probably looking for.

Baden-Württemberg – the Black Forest

The south-western region of Germany from Karlsruhe to Basel is considered by many travellers its most enchanting. The pace of life is slower and the villages and towns dotted round the forests really are as attractive as the tourist brochures make them look. The main towns of this region are Heidelberg, Freiburg, Tübingen, Baden-Baden and Stuttgart. The first three are picturesque old university towns and worth a day or two; unless you've time, forget Baden-Baden as it's very expensive, and Stuttgart is mostly an industrial city. A day trip from Heidelberg to Freiburg, Donaueschingen and Offenburg is a good 'pushed for time' introduction to this area.

Heidelberg

Famous for its university and magnificent castle, most of Heidelberg's sights can be seen in a day, but are nevertheless well worth seeing. Start your tour at the MARKTPLATZ and take in the HEILIG-GEIST KIRCHE and HAUS ZUM RITTER, a Renaissance mansion house, now a hotel and restaurant. The OLD UNIVERSITY has an interesting STUDENTS' JAIL which proves that graffiti weren't a twentieth-century invention. From here cross the Karl-Theodor Bridge over the River Neckar and take the PHILOSOPHER'S WALK to the 1,400-foot Heiligenberg. Apart from a good view of the town, there are reconstructed Roman ruins and the twelfth-century ST STEPHEN'S CLOISTER.

Inside the amazing SCHLOSS (castle) is the GERMAN APOTHECARY MUSEUM with interesting reconstructions of laboratories of the seventeenth century.

The tourist information office, just outside the station, is open Mon.–Sat.: 9 a.m.–7 p.m., Sun.: 2 p.m.–7 p.m. They run an accommodation-finding service for a small fee and supply you with leaflets and maps. Ask for 'All Around Heidelberg'. AMEX is at Friedrich-Ebert Anlage 16. Unitra, the student travel centre, is at 117 Hauptstrasse.

Hotels tend to be expensive as Heidelberg gets its fair share of middle-class, middle-aged tourists, so they don't exactly cater for eurorailers in a big way. Still, there's a youth hostel at Tiergarten-strasse (Tel. 42066), on bus route 11 with connecting tram at night, and a campsite at Heidelberg–Schlierbach (Tel. 802506).

Use the Mensa restaurants for meals: there's one off Universi-tätsplatz and another in Marstallhof – or a student inn. These are dotted all round the city.

Freiburg

An attractive city of 170,000 people which has fully recovered from its heavy wartime destruction and is restored and as picturesque as ever. Though the university is the source of most young Frei-burghers' social life, the summer schools based there make sure things don't grind to a halt outside term-time.

Two blocks down Eisenbahnstrasse from the station is the tourist information at Rotteckring 14. They'll arrange accommodation for you, or, if you're staying more than two days, you can get into private accommodation.

The Altstadt (Old Town) has at its centre the MÜNSTER – the beautiful medieval cathedral with its intricate carvings and gar-goyles. Opposite the cathedral to the south is the sixteenth-century KAUFHAUS (merchants' hall), and nearby is the RATHAUS (town hall) made out of two old patrician houses. Medieval and baroque art of the Upper Rhine can be seen in the AUGUSTINER MUSEUM.

There's a youth hostel and a campsite in Kartäuserstrasse at 151 and 99 respectively (Tel. 67656 and 35054). With woods and forests all around, you shouldn't be stuck for a place to pitch your tent, but if things are desperate see the Bahnhofmission at the station.

The last week of June sees the Wine Festival; Baden white wine is well worth trying, and Freiburg has many wine bars and cheap (by German standards) eating places. Concentrate on the university area and Augustinerplatz; note that there's a Mensa on the corner of Werderring and Bertoldstrasse.

Tübingen

The University of Tübingen, founded in 1477, still makes use of the town's Renaissance castle (SCHLOSS HOHENTÜBINGEN) and though you can't enter it, you can get a good view over the Old Town and the Neckar from its gardens. In the centre there are old gabled houses and a fifteenth-century church, STIFTSKIRCHE. In the Neckar on a man-made island is the PLATANENALLEE – an avenue of plane trees which makes a good walk. Reach it via the Eberhard Bridge.

The youth hostel is at Gartenstrasse 22/2 (Tel. 23002), ten minutes from the station, and there's a campsite on the banks of the Neckar (Tel. 23343). The university Mensa is on the corner of Wilhelmstrasse and Keplerstrasse and is open for lunches and dinners.

The Rhine Valley

The section of the 820-mile-long Rhine that flows through Germany is considered the most scenic, and the popular image of sailing down the Rhine is a pleasure cruiser passing vineyards, castles and cliffs. This is founded on truth but is somewhat idealistic as the Rhine today is still Europe's main commercial waterway and as such takes its fair share of barges and freight loads. Köln–Düsseldorfer lines run boats from Frankfurt to Düsseldorf which give a 50 per cent discount to Inter Railers and is free to Eurail card holders. The most attractive segment of the journey is from Rüdesheim to Koblenz, or vice versa; stop off at Oberwesel or Bacharach (spend the night in a castle youth hostel).

Cologne (Köln)

The main reason for stopping off at Cologne is undoubtedly the cathedral (KÖLNER DOM) which took from 1248 to 1880 to complete; see the fourteenth-century stained-glass windows, altarpiece and the Shrine of the Magi. In the Second World War, 90 per cent of Cologne was razed to the ground, but amazingly the cathedral escaped almost intact.

Other things of interest are the ROMAN-GERMANIC MUSEUM exhibiting Cologne's Roman remains and the WALLRAF-RICHARTZ-MUSEUM/MUSEUM LUDWIG with its impressive collection of German works. Even if you can only afford a few hours you should have no problems, as everything is very near the station.

STATION FACILITIES

	HAUPTBAHNHOF
Train information	All hours (Tel. 2761)
Reservations	Mon.–Sat.: 6.30 a.m.–9 p.m., Sun.: 8 a.m.–4 p.m.
Tourist information	Mon.–Sat.: 8 a.m.–9 p.m., Sun.: 9.30 a.m.–7 p.m. Located directly opposite cathedral Unter Fetterhennen, 19
Foreign exchange	7 a.m.–9 p.m.
Left-luggage lockers	Always accessible
Left-luggage store	All hours
Waiting room	In restaurant (with ticket only)
Bar, Buffet	7 a.m.–9 p.m. 'Milchstube','Bierfass', all hours except 4 a.m.–5 a.m. 'Treffpub'
Restaurant	8 a.m.–10 p.m. – 'Terrassen' and 6 a.m.–10 p.m. – 'Gaststätte'
Shops	Regular hours in pedestrian mall
Post office	7 a.m.–10 p.m. Nord Tunnel

Daily trains to: Düsseldorf (½ hour), Hamburg (4½ hours), Copenhagen, Hanover (3 hours), Mainz (1¾ hours), Frankfurt (2¼ hours), Würzburg (4 hours), Nürnberg (5 hours), Stuttgart (4 hours), Vienna, Munich, Innsbruck, Zürich, Basel (5 hours), Paris, Brussels (3 hours), Rotterdam (3½ hours), the Hague (4 hours), Amsterdam (3 hours).

The youth hostels are at Siegesstrasse 5a (Tel. 814711) and Konrad-Adenauer-Ufer, and there are cheap(ish) hotels in the side streets a few blocks from the cathedral. Tourist information will also find rooms from about 24 DM upwards. Transalpino is at Hohenzollernring 47 (Tel. 219803). Salzgasse in the Old Town is where to go for eats, and there are all the usual excellent department stores with food halls for buying groceries.

The Moselle Valley

Less commercial, and some say less scenic, is the Moselle region where wine making is the main regional industry, apart from tourism. Boats run between Trier and Koblenz (KD lines with the same reductions as on the Rhine). The towns to get off at are: BERNKASTEL-KUES, TRABEN-TRARBACH and COCHEM. You can hire bikes at one of these stations and return them at another. This is the region for wine tasting – ask at the tourist information offices for tours of the local cellars.

Trier

Germany's oldest city and one-time capital of the Western Roman Empire (with Roman baths, arches and amphitheatre remains to prove it), Trier has many interesting churches and museums, as well as the house where Karl Marx was born. Tourist information is next to the Porta Nigra, the youth hostel is at Maarstrasse 156 (Tel. 41092) and the campsites are at Monaisestrasse (Tel. 86210) and Luxemburgerstrasse 8 (Tel. 86921). The Mensa is across the Kaiser-Wilhelm Brücke and is open only for lunch.

Munich (München)

Munich is the capital of Bavaria and is regarded as the ultimate West German city. It is beautifully landscaped, tastefully decorated, carefully laid out and has a glut of things to do and see.

Ruled for over 650 years by the Wittelsbacher family who brought the world-famous art collections and rich architectural heritage to the city, Munich seems to have continual festivals all the year round: Fasching with its masked carnivals from January to February; the beer inaugurations in March; the summer season of concerts and operas from May to August; the famous Oktoberfest beer festival lasting from September to October, followed not long after by the Christmas markets. And this doesn't even take into account the countless student-based activities going on round SCHWABING, Munich's lively Latin quarter.

STATION FACILITIES

	MÜNCHEN HAUPTBAHNHOF
Train information	6 a.m.–11 p.m. (Tel. 592 991)
Reservations	5.30 a.m.–12 midnight in 'ABR Reisebüro'
Tourist information	Mon.–Sat.: 8 a.m.–11 p.m., Sun.: 1 p.m.–9.30 p.m.
Foreign exchange	6 a.m.–11 p.m.
Bar, Buffet	6 a.m.–10 p.m. 'Milchstube'
Cafeteria	6 a.m.–12 midnight
Restaurant	6 a.m.–12 midnight
Left-luggage lockers	Always accessible with valid ticket
Left-luggage store	6 a.m.–12 midnight
Shops	6 a.m.–10 p.m.
Waiting room	All hours
Post office	Mon.–Fri.: 7 a.m.–9 p.m., Sat.: 8 a.m.–9 p.m.
Station shuts	1 a.m.–4.30 a.m. Enter with tickets from Arnulfstrasse side

Daily trains to: Paris, Brussels, Stuttgart (2 hours), Mainz (4½ hours), Zürich (5 hours), Bologna, Florence, Milan, Venice, Vienna, Innsbruck (2¼ hours), Salzburg (1½ hours), Cologne, Düsseldorf, Hamburg, Würzburg (2½ hours), Frankfurt (4 hours) and Nürnberg (1¾ hours).

TOURIST INFORMATION

The Fremdenverkehrsamt (tourist office) (Tel. 239 1259) is at the front of the Hauptbahnhof, opposite platform 11, and is open Mon.–Sat.: 8 a.m.–11 p.m., Sun.: 1 p.m.–9.30 p.m. The staff are helpful, fluent in English and will supply you with maps and pamphlets and find you a room for a small charge. Get the monthly programme of events and the 'Young People's Guide to Munich'.

Munich's city transport system is one of the best in Europe, and also one of the most complicated. There are buses, trams, the U-Bahn and the S-Bahn. Note: Rail pass holders get free travel on the S-Bahn. There are various passes, including a 24-hour tourist one. You need only one ticket even if your journey takes in the tram, bus and underground systems. For further information, pick up leaflets at the underground at Hauptbahnhof, or S-Bahn stations.

● **Addresses:**
POST OFFICE: Bahnhofplatz 1 (opposite station). Open 24 hours. Also poste restante here.
UK CONSULATE: Amalienstrasse 62.
US CONSULATE: Königinstrasse 5.
CANADIAN CONSULATE: Max-Joseph Strasse 6 (Tel. 558531).
AMEX: Promenadeplatz 3, Mon.–Fri.: 9 a.m.–6 p.m.
MEDICAL HELP: Try university clinic at Ismaningerstrasse.
TRANSALPINO: Schwanthalerstrasse 2–6 (Tel. 557165), Mon.–Fri.: 9 a.m.–5.30 p.m.
STUDIOSUS-REISEN (Student Travel): Amalienstrasse 73 (Tel. 52380).

SEEING

MARIENPLATZ – the attractive pedestrian zone – is at the centre of Munich. The neo-Gothic TOWN HALL is located here (look out for the 11 a.m. glockenspiel show), as is the old town hall (ALTES RATHAUS). Just off Marienplatz is the twelfth-century church of ST PETER. If a white disc is out on the platform, climb its tower for a view extending to the Alps (a red disc means you'll just see over

Munich). Also near here is the FRAUENKIRCHE; this church, with its green onion-topped twin towers, is the symbol of the city and houses various works of art, tombs and relics as well as the mausoleum of Emperor Ludwig IV. ST MICHAEL'S CHURCH and the baroque THEATINER CHURCH are also worth a look. Eight blocks west of Marienplatz is KARLSPLATZ, the main square of Munich. All the city transport starts from here and SONNENSTRASSE, the main shopping street, begins. The palace of the Bavarian rulers (the RESIDENZ) houses a spectacular array of riches. Tours leave Tues.–Sat.: 10 a.m.–4.30 p.m., Sun. till 1 p.m. North of the Residenz is the university area (Schwabing) with Leopoldstrasse at its centre. Nothing much goes on in daytime here, but it's a lively place at night. To the east of Schwabing lies the ENGLISH GARDEN, ideal for sunbathing (nude!) and picnicking.

The ALTE PINAKOTHEK is one of Europe's finest art galleries. It specializes in early German, Flemish and Italian works and it's free on Sundays (closed Mondays). The NEUE PINAKOTHEK concentrates on modern art.

The DEUTSCHES MUSEUM is located on an island in the Isar River; it is the largest technical museum in the world (with lots of buttons to push), and has exhibits such as U-boats, a Messerschmitt jet fighter, a planetarium and old locomotives. The BAVARIAN NATIONAL MUSEUM gives a good introduction to what makes Bavaria different from the rest of Germany and has the most extensive collection of arts and crafts in the world (closed Mondays but open till 5 p.m. even on Saturdays).

SLEEPING

Munich is busy all year, particularly during the Oktoberfest when beds are very scarce. Still, there are plenty of places if you know where to look. Expect to pay about 25–35 DM for student accommodation, 25 DM at youth hostels and up to 60 DM in pensions. Ask at tourist information for the Accommodation Guide to Munich.

The cheapest sleep to be had is at the Youth Camp (Jugendlager Kapuzinerhölzl) at Kapuzinerhölzl (Tel. 1414300); open July–August, 5 p.m.–9 a.m. For 6 DM you get an air mattress, blankets and a place in the circus tent, not to mention tea in the mornings and evenings. You won't get turned away. Take U-Bahn line U1 to Rotkreuzplatz, then tram 12 to Botanischer Garten.

• **Youth hostels:** Wendl-Dietrich Strasse 20 (Tel. 131156) is large but strictly run; the one at Burgweg 4–6, Pullach (Tel. 7930643), is more fun, but this renovated castle fills up early. Take S-Bahn 7 to Pullach. Haus International, Elisabethstrasse 87 (Tel. 185081), is good but more expensive, so share in a large room to bring down the price. Finally, there's Jugendgästehaus at Miesingstrasse 4 (Tel. 7236550).

Some of the cheapest pensions are located in Schillerstrasse and Landwehrstrasse. Try Pension Schiller (Tel. 592435) at Schillerstrasse 11; further down the street at No. 32 there's Pension Bergbauer (Tel. 591005). Pension Alpina (Tel. 5380722) at Landwehrstrasse 49 has about thirty beds and does doubles for about 60 DM. The campsite, which is well equipped, is at Zentrallandstrasse 49 (Tel. 7231707), open March–Oct. Take U-Bahn to Implerstrasse, then bus 57.

EATING AND NIGHTLIFE

Bavarian cooking is tasty, filling and not for the weight-conscious. Munich's speciality is Weisswurst – a sausage made of veal and parsley. You can buy it at any number of stalls and eat it as a quick snack with a beer to keep you going. The VIKTUALIENMARKT is an attractive sight, but it's invariably cheaper to buy your supplies from one of the superb food halls of the department stores, Kaufhof Hertie or Deutscher Supermarkt. The displays and high standards in these places really open your eyes if you've been weaned on dull supermarkets at home.

The student canteens (Mensas) have cheap lunches at Arusstrasse 17 or Leopoldstrasse 13, open 12 noon–2 p.m., and all over Schwabing you'll find reasonably priced eating places. A quarter of the world's beer comes from Bavaria, and Munich is at the heart of this with its social life revolving round the beer halls and gardens. These are good places to eat, drink and make new friends. Avoid the touristy Hofbräuhaus as you're unlikely to meet the locals there; try instead the beer gardens in the English Garden or Schwabing. Augustinerkeller at Arnulfstrasse 52, Donisl at Marienplatz, and Hundskugel (Munich's oldest pub) at Hoherstrasse are more representative.

For nightlife, Schwabing is the area to head for. Studiosus-Reisen, Amalienstrasse 73, have tickets for concerts, theatres, etc., with reductions. There's music and dancing at The Drugstore, Feilitzschstrasse 12, and the unviersity have occasional 'events' such as open-air discos outside term-time which you can go along to if you can pass yourself off as a German student.

• **Excursions:** 22 km north-west of Munich is the concentration camp of DACHAU built in 1933. A visit here will put into perspective the atrocities that were committed and will leave an impression with you that all the opulence of Munich can't take away. The old administration block is now a museum, and a film in English is shown twice a day. Get there on the S-Bahn (free to Inter Railers): line 2 (Peterhausen) to Dachau, then bus 3 or L1 to the camp.

In contrast, the OLYMPIC VILLAGE of the 1972 Olympic Games shows you a healthy twentieth-century German venture. The stadium is impressive and you can go for a swim in the pool Mark Spitz used to win him his five gold medals. Take the bus or underground.

NYMPHENBURG PALACE AND PARK is Munich's Versailles. Home of the Bavarian kings, situated in a 495-acre park, the palace makes a pleasant day trip. Closed Mondays. Another idea for a trip is Europe's largest zoo, Hellabrunn, 6 km south of the city.

The Alps and the Romantic Road

The Romantische Strasse is the name for the undeniably scenic stretch from Füssen to the vineyards of Franconia. The towns en route are very picturesque, and this is the route to take for fairytale castles and medieval churches set among rolling green hills.

To get to those hidden little corners of Bavaria, the train is not the best way: use the Europabus 'Romantische Strasse'. They offer two alternative routes: Füssen to Würzburg, and Munich to Wiesbaden. Inter Railers get 25 per cent discount (free to Eurail card holders). Make further inquiries at the Starnberger Bahnhof part of Munich station.

Places of note en route are: NÖRDLINGEN with its perfectly preserved circular medieval fortifications and fifteenth-century St George's Church; DINKELSBÜHL, also with a St George's Church which is a Gothic masterpiece, 'Deutsches Haus' and Old Town Hall; ROTHENBURG – visit the Rathaus, St Jakob's Church and the Folterkammer (torture chamber); and WÜRZBURG.

Würzburg

In the heart of wine country, Würzburg is *the* baroque city of West Germany. The Franconian RESIDENZ is the magnificent palace of the prince-bishops and is the main sight of Würzburg. Open Tue.–Sun.: 9 a.m.–5 p.m. The MARIENBERG FORTRESS, another of the princes' homes, is on the other side of the River Main, which intersects the town. Near the fortress is the KÄPPELE, an ornate baroque church which allows you an excellent view from the top. The MAINFRÄNKISCHES MUSEUM houses sculptures and carvings and is located in the Marienberg Fortress.

STATION FACILITIES

	HAUPTBAHNHOF
Train information	7 a.m.–9 p.m.
	(Tel. 50 656)
Reservations	7 a.m.–9 p.m.
Tourist information	Mon.–Sat.: 8 a.m.–8 p.m.
	Pavilion outside station
Foreign exchange	Mon.–Fri.: 6 a.m.–9 p.m., Sat.: 9 a.m.–1 p.m.
	(in next building along)
Café	Mon.–Fri.: 7 a.m.–8 p.m.
	Sat.: 7.30 a.m.–2.30 p.m.
	Sun.: 11 a.m.–6 p.m.
Restaurant	6.30 a.m.–0.30 a.m.
Bath, Shower	6 a.m.–10 p.m.
Left-luggage lockers	Always accessible
Left-luggage store	Mon.–Sat.: 8 a.m.–5 p.m.
Waiting room	In restaurants
Shops	Regular hours
Post office	Mon.–Fri.: 6 a.m.–9 p.m.
	Sat.: 6 a.m.–8 p.m., Sun.: 9 a.m.–8 p.m.
	(in next building along)

Daily trains to: Nürnberg (1 hour), Vienna, Munich (2½ hours), Stuttgart (2¼ hours), Mainz (2¼ hours), Paris, Cologne (4 hours), Frankfurt (2¼ hours).

TOURIST INFORMATION

Located just in front of the station and in the centre at the Haus zum Falken, by the Marktplatz: Mon.–Thurs.: 8 a.m.–5 p.m., Fri.: 8 a.m.–12 noon. They'll find you a room for 2 DM.

SLEEPING AND EATING

The two youth hostels are: Burkarderstrasse 44 (Tel. 42590) and Frau-Holle-Weg 27, Heidingsfeld (Tel. 705913), just outside the town. Watch out for their early curfews! The campsite is at Mergentheimerstrasse 13B (Tel. 72536). Tram 5 gets you there.

Eat at the university Mensa in the Studentenhaus at the corner of Münzstrasse and Jahnstrasse. Open for lunch and dinner on weekdays.

West Berlin

There is literally no other city in Europe, or elsewhere, like West Berlin. This capitalist outpost was once as beautiful and cosmopolitan as Paris or London, but was reduced to rubble in the Second World War. Then in August 1961 the city was cut in two by the notorious Wall which split life on either side between the two political polarities. With a background as dramatic as this, it's only to be expected that West Berlin is a city of extremes and contradictions, the most interesting one being that West Berlin is actually in East Germany, 110 miles from the West German border. This was the city at the heart of the Cold War of the mid-twentieth century, and that alone makes it significant enough for a visit – it's not so much the sights that are worth coming for, as the atmosphere.

STATION FACILITIES

	BERLIN BAHNHOF ZOO
Train information	6 a.m.–10 p.m.
Reservations	Mon.–Fri.: 6 a.m.–9 p.m.
	Sat. and Sun.:
	8 a.m.–4 p.m.
Tourist information	In Europa Centre, 7.30 a.m.–10.30 p.m.
Foreign exchange	Mon.–Sat.: 8 a.m.–9 p.m., Sun.: 10 a.m.–6 p.m.
Left-luggage lockers	Available, but quite small
Restaurant	6 a.m.–12 midnight
Post office	Always open
Station shuts	12 midnight–5 a.m.

• **Getting there:** The following places are the checkpoints between West Germany and East Germany: Büchen–Schwanheide, Bebra–Gerstungen, Helmstedt–Marienborn, Hof–Gutenfürst and Ludwigsstadt–Probstzella. As you've to travel more than 100 miles of East German territory, you'll be issued with a transit visa at the checkpoint. There's no limit to the foreign currency you can take into East Germany (including West German Marks), but you must not take any East German Marks either into or out of East Germany. Keep receipts for everything you spend.

Rail passes are *not* valid past the East German border. Buy a ticket on the train (50–60 DM) or, if you're organized, buy your ticket from the nearest Student Travel Centre; Transalpino tickets save you a bit.

There are good connections from West Germany to West Berlin, and you should experience no difficulties at any stage of this trip (you won't get roughed up just because you pass briefly through a Communist country, contrary to popular myth). Get off at Bahnhof Zoo in the centre.

TOURIST INFORMATION AND ADDRESSES

TOURIST OFFICE: On the Budapesterstrasse side of the Europa Centre, open daily 7.30 a.m.–10.30 p.m. Accommodation service for a small fee. Ask for the leaflet 'Tips for Young Berlin Visitors'.

Among other bits of interesting information, it lists 20 or so cheap pensions.

POST OFFICE: Bahnhof Zoo. Twenty-four hours. Also poste restante here.

AMEX: Kurfürstendamm 11 (2nd floor), Mon.–Fri.: 8.30 a.m.–5.30 p.m., Sat.: 9 a.m.–12 noon.

ARTU REISEBÜRO: Hardenbergstrasse 9. Student Travel office selling Transalpino tickets back to Bundesrepublik, and IUS card. Open Mon., Tue., Thur., Fri.: 9.30 a.m.–2 p.m., 3 p.m.–7 p.m., Wed.: 10.30 a.m.–2 p.m., 3 p.m.–6 p.m.

UK CONSULATE: Uhlandstrasse 7.

US CONSULATE: Clayallee 170.

CANADIAN CONSULATE: Europa Centre (12th floor), Tel. 261 161.

SEEING

Ironically, the WALL is one of the tourist attractions of today. You can stand on wooden pedestals at various points and look over into East Berlin – the one at the Brandenburg Gate gives a particularly clear view. If this whets your appetite and you want to go over and spend a day 'behind the Iron Curtain', do the following: take the underground to Bahnhof Friedrichstrasse, or get yourself to Checkpoint Charlie. If you're going in for just the day (i.e., you'll be back by midnight), you need to show your passport and then change about 30 DM to East German Marks (and you must spend all this over there). You're not allowed any Western printed matter (we've had the *Economist* and *Cosmopolitan* firmly taken off us) and there are strict dos and don'ts as to what you can and can't take in and out. Near the checkpoint is the MUSEUM OF THE WALL which tells its story. For details on East Berlin, see the chapter on East Germany, above.

KAISER-WILHELM GEDÄCHTNISKIRCHE: this church is the focal point of the city, and in many ways tells its story. It's been built, bombed, rebuilt and preserved and is as much a mixture of old and new as Berlin itself. TIERGARTEN is a beautiful park, next to the city zoo which has more species than any other in the world. Next to the zoo is the world's most extensive collection of fish and reptiles in the

Aquarium on Budapesterstrasse. SCHLOSS CHARLOTTENBURG lies a few miles north-west of Berlin. This seventeenth-century palace houses several galleries and museums and is the best example of Prussian architecture you'll find around Berlin (closed Mondays). DAHLEM MUSEUM is a complex of seven museums (closed Mondays), so you're bound to find something to interest you. The BAUHAUS MUSEUM with exhibits of the school's designs (closed Tuesdays and Wednesday mornings), and the photographic story of German nineteenth- and twentieth-century history at the REICHSTAG BUILDING are both interesting visits.

SLEEPING

Finding a bed isn't easy and this is one city where you would be really wise to book ahead; write about two to three weeks in advance, to the Tourist Board: Verkehrsamt Berlin, Europa Centre, 1000 Berlin 30, stating how much you can pay. If you aren't organized enough to plan ahead, don't worry; ask at tourist information for their map of Berlin with all the hotel and hostel listings.

• **Youth hostels:** Hermsdorferdamm 48, Berlin 28 (Tel. 404 1610) is well out of the town centre, but good. Needs a month's advance booking. Alternatively, try Bayernallee 36, Berlin 19 (Tel. 305 3055); Kluckstrasse 3, Berlin 30 (Tel. 261 1097) is central.

• **Pensions:** The area round Fasanenstrasse, Uhlandstrasse and Meinekestrasse is your best bet. Also on Carmerstrasse, Grolmann-strasse and Knesebeckstrasse. Try Pension Savoy (Tel. 881 3700) at Meinekestrasse 4; just next door are Pension Zeinert (Tel. 881 3319) at No. 5 and Pension Witzleben (Tel. 881 6395) at No. 6. For good doubles try Pension Fisher at Nürnbergerstrasse 24A (Tel. 246 808), near the station.

• **Camping:** Zeltplatz Kladow 1 and 11, Krampnitzer Weg 111/117 (Tel. 365 2797). Zeltplatz Dreilinden, Albrechts Teerofen (Tel. 805 1201).

If you're desperate, the Bahnhof Mission in the station will help out, or go out to the Grünewald and sleep there.

EATING AND NIGHTLIFE

The department stores have good cafeterias and there are fast-food chains and sausage stands. Try Zum Ambrosius at Lützowplatz for traditional German meals at reasonable prices.

Berlin's a big cultural centre and there's always plenty happening in the evenings. Festival follows festival and the student community is large and active. Head off to the area round Konstanzerstrasse, Düsseldorferstrasse, Joachim-Taler Strasse and Lietzenburger-strasse. With literally thousands of pubs, clubs and discos you should find something to occupy you. In the Irish Pub on Eisena-cherstrasse you're guaranteed to meet a fellow Brit, and in Leierkasten on Zossenerstrasse you'll bump into the local students. 'Tip' – the bi-weekly listing of what's on, is worth buying if you're staying a while.

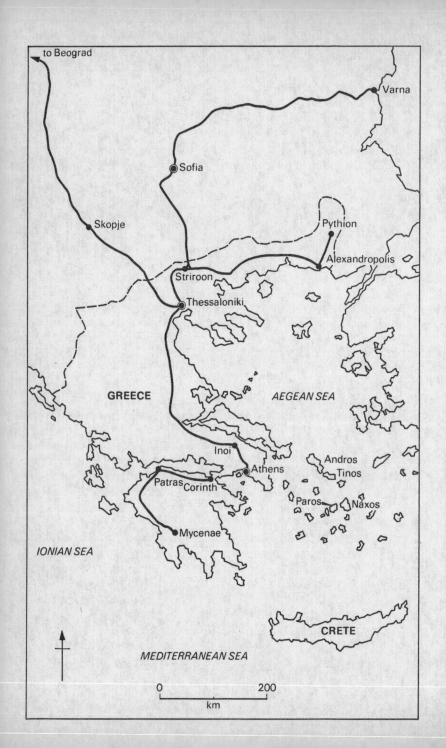

GREECE

Entry requirements	Passport
Population	9,000,000
Capital	Athens (pop.: 2,750,000)
Currency	Drachma
	£1 = approx. 165 dr.
Political system	Republic
Religion	Greek Orthodox
Language	Greek (some English and French spoken)
Public holidays	1, 6 Jan.; Shrove Monday; 25 March;
	Good Friday; Easter Sunday; Easter Monday;
	1 May; 11 June; 15 Aug.; 28 Oct.; 25, 26 Dec.

Every year, Greece acts like a magnet to thousands of eurorailers from the north. So many come that the summertime population increases by about 50 per cent. The islands in particular offer the best under-30 social scene you're likely to find. Ironically, it's much easier to get to know Germans and Swedes here than Greeks, and you get to know them very well indeed if you share the same nudist beach for long enough. It's difficult to have a bad holiday in Greece, the birthplace of Western civilization, which provides a haven not only for lovers of nature, but also for those interested in history, archaeology and the arts.

Greek history begins about 2,500 BC with the Minoan civilization on Crete, a thousand years before the Mycenaeans got it together on the mainland. The classical period began during the eighth century BC and reached its peak in fifth-century BC Athens. As independent city-states the Greeks shared the same culture, but were always at each other's throats, until Alexander the Great sorted them out during the third century BC, uniting former rivals and himself conquering a world empire. By the fifth century AD, Greece had become part of the Byzantine Empire, and was eventually conquered by the Turks in the fifteenth century. The War of Independence in 1821 started the formation of the modern Greek state, a process which ended in 1947 with the return of the Dodecanese. They still play cricket on Corfu which, along with other Ionian islands, was under British rule till 1864. After the Germans pulled out in 1944, civil war broke out and continued for five years, seriously hindering Greece's postwar recovery. Away from the beaches, things are less serene. Relations with Turkey remain as strained as ever, particularly after the invasion of Cyprus in 1974. High inflation and low per capita income compared with other EEC countries characterize the economy. Greece's recent history is almost as complex and unstable as her past. If stuck for conversation, it's a safer bet to have a crack at the Turks than to discuss the monarchy (of her six kings since independence, four have been deposed and one assassinated).

● **Getting there:** Travelling there by train is still the cheapest way of getting to Greece, the islands and the sun. Charter flights become more expensive every year and offer little in the way of flexibility. No matter how bad things might sometimes seem by train, console yourself with the knowledge that they would have been a lot worse by bus. But there are problems in going by train, not least of which is deciding on your route.

● **The Belgrade–Athens run:** Nearly all ex-eurorailers have their own version of this recurring horror story. In theory, the journey through Yugoslavia seems attractive enough, especially when weighed against the ever-increasing ferry fares from Brindisi to Patras. In reality, the story is often very different: trains are nearly always late on departure from Belgrade – that is, if they depart at all. When and if they do, it's no exaggeration to say that they can be ten hours or more late on arrival at Athens. If you think that's bad enough, there's worse to come. The authorities take the view that eurorailers are a sub-species and make no effort to provide anything like the number of coaches needed for what must be one of the busiest lines in Europe during the summer. If you're lucky, there's water for two or three hours; if not, we hope you have a good bladder. If you travel in midsummer you're likely to end up on the floor, or standing with your head out of a window to escape the smell of the loos, unless you heed this good advice:

1. If you can travel out of season, do so or at least try to avoid mid-July/August.
2. Go for the fastest train possible – it's well worth the supplement. Try and get on the through-train from Munich or Vienna, or travel overnight in a couchette/sleeper.

3. Reserve a seat well ahead of time or, if that's not possible, arrive early and look for German or Austrian coaches.
4. Take along plenty to eat and *drink*. Remember: the trains aren't air-conditioned and you don't know how long a train may stop en route.
5. Don't make arrangements to meet someone at the other end or keep your schedule too tight unless you can't avoid it.
6. Go on board determined to make friends, and try and look on the whole episode as an educational experience.

When you reach Thessaloniki, things pick up no end. When it comes to soft drinks and refreshments, it's a seller's market, a fact which the keen-eyed but smiling traders know all too well as they descend on those who had set off unprepared.

● **The Italian run:** The problems faced by travellers in Italy are normally a considerably watered-down version of those faced in Yugoslavia. Trains are crowded and the toilets dirty. Your real problems start at Brindisi, beginning with the mile walk straight down to the docks.

Unfortunately, there are no reductions with the Inter Rail, so anyone under 26 will have to pay the normal student deck-class fare. It's best to shop around as there are several rival companies offering different deals, many of which send their punters to meet the trains at Brindisi station. None of them is cheap and prices rise dramatically each year. Expect to pay about 65,000 L plus a port tax of about 8,000 L. Some ferries stop off at Corfu, which is an optional extra worth thinking about. If you intend stopping off there, tell them when you buy your ticket, as it's an extra 2,000 L or so port tax. There's no way round these extra port taxes and supplements, and it's the same at the Greek end of the operation. One of the best lines is the Hellenic Mediterranean Lines (HML)/Adriatica Lines. From the pier, take your ticket and passport to the police station (second floor), where you'll get the necessary stamps. Those travelling on Transalpino are OK as your ticket includes the boat fares. Eurail Pass holders have to pay a supplement of 20,000 L when travelling between 10 June and 30 September, but apart from this one extra you get to travel free providing you stick to the deck (seats are extra).

How eventually you decide to go depends largely on your tolerance level, what type of ticket you hold, and how much you can afford.

GREEK RAILWAYS
(Organismos Sidirodromoń Ellados, OSE)

A quick look at any rail map will show you that Greece's network is hardly a match for northern Europe's. Only the major cities are connected, and the few trains there are will seem slow except by East European standards. The international long-distance trains are somewhat optimistically called 'expresses'. Some of these require a small supplement of about 100 dr. Local trains are slow enough to enable you to strike up lasting friendships. (By the time you arrive you'll feel as if you were born with your fellow travellers.) There are no Inter Rail bonuses in Greece, but always ask for student discounts.

● **Eurail bonuses:** Free:
—Eurail Pass and Eurail Youthpass travellers can use steamers (*Appia, Egnatia, Espresso Grecia, Castalia*) operated by the Hellenic Mediterranean and Adriatica di Navigazione between Patras and Brindisi and vice versa. However, between 1 June and 30 September, they must pay a £5 ($8) high-season surcharge. During July and August, advance reservation, which costs £1.20 ($2), is recommended. Special accommodations (airline-type seats or cabins) and port taxes are extra. Before boarding, all passengers must check in at the Shipping Line Office at the pier. Passengers who wish to break their voyage at Corfu must declare their intention of 'stop over' upon delivery of the ticket.

Reduced fares:
—30 per cent reduction on the published full fares of the Adriatica Line between Piraeus–Venice or Alexandria and vice versa, on the *Espresso Egitto*. Contact the local Adriatica offices.

TRAIN INFORMATION

English is spoken by information officers at all major stations. Also pick up the Tourist Board's booklet, 'General Information about Greece'.

• **Reservations:** Wherever else in Europe you may decide against not reserving, it's well worth thinking about it here. The rule is to book a seat as far in advance as possible for international trains. It pays to be organized here; hundreds aren't. It's not possible to reserve on internal routes within Greece.

• **Night travel:** Couchettes and sleepers are both cheap by European standards. If you can get one, go for it.

TOURIST INFORMATION

For information about the country, accommodation and the main sights, see the National Tourist Organization of Greece (NTOG). For any other local information see the tourist police. Don't be put off by their name. Their role is to help you find accommodation and sort out your problems.

• **ISIC bonuses:** Up to 50 per cent off internal flights and ferries, up to 80 per cent on theatres and museums. For further information contact Student Travel Service, 1 Fillellinon St, Athens.

• **Money matters:** 1 drachma (dr.) = 100 lepta.
Banking hours are Mon.–Fri.: 8 a.m.–1.30 p.m. Some branches are open till 2.30 p.m., but don't rely on it. Also a word of warning: if you still have some dinar left over from Yugoslavia, you can only change them at the National Bank of Greece. It's best to change all your drachma before you leave Greece. All banks give the same rate and there are no commission charges. You can also change money at the Post Office (ELTA) and the Telecommunications Organization (OTE).

• **Post offices:** Stamps can also be bought from kiosks, but with a 10 per cent surcharge.

• **Shops:** Open Mon., Wed., Sat.: 8 a.m.–2.30 p.m., Tue., Thur., Fri.: 8 a.m.–1 p.m. and 5 p.m.–8.30 p.m. Supermarkets tend to close at 2 p.m. or 3 p.m.

• **Museums:** Open in winter 9 a.m.–3.30 p.m.; summer 7.30 a.m.–5.00 p.m. They tend to close on Mondays or Tuesdays, and give free admission on Thursdays and Sundays.

SLEEPING

Greece presents the greatest variety of possibilities in all of Europe. Hotels are graded A, B, C, D and E. For a C-class hotel, expect to pay at least 700 dr. each. Student hostels are open to any paying customers. Many also offer sleeping on the roof during summer. The youth hostels are nothing to get excited about. As usual, to stay you need an IYHF card. It's possible to get one in Athens if you haven't already got one. Some pensions and hotels charge 10 per cent extra for short stays during high summer and charge extra for showers. Off season, the boot's on the other foot and it's worth bargaining to get the price down. All hotel prices are fixed and should be posted at the reception. Expect to pay an extra 100 dr. tax in the summer.

The National Tourist Board issues a list with all the official campsites and facilities, but unfortunately not the prices, which vary greatly. Expect to pay at least 250 dr. per person. Also on the outskirts of some towns there are unofficial camps with fewer facilities.

On the islands, accommodation is hopelessly inadequate. Camping is illegal on many islands but nearly everyone is forced to do it at some stage as during July and August all the hotels and private rooms are full. The police are stepping up action and the official policy of NTOG now is that you can't come to Greece by cheap charter flight without having prebooked accommodation. Use your own discretion, but if you're camping illegally keep the place clean.

EATING AND NIGHTLIFE

Don't expect to eat as cheaply as you would have done a few years ago as high inflation continues to push up prices. Even old hands sometimes get a shock when they convert the bill into sterling or dollars. Unfortunately, some small shops and bakeries operate a two-tier price system (one for tourists, one for the locals), so if prices aren't marked, ask first. If you're going to the islands it's easy to live off bread, cheese and water melon (karpouzi) during the day, and eat out at night. If you need that added luxury of a cup of coffee for breakfast to see you through the day, be sure to ask for Nescafé or you'll end up with sweet Greek coffee instead. (Don't make the mistake of calling it Turkish.)

When eating out, as often as not you'll be ushered into the kitchen. Take your time, as this is the local custom of choosing. Arni is lamb; moschari, veal; chirino, pork; kotópoulo, chicken. Avoid the fish unless you've got plenty of money or are on the islands where it's fresh. Moussaka is a combination of meat with potato or eggplant, in tomato sauce. Dolmades are minced meat and rice wrapped in vine leaves and are delicious hot or cold. Eating out is a leisurely affair and gives one the opportunity in the islands of seeing what people look like with their clothes on. If you're down on your luck, there's always a souvlaki stand (meat kebab wrapped in bread) not far away. For drinks, don't overdo it with ouzo (the local aniseed spirit), or you'll know all about it the next morning. For the evening meal, try at least one bottle of the local retsina (with resin) before returning (as most do) to the aretsinato wine. During the summer months, the Athens Festival takes place. This includes open-air performances in the Herodes Atticus Odeon – an experience you're not likely to forget. For details on this and other events, contact the Athens Festival Box Office, 4 Stadiou St. There are numerous local festivals celebrating everything from Easter to wine. The Greeks use any excuse to have one, as they love to let their hair down and dance. Once a bouzouki gets going, anything can happen. Nightclubs are dull and expensive by comparison. Films are shown in their original language, and are always cheaper in the suburbs.

Northern Greece

If you're entering Greece from Yugoslavia or Bulgaria, your first main centre will be Thessaloniki. This is Greece's second city, founded in 315 BC, but unless you're desperate for a break there's not that much in Thessaloniki to merit stopping off. If you do though, take a stroll through the OLD TURKISH QUARTER, visit the ARCHAEOLOGICAL MUSEUM and the third- and fifth-century churches of ST GEORGE and ST DEMETRIUS.

Northern Greece is real 'spaghetti western' country. The mountains are rugged and the scenery wild and untamed. The two provinces of this area are Macedonia and Thrace.

South-east of Thessaloniki is the self-governing monastic commune of Mount Athos (no female has been allowed in for 900 years). If you want to visit, you'll have to go through your embassy and be able to give a sound reason for your visit.

To see some exceptional early Christian art and visit six Byzantine monasteries is much easier – just get yourself to METEORA, north of Kalambaka (take the bus from there).

The Peloponnese

The most southerly part of Greece's mainland is separated from the central belt by the Isthmus of Corinth. The Peloponnese has remnants of every people who have ever occupied that land: Greeks, Turks, Franks and Venetians. It is an untouristy region and on the main circular line from Patras to Athens lie Kalamata, Tripolis, Argos and Corinth. Near Argos lies the delightful town of Nafplio which is as yet unspoilt. (There's a good youth hostel in the town which does not require a YHA card.)

The main town is CORINTH, though there are two Corinths: the new town, which has nothing much to recommend it, and the old town which has. The station will leave you in the new town, but buses leave every half-hour for 'Arhea Korinthos'. Here you can see columns from the sixth-century Temple of Apollo and the rostrum from which St Paul preached Christianity to the Corinthians. If you're staying overnight in New Corinth, try Hotel Akti (Tel. 2337) down by the sea.

Just down the line is MYCENAE which dates back to 3,000 BC and is one of Greece's high spots for archaeologists. Many of the treasures found here are now in Athens, but you can still see the 'Gate of the Lions', royal tombs and the 'Treasure of Atreus'. The youth hostel is at Athens-Fihtia (Tel. 66224). They offer beds for 400 dr., or the roof for half that.

Still going south, you'll come to EPIDAURUS whose main attraction is the well-preserved fourth-century BC amphitheatre, in which classical Greek dramas are staged during the summer.

Don't bother with SPARTA (there's not much left); but MYSTRA, 7 km away (50 dr. bus journey), has an impressive display of Byzantine churches, palaces and a castle.

PATRAS is the largest town of the Peloponnese. It's where you're likely to land if you take the ferry to Greece from Brindisi, southern Italy. There's not that much to see here, but if you've time to kill waiting for a ferry, visit the VENETIAN CASTLE, ARCHAEOLOGICAL MUSEUM, MUNICIPAL THEATRE and churches of PANTOKRATOR and AGIOS ANDREAS.

Trains run (though not very often) to OLYMPIA, site of the first Olympic Games. See the stadium, the excellent museum, and stay in the youth hostel (Tel. 22580).

Athens

Athens, 'the cradle of Western civilization', can offer you what is generally considered to be the high spot of a European tour: a visit to the 'high city' of the ancient Greeks, the Acropolis. It can also offer you dirty, squalid accommodation, unbearable heat, so-so food, and street after street of ugly concrete blocks. Modern Athens has nothing much to offer, but it's all worth while when you climb up to see the classical beauty of the white-stoned Parthenon, Temple of Athena and the beginnings of Western drama, the Theatre of Dionysus. If you're going island-hopping, Athens – or rather Piraeus, its port – is your starting point. Ferries leave from here for scores of islands (there are 1,500 to choose from in the Aegean and Ionian seas), and the average fare for a deck passenger on a 5-hour sail is about 1,200 dr.

STATION FACILITIES

If you're travelling to the Peloponnese or Patras (for the ferry to Italy) use the Athinai-Peloponnese station, adjacent to the Larissa station (six Patras trains daily).

	ATHINAI LARISSA
Train information	6 a.m.–11.30 p.m. (Tel. 522 2491)
Reservations	At OSE office, Karolou 1–3
Tourist information	7 a.m.–12 midnight at tourist police station
Foreign exchange	7 a.m.–7 p.m.
Left-luggage office	6 a.m.–12 midnight
Restaurant	5 a.m.–12 midnight
Post office	Mon.–Fri.: 6 a.m.–8 p.m., Sat.: 7 a.m.–8 p.m. Sun.: 2 p.m.–7.30 p.m.

Daily trains to: Thessaloniki, Belgrade–Trieste–Venice, or Belgrade–Munich–Dortmund.

TOURIST INFORMATION

The tourist police are at the station, and there's an information desk in the National Bank of Greece on Syntagma Square (Tel. 32 22545), open Mon.–Sat.: 8 a.m.–8 p.m. The main office of NTOG is at 2 Amerikis St (Tel. 32 23111). Pick up the free map and leaflets on campsites, hostels, etc. They don't operate an accommodation-finding service, so basically you're on your own. The headquarters of the tourist police is at 7 Singrou Avenue, and to call them for help dial 171. A good source for information on museums and shop hours is the *Athenian* which is published in English.

• **Addresses:**
POST OFFICE: 100 Eolou St, near Omonia Square. Also Syntagma Square.
OTE OFFICE (main telephone office): 28 Oktavriou No. 85, open 24 hours.
AMEX: 2 Syntagma Square, weekdays: 8.30 a.m.–5.30 p.m., Sat.: 8.30 a.m.–1.30 p.m.

UK EMBASSY: 1 Plutarchou (Tel. 736211).
US EMBASSY: 91 Vasilias Sofias (Tel. 712951).
CANADIAN EMBASSY: 4 Loannou Genadiou St (Tel. 7239511).
AUSTRALIAN EMBASSY: 15 Messogheion Avenue (Tel. 3604611).
FIRST AID: 21 Tritis Septemvriou (Tel. 150).
TRANSALPINO: 28 Nikis St (Tel. 3220503)

● **Getting about:** Looking at the taxis' tariffs, they seem a huge bargain, but by the time you've been ripped off – which seems to happen to most tourists – they don't work out as such a hot idea. The buses and trolley-buses, when they're not on strike, are OK but usually packed. You can take a bus out to the nearby beaches from the bus station in the centre of town.

SEEING

Athens reached its zenith around 400 BC when Plato, Socrates and Aristotle were strolling around the Acropolis which today is the heart of the city. What's worth seeing in Athens – the antiquities – are all clustered round the old town, or PLAKA district. The ACROPOLIS should be seen as soon as it opens (9 a.m.) before the hordes swarm up and destroy its atmosphere. The PARTHENON, the temple dedicated to the goddess Athena, is held up as the epitome of architectural perfection. See also the ERECHTHEION, TEMPLE OF ATHENA NIKE and the PROPYLAEA, the gates to the ancient city. The ACROPOLIS MUSEUM is a must. It contains some of the finds: statues, friezes, etc.

The Acropolis stays open till 8 p.m. weekdays, 4.30 p.m. on Sundays, when it's free. Entrance is 100 dr. (50 dr. on ISIC). PNYX HILL offers a beautiful view of the Acropolis, and there's a *son et lumière* show here at 9 p.m. each night.

The ancient AGORA, north of the Acropolis, was the marketplace and still has the remains of the old administrative centre. The TEMPLE OF HEPHAISTOS is considered the best preserved in Greece. This site opens at 8 a.m. and is well worth a visit.

The NATIONAL ARCHAEOLOGICAL MUSEUM, 28 Oktomuriou St, has the best collection of ancient Greek artefacts in the world: gold death-masks, vessels, jewellery, statues, tombstones, frescoes, etc., dating from 1500 BC. Open 8.30 a.m.–7 p.m. weekdays, 10 a.m.–4.30 p.m. Sundays. Closed Mondays.

SYNTAGMA (Constitution) Square, is the centre of modern Athens. This is where you'll find the hotels and cafés you can't afford. Constitution Square is flanked on one side by the Greek Parliament. From here take Amalias Avenue for the attractive NATIONAL GARDENS and HADRIAN'S ARCH. Also in this direction lie the PRESIDENTIAL PALACE and the OLYMPIC STADIUM.

The famous FLEA MARKET on Ifestiou St makes a colourful walk and can produce some good bargains in equipment and leather goods – but barter.

SLEEPING

There are literally hundreds of places to stay in Athens that fall into the economical category, and even though it's up to you to find your own room, unless you're arriving very late on an August night you should be OK. That's not to say that these places are clean, friendly or have even the bare essentials, but they are cheap.

Head first for the Plaka as it's not only an attractive central place to stay (right underneath the Acropolis) but also one of the cheapest districts. Basically, the nearer to Syntagma Square you end up, the more you can expect to pay.

You may well find young blokes from various student hostels (unofficial ones, some of which are fairly grotty) joining the trains just before Athens extolling the virtues of their establishments and handing out leaflets. Don't be put off by them all – the Joy on Ferron 38 (Tel. 8231012) is particularly OK, and near the station.

If you aren't completely numbed by the long, gruesome journey (particularly if you're hot off the notorious Belgrade–Athens run), try cutting right back on expenses and sleep on the roofs. Many hostels offer you a place for 300 dr. or less, and at least it's cool. For a single, on average, expect to pay 400–700 dr., doubles 900 dr. and dormitory beds 400 dr.

Try: Student's Inn, 16 Kidathineon (Tel. 3244 808) – the cleanest, best-equipped and most reasonably priced place we've ever found in Athens. Clare's House, 16a Frynichou St (Tel. 3229284) – attractive converted house, a bit more expensive. John's Place, 5 Patrou St (Tel. 3229719) – clean and comfy. Tony's Pension, 26 Faharitsa St (Tel. 9236370), is OK, as is Pension Propilea, 28 Propileon St, just round the corner and under the same management. The youth hostel at 57 Kypselis St (Tel. 8225860) is always pretty busy and not too central, but it's cheap. For hotels, try round Apollonos St or Hotel Eva, 31 Victoros Ougo (Tel. 5223079) near the station. The nearest campsite is quite far out: 190 Athinon Avenue, Peristeri (Tel. 5814114); it is generally not worth the hassle of getting there, but if you must, take bus 67, 68 or 150.

If you're still stuck for a bed, drop into the ISYTS student centre at 11 Nikis St, and they'll help you out.

EATING AND NIGHTLIFE

The advice is easy – head for the Plaka. There are lots of restaurants, bars and discos there. The port of Piraeus is also lively at night, particularly Zea Marina, and in the National Park people gather on summer evenings to see performing artists.

For cheap eats, fill up on the shish kebabs (souvlaki) and dolmades (vine leaves stuffed with meat). Avoid the fruit from stalls as it's overpriced and the quality suspect. Try Xynos or Aerides in the Plaka.

• **Excursions from Athens:** 69 km away is the amazing TEMPLE OF POSEIDON on Cape Sounion. It dates back to 500 BC and is dedicated to the God of the Sea. Like the Acropolis, get there as early as possible; buses leave from Mavromateon St on the hour.

For DELPHI, take the local train to Levadia and take the bus direct from there. This is the site of the Delphic Oracle and was the holiest place in Greece. Little is left of the Temple of Apollo but there's still a 400 BC theatre and the stadium where the Pythian Games were held.

The Islands

For many, Greece is the islands. In fact, it is so for very many. Each year quiet fishing villages are becoming tourist-saturated, and while some remote islands probably still have a decade or so to go before they're turned into mini Majorcas, many have only a year or two, and some are there already. For a remote haven, choose an island which has only a weekly sailing from Piraeus – the fewer the ferries, the less the crowds. Another way to find a 'goodie' is to ask backpackers. Three things to bear in mind:

1. Buy your ticket from one of the agencies in Piraeus, not on the boat – they charge 20 per cent surcharge.
2. Unless you enjoy a good strong gust knocking your tent down or throwing sand up in your face, avoid the southern Aegean islands in August. They can receive the incredibly strong meltemi (southern wind) which can really muck up your sunbathing and sightseeing.
3. If you plan on going far afield, go for an overnight boat as it costs no extra to sleep on deck and saves you the price of a night's accommodation at the other end.

The Argo Saronics

These islands are within 4 hours of Athens, and consequently are among the most touristy and expensive. AEGINA is the closest to Athens. Look for bed and food around the port in Aegina town and admire the view from the TEMPLE OF ATHENA. The bay of Agia Marina has the best beaches but is packed out with Athenians at weekends.

POROS is packed out in summer, but for a reason. It has beautiful beaches and lush pinewoods. The tourist information in the town of Poros will help you find a bed – avoid hotels. See the MONASTERY OF KALAVRIA.

HYDRA, 3½ hours from Piraeus, is one of the beautiful people's islands, consequently the prices, especially along the harbour, are crippling. For a truly memorable view, climb up to the hilltop monastery of AGIA TRIADA. Hydra is all you expect a Greek island to be: narrow winding streets, donkeys (no cars allowed), beaches and blue sea and sky. The tourist police (Tel. 52205) will find you rooms, which are cheaper at the other side of the town.

SPETSES is a small wooded island of great charm with AGII ANAR-GIRI as its best beach. The harbour town of Spetsai has the two cheap hotels (the Acropole and the Saronicos) and the tourist police on Botassi St.

The Cyclades

These are the most visited of the Aegean islands. There are 211 of them in all, but it's still possible to find a few of the inhabited ones that will offer you relative 'splendid isolation'. The 'dry islands' of SIFNOS, SIKINOS, SERIFOS and MILOS are relatively quiet, but their landscape is rather arid. ANDROS and TINOS are very attractive and large enough to allow the tourists to spread themselves out. MYKONOS is *the* Greek island. It's very beautiful, very very touristy, very expensive and very gay. There are nude beaches (the Paradise beach and Super Paradise – but watch out, boys, as they are mostly gay) and countless discos, clubs and restaurants. There's also what was there before the thousands of tourists: whitewashed houses, windmills and 365 churches. There's a youth hostel and a few reasonably priced hotels: the Philip (Tel. 22294), the Apollon (Tel. 22223) and the Kakboni (Tel. 22475).

There are boat trips (73 dr.) from Mykonos to DELOS, ancient religious centre of the Greek world, where you can see the ruins of the Sanctuary of Apollo, the Terrace of Lions and the archaeological museum.

PAROS is almost ruined now, and all that makes it worth the trip is its beautiful old church, Panagia Ekatontapiliani.

NAXOS is considered by many the most beautiful of the Cyclades islands. Its capital, Naxos town, has cheap rooms and tavernas. See the beautiful old Venetian quarter, the CASTRO. APOLLON and AGIA ANNA have the best beaches.

IOS is the students' island: lots of guitar-strumming, pot-smoking, bead-wearing types on the beaches, and plenty to do at night. Don't let this put you right off – it's a pretty island. Try for a room in the village of Ios.

Santorini

4,000 years ago, a massive explosion left the outer rim of a volcano which became Santorini. From the harbour, climb (or take the donkey) up to the town of THIRA where you can find rooms at reasonable prices. Alternatively, the youth hostel (Tel. 22722) offers a very good deal. The best beaches are Kamari, Monolithos and Perissa with its black sand. There are ruins from the Minoans, Romans and Venetians. The boat trip out to the little island of Mikra Kameni, where the volcano started and smoulders still, is worth it.

The Sporades

Some of the quietest islands in Greece are the Sporades, as they're further off the beaten track than the others. You approach them by boat from Kymi, Agios Konstandinos or Volos which you reach by bus from Athens.

SKIATHOS is the most touristy, but that's because it's very beautiful. Stay in Skiathos town at Hotel Avora, 3 Antipl. Laskou St, if you can. KOUKOUNARIES is a superb beach surrounded by pine groves.

ALONISSOS is the smallest island. From the port of Patitiri, head for Marpounda or Kokinokastro where there's a good beach and some archaeological remains.

SKOPELOS has cheap rooms in its town and good beaches at STAFILOS and AGNONDAS. Inland lie the ruins of the medieval bishops' palace, and many churches and monasteries with icons.

SKYROS is the most beautiful and unspoilt island of the Sporades. Flat-topped white houses stand on the cliffs and folk crafts still flourish. The long dark sand beach is wonderful, and there are countless little coves for swimming and sub-aqua jaunts. Try Baloti (Tel. 91386) or the Vassale Restaurant for a room, and change money at Stam Sarri on Agoras St.

North-east Aegean

If you don't mind going a bit further out of your way, the islands off the mainland of Turkey have their rewards: Samos, Lesbos and Chios are the three most popular. SAMOS is heavily wooded with a rocky coastline and a good beach resort, Kokari. LESBOS is a mass of olive trees and has some incredible, traditionally designed buildings in its port of Methymna. CHIOS has an interesting old monastery, the Nea Moni, plus all the usual Greek island charms.

The Dodecanese (South-east Aegean)

These are the most easterly islands of Greece, a few miles away from Turkey. The boat trip from Piraeus can take up to 20 hours, so unless you've a bit of time to spend – think again. You're rewarded for your efforts by superb beaches, mountains, medieval buildings and an air of historical importance which you don't find in any other group of islands.

The two main islands are RHODES and KOS, the latter of which is regarded as the birthplace of modern medicine as it was a healing centre of wide acclaim. The Knights of St John captured them in the fourteenth century, and after them the Turks, Italians and Greeks moved in.

RHODES: if you avoid the main town of Rhodes to escape from the package tourists, you're OK. In Rhodes town, see the medieval Turkish quarter, the Suleiman Mosque, and the Grand Masters' Palace. The tourist police and tourist information will help you out, and you shouldn't find accommodation too bad. There's a youth hostel and several cheap places in Apellou St. The ferries to Israel stop at Rhodes, but only for a couple of hours; you can wait for the next boat provided you say so when you book.

LINDOS, along with Kameiros and Ialissos, has archaeological remains and is a particularly picturesque town, but the package-deal customers are here in swarms in summer.

KOS comes very high in the list of archaeological sites and is a fascinating island: great beaches, mosques, a Crusader fortress, mansions and a wonderful atmosphere. In the town, try the Asklepeion (Tel. 28616) or the Kalimnos (Tel. 22336) for a room, but camping, though not legal, is idyllic. There is an official campsite, however; the tourist police will tell you how to get there. On the outskirts are the ruins of Hippocrates' medical school and sanctuary.

Crete

This is the most varied of all the islands, from the barren mountains to the beautiful old cities. Crete is divided into four regions with Agios Nikolaos, Rethymnon, Hania and Heraklion as their capitals. HERAKLION (Iraklion) is the main port of Crete with connecting ferries to Piraeus. Apart from the amazing ARCHAEOLOGICAL MUSEUM off Eleftherios Square, the city has little to recommend it. If staying, try the youth hostel (Tel. 286281) or one of the places in Handakos St. From Heraklion you can visit the Minoan ruins at KNOSSOS or PHAESTOS, or the beach at PLAKIAS.

In western Crete look out for RETHYMNON with its Venetian and Turkish buildings. There is a youth hostel at No. 7 Pavlou Vlastou (Tel. 22848), and the tourist office is on 100 Kountouristou St (Tel. 29148). In HANIA (Chania), the elegant capital of Crete, the architecture makes you feel you're more in Turkey than in Greece. Try the harbour area for rooms, or the youth hostel (Tel. 53565). For the high spot of your Cretan trip, walk along the 18 km SAMARIA GORGE, the largest one in Europe. Take the bus to OMALOS for this five-hour walk.

In eastern Crete AGIOS NIKOLAOS is the tourist trap. It's very picturesque but often short of rooms. Try the youth hostel (Tel. 22823) or pester the tourist police till they come up with something. SITIA, east of the city, is near the fantastic palm beach of VAI, and the youth hostel (Tel. 22693) can usually squeeze you in.

The Ionian Islands

These are the islands off the north-west coast, lusher than most, with Corfu as its main tourist trap.

Corfu

If you're taking the ferry from or to Italy, chances are you'll stop off here. Take the opportunity if you've a day or two to spare, particularly if you can avoid the terrible crush months of July and

August. Corfu doesn't look terribly Greek; in some ways it's more like the French Riviera. The Venetians, French and British have all occupied the island and left their colonial marks in the buildings, food and people.

When you disembark, turn left to the Old Port; the road to the right of the Hotel Constantinopolis is where to start your search for a cheap bed. The tourist police, 35 Arseniou St, will fix you up in a private home if they like the look of you. Tourist information is in the post office building between Mantzaran and Dessila streets. The youth hostels are far out and invariably full. See Mon Repos where the Duke of Edinburgh was born. For your evening meal, the Old Port area is good and there's Greek folk dancing at the Fortress at 9 p.m.

You can rent mopeds for 600 dr. and get to the best beaches that way. Beware of some of the cheap food stalls as food poisoning seems to be a recurring hazard on the island.

PAXÍ and its little neighbour ANTIPAXÍ are becoming more touristy than is desirable due to their proximity to Corfu, but these small islands still have a lot of charm, and the sandy beaches of Antipaxí make ideal campsites.

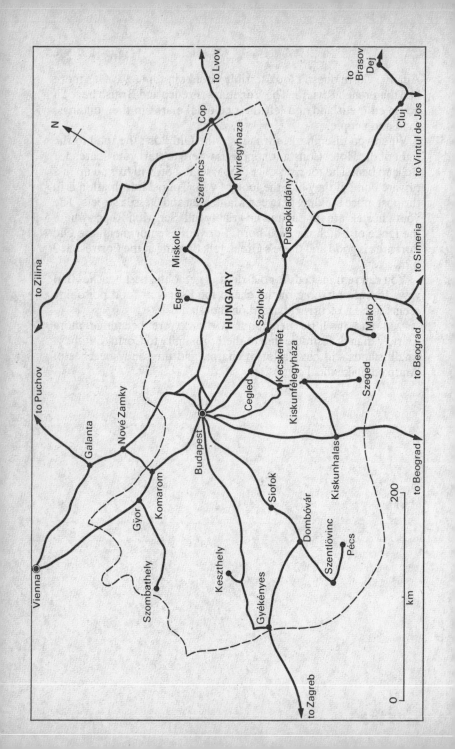

HUNGARY

Entry requirements	Passport and advance visa
Population	10,713,000
Capital	Budapest (pop.: 2,064,000)
Currency	Forints
	£1 = approx. 64 ft.
Political system	Socialist People's Republic
Religions	Catholic and Protestant
Language	Hungarian (some German and English understood)
Public holidays	1 Jan.; Easter Monday; 4 April; 1 May; 20 Aug.; 7 Nov.; 25, 26 Dec.

During the ninth century, seven tribes of mounted Magyars began riding eastwards, until they were stopped by the Holy Roman Empire in what is now Hungary. Gradually they began to settle down and became converted to Catholicism. Then during the fifteenth century, just when things were beginning to take off, the Turks turned up. A century and a half later, the Austrians took over and in 1867 after several uprisings they agreed to grant Hungary equal status under the joint monarchy of the Austro-Hungarian Empire. Things fell apart at the outbreak of the First World War, and Hungary went it alone until 1945. Two years later the Communist Party, aided by the Russians, took power. Since then, Hungary has been linked with the Soviet Union, despite the attempted counter-revolution of 1956. Travel within Hungary can be very slow, so think twice before heading off to explore every corner. Fortunately, the areas which have most to offer are the most accessible. If you only have time to visit one country in Eastern Europe, you can't go far wrong with Hungary. The people are friendly, the prices are cheap and every effort has been made to preserve the past in a country which is marked more by its similarities to the West than its differences.

HUNGARIAN STATE RAILWAYS
(Magyar Államvasutak, MÁV)

Trains are considerably slower than they are in the West, as well as being crowded in the summer. There are often long gaps between services, too, but with patience it's possible to explore nearly all the larger towns and tourist centres on an Inter Rail or BIJ ticket. Trains marked 'Sebesvonat' make only a few stops at major centres; other fast trains are marked 'Gyorsvonat'. The ultra-slow local ones ('Személyvonat') are noisy and fun but take an age to get anywhere. Bear in mind when making your plans that the railway network is very centralized and that it's always easier to enter or leave Hungary via Budapest. As in other countries, Transalpino holders can break their journeys at any point without having to get their ticket stamped. As with the rest of Eastern Europe, queueing is a way of life, and unavoidable during the summer. Whenever possible, make your seat reservations in advance, either at the IBUSZ office when you arrive, or at the MÁV booking office at Népköztársaság 35, Budapest (Mon.–Sat.: 9 a.m.–5 p.m.). It's worth keeping an eye out for any trains with new carriages, as they are a vast improvement on the old rolling stock.

• **Inter Rail bonuses:** Free entry to Metró Museum, Metró Station Deák Ferenc tér, Budapest; Transport Museum, Városligeti-Körut 11, Budapest V; and Horse Carriage Museum, Párad Fürdö.

TRAIN INFORMATION

Some of the information staff often speak a little English; if not, German is the best back-up. If you're getting nowhere, try and get your tongue round: 'Melyik vágányról indul a . . . vonat?' (From which track does the train to . . . leave?)

• **Reservations:** (Helyjegy) To be sure of a seat, it's best to reserve at least two or three days in advance. This is obligatory on some international (Nemzetközi gyorsvonat) and other express trains.

• **Night travel:** Where necessary, Hungary borrows sleepers and couchettes from other East European countries.

• **Eating on trains:** All long-distance trains have either a buffet car or mini-bar. Station buffets are particularly good value, however.

TOURIST INFORMATION

All towns have their own local tourist information offices (Idegen-forgalmi Hivatal) in addition to the state-run IBUSZ offices which deal with all aspects of travel and accommodation.

• **IUS bonuses:** 25 per cent off other East European train fares. For further information, contact Express, Szabadság tér 16, Budapest.

• **Money matters:** 1 forint (ft.) = 100 fillérs.
Banking hours are generally 9 a.m.–5 p.m., though the Hungarian National Bank closes at lunchtime. There's no minimum daily exchange amount, so only change money as you need it. Bank notes cannot be taken out of the country. Commission charges are very low (usually 1 per cent) and it's definitely not worth the risk of exchanging on the black market.

• **Post offices:** Open Mon.–Fri.: 8 a.m.–4 p.m.; Sat.: 8 a.m.–1 p.m. Stamps can also be bought from tobacconists.

• **Shops:** Most shops are open 10 a.m.–6 p.m., with food shops opening at 7 a.m. Late-night opening on Thursdays is usually to 8 p.m. On Saturdays 9 a.m.–2 p.m. is the norm and many tobacconists and pastry shops also stay open on Sundays. On Mondays in Budapest prices are reduced at the Centrum department stores.

• **Museums:** Open 10 a.m. till 6 p.m. (Closed Mondays.) Admission is between 2 and 5 ft.

SLEEPING

IBUSZ and the local tourist offices will fix you up in a private house for about 250 ft. per night. These are your best bet, so ask for the IBUSZ leaflet on accommodation in private homes. They are graded into A, B and C, depending on the tourist potential of the area. In small towns, look for the sign Szoba Kiadó and don't be afraid to accept offers of a room if you're approached on the street. If you're out of luck, the student travel service Express have several hostels and cheap student hotels. There's no need to be a member of the IYHF, and it's possible for couples to get a room to themselves.

Most hotels, especially the budget ones, are booked out months in advance and are expensive for what you get.

Camping is a realistic possibility; ask for a camping map from IBUSZ. There are over a hundred sites, graded from 1 to 3, depending on the facilities offered. For more detailed information contact the Hungarian Camping and Caravanning Club at Kálvintér 9, Budapest 1088 (Tel. 177280). During the summer, Hungary's population almost doubles and queues for accommodation can be frustrating. If you've a wet day in Vienna, go to the IBUSZ office at Kärntnerstrasse 26, where it's possible to reserve accommodation ahead of time. Also if you plan on staying at any of the Express hotels or hostels in Budapest and will be arriving before 6 p.m., you're given priority if you have an Express Student voucher, available from Ökista in Vienna. Wherever you end up, don't forget that you must register with the police (Keokh) within 24 hours of having your visa stamped, unless you're going through official booking services, where they do it for you.

EATING AND NIGHTLIFE

Hungarian food is excellent by any standards, and furthermore it's cheap. Try pörkölt (a pork stew with paprika), paprikás csirke galuskával (chicken with a sour cream paprika sauce) or goulash, with somlói galuska (sweet dumplings in rum and orange sauce) or rétes (strudel) to follow. The cheapest places are the self-service restaurants. Choose and pay the cashier, then collect your food. Look out for the tourist menus as they're normally exceptionally good value; if you're really broke and don't mind standing up, try any bisztró. Unlike the rest of Eastern Europe, Hungary has quite a bit of nightlife, particularly in Budapest. There are student discos and open-air concerts, as well as nightclubs.

Budapest

The heart of the capital is the Danube, looking far more impressive than it does in Vienna, and spanned by a nice collection of bridges. Buda, south of the river and set among gentle hills, is a mixture of winding medieval streets, viewpoints over the city and neat suburbs; Pest is the centre of commerce and government. The two were united, along with Óbuda, in 1873, to become Budapest. There's plenty to see and do and because food and transport are incredibly cheap by Western standards it allows your lifestyle, for once, to rise above its usual humble level. A taxi, a cruise up the Danube and a good meal while afloat will only cost you about 300 ft. All in all, Budapest is more lively, cosmopolitan and Westernized than any other East European city.

STATION FACILITIES

There are three main stations: Déli (south) which serves the south-west, Keleti (east) and Nyugati (west). They are well equipped by Eastern European standards, and you shouldn't find anything too out of the ordinary here. If you are stuck, remember 'palyaudvar' means 'station'.

TOURIST INFORMATION

There are IBUSZ offices in all the stations (daily 8 a.m.–6 p.m.). In addition there are offices at V, Felszabadulás tér and Petófi tér 3. The latter is open 24 hours and also operates a currency exchange and accommodation service. Budapest Tourist, which arranges private accommodation, is at V, Roosevelt tér 5–6 (open Mon.–Sat.: 8 a.m.–9 p.m., Sun.: 2 p.m.–8 p.m.). They also have offices near the two main stations: Baross tér near Keleti, and Bajcsy Zsilinszky u 55, near Nyugati. If you're sick of queues and know exactly what you want to ask, you can phone in to tourist information (Tel. 224052 or 315346).

● **Addresses:**
MAIN POST OFFICE and International Telephone Exchange is on the corner of Petófi Sándor u and Martinelli tér (poste restante Városház u 18), open Mon.–Fri.: 7 a.m.–9 p.m.; 7 a.m.–7 p.m. Saturday and in the morning only on Sundays and public holidays. Twenty-four-hour post offices are sited at Keleti and Nyugati stations.
UK EMBASSY: Harmincad u 6 (Tel. 171430).

US EMBASSY: Szabadság tér 12 (Tel. 124224).
CANADIAN EMBASSY: Budakeszi u, 55/D P/8 (Tel. 365728).
EXPRESS: Student Travel Centre, Szabadság tér 16, sell IUS cards, book student hostels, tours etc.

• **Getting about:** Public transport is efficient and very cheap. Buy tickets in advance for buses, trolley-buses (blue) and trams (yellow) from Trafik shops. The underground is also useful – insert 1 ft. into machines on entry for any length journey. Some tram services run all night. Even taxis are relatively cheap if there's a crowd of you – about 40 ft. per mile.

SEEING

The old town of Buda has at its centre VÁRHEGY, Castle Hill, with its painted baroque houses and students' and artists' quarter. Crowning the hill is the thirteenth-century MATTHIAS CATHEDRAL where the Hungarian kings were crowned. The ROYAL PALACE, virtually destroyed in 1944, is now rebuilt and houses two important museums: the HISTORICAL MUSEUM OF BUDAPEST and the NATIONAL GALLERY with its impressive collection of Hungarian art. The Margaret Bridge takes you to MARGARET ISLAND, lying in the middle of the Danube. The island is a recreation park and often has outdoor concerts and plays on summer evenings. For the best views over the city, cross the Elizabeth Bridge and climb Gellert Hill to the Liberation Monument. You can get a bus back if you're shattered. The floodlighting on summer evenings makes a walk by the riverside well worthwhile.

ST STEPHEN'S BASILICA is the impressive church on Pest beside the PARLIAMENT. A walk through the twenty-seven courtyards of this complex when the sun is setting over the Buda hills can be truly memorable. Two other museums of exceptional quality are the FINE ARTS and the HUNGARIAN NATIONAL. The Fine Arts is in Városliget (the City Park) which has rowing boats for hire on the lake, and amusement parks. If you want to cleanse the pores of the grime of train travel, try an authentic Turkish bath. It's only around 45 ft. and includes a massage. Try the old Ottoman baths of Király Fürdö on Föutca 85 or Rudás Fürdö at Döbrentei tér 9.

SLEEPING

Budapest gets busy in summer, so don't hang about getting organized on the bed front. Head for either the student accommodation office at Hotel Universitas, Irinyi József u 9, or the IBUSZ or Budapest Tourist Offices mentioned under tourist information, above. Private accommodation is your best bet: expect to pay anything up to 200 ft. each. The Alien Registration police office is Keokh, Népköztársaság u 12, open 8 a.m.–1 p.m., weekdays. You don't need to bother with this if you book through IBUSZ or an official set-up. If Hotel Universitas is full they'll give you alternatives in the same area.

Camping out is illegal but easy to get away with (and even if you are caught you won't be sent off to Siberia, so don't worry). Try the park on the Buda side of the Petófi Bridge.

The two official campsites are a good last resort as they're rarely full to capacity. Hárshegy is at Hárshegyi u 5 (Tel. 151482) and Római camping, Szentendrei u (Tel. 887167). Both cost around 100 ft. per person if you've a tent. Hárshegy also have four-bed bungalows around 500 ft. Check their availability through Budapest Tourist.

EATING AND NIGHTLIFE

Hungarian cuisine is one of the best in Europe and in Budapest you can eat well in any price range. Fixed menus for lunch are common and rarely cost more than 60 ft. but you have to ask for them as they are not always displayed. Look out for places called bisztrós, büfés, self-services and grills for even lower prices. One night at least, though, have a real blow-out. Even in a tourist trap, with gypsy music, wine and all the trimmings, there should be change from 400 ft.

Try: Fehér Galamb, Szentháromság 9, down from Matthias Cathedral, an excellent cheap restaurant and wine cellar.

Hungaria Restaurant, Lenin Krt. Amazing fin-de-siècle decor, gypsy music and dancing. The carp from Lake Balaton are a speciality here.

Century Restaurant (Százéves), Pesti Barnabás u 2, just off Vaci u. More than one century of atmosphere, music and memorable erdélyi káposta (stuffed cabbage with spiced minced pork and soured cream).

The meals on the Danube are good, too. Boats leave from below the Duna Hotel at 5.30 p.m. and 9 p.m. and the cruise lasts two or three hours – plenty of time to enjoy the meal knowing it won't break the bank. Wine cellars (borok) often serve good meals and the Hungarian wines, particularly Tokaji and Egri Bikavér (Bull's Blood), are quite something.

The other 'must' is a visit to a sixteenth-century pastry shop, known worldwide. Ruszwurm (Szentháromság 7, opposite the Matthias Cathedral) has its own varieties of cakes and strudels plus original furnishings and bread sculptures.

The *Express Cocktail Ship* is another Danube cruiser which attracts the students. There's rock, dancing and boozing, all for 60 ft. The boat leaves from Duna Hotel at 10 p.m. on Wed., Fri. and Sat. nights. The Ifjúsági Park (Youth Park) near the castle has an open-air dance floor, and local rock bands perform there till midnight. For student discos, try the Vár Klub, next to the Matthias Cathedral. There's traditional folk dancing in Buda Park, and a list of events is published in 'Coming Events in Budapest'.

The Danube Bend

This has Hungary's most spectacular scenery and it's possible to see some of it on a day trip from Budapest. The Danube makes a dramatic sweep south, about fifteen miles from Budapest, and the mountain scenery and villages up here are the best you'll find in the country. Boats leave the capital from Vigadó tér dock at 7 a.m. and 7.30 a.m. every day – later boats make it possible for you to stop off and sightsee before continuing your journey. (Further information on boats is available from Dunatours, Bajcsy Zs. u 17.) The journey to Esztergom, the heart of medieval Hungary, takes 5 hours so it's best to take a single and return to Budapest by bus (to Szentendre) and then suburban train.

SZENTENDRE is an old Serbian market town and artists' hangout. Lots of small museums (Margit Kovács ceramics collection is superb), churches and baroque houses. The main square (Karl Marx tér) is the venue for a summer festival, and the OPEN-AIR MUSEUM (near Angyal St) has examples of traditional buildings from all over the country. The tourist office is by the Danube at Somogyi Bacsó part. 6.

VISEGRÁD is right on a bend among the mountains. This was a Middle Ages stronghold and has a FORTRESS and ROYAL PALACE. Its rich past makes it popular with tourists but you won't find any cheap commercialism, so eat in the restaurants without any fear of being ripped off. Tourist information is on the Danube Embankment.

ESZTERGOM has some of the oldest and best-preserved remains in Hungary. This was the residence of the Magyar kings from the tenth to the thirteenth centuries. Take in the CHRISTIAN MUSEUM and ROYAL PALACE remains, but most of all visit the BASILICA, the largest cathedral in the country. For 5 ft. you can climb to the dome and walk around outside it to enjoy superb views over the surrounding country and into Czechoslovakia. Tourist information is at Széchenyi tér 13.

The Hungarian Plain

East of the Danube lies the dusty central plain which is real Hungarian peasant land. An in-depth exploration of this region will still produce pockets of rural life virtually unchanged for generations. Trains run through the Plain and the Budapest–Kelebia line stops off at the main settlements like Kecskemét and Szeged.

KECSKEMÉT, home town of Kodály, has only a small area of old town left, but what there is is good. Walk along BÁNK BÁN and János Hoffman streets. The TOWN HALL on Kossuth tér is another typical building.

SZEGED, near the Yugoslav frontier, was completely destroyed by flood in 1879, but the town today still has something to say of its rich past when it was under Turkish and, later, Austrian rule. See the DÓM TÉR where the VOTIVE CHURCH is, and Hungary's best Greek Orthodox Serbian church on the north side of the square. The local tourist information office is at Victor Hugo u 1, but you're best to try Express at Kijyo 3.

EGER, in the north-east, is Hungary's Bordeaux. This is where the good red wine (Bull's Blood) you've been knocking back in Budapest originates. Tourist information at Bajcsy Zsilinszky u 9 will give you a map and information, and should you decide to stay they'll help out on accommodation. DOBÓ ISTVÁN SQUARE is the town centre; just north of this is the CASTLE. The Kazamata Restaurant in the centre, by the neo-classical CATHEDRAL, is exceptionally good value and the wine is a knock-out. Eger is a good place to base yourself if you fancy delving into the forests and villages of inner Hungary for a while, and there are various cheap hotels and campsites.

Western Hungary – Lake Balaton

TRANSDANUBIA, the western region of Hungary, is the most scenic area after the Danube Bend. Here is Europe's largest lake, with rolling hills and vineyards interspersed with picturesque old towns. This is the region you'll pass through if you're coming in from Austria, and if you've hit a good spell of weather this is where to break your journey, as there are good beaches and everything you need for a few days' beach-bumming, Hungarian-style.

SIÓFOK, on the southern shores of Lake Balaton, is a bit like Torremolinos for us; but if it's company you're after, head there. KESZTHELY has more to offer. Apart from its beaches, there are various things to see: the first European agricultural college, GEORGICON; the HELICON LIBRARY, with many rare books and antiquities; and the BALATON MUSEUM.

TIHANY and BALATONFÜRED are on the northern shore and are quieter and prettier. Tihany has Celtic and Roman ruins and a beautiful yellow ABBEY looking down on the peninsula. The OPEN-AIR MUSEUM gives a good idea of the Balaton folk traditions, and the thatched-roof houses set among the hills add to the charm.

Balatonfüred is a health spa which tends to attract wealthy Hungarians and Russians. See the MEDICINAL SPRINGS, busy HARBOUR and ROUND CHURCH.

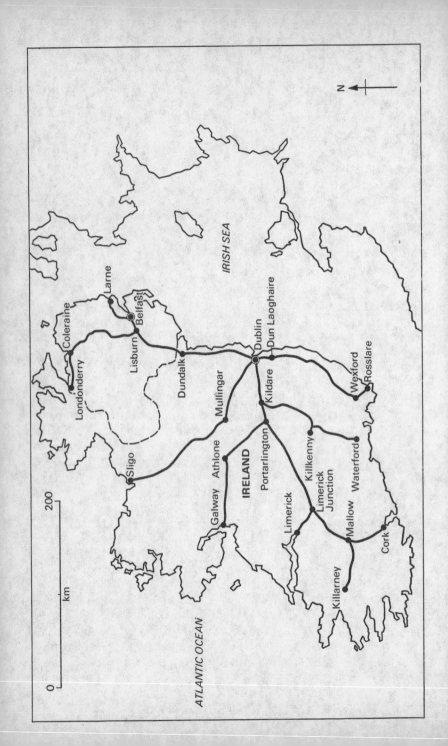

IRELAND

Entry requirements	Passport (not necessary for UK nationals)
Population	3,500,000
Capital	Dublin (pop.: 997,000)
Currency	£1 = approx. 121.5 Irish pence
Political system	Parliamentary Democracy
Religion	Roman Catholic
Languages	English and Irish
Public holidays	1 Jan.; 17 March; Good Friday; Easter Monday; first Monday in June; first Monday in August; last Monday in October; 25, 26 Dec.

Irrespective of when you plan to visit Ireland, prepare for the worst: the chances are you'll soak up more than its history and folklore. The Romans never conquered Ireland and as a result the Celts, themselves immigrants, were able to develop a native culture free from outside interference until the arrival of St Patrick in the fifth century. Ireland then became a centre of culture and learning at a period when the rest of Europe was suffering under the barbarian invasion following the collapse of the Roman Empire. This period of peaceful progress was interrupted by the Vikings who repeatedly raided the coast throughout the ninth and tenth centuries. After finally defeating the Norsemen, the Irish began fighting it out among themselves and thereby gave the Normans an opportunity to extend their influence beyond England. By the Tudor period, parliament was in the control of a British minority who gradually replaced the Irish Catholic landlords with Protestants from Scotland and England. The nineteenth century began with Ireland as part of the United Kingdom, but the subsequent failure of the potato harvests (1845–8) helped forward the cause of Irish nationalism, as well as leading to mass emigration. By 1914, home rule was passed and, seven years later, the Irish Free State was born, with the exception of the six counties of Northern Ireland. Finally, in 1937, Ireland (Eire) became a fully independent country. Trains will get you to all the main centres, but the best way to get to grips with her past is to hire a bike and explore the glut of prehistoric and medieval monuments. The Irish are justifiably proud of their hospitality, and although not every Irishman is another W. B. Yeats, most have the 'gift of the gab' and are only too happy to pass the time of day with you.

• **Getting there:** The shipping lines which operate regular sailings from Britain to Ireland are Sealink and B & I. If you're a student, B & I offer the best deal on their daily service from Liverpool to Dublin with 25 per cent discount if you buy your ticket at USIT, 52 Grosvenor Gardens, London SW1 (Tel. 01–730 8111) just beside Victoria Station, and 50 per cent if you buy a Travel-Save Stamp with your ISIC. If you're not a student, check all the other prices. Transalpino offer a train/ferry ticket from London to Dublin for about £50 (see Transalpino notes, page 27) on an ISIC which is the best value of all. Irish Continental Line operates Le Havre–Rosslare and Cherbourg–Rosslare, while Brittany Ferries operate Roscoff–Cork. Eurail Pass holders get to travel free on both services to Rosslare which is a considerable saving as the normal fare is around $90.

IRISH RAILWAYS
(Coras Iompair Eireann, CIE)

Eurail Passes are valid in the Republic, but unfortunately Ireland is still considered part of Britain as far as the Inter Rail's concerned, and you have to pay half fare if you bought your ticket in the UK. The Irish Railways' Rambler tickets are an alternative, but they're quite pricey at around £50 for eight days and £60 for fifteen. You're better to get a Travel-Save Stamp (£5) with your ISIC, as this entitles you to half-price travel on any train or long-distance bus in Eire. You can get these stamps from USIT in either London or Dublin. Trains are reasonably fast around the Dublin area and to major towns, but don't expect speeds similar to those on the continent.

• **Eurail bonuses:** Free:
—Ferry crossings on the Irish Continental Line between Rosslare (Ireland) and Le Havre (France) 21 hours or Cherbourg (France) 17 hours, and between Cork (Ireland) and Le Havre (France) 21½ hours. If cabin accommodation is requested an extra charge will

be made. Port taxes are extra and payable in Irish pounds. During July and August advance reservation is recommended. It is compulsory if cabin accommodation is requested. Check the sailing schedule always.

TRAIN INFORMATION

• **Reservations:** Are not necessary. If you want to make one, you must do so by 5 p.m. on the preceding day.

• **Night travel and eating on trains:** There are no night services in Ireland. Most long-distance trains have catering facilities ranging from bar service to set meals.

• **Bikes:** Are often the only way to get to the local hostel and see the neighbourhood. They cost about £4 a day from most towns.

TOURIST INFORMATION

There are seventy-six offices scattered throughout Ireland which are open Mon.–Fri.: 9 a.m.–6 p.m., Sat.: 9 a.m.–1 p.m. Each office gives information on its own region as well as for all of Ireland. They have a good selection of maps and literature.

Not all of Ireland is run as efficiently as the tourist board, so use their offices fully while you have the chance.

• **ISIC bonuses:** With the ISIC you can get a CIE Travel-Save Stamp ticket. This entitles you to 50 per cent off all journeys, also reductions to some cinemas and theatres.

• **Money matters:** 1 Irish pound (£1) = 100 pence (p.).
Banking hours are Mon.–Fri.: 10 a.m.–12.30 p.m., 1.30 p.m.–3 p.m. with an extension to 5 p.m. on Thurs. in Dublin. For the rest of the country late-opening days vary. The British have approximately a 30 per cent advantage with sterling against the Irish pound.

• **Post offices, shops and museums:** Tend to work around a 9 a.m.–5.30 p.m. routine. Museums vary the most, so always check with the nearest tourist information office.

SLEEPING

Hotels can be expensive so your best plan is to stick to bed and breakfast (B&B) and hostels. For advance information on youth hostels contact An Oige, 39 Mountjoy Square, Dublin (Tel. 745734).

Ask at tourist information for their leaflet on Irish Homes (50p). This lists all the approved B&Bs. If you require it, they'll book you a bed by phone for a small charge. Youth hostels tend to be situated in the most scenic parts of the country but are not always near a station. Beds cost between £2 and £4, depending on the hostel. Camping costs about £3 a tent on official sites, and is only for those who don't mind getting wet. (Tourist information provide a booklet priced 50p.)

EATING AND NIGHTLIFE

Food can be expensive in Ireland, even in the shops. Some restaurants outside Dublin shut by about 9 p.m., so eat early. For bargains you'll have to turn to Chinese and Indian food, or live off fish'n'chips. Ask at tourist information for their useful booklet 'Special Value Tourist Menu 1985', which lists many restaurants throughout Ireland, that provide enjoyable three-course meals at fixed prices. The only time you're likely to get the chance of traditional Irish cooking is in a guesthouse or B&B where, if you're lucky, Irish stew or boiled bacon and cabbage may appear on the menu (if you consider this luck!). Some guidebooks politely call Irish food wholesome, rather than basic which is perhaps a more apt description. When it comes to drinking, it's a very different question. The pub is the cornerstone of Irish nightlife; wherever you are, there will be a pub nearby. Ask about to discover which pubs have folk music and dancing, and where the best draught Guinness is.

Dublin

There's no denying Dublin has character. The contrast of the elegant eighteenth-century quarter with the damp dingy slums only a mile or two away is as much a comment on the Irish mentality as anything. This is the setting James Joyce used for *Ulysses* – his own home town. It's a rich experience, so don't try and hurry it.

STATION FACILITIES

Dublin has two main stations: Connolly, with northbound trains, and Heuston Station for trains to the south and west.

	CONNOLLY STATION
Train information	Mon.–Sat.: 7.30 a.m.–8.30 p.m.
	Use Booking Office on Sundays
	(Tel. 787777)
Reservations	Mon.–Sat.: 7.30 a.m.–8.30 p.m.
	Sun.: 7.30 a.m.–10.30 a.m., 4.30 p.m.–8.30 p.m.
Left-luggage store	Mon.–Sat.: 7.30 a.m.–9 p.m.
	Sun.: 8 a.m.–9 p.m.
Restaurant, Buffet	Mon.–Sat.: 7.30 a.m.–7.30 p.m.
Shops	Mon.–Sat.: 7.30 a.m.–7.30 p.m.

	HEUSTON
Train information	Mon.–Sat.: 7 a.m.–9 p.m.
	Sun.: 8 a.m.–9/10 p.m.
	(Tel. 771871)
Reservations	Mon.–Sat.: 7 a.m.–9 p.m.
	Sun.: 8 a.m.–9/10 p.m.
	(Tel. 771871)
Left-luggage store	Mon.–Sat.: 7.30 a.m.–9 p.m.
	Sun.: 8 a.m.–9 p.m.
Restaurant	Mon.–Sat.: 7.30 a.m.–7.30 p.m.
	Sun.: 8.30 a.m.–10.30 a.m., 5 p.m.–8 p.m.
Shops	7.30 a.m.–7 p.m.

Daily trains to: Belfast, Sligo, Rosslare (Connolly); Cork, Galway, Limerick (Heuston).

TOURIST INFORMATION

Main office: 14 Upper O'Connell
St (Tel. 747733), open Mon.–
Sat.: 8.30 a.m.–6 p.m. Money
exchange facilities provided
Mon.–Sat.: 8.30 a.m.–6 p.m.;
there is also a branch at the ferry
pier at Dun Laoghaire, and at
Dublin Airport.

● **Addresses:**
GENERAL POST OFFICE: O'Connell
St, open daily till 8 p.m.
AMEX: 116 Grafton St, open
Mon.–Fri.: 9 a.m.–5 p.m., Sat.: 9 a.m.–12 noon.
USIT (IRISH STUDENT TRAVEL AGENCY): 7 Anglesea St, open Mon.–
Fri.: 9.30 a.m.–5.30 p.m., Sat.: 10 a.m.–1 p.m.
UK EMBASSY: 33 Merrion Rd (Tel. 695211).
US EMBASSY: 42 Elgin Rd, Ballsbridge (Tel. 688777).
CANADIAN EMBASSY: 65–68 St Stephen's Green (Tel. 781988).
TRANSALPINO: 24 Talbot St (Tel. 742382)

● **Getting about:**
City buses operate from 7 a.m. to 11.30 p.m. Many of them start
from O'Connell Street in the centre. You won't need them for
sightseeing as it's all easily negotiated by foot ('shanks's pony' as
they call it). If you're there for a while and can claim to be pursuing
an educational or cultural project, make inquiries at tourist
information for the 'Youth and Educational Travel Concession
Ticket', looking earnest and intellectual.

SEEING

Start with O'Connell Street and your visit to the tourist office, then
head for TRINITY COLLEGE, the university which has produced such
men as Thomas More and Oscar Wilde, and see the beautiful
LIBRARY which is the home of one of the world's most outstanding
illuminated manuscripts: the eighth-century 'Book of Kells'.

At Castle Street is, predictably, DUBLIN CASTLE. It's thirteenth-century, and next to it is the CITY HALL. As far as churches go, CHRIST CHURCH (started in 1038), and the twelfth-century ST PATRICK'S CATHEDRAL are the names to look for.

The most elegant buildings of Dublin are said to be the CUSTOM HOUSE, on the north bank of the River Liffey, and the Bank of Ireland in College Green (formerly Parliament House).

The NATIONAL MUSEUM (closed Mondays) on Kildare Street is good for early historians, and the NATIONAL GALLERY is mainly a collection of old masters. The JOYCE MUSEUM at Martello Tower (a little way out at Sandycove) looks at the life and works of the Irish author, James Joyce. Pick up the 'Ulysses' map from tourist information. For a breath of fresh air, head for ST STEPHEN'S GREEN or PHOENIX PARK. Across the river from Phoenix Park is KILMAIN-HAM JAIL. The jail is restored and is now a historical museum, with conducted tours on Sundays from 3 p.m. to 5 p.m. and on Wednesdays from 10 a.m. to 12 noon and 2.30 p.m. to 4 p.m. For a few free pints of Guinness, go to their brewery at JAMES' GATE, watch the film about its production, then sup up.

SLEEPING

You can expect to pay between £10 and £15 in a hotel, so head for the student and youth hostels. Go round to the Irish Student Travel Service, 7 Anglesea St (Tel. 778117) if you're out of luck, and a word of warning: if you were thinking of a free night in Phoenix Park, bear in mind that the President of Ireland stays there, so there are pockets of police to contend with.

International Student Accommodation and Activity Centre (ISAAC), 2–4 Frenchman's Lane (Tel. 788159), is a very central old warehouse and the best deal in Dublin at around £5 a night. Also try The Young Traveller at St Mary's Place (Tel. 305000). It's a lot cleaner, but expect to pay £8 for B&B.

• **Youth hostels:** 39 Mountjoy Sq. (Tel. 745734) and 78 More-hampton Rd, Donnybrook (Tel. 680325), are both very good and cheap. The YWCA at Radcliffe Hall, St John's Rd (Tel. 694521), is also worth checking out.

● **Bed and breakfasts:** Try Upper Gardiner St where there are a few, or any along the Clontarf road, with views out to Dublin Bay. Particularly good is Mrs McKenna at 110 Sandford Rd, Ranelagh (Tel. 971375), as she always makes you feel very welcome.

EATING AND NIGHTLIFE

There are the usual soulless fast-food chains in the centre, and also quite a few pubs now offering excellent-value lunches. If you're in town for a while, it's worth buying the tourist board's booklet 'Special Value Tourist Menu' which has a good choice of eating places in Dublin, offering three-course meals at fixed prices.

Anywhere around the university is your best bet, with restaurants catering for the student market. Try Newman House, 86 St Stephen's Green; it's good, cheap and filled with students who can act as a mine of information. Closed in August. Bewleys have cafés in Grafton St, South George St, and Westmoreland St, all doing good meals at reasonable prices.

This is the home of the pub. It's at the centre of Ireland's social life, and the atmosphere in a good Dublin local takes some beating. O'Donoghue's, Merrion Row, is always lively, as is the Baggot Inn, Baggot St. Lincoln's Inn behind Trinity College is a students' haunt. Davy Byrne's on Duke St was a Joycean pub, now populated with young Dubliners. All pubs shut at 11.30 p.m. McGonagle's, South Anne St, is a rock club which isn't as expensive as most. 'In Dublin' lists all current events.

The South-east

Counties Wexford, Wicklow, Kilkenny and Tipperary.

The WICKLOW MOUNTAINS lie only ten miles from Dublin, and a day or two exploring this mountainous area from the base towns of Glendalough (with its eighth-century monastery) or Wicklow can be rewarding. ENNISCORTHY is a small town in the Slaney valley and on the main line south from Dublin. It was a storm centre during the 1798 rebellion against the British. The sixteenth-century castle is now a folk museum, and if you hit it in the first week of July, expect an even-better-than-usual atmosphere, as the Strawberry festival livens things up considerably. In WEXFORD see the BULL RING and ruins of the twelfth-century SELSKAR ABBEY, and ask for information on the free guided walking tours at tourist information on Crescent Quay. WATERFORD, about an hour from Rosslare where the Fishguard ferry deposits you, is famous for its crystal, but apart from this and its impressive eighteenth-century CHRIST CHURCH CATHEDRAL there's not a lot doing, so head for KILKENNY and see the thirteenth-century cathedral of ST CANICE with its adjacent Round Tower, and the dominating, beautiful CASTLE. The tourist office at Shee Alms House, Rose Inn St, will fix you up with a bed. CASHEL, in County Tipperary, was a medieval ecclesiastical centre and CORMAC'S CHAPEL is the finest remaining example from this period of architecture. Rising majestically over the town, the famous ROCK OF CASHEL crowned with a magnificent group of ruins is one of Ireland's great historic sites.

Cork

3½ hours on the main line from Dublin, Cork is a convenient stopover for exploring the south-west. See the Gothic cathedral of ST FINNBARR and, as a contrast, the modern CHRIST THE KING CHURCH. If you're musically inclined, ST ANNE'S CHURCH offers you the opportunity to play its bells. The tourist office on Grand Parade St (open 9 a.m.–7 p.m. in summer) have guided walking tours two evenings each week in July and August. Head for the university area for B&B, or the youth hostel at Redclyffe, Western Rd (Tel. 432891).

From Cork it's only six miles to the famous BLARNEY STONE in Blarney Castle where legend has it you acquire 'the gift of the gab' once you've paid your £1 and kissed the stone.

The South-west

The south-west – West Cork and Kerry – has Ireland's highest mountains, lakes, forests and a rugged coastline. Seventeen miles from Cork is KINSALE, the culinary capital of Ireland. A pretty, small fishing village with a twelfth-century church and good youth hostel (Tel. 021 72309).

KILLARNEY is the jewel of this part of the world. It is incredibly scenic and only 1½ hours from Cork. Walk round the beautiful BOURNE VINCENT MEMORIAL NATIONAL PARK and see the folk museum in MUCKROSS HOUSE there. Use the tourist office in the town hall to help you find a room, as beds can be very scarce in summer in this, the most visited part of Ireland.

The coastal road, the Ring of Kerry, is beautiful, winding its way between the sea and hills, but this would take you off the rail tracks, so only indulge if you need a few days off. Half an hour from Killarney is TRALEE, the capital of the 'Kingdom of Kerry', which in late August plays host to the world during the Festival of Kerry – a week of sport, music and song – culminating in the crowning of the Rose of Tralee. DINGLE is the gateway to the Gaelic Irish-speaking districts, and quiet, unspoilt countryside where one can unwind in an archaeological wonderland. Ferries run from DUNQUIN to the remote seven islands in the Atlantic called the Blaskets – don't go there if you get lonely easily.

Limerick

Ireland's fourth city is on the River Shannon. A port town with Georgian houses and elegant buildings like the CUSTOM HOUSE and TOWN HALL. KING JOHN'S CASTLE was built in 1210, and nearby stands the twelfth-century ST MARY'S CATHEDRAL. The town is famous for its beautiful hand-made lace, and the Limerick Lace Collection can be seen in the CONVENT OF THE GOOD SHEPHERD in Clare St. For a cheap B&B, try anywhere along the Ennis road.

Eight miles from Limerick City on the main Shannon Airport/ Ennis/Galway road stands the fully restored fifteenth-century BUNRATTY CASTLE which houses a superb collection of fourteenth-seventeenth-century furniture and furnishings. It is open to visitors daily, and medieval banquets and entertainments are held twice nightly. The FOLK PARK in the grounds of the castle contains farmhouses and cottages, a forge and other typical features of the traditional way of life.

Galway

Galway is a seaport and university town which was ruled in the sixteenth century by Anglo-Norman tribes, and made her money in dealings with the Spanish wine trade.

TOURIST INFORMATION AND ADDRESSES

IRISH TOURIST OFFICE (Tel. 63081): One block east of the station, off Eyre Sq. Also on the Promenade.
POST OFFICE: Eglinton St. Open Mon.–Sat.: 9 a.m.–6 p.m.
USIT (STUDENT TRAVEL): University College, New Science Building, Galway (Tel. 24601).

SEEING

Eyre Square, where the station is, is the city centre. Note the SPANISH ARCH, the gateway of the old town. LYNCH'S CASTLE, down Shop St, is fourteenth-century, as is the CHURCH OF ST NICHOLAS. Walk round by the banks of the River Corrib and see the salmon jump at SALMON WEIR BRIDGE in the spawning season, and in the summer evenings check out the *Seoda*, a traditional music presentation in the Irish-speaking theatre (Taibhdhearc Na Gaillimhe) on Middle St. In late July the GALWAY FAIR comes to town.

SLEEPING, EATING AND NIGHTLIFE

B&Bs are your best bet as there's no hostel and the campsites are all far out: Mrs Barret, 7 St Mary's Ave. (Tel. 23249). If you've come in a busy period, try the seaside suburb of Salthill.

There is a selection of eating places in the 'Special Value Tourist Menu' booklet, and there's plenty of fish'n'chip shops to keep you going. Cullen's Bar, Forster St, and Crane Bar, also Forster St, are lively at night and have traditional music.

• **Excursions from Galway:** Three hours on the boat takes you out to the remote and fascinating ARAN ISLANDS: Inishmore, Inishmaan and Inisheer. Life out here is primitive, and the prehistoric forts and remains add to the atmosphere.

The North-west

Counties Mayo, Sligo and Donegal lack the charm, and warmer climate, of the south. They are serious counties, full of prehistoric remains and reminders of their turbulent past with the British. WESTPORT, in Clew Bay, is worth stopping at to see the beautiful estate of the Marquess of Sligo, two miles from the town. WESTPORT HOUSE is his Georgian mansion, open to the public April–Sept., full of beautiful things. You'll find Westport a busy place on the last Sunday in July, but all those people climbing CROAGH PATRICK aren't tourists, they're pilgrims as this is where St Patrick is said to have fasted and prayed. The tourist office and post office are in the Mall, and for a room try the places along Distillery or Castlebar Road.

SLIGO, the county of W. B. Yeats, is incredibly rich in archaeological sites and atmosphere. This is the main town of north-west Ireland, with its population of only 14,000. The tourist office at Temple St will give you help and information on sights and accommodation, and they have guided walks at 11 a.m. every day.

The main sight of the town is the ruined thirteenth-century Dominican friary, Sligo Abbey. For B&B, look along Wolfe Tone St.

COUNTY DONEGAL is not served by rail, but if you want to do a bit of hitching this region will provide you with an unspoilt, wild and beautiful terrain. Use the coastal youth hostels, and take warm clothes.

For Northern Ireland see United Kingdom.

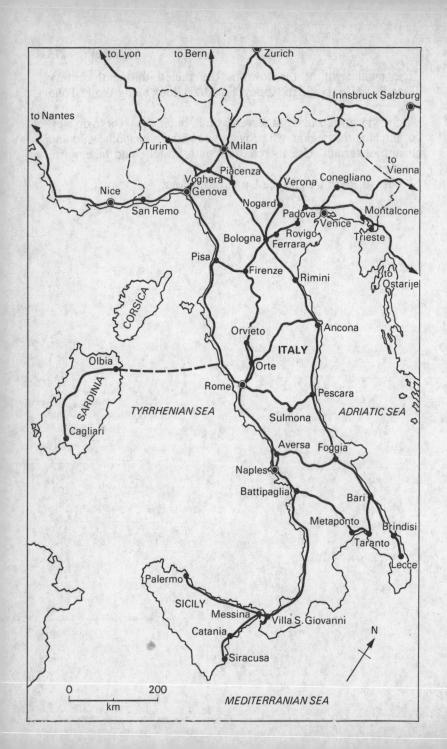

ITALY (Italia)

Entry requirements	Passport
Population	57,000,000
Capital	Rome (pop.: 3,800,000 +)
Currency	Lira
	£1 = approx. 2,325 L
Political system	Republic
Religion	Roman Catholic
Language	Italian (English spoken in some major cities)
Public holidays	1, 6 Jan.; Easter Monday; 25 Apr.; 1 May; 1 June; 15 Aug.; 1, 7 Nov.; 8, 25, 26 Dec.

We always think of Italy as a spoilt child. The chances are you're going to be annoyed, frustrated and overwhelmed, and yet your greatest eurorailing stories will probably originate here. Whatever your personal feelings on Italians are, you've got to admit they have style. Who else could make a full-scale drama out of a potentially normal situation like seeing a relative off in a train; or challenge a restaurant bill with the gusto of life and death?

Italy's history is dominated by three familiar themes: Empire, Church and the Renaissance, all of which have played a major role in the forming of European culture. From the eighth century BC onwards, there were Greeks in southern Italy and Sicily, and Etruscans in the north. By the third century BC, the Romans were on the move, conquering an empire which was to reign supreme over much of the barbarian world, until its downfall in the fifth century AD. As the civil power of Rome declined, it found a new role as the centre of the Christian Church. Italy became disunited and power was left in the hands of local lords, each seeking control of provincial kingdoms. Even the Pope and the Holy Roman Emperor could not agree as to who ruled what. Eventually the Pope, fed up with the whole affair after the city-states refused to submit to his authority, moved base to Avignon (1303–77). After this period of internal strife, the Kingdom of Naples and powerful city-states such as Venice and Florence, provided patronage for the arts. Among other factors which gave rise to this fifteenth-century Renaissance was the new humanism which produced men like Leonardo da Vinci and Michelangelo. Disunity and continued rivalry led to outside intervention by Spain and Austria and finally by Napoleonic France. This foreign domination created the desire for unity, initially under Garibaldi, leading to the ultimate unification of all Italy in 1870. After the First World War, Mussolini and the Fascists rose to power, which eventually brought about an alliance with Hitler during the Second World War. Since then, industrialization and emigration have characterized the economy, particularly in the south where poverty continues to be a problem.

ITALIAN STATE RAILWAYS
(Ferrovie dello Stato, FS)

On paper, the Italian rail network should be one of the best in Europe. In reality, it's just like the rest of Italy: pretty inefficient. Most Italians accept that trains always run late and they thrive on the bureaucracy and confusion of the whole system.

If you set out prepared for anything, you won't be surprised when a grandmother tries to board a busy train through your window, and ousts you into the corridor while she grabs your seat. Social friction within Italian society can only be worsened by the railways which ensure that those with money are provided with everything imaginable, while second-class passengers don't even get loo paper. In peak season second class gets incredibly busy on the main lines, so either move early for a seat or, if it is a long trip, reserve. If there's a group of you, set one the task of getting in pronto without a rucksack to get some seats; then the rest can follow at leisure.

The best of the non-supplement trains are the long-distance Espressos. They run frequently between Rome, Florence, Venice, Milan and Naples. Away from the main centres, things are not so rosy as you'll have to depend on the Direttos which stop at most stations or, even worse, the Locales which stop at every station. If this happens, turn the experience to your advantage as many of the stations which were built in the nineteenth century are among the finest examples you're likely to find in Europe. The Rapido is the top of the ladder for second-class travel, but for this privilege you'll have to pay a special supplement of about 30 per cent of the normal fare plus 2,000 L for a seat reservation. (Some Rapidos are first class only, so always check before boarding the train.) If you've always wanted to travel on a TEE, wait until you're out of Italy as you'll have to pay through the nose: 80 per cent more to travel on first class, plus a speed supplement. The station manager's office is always interesting as there's a 50/50 chance there'll be either a crucifix or a picture of Karl Marx over his desk.

The Italian Kilometric Ticket (no age restrictions) is valid for up to 20 trips, totalling up to 3,000 km, and can be used by as many as five different people. If this is the case, each trip is calculated by multiplying the distance travelled by the number of adults. This pass can be bought from every large station in Italy as well as from any Compagnia Italiana Turismo (CIT) office, and costs around 200,000 L for first class, 120,000 L for second class. Alternatively, it's possible to buy it from Italian State Railways in New York, 666 Fifth Ave., NY 10113 (Tel. 212 397 2667) for around $160 and $90 respectively. It's well worth thinking about if you're travelling in a group, but difficult to justify individually as 3,000 km is a long way in Italy.

● **Inter Rail bonuses:**

FROM	TO	REDUCTION %
Civitavecchia	Olbia	20
Civitavecchia	Cagliari	30
Civitavecchia	Porto Torres	30
Genoa	Olbia	30
Genoa	Porto Torres	30
Naples	Palermo	30
Naples	Cagliari	30

● **Eurail bonuses:** Free:
—Eurail Pass and Eurail Youthpass travellers can use steamers (*Appia, Egnatia, Espresso Grecia, Castalia*) operated by the Adriatica di Navigazione and Hellenic Mediterranean Lines between Brindisi and Patras and vice versa. However, between 1 June and 30 September, they must pay a £5 ($8) high-season surcharge. During July and August, advance reservation, which costs £1.20 ($2), is recommended. Special accommodations (airline- type seats or cabins) and port taxes are extra. Before boarding, all passengers must check in at the Shipping Line Office at the pier. Passengers who wish to break their voyage at Corfu

must declare their intention of 'stop over' upon delivery of the ticket. Holders of tickets for Corfu (as final port of destination) can in no case continue their voyage to Patras.

Reduced fares:
—About 20 per cent reduction on first-class fares for holders of Eurail Pass and on second-class fares for holders of Eurail Youthpass on the Steamship Company Tirrenia between Naples and Palermo, Naples and Malta, Syracuse and Malta and for crossings to Sardinia.
—20 per cent reduction on the normal fares of the Steamship Company DFDS between Genoa and Tunis, Genoa–Alicante and Málaga.
—30 per cent reduction on the published full fares of the Adriatica di Navigazione between Venezia–Piraeus–Alexandria, on the *Espresso Egitto* and/or its return. Contact the local Adriatica offices.

The following half-price reductions are granted by Europabus on transportation costs only and by local offices in Europe.
266 Venice–Florence
267 Florence–Rome
268 Rome–Naples–Pompeii–Sorrento–Amalfi
269 Palermo–Agrigento–Syracuse–Taormina–Palermo

TRAIN INFORMATION

The FS information officers generally speak English, but aren't too helpful, as they get fed up with the long queues in the summer; so try and use your timetable whenever possible.

• **Reservations:** Are optional on all non-supplement trains and can be made up to six hours before departure. It's a good idea to do this on runs between major cities, as the trains are always mobbed. It's also possible to reserve a seat on the boat train from London to Italy or vice versa.

• **Night travel:** This is a good move in Italy where prices are low and distances often long. You can get a couchette from Paris to Rome or vice versa for about 14,000 L. Within Italy, they are either first-class four-berth or second-class six-berth. Don't expect too much for your money – couchettes are often old and dirty. Avoid bottom bunks as headrests take up space, and it's even stuffier down there since the air conditioning rarely works. If you prefer to go up-market, there are also sleepers run by Wagons-Lits. If you're asked to give up your passport for the night, don't worry as this is standard practice.

• **Eating on trains:** There are expensive mini-bars on all major trains.

• **Scenic tips:** Without doubt, the finest way of arriving in north Italy is from Switzerland. The Bern–Brig–Milan and the Zürich–Lugano–Milan runs offer some of Europe's most spectacular Alpine scenery. If you plan on arriving from Austria, you won't be disappointed either, as the runs from Innsbruck–Bolzano to Verona and Villach–Udine to Venice also offer some fine mountain views. One of the most popular routes is from Nice in France down to Pisa – which is no wonder, as there's a lot more than just the Mediterranean coast to feast your eyes on (the train makes its way past most of the Riviera beaches). Further down the same line, anywhere around the Bay of Naples has excellent coastal views, particularly along the narrow-gauge line to Sorrento, though this is a private railway. If you're arriving at Brindisi from Greece, there are three very different but equally scenic routes to choose from: along the southern coast to Catania in Sicily; up the Adriatic coast to Rimini; or over the mountains to Naples via Taranto.

• **Bikes** and scooters can sometimes be hired from local tourist offices.

TOURIST INFORMATION

Italy is divided into twenty regions. Each region's capital city has its own tourist board called Assessorato Regionale Turismo (ART). Each of these regions is divided into provinces which, in turn, have their own tourist offices, Ente Provinciale Turismo (EPT). Apart from promoting general tourism in their areas, the EPTs also publish free maps, brochures, etc., as well as helping with accommodation problems. For everyday purposes, look for the local tourist offices, Azienda Autonoma di Soggiorno e di Turismo (AAST). They have exactly the same function as the EPTs except they're limited to a particular town or resort. Before you set off to Italy, it's well worth writing in advance to their State Tourist Office (ENIT) at 1 Princes Street, London W1R 8AY, or Italian Government Travel Office, 630 Fifth Ave., New York, NY 10020, asking them to send you their excellent free 'Travellers' Handbook 1985' which contains everything you will need to know.

• **ISIC bonuses:** Free entrance to all state-run museums and antiquities. Between 20 and 50 per cent discounts on sea travel. For further information, contact STC Viaggi per la Gioventù, Via Nazionale 172, Rome.

• **Money matters:** The only unit of currency is the lira, for which there are notes for everything between 500 and 100,000 lire.
Banking hours are Mon.–Fri.: 8.30 a.m.–2.30 p.m.
Some exchange agencies (cambio) give a better rate: you will have to shop around. On 1 August 1984 the gettone (Italian phone token used as currency) was revalued and is now used as the equivalent of 200 L.

• **Post offices:** Open 8.30 a.m.–2 p.m. Letters can be sent to poste restante by adding 'Fermo Posta' to the name of the locality. On delivery at the central post office, you'll have to pay a small charge. Stamps are also sold at tobacconists'.

• **Shops:** Open from 8.30/9 a.m.–1 p.m. and from 3.30/4 p.m.–7.30/8 p.m., except in northern Italy where the lunch break is shorter and shops close earlier. Most stores take a half day on Monday, generally opening at about 3.30 p.m. Supermarkets can be difficult to find so, if you see one, use it.

For opening times of museums, check at the local AAST office. Many are shut on Sunday afternoons, Mondays and public holidays. Also, many churches shut between 12 noon and 3 p.m. N.B. Most churches, especially the major cathedrals, will not admit people wearing shorts or with uncovered shoulders (or girls with short skirts).

SLEEPING

There is a vast array of hostels, hotels and pensions in Italy to choose from; each one has its own fixed charges, mostly 12,500–30,000 L, as worked out by the provincial tourist boards. These charges vary according to the grade and the season (hotels 1–5, pensions 1–3). Always check behind the door to see if it includes IVA (Italian VAT), breakfast, and a shower, as these are often extra. There are fifty-two youth hostels scattered throughout Italy (open for IYHA members only), as well as numerous student hostels in all the main towns (open to everyone). For further information on youth hostels in Italy contact Associazione Italiana Alberghi per la Gioventù, Palazzo della Civiltà del Lavoro, Quadrato della Concordia, 9–I–00144 Roma EUR (Tel. 5913702). Hostels are not automatically your best bet as many operate an evening curfew and shut during the siesta period. We've found inexpensive hotels are more reliable in their cleanliness and flexibility. Look for the signs Pensione, Albergo, Locanda and Soggiorno. Girls have another option by staying at the local Casa Famiglia which are run by nuns and offer a bed for about 10,000–18,000 L. Wherever you stay, don't be afraid to give up your passport when you check in as this is standard practice. If you're determined to save as much as you can, camping represents another alternative. The local AAST office has information on the prices of the nearest sites but, for the amount you save, it's often a lot more convenient to stay at a cheap pension in the centre.

EATING AND NIGHTLIFE

Finding a supermarket or a public toilet can be a problem in Italy. You may be forced into a café with high prices and an old crone posted outside the toilet demanding 200 L. To avoid this it's best to be organized. In general, the breakfast at a hotel or pension isn't worth it, as all you're likely to get is a cup of coffee and a roll (it's normally cheaper at the local bar). If you can do without breakfast, go straightaway to the nearest supermarket or local market. In the evening rosticcerie, trattorie, tavole calde and osterie represent the best value. Cheap restaurants can be found quite easily and the standard of the cooking is incredibly high, even on a fixed-price

8,000 L menu. In fact, Italy represents one of the best deals in Europe for good cheap meals. The pizza stalls give you a cheap and tasty lunch, and in the evening, especially in Rome, you're spoilt for choice. Some places bump up the bill if you've chosen to sit outside to eat your meal, so check first. When your bill comes, check it. The reason so many Italians stage melodramas with the waiter is that the arithmetic is often dodgy, and never in your favour. Snacks and afternoon coffees are a bad idea: they inevitably end up costing as much as a meal, so bear this in mind when you're at the supermarket. Expect to pay 10,000–20,000 L for a full meal with wine in a trattoria, and 8,000–12,000 L for the menu turistico.

The evening meal is a leisurely and latish affair, and once it's over most Italians wander round to a few cafés and bars, soaking up the local colour. As Luigi Barzini comments in *The Italians*:

> The show can be so engrossing that many people spend most of their lives just looking at it. There are usually café tables strategically placed in such a way that nothing of importance will escape the leisurely drinker of espresso or aperitivo.

The disco and nightclub news is not startling, but there are a few flash – and expensive – places in the main cities. Musical and cultural events are thick on the ground in places like Rome, Florence and Milan. Pick up the 'What's On' from the local tourist office of whichever centre you're in, and make use of your ISIC whenever you can.

Northern Italy

The north is where the money's made, and to a large extent stays. Parts of it are therefore industrial, and prices tend to be higher, but there are too many interesting towns in this area simply to head south regardless. Its regions include PIEDMONT where Turin is; the DOLOMITE RANGE (part of the eastern Alps); LOMBARDY, dominated by Milan; EMILIA-ROMAGNA where Ferrara, Parma and Bologna are located; the ITALIAN RIVIERA where Genoa and the resort towns lie; and VENETO, the region of beautiful Renaissance towns such as Verona, Padua, and its crowning glory – VENICE.

Piedmont and Trentino – Alto Adige

TURIN is more of a stopping-off place than a tourist centre. It's on the main line to Rome, Florence, Naples and Paris and is one of Italy's main industrial centres. The old SIXTEENTH-CENTURY QUARTER, however, is attractive enough to merit a visit, as is the former ROYAL PALACE, the PALAZZO MADAMA and the very good EGYPTIAN MUSEUM and ANCIENT ART MUSEUM in the baroque Palace of the Academy of Sciences. Climb up the emblem of the city, the MOLE ANTONELLIANA, and look over the city from its 548-foot height. The tourist office is at Via Roma 222 and there's an information office at Porta Nuova.

The DOLOMITE REGION towns are a mixture of Roman ruins, medieval castles and baroque churches. The backdrop of the pink-coloured Dolomites and the proximity to Austria and Switzerland make this region feel like a totally different country. BOLZANO is on the main line from Munich, and is more Austrian than Italian in its language and character. This is the capital of the Alto Adige area and was part of Austria's south Tyrol till 1918. Tourist information is on Piazza Walter 22 and 8, where the GOTHIC CATHEDRAL stands. The MUSEO DELL'ALTO ADIGE has a rare collection of local wooden sculptures and paintings and the village of GRIES, across the River Isarco, makes a lovely walk. BRUNICO, half an hour from the Austrian frontier, still feels like a part of Austria. The dominating Tyrolean CASTLE OF BISHOP BRUNO was built in 1251. Walk for half an hour to the PLAN DI CORONES for an incredible Alpine view. TRENTO, half an hour from Bolzano on the line to Verona, is another Roman town on the Brenner route. Unlike Brunico, this town feels very Italian and, even though the inhabitants were Austrians till 1918, they now consider themselves true Italians. Walk down VIA BELENZANI and look at the Renaissance and Venetian palaces, the baroque church of SAN FRANCISCO

SAVERIO, and the thirteenth-century bishop's house, IL CASTELLO DI BUON CONSIGLIO (the Castle of Good Counsel).

Lombardy

This region stretches from the Italian-Swiss border and Lombardy lakes to the plains of the Po River valley, taking in places such as Como, on Lake Como, Bergamo, Mantua (Mantova) and its main city, Milan.

COMO is an ancient silk-producing city on the southern tip of Lake Como. Its architecture is very rich and you should head for the PIAZZA DEL DUOMO to see the old PRETORIAN PALACE called Il Broletto (1215). Next to this is the PALAZZO DEL COMUNE, and the Renaissance Gothic DUOMO from 1396. The Romanesque church of SAN FIDELE is reached by taking Via Vittorio Emanuele. Tourist information is on Piazza Cavour, and at the station.

BERGAMO is divided into two: the lower city, built under the Fascists in the 1920s; and the upper city, a medieval settlement reached by funicular. Apart from the PALAZZO DELL'ACCADEMIA CARRARA with its collection of sixteenth-century art and furniture, forget the lower city. Once you've taken the funicular up head for the Piazza Vecchia where the PALAZZO DELLA RAGIONE stands. Opposite this is the PALAZZO NUOVO. The cathedral has a fifteenth-century interior and nineteenth-century exterior. VIA ROCCA takes you to a park which has a medieval lookout post from where the view over the Bergamasque valleys is particularly good. Tourist information is on Viale V. Emanuele II.

MANTUA was one of *the* Renaissance courts, ruled as it was for 400 years by the Gonzaga family. Their sumptuous palace (PALAZZO DUCALE) is on Piazza Sordello. There are over 500 rooms, including the miniature suite specially constructed to house the court dwarfs. It's free on ISIC, closed Mondays and open weekday mornings and Saturday afternoons. Opposite the palace is the medieval CATHE-DRAL which is impressive enough, but pales into insignificance beside the beautiful Renaissance CHURCH OF SANT'ANDREA. The

PALAZZO DEL TÈ was the Gonzagas' summer home, built in the early sixteenth century (closed Mon. and Sun. p.m.). The artist who painted the frescoes decorating the rooms here was Giulio Romano, and you can visit his sun house on VIA C. POMA, which is still well preserved. Tourist information is at Piazza Mantegna 6 and Piazza Sordello 23; watch out for their 1 p.m.–3.30 p.m. siestas. For cheap beds, try Locanda La Torretta, Via Leon d'Oro 13 (Tel. 322718), or the youth hostel Ostello Sparafucile (Tel. 322 415), a renovated medieval castle, open Mar.–Oct.

Milan (Milano)

Most eurorailers don't get off at Milan, or if they do they stay in the station till their connection comes. We're not totally condemning this as there's no denying Milan's not exactly Venice in the sightseeing stakes, but it's got a lot more than most people realize, and as the rich man of Italy (every third building seems to be another bank), it has the perks of a high living standard (and higher standards of cleanliness) and more things going on in the evenings than elsewhere.

STATION FACILITIES

There are three stations in Milan (Centrale, Lambrate and Garibaldi). The last two are mostly used for local traffic and are less important. We consider the Centrale station to be one of the most impressive in Europe, if only for its sheer size alone, which reflects past Italian confidence in their railway system. Despite its headline news in November 1983, the fire at the station was a small affair and has only really affected the train information desk. The temporary desk keeps the same hours but with much longer queues, so it's best to use the timetables posted up within the main hall.

	MILANO CENTRALE
Train information	7 a.m.–11 p.m.
	(Tel. 222 441)
Reservations	7 a.m.–10 p.m. (6.30 p.m.–10 p.m.
	for couchettes and sleepers)
Tourist information	9 a.m.–12.30 p.m., 2.30 p.m.–6.30 p.m.
Foreign exchange	7 a.m.–9 p.m.
Left-luggage store	7 a.m.–10.30 p.m.
Bar, Buffet	7 a.m.–12 midnight
Restaurant	11.30 a.m.–11.30 p.m.
Bath, Shower	7 a.m.–10.30 p.m.
Post office	Mon.–Fri.: 8 a.m.–2 p.m.
	Sat.: 8 a.m.–4 p.m.

Daily trains to: Bern (4½ hours), Basel (5½ hours), Paris, Luxembourg, Vienna, Venice (3 hours), Frankfurt, Florence (3¼ hours), Rome (6½ hours), Bologna (2 hours), Brindisi, Naples, Nice (4¾ hours), Genoa.

TOURIST INFORMATION AND ADDRESSES

The Provincial Tourist Board is at Palazzo del Turismo, Via Marconi 1 (Tel. 809662), open Mon.–Fri.: 8.45 a.m.–6 p.m.; Sat.: 9 a.m.–5.30 p.m. (closed Sundays). For information on Milan, go to the Duomo then walk to the left side of the square under the arches (opposite the Galleria Vittorio Emanuele). They will supply you with a free map of the city which marks the metro and main train/bus lines. Another useful free map gives locations of all the hotels and pensions within the commune. Get the free guide 'Tutta Milano' in English.

POST OFFICE: Stazione Centrale or Via Cordusio 4; also poste restante.

AMEX: Via Vittore Pisani 19, near central station; open Mon.–Fri.: 9 a.m.–6 p.m., Sat.: 9 a.m.–12.30 p.m.

UK CONSULATE: Via San Paolo 7 (Tel. 803442).

US CONSULATE: Piazza della Repubblica 32 (Tel. 652841).

CANADIAN CONSULATE: Via Vittore Pisani 19 (Tel. 6570451).

AUSTRALIAN CONSULATE: Via Turati 40 (Tel. 6598727).

24-HOUR CHEMIST: Tel. 871442 or 192.

TRANSALPINO: 5 Via Locatelli (Tel. 6592041) and in Stazione Centrale (marked 'Wasteels BIJ').

SEEING

The CATHEDRAL (Duomo), the white marble monument of Milanese wealth with 135 spires and over 2,000 sculptures inside and out, is the finest piece of Gothic architecture in northern Italy. It was started in 1386 and not completed till 1813. Ascend to the roof for the view. It's at Piazza del Duomo, though you'd have a job missing it. The famous opera house, LA SCALA, with perfect acoustics has been the scene of many a Verdi or Rossini première, and there's a museum there showing costumes, manuscripts and other operatic memorabilia. It's north of the Duomo, through the gallery, on Piazza della Scala. The BRERA PALACE AND ART GALLERY, a few blocks north of La Scala on Via Brera, is Milan's finest gallery. Housed in a seventeenth-century palace is a varied collection of Italian art and a library of books and manuscripts. The POLDI-PEZZOLI MUSEUM is a private collection with some rare sculptures, paintings and tapestries (closed Mondays), Via Manzoni 12.

The MUSEUM OF ANTIQUE ART is housed in the fifteenth-century SFORZA CASTLE (closed Mondays). Among its collection is Michelangelo's 'Rondanini Pietà' – his last, unfinished work. Enter from Corte Ducale, Piazza Castello. Behind the castle is the SEMPIONE PARK. SANT'AMBROGIO BASILICA, dating back to the fourth century, houses religious treasures and a few dead saints as well as a jewel-studded ninth-century altar, and if you'd like to see the rapidly decaying masterpiece, Leonardo's 'Last Supper', go to the convent next to SANTA MARIA DELLE GRAZIE.

SLEEPING

You shouldn't encounter many hassles in finding a reasonably priced room in Milan, even in summer – and you won't have to walk far either as there are plenty of suitable places just north or west of the station. The tourist office will help you out if you've hit a fluke blackspot. There's a youth hostel, the Ostello per la Gioventù AIG Pier Rotta at Viale Salmoiraghi 2 (Tel. 367095); it's clean, cheap and on the main underground line.

For pensions in the 20,000–35,000 L range, try: Pensione Italia, Via Vitruvio 44 (Tel. 873697), practically in the station it's so close. Pensione Cuba, Via Ricordi 14 (Tel. 2716470); Pensione Lippi, Via

Lippi 48 (Tel. 2361205), and Pensione Soperga, Via Soperga 19 (Tel. 278228) are also close to the station and cheap. More centrally, there are a few pensions in Via Dante at 25,000 L per double.

In recent years Milan has been taking over from Paris as Europe's foremost city for fashion and design. Consequently, many English-speaking models have been lured by the prospect of fame and fortune. If you've been travelling on your own and miss English-speaking company, try the American Hotel, Via Finocchiaro Aprile 2 (Tel. 666441) or Hotel Brussels, Piazza Castello 13 (Tel. 809361).

EATING AND NIGHTLIFE

There are trattorie and rosticcerie all over the city. The speciality of Milanese cooking is that they use butter, not olive oil as they do elsewhere in Italy. With the amount of money knocking about Milan, the Milanese tend to eat out a lot, so restaurants are more expensive here than elsewhere. For a cheap meal near the centre try Big Burgy, just out from San Babila underground station, or, even better, Ciao, just down the road at Corso Europa 12. If you want to go up-market without paying up-market prices, try Pane e Farina at Via Pantano 6 (Tel. 803274). For an interesting evening and a closer look at some of Milan's large transvestite community try Scimmie at Via Ascanio Sforza 49.

Emilia-Romagna

This is the region from the southern Po Valley to the Apennine Mountains north of Tuscany. Its towns are medieval and Renaissance: Parma, Ferrara, Ravenna and Bologna. It has the richest cuisine in Italy, where tortellini, tagliatelle and Bolognese sauce originated, and from Parma has come Parma ham and Parmesan cheese.

PARMA, in the centre of the huge plain south of the River Po, is

known for its architectural and gastronomic delights. PIAZZA GARI-
BALDI is the old town centre with the TOWN HALL, CLOCK TOWER and
GOVERNOR'S PALACE. The DUOMO (Cathedral) is Romanesque and
on its cupola is Correggio's 'Assumption of the Virgin Mary'. The
church of the MADONNA DELL STECCATA in Piazza Marconi is
sixteenth-century and has been restored since its Second World
War bombing. The PALAZZO DELLA PILOTTA is now the city's
museum, and the NATIONAL GALLERY looks at the school established by Correggio in Parma, as well as the medieval–Renaissance
Italian works. Tourist information is at Piazza Duomo 5. There's a
student hostel both here and at Ferrara.

FERRARA today is an agricultural and industrial centre, but
hopefully you'll visit it to see what's left of one of the Renaissance's
cultural centres. It was an independent duchy ruled by the dukes of
Este, and in their courts flowered some of the most gifted
philosophers, artists and writers of the Renaissance movement. The
CASTELLO ESTENSE (the Duke's Castle) dates back to the fourteenth
century. This fortress, surrounded by a moat and complete with
dungeons and a beautiful chapel, is open to the public. The town's
CATHEDRAL is of the twelfth century and stands opposite the
thirteenth-century PALAZZO COMUNALE. The PALAZZO SCHIFANOIA,
down Via Scandiana, is where the dukes went for amusement; it's
now a museum; the archaeological museum is in the Renaissance
PALAZZO DI LUDOVICO IL MORO. Tourist information is at Largo
Castello 28.

RAVENNA was the sixth-century western capital of the Byzantine
Empire, and the early Christian mosaics are outstanding. Ravenna
is an hour down the line from Ferrara, and two hours from Bologna.
The tourist office at Via Salara 8 will supply maps, information and
accommodation help. SAN VITALE, the octagonal church, contains
some mosaics, but across the cloister is the TOMB OF GALLA PLACIDIA
with the best mosaics in Ravenna. Dante is buried in the grounds of
the CHURCH OF SAN FRANCESCO. The high spot of Ravenna is a visit
to the seventh-century church of SANT' APOLLINARE IN CLASSE (bus 4
from the station). The beaches are good, but often mobbed in
summer. There's a youth hostel on Via Aurelio Nicolodi (Tel.
420405). It's good, cheap and reached by bus 1. For camping, head
to Marina di Ravenna, and for a hostel try Albergo Minerva, Via
Maroncelli 1 (Tel. 34543), just to the right of the station. There's a
student refectory at 8 Via Oberdan.

Bologna

The oldest university town in Europe (1076), one of the gastronomic centres of Europe, a Renaissance city of culture and learning, and today as red and communist as Moscow. This is where some eurorailers met a tragic death in August 1980 when the station was bombed. Things are back to normal now, and what's left of the station still stands on the northern edge of Bologna and carries trains running to Florence, Venice, Rome, Vienna, Sicily and other destinations.

STATION FACILITIES

	BOLOGNA CENTRALE
Train information	8 a.m.–8 p.m.
Reservations	7 a.m.–9.45 p.m.
Tourist information	Mon.–Fri.: 9 a.m.–12.30 p.m., 2 p.m.–6 p.m.
	Sat.: 9 a.m.–12.30 p.m.
Foreign exchange	8 a.m.–10 p.m.
Left-luggage store	All hours
Cafeteria	Thurs.–Mon.: 11 a.m.–3 p.m., 7 p.m.–10 p.m.
Restaurant	11 a.m.–12 midnight (upstairs)
	7 a.m.–12 midnight (downstairs)

TOURIST INFORMATION AND ADDRESSES

Apart from the one at the station, there are offices at Via Leopardi 1, Via Marconi 45, and Piazza XX Settembre. General siesta-time is 12.30 p.m.–3.30 p.m. They'll help out on accommodation as well as providing the usual services.

POST OFFICE: Piazza Minghetti, Mon.–Sat.: 8 a.m.–9 p.m., Sun.: 8 a.m.–2 p.m.

STUDENT TRAVEL OFFICE: CTS, Via delle Belle Arti 20 (Tel. 264862).

24-HOUR CHEMIST: Tel. 192.

SEEING

The main street is VIA UGO BASSI with at one end the pedestrianized PIAZZA MAGGIORE where three Gothic structures tower up and supply shade to sit under. The PALAZZO COMUNALE is a complex of palaces which contains the municipal art gallery. Seven churches joined into another conglomeration is what you find at the BASILICA SANTO STEFANO; the octagonal church of the Holy Sepulchre, the eleventh-century church of the Crucifix and the church of St Peter and St Paul all merit a look. The courtyard behind the Holy Sepulchre has the BASIN OF PILATE where Pontius Pilate is said to have washed his hands when symbolically absolving himself of responsibility.

SLEEPING, EATING AND NIGHTLIFE

The scope isn't huge in Bologna for budget beds. The cheapest place in town is the Dormitorio Comunale on Via Sabatini 2. It has replaced the old hostel, but we can't vouch for it. Try Locanda Neva behind the station on Via Serra 7, Pensione Fiorita, Via San Felice 6 (Tel. 229560), or Pensione Marconi, Via Marconi 22 (Tel. 262832).

Eating's a totally different proposition: the only headache here is deciding where to go, as there are simply so many likely places. The cooking is terrific, and it's almost unheard of to have a bad meal. Though there is a university refectory, this is one place it'd be a shame to use as there are so many family-run trattorie. Try Sancho Panza, Via Albari 2, or the Trattoria at Via Broccaindosso 21A. If you're there in term-time, ask students in the university refectory for an idea of what's on; and pick up the rest of the events from tourist information.

The Italian Riviera – Liguria

From the French Côte d'Azur to Tuscany lies the Italian Riviera. It's not quite as flash as its French counterpart, but it's cheaper, which results in some of the bigger resorts being packed out in summer. Genoa is the main town of this region, though it's hardly a resort. There's a very comprehensive line serving the Riviera which starts at Marseille in France, passes through the border at Ventimiglia and serves places like Bordighera, San Remo, Alassio, Albenga and Genoa. There are at least twenty-four trains a day, so hopping from one place to the next till you find the one you like best is easy. Each town has a tourist information office (Azienda di Turismo) and they'll help out on accommodation.

BORDIGHERA was a favourite among European royals and the English aristocracy in the nineteenth century. The oldest part of the town is on the hill, and along the shore is the new town. Bordighera is an attractive garden-filled resort which prides itself on its abundant palm trees (they supply the Vatican with palms on Palm Sunday). Prices tend to be high here, so try sleeping on the beach (in an unobtrusive place as the police aren't at all keen on this practice) and avoid the restaurants without fixed menus.

SAN REMO is the Riviera's largest resort, but unless you've money to waste in the Casino, stick tight to the beach. There are plenty of pizzerias and cafés, but this resort is one of the most commercialized and we're not recommending it too highly.

ALASSIO has a good mile-and-a-half beach. The new town's pretty grim, but the old town down by the beach is lovely. This used to be another haunt of the wealthy British, and there's tennis, golf and skiing on offer.

ALBENGA was a strategic Roman port and you can visit the ROMAN NAVAL MUSEUM here and see the remains of a Roman ship sunk in the first century BC. Today it is a market town and is more down-to-earth, and Italian, than many of the surrounding resorts.

Genoa (Genova)

The largest port of northern Italy with a medieval harbour-quarter, Renaissance upper town of merchants' palaces and, above all this, modern Genoa. Crowning this is the CIRCONVALLAZIONE A MONTE, a boulevard which winds its way in and out of the hills, giving a superb panorama over the city. Genoa became an important artistic centre in the sixteenth and seventeenth centuries when Flemish masters, including Rubens and Van Dyck, came over to paint the wealthy merchants' portraits. This is also the birthplace of Christopher Columbus.

STATION FACILITIES

Genoa has two stations: Porta Principe and Brignole. Northbound trains leave from Principe, southbound from Brignole. Through-trains stop at both, except those going north-west (Milano–Nice) which stop only at Principe. There are inter-station connecting trains at least every thirty minutes.

	PORTA PRINCIPE	BRIGNOLE
Train information	7 a.m.–11 p.m. (Tel. 284 081)	7 a.m.–11 p.m. (Tel. 284 081)
Reservations	7 a.m.–10 p.m.	7 a.m.–10 p.m.
Tourist information	Mon.–Sat.: 9 a.m.–12 noon 3 p.m.–7 p.m.	Mon.–Sat.: 8 a.m.–12 noon 4 p.m.–7 p.m.
Foreign exchange	Mon.–Fri.: 8.20 a.m.–1.20 p.m.	See train information
Left-luggage store	All hours	All hours
Cafeteria	11.30 a.m.–3.30 p.m. 7 p.m.–11 p.m.	6 a.m.–9.30 p.m.
Restaurant		11 a.m.–5 p.m.
Bar, Buffet	7 a.m.–11.30 p.m. (summer) 7 a.m.–11 p.m. (winter)	6 a.m.–9.30 p.m.
Post office	Mon.–Sat.: 8 a.m.–10 p.m. Sun.: 8 a.m.–12 noon	Mon.–Fri.: 8.15 a.m.–10 p.m. Sat.: 8.15 a.m.–2 p.m.

Daily trains to: Luxembourg, Frankfurt, Milan (1½ hours), Venice (4½ hours), Bologna (3 hours), Florence (4½ hours), Rome (5½ hours), Naples, Nice (3 hours).

TOURIST INFORMATION AND ADDRESSES

At the railway stations and the main office at Via Roma 11.
POST OFFICE: Palazzo Poste, Via G. Boccardo 2.
UK CONSULATE: Via XII Ottobre 2, 13th floor (Tel. 564 833).
24-HOUR CHEMIST: Piazza Acquaverde (Principe Station).

SEEING

Get hold of a map as it's a confusing city. Walk down VIA GARIBALDI and see the elegant sixteenth-century palaces. The PALAZZO BIANCO is now an art gallery with a Flemish collection. See the gallery and fine frescoes of PALAZZO CATALDI and the antiquities in PALAZZO DORIA TURSI. VIA BALBI and VIA CAIROLI are fine examples of old Genoa, as is PIAZZA DE FERRARI. SAN LORENZO CATHEDRAL was started in the twelfth century and finished in the sixteenth.

SLEEPING, EATING AND NIGHTLIFE

The youth hostel's your best bet. It's at Via Cinque Maggio 79 (Tel. 387370). Tourist information will come up with plenty of pension suggestions and you shouldn't find any problems. The Hotel Astoria on Piazza Brignole (Tel. 893991), near Brignole Station, does some reasonable rooms (go for ones without baths). There's a student hostel too.

There are scores of pizzerias and restaurants, and the prices all seem very much on a level in all quarters of the town, so go for one that's handy and displays its menu with prices quoted. Try the regional specialities of cima Genovese (stuffed cold veal) and pandolce (orange-flavoured cake).

Veneto

Veneto encompasses the north-eastern section of the Po Valley to the Dolomites and coastal resorts. This is the region around what many consider to be the most beautiful city in the world, Venice. Apart from this, there are the art towns of Padua and Verona close by.

Venice (Venezia)

Venice is absolutely unmatched by anything else in Europe; there really is nowhere else like it. It's a 'must' on any European tour, and it's worth all the crowds and higher-than-normal prices, because you'll never forget it. The town consists of 117 islets connected by 400 bridges with 150 canals winding their way through the maze. There are no cars, only boats.

The history of Venice is long and colourful. Her buildings reflect her glorious past when she, as an independent city-state, ruled over most of the Mediterranean. During the Renaissance, Venice was *the* trading port with the Middle East, and she became the centre of European commerce. The doges (the city dukes or rulers) had enough money not only to build sumptuous palaces and churches, but also to commission large-scale works of art from the Venetian school (Titian, Tintoretto, etc.) and patronize science and the arts. Their 1,000-year independence came to an end in 1797 when Napoleon gave Venice to the Austrians. When Italy was united, Venice joined on, and its popularity as a tourist trap of the twentieth century has brought it new wealth, much of which is used to prevent the entire city sinking and being lost for ever.

STATION FACILITIES

The station is situated at the west end of the town right on the Grand Canal. It's easily possible to walk everywhere by foot, but it's more fun to take the vaporetti (waterbuses) from outside the station. Nos. 1, 2 and 5 take you down the Grand Canal to San Marco Square.

SANTA LUCIA, VENEZIA	
Train information	6 a.m.–10 p.m. (Tel. 715555)
Reservations	7 a.m.–10 p.m.
Tourist information	8 a.m.–8 p.m.
Foreign exchange	Mon.–Sat.: 8 a.m.–7 p.m. Sun.: 8 a.m.–1 p.m.
Left-luggage store	All hours
Bar, Buffet	6 a.m.–9 p.m.
Waiting room	All hours
Post office	Mon.–Sat.: 8.30 a.m.–1.30 p.m.

Some trains stop only at Venezia–Mestre on the mainland, so check. To reach Venezia Santa Lucia from Mestre, there are both trains and buses.

TOURIST INFORMATION

At the station and near San Marco Square at Ascensione 71F. There's also a student tourist office (CGTS) at Calle del Fabbro 3252, near Ponte Foscari. They'll also help out with accommodation and student travel.

● **Addresses:**
POST OFFICE: Fondaco dei Tedeschi.
AMEX: San Marco, 1471 San Marco. Mon.–Fri.: 9 a.m.–6 p.m., Sat.: 9 a.m.–12.30 p.m.
UK CONSULATE: PO Box 679, Accademia 1051 (Tel. 27207).
FIRST AID: (Tel. 3000).

● **Getting about:** The waterbuses (vaporetti) cover all Venice. A trip on Line 4 is good, as it takes in quite a few sights. They run every 10 minutes from 5 a.m. to 12 midnight. Fares are around the 2,000 L mark. There are also a few buses, but their routes are restricted. The gondolas look beautiful, but at 60,000 L an hour it's not surprising we haven't seen too many eurorailers on them.

SEEING

Venice is a place to wander in. There are so many little winding back-streets and alleys, unexpected quiet squares and little humpback bridges that this is the easiest place in Europe to get lost in (no wonder Venice's famous son Marco Polo was so good at exploring). The sights that you can't miss are as follows:

1. ST MARK'S SQUARE: The city revolves round this incredible piazza. ST MARK'S BASILICA and the DOGES' PALACE are here, as are the LAW COURTS, the beautiful CLOCK TOWER and the OLD LIBRARY – now an archaeological museum. The PIAZZETTA leads off from the square to the GRAND CANAL.
2. ST MARK'S BASILICA: This amazing Byzantine church, built in the eleventh century, is a riot of gold, marble and mosaic. It was originally the chapel for the doges, and became the city cathedral in 1807. The four massive bronze horses over the doorway were brought over from Constantinople after it was raided in 1207. (Girls: bring a shawl to cover your shoulders and arms; men: wear long trousers to be let in.)
3. DOGES' PALACE (Palazzo Ducale): This pink-and-white fairytale palace was the home of the Venetian government and the rulers of the republic. (Note the Tintoretto in the Grand Council Chamber.) The connecting bridge between the palace and the prison is known as the BRIDGE OF SIGHS.
4. THE ACADEMY OF FINE ART (Galleria dell'Accademia) has the best of the Venetian school's work: Canaletto, Tintoretto, Bellini, Veronese, etc. Closed Mondays. Free on ISIC.
5. CHIESA DEI FRARI: After St Mark's, this is Venice's most prized church. It houses two Titians and a Bellini. Next to it is the SCUOLA DI SAN ROCCO with a collection of fifty-six Tintorettos on biblical themes.
6. SCHOOL OF ST GEORGE: Beyond St Mark's Square at Calle dei Furlani. A frieze of paintings by Carpaccio – beautiful, and usually much quieter than the other museums.

• Excursions: Just north of Venice lies the LIDO, the beach resort of the rich and famous. Wander past the villas, casino and hotels, and imagine it as it was when Thomas Mann used it to inspire his novel,

Death in Venice. Also worth a trip is the island of MURANO where Venetian glass is blown; BURANO, a colourful little fishing village; and TORCELLO with its Byzantine cathedral.

SLEEPING

Here the problems start, especially in August. It's a seller's market and don't they know it. Rooms here cost about 30–50 per cent more than elsewhere in Italy, so get into Venice early, leave your rucksack off at left luggage, and start out. The area near the station is as good as anywhere to look; just keep going from one pension to another. Tourist information at San Marco will try and get you a room, but the station branch don't bother. If all else fails, there's always sleeping at the station, though it can get a bit rough sometimes.

● **Hostels:** The youth hostel is on the island of Giudecca at Fondamenta delle Zitelle 86C (Tel. 38211). Also out here are a few pensions and a religious hostel, Istituto Canossiane, Ponte Piccolo 428 (Tel. 22157). Reception opens at 4 p.m., and it's around 12,000 L each. Istituto Ciliota at San Stefano 2976 (Tel. 704888) caters for women and married couples only. Finally there's Domus Covanis, Dorsoduro 899, on Rio Foscarini (Tel. 87374). It's clean and convenient.
For camping, head to the beach on Litorale del Cavallino.

● **Hotels and pensions:** Don't attempt to stay in a single room – it'll cripple you financially. If you are travelling alone, find a partner quick, or head for a hostel. We suggest the Lista di Spagna near the station as there are many cheap pensions in this area. Locanda Stefania, Fondamenta Tolentini, 181A (Tel. 703757), is across the bridge at the station. Doubles cost around 30,000 L. Locanda Riva Castello 5310 (Tel. 27034) is a safe bet, with a very friendly owner; his café does the cheapest spaghetti in Venice and a really excellent pizza. Locanda Corona, Calle Corona 4464 (Tel. 29174) is very central. Locanda Ca' Foscari, Dorsoduro 3888 (Tel. 25817) is clean and reasonably priced.

EATING AND NIGHTLIFE

There are quite a few fixed-price menus floating about and the food markets provide all you need for picnics. The main market is at the foot of the Rialto Bridge. For trattorie the best area is Dorsoduro; there's a particularly good one at Dorsoduro 3922. If you're hard up and can't afford to eat at a trattoria, try the railworkers' café to the right of the station (Mensa Dopolavoro Ferroviario), or the students' Mensa at the end of Calle della Frescada.

Verona

It's not surprising Shakespeare chose Verona as his setting for *Romeo and Juliet* as it is a romantic city of palaces, churches, gardens and vineyards. It's about midway on the line from Milan to Venice and a popular destination with eurorailers. From the station it's a 15-minute walk to the centre of Verona, so take the bus No. 2 to the PIAZZA BRA where the incredibly preserved ROMAN ARENA is. Tourist information is at Via della Valverde 34 (open Mon.–Fri.: 9 a.m.–12 noon, 3.30 p.m.–6.30 p.m., Sat.: 9 a.m.–12 noon). At the PIAZZA DELL' ERBE are the Veronese merchants' palaces, and just close by at PIAZZA DEI SIGNORI are the tombs of the Scaligeri, Verona's medieval enemies. Their house was the CASTELVECCHIO, now a museum. The Romanesque church of SAN ZENO MAGGIORE is worth seeing for its bronze door-panels and the altar-piece by Mantegna.

For a bed, try the Istituto Don Bosco, Via Provolo 16 (Tel. 591300), or for women the Casa della Giovane, Via Pigna 7 (Tel. 24978). Pensione Marina, Via Ponte Nuovo 5 (Tel. 25968) do doubles for about 30,000 L, and there's camping at the aptly named Romeo and Juliet site on Via Bresciana 54 (Tel. 989243). Also newly opened is the hostel at Salita Fontana della Ferro 15, just across the Ponte Pietra, and with beds at 6,000 L a night it's good value.

Try Trattoria alla Canna at Via Scrimiari 5, or Cucina Cristo at Piazzetta Pescheria for cheap set menus. Wash it down with the local Soave or Valpolicella wine. During the summer there are sometimes performances of opera and Shakespearean dramas in the 22,000-capacity Roman Arena. Seats start at about 12,000 L, but it's an experience you won't easily forget (check with tourist information).

Padua (Padova)

About 1½ hours from Venice lies Padua, the famous thirteenth-century university town. Tourist information is near the station. Pick up maps here, and make use of the accommodation service, which is free (open 9 a.m.–12.30 p.m., 3.30 p.m.–7 p.m., closed Saturday p.m. and Sunday). There also is a downtown office at Riviera Mugnai 8. The CAPPELLA SCROVEGNI is *the* sight of Padua: Giotto's masterpiece of medieval art that shook the artistic theories of the time. Next door is the CHIESA DEGLI EREMITANI where Mantegna's frescoes hang. Further up Corso Garibaldi is the university with its famous anatomical theatre. IL SANTO is the church dedicated to St Anthony, built in a mix of about six architectural styles. The SCUOLA DI SANT'ANTONIO contains four Titians also dedicated to this saint, the patron of Padua.

Accommodation shouldn't be a problem. The youth hostel here is a renovated medieval castle. It's at Porta Legnano in Montagnana, an hour's bus ride from 42 Via Trieste. In town, try the Ostello Città di Padova at Via Aleardi 30 (Tel. 28369). For food, go to the excellent food market, the Salone, near the university, or try one of the three Mensas: at Via San Francesco 122 (closed August), Via Padovanino, or Via Leopardi.

Tuscany

Italy's wealthiest region in every way. This was the birthplace of the Renaissance and, apart from the mountains and coastal beaches, it offers some of the finest old art cities in the world: Siena, Pisa and the Renaissance town itself, Florence. The countryside is beautiful – without the south's poverty or the north's heavy industry, and the trains serve even the smallest towns.

Florence (Firenze)

The Medici family made Florence the central point of the Renaissance, and her citizens included names like da Vinci, Botticelli, Michelangelo, Galileo and Machiavelli. The legacy lives on in today's Florence, and even the pot-smoking, guitar-strumming crowd that camp outside the Uffizi in summer can't take away from the centuries of elegance and careful detail that make this a pilgrimage centre for artists the world over. There are enough churches, galleries, palaces and museums to interest everyone, but there aren't enough beds, so come early to Florence, and avoid joining the throngs of August station-sleepers who wake up to find they've lost more than a good night's sleep.

STATION FACILITIES

	FIRENZE SANTA MARIA NOVELLA
Train information	8 a.m.–8 p.m. (Tel. 278785)
Reservations	7 a.m.–9 p.m.
Tourist information	10 a.m.–8.30 p.m.
Foreign exchange	8 a.m.–12 noon, 1 p.m.–7 p.m. in train information
Left-luggage store	All hours
Bar, Buffet	5.30 a.m.–11.20 p.m.
Restaurant	11.30 a.m.–9 p.m.
Shops	8 a.m.–12 noon, 5 p.m.–7.30 p.m. except Wednesdays and Sundays

Daily trains to: Bologna, Venice, Munich, Vienna, Frankfurt, Pisa, Rome, Naples, Sicily, Paris, Milan.

TOURIST INFORMATION

The main tourist office is at Via A. Manzoni 16, open 8.30 a.m.–1.30 p.m., 4 p.m.–6 p.m., closed Saturday p.m. and Sundays. The station branch deals with accommodation (commission 1,000 L), but the queues are long. The city tourist office is at Via Tornabuoni 15 (Tel. 216544).They give out good maps of the city.

● **Addresses:**
POST OFFICE: Via Pellicceria. Also poste restante and telephones. Open Mon.–Sat.: 8.15 a.m.–7.30 p.m.
AMEX: c/o Universalturismo, Via degli Speziali 7r, Mon.–Fri.: 9 a.m.–12.30 p.m., 3.30 p.m.–7 p.m., Sat.: 9 a.m.–12 noon.
UK CONSULATE: Palazzo Castelbarco, Lungarno Corsini 2 (Tel. 212594).
US CONSULATE: Lungarno Vespucci 46 (Tel. 298276).
STUDENT TRAVEL: CGTS, Via delle Terme 53r. Open 9.30 a.m.–12.30 p.m., 3 p.m.–6 p.m., closed Saturday p.m. and Sundays. They also help out on accommodation and city information.
24-HOUR CHEMIST: At the station.

SEEING

The DUOMO is the amazing multicolour cathedral with the huge dome which takes up a good chunk of the centre. It was started in 1296 and finished in 1434 – the dome was hailed as the wonder of the fifteenth century, but the façade of the cathedral today is only nineteenth-century. Climb the 464 steps for an unrivalled view over Florence. The CAMPANILE was Giotto's idea and the BAPTISTRY is Romanesque and noted for its bronze doors by Ghiberti. The next sight of Florence has got to be the UFFIZI, one of the world's greatest art galleries housed in a Renaissance palace. There's such a glut of sheer genius here, you really can't cope; visit it more than once and try to avoid the crowds. It isn't quite the same trying to study the finer points of a Leonardo with school parties whizzing past and real art enthusiasts elbowing you out of the way to get a closer look. It's open Tues.–Sat.: 9 a.m.–7 p.m., Sun.: 9 a.m.–1 p.m. Still, we must be grateful we still have the Uffizi to visit, as Hitler ordered the collections to be destroyed in 1945, and the terrible flood of 1966 badly damaged many of its treasures.

Across from the Uffizi is the PALAZZO PITTI, a fifteenth-century palace which the Medicis used during the sixteenth century. You can wander round it today and see the Raphaels, Rubens, Titians, and on its ground floor the ROYAL APARTMENTS and MUSEUM OF

GEMS. The medieval BARGELLO PALACE holds the NATIONAL MUSEUM, an important sculpture collection (closed Mondays), and if you, like thousands of others, came to Florence to see Michelangelo's 'David' you'll find him in the GALLERIA DELL'ACCADEMIA on Via Ricasoli (also closed Mondays). The massive PALAZZO VECCHIO was the Medici residence from the fourteenth to the sixteenth century. Inside it's sumptuous – not surprisingly, they got the cream of Renaissance artists to decorate it. It's at Piazza della Signoria (closed Saturdays). The other palace you ought to see is the MEDICI on Via Cavour. They lived here from 1460 to 1540. There's a tiny chapel on the first floor, and a Medici Museum downstairs which is free on Sundays.

As far as churches go, take in the Medicis' Renaissance parish church, ST LAURENCE'S. Most of them are buried here in the MEDICI CHAPELS (closed Mondays), and there's a LIBRARY considered to be Michelangelo's architectural masterpiece. SAN MARCO is worth seeing for the monks' cells which Fra Angelico painted his unique shade of blue, and the BRANCACCI CHAPEL of Santa Maria della Carmine has some beautiful Masaccio frescoes. Giotto has some work in SANTA CROCE and next to this is the interesting PAZZI CHAPEL.

The PONTE VECCHIO was the only bridge to survive 1944's bombs. It dates back to 1345 and is famous for the gold- and silversmith shops that line it. The STRAW MARKET (Mercato Nuovo) makes a good shopping trip, and the BOBOLI GARDENS, behind the Pitti Palace, are good for a picnic and sunbathe; they close at night, however, so a free sleep is impossible.

SLEEPING

Use the station tourist office and stress your price range. Florence is more expensive than average (though not up to the extortionate Venetian levels), so be prepared to spend about 10,000 L in a hostel, 20,000 L in a pension and about 20,000 in a hotel for a single. Showers are invariably an extra 1,000 L and breakfast is rarely included.

• **Hostels:** The youth hostel is at Viale Augusto Righi (Tel. 601451) with around 400 beds, but it's for IYHF members only and costs

8,000 L a night. Reception opens at 2 p.m.; take bus 17B from the station. Pio X-Artigianelli, Via dei Serragli 106 (Tel. 225044). Near the Pitti Palace, about 8,500 L in triples, and 4 p.m. reception. Ostello S. Monaca, Via Santa Monaca 6 (Tel. 268338), 8,000 L. Drop off bags 1 p.m.–3 p.m.

● **Pensions:** There are a glut of suitable places within five minutes of the station. The only problem is that this is common knowledge, so get there early. If you come up with nothing in this area, drop off your pack if it's heavy as the other pensions are a good walk away. From the station, turn left then try places along Via Nazionale, Via Fiume, Via Fuenza, Via 28 Aprile, Via Guelfa and Via Cavour. We've tried the following and found them OK: Locanda Nella, Via Fuenza 69 (Tel. 284256); Locanda Mia Cara at No. 58; Pensione Beatrice, Via Fiume 11 (Tel. 216790). Also try Locanda Sampoli at Via S. Gallo 39 (Tel. 480316).

Outside this section try Locanda Aldini,Via Calzaioli 13 (Tel. 214752), near the Duomo, or Pensione Davanzati at Via Porta Nossa 15 (Tel. 283414).

● **Camping:** Viale Michelangelo 80 (Tel. 6811977) is a site open April–Oct. – bus 13 from the station (good views of Florence); and for all-year camping try Camping Camerata next to the youth hostel (Tel. 610300).

EATING AND NIGHTLIFE

The Santo Spirito–San Frediano quarter has more economy restaurants than elsewhere, but really Florence isn't geared up for subsistence-level living.

The Trattoria Casalinga on Via Michelozzi 4r, Via Guerla and Via Frescolana do really cheap and good meals; a favourite of ours (for a splurge) is Trattoria ZaZa at P. Mercato Centrale 26. If you've really reached rock bottom, Casa San Francesco on Piazza Sant' Annunziata, run by Franciscans, will do you a full meal for about 4,000–6,000 L. The university Mensas are on Via San Gallo 25 and Via dei Servi 66–68. For picnic food, the Mercato Centrale, near San Lorenzo, is your best bet. There are also a number of fast-food chains and, of course, ice-cream parlours. Florence is reputed to have the best gelati in Italy. Vivoli, on Via dell' Isola delle Stinche, is still held by many to produce the world's best. Use the take-away pizza places for economy shopping.

During July and August there are bi-weekly classical concerts held in the Pitti Palace courtyard, and there's a music festival in May. On 24 June there are fireworks on Piazzale Michelangelo after the parade in sixteenth-century costume, and the soccer match of the afternoon. On most summer nights, groups of students and travellers congregate on the Ponte Vecchio, and at the Duomo and Piazzale Michelangelo.

Siena

Siena is Tuscany's second art city, but while Florence is Renaissance, Siena is medieval. It's 1½ hours from Florence, and there are about ten daily trains arriving at Via Empoli. (Trains from Rome arrive at Via Chinsi, and you have to change at these stops unless you're talking a direct train.) The heart of the city is the PIAZZA DEL CAMPO, where the Palio (an inter-district horse-race) is held as part of the 2 July and 16 August celebrations, with fifteenth-century costume parades and all-night dances following on. The closest you'll get to the centre by bus from the station is Piazza Matteoti; walk the rest. The Gothic TOWN HALL and bell tower are in this piazza, and in the PIAZZA DEL DUOMO (bus 1: tickets at station) is ST CATHERINE'S CATHEDRAL with its museum of art and sculpture opposite. The CHIGI SARACINI PALACE is today a music academy, but on request they'll show you round the Renaissance apartments and gallery of Tuscan paintings. Further along you'll come to PIAZZA SALIMBENI with its four palaces dating from the thirteenth to the sixteenth centuries.

Cheap rooms are a bit of a problem here, but you can try Locanda Garibaldi, Via G. Dupré 18 (Tel. 284204). It's central and the cheapest in Siena. Or ask tourist information: they're at Piazza del Campo 5 (Tel. 280551). There's no shortage of good trattorie, and the Mensa Universitaria is on Via Sant' Agata.

Pisa

Head straight for the PIAZZA DEL DUOMO with its famous Leaning Tower which Galileo used in his experiments. Also here is the tourist office, though the main one's at Lungarno Mediceo 42. Beside the tower is the CATHEDRAL AND BAPTISTRY, and the nearby CAMPO SANTO is a twelfth-century cemetery built by the Crusaders.

Lodgings are difficult if you arrive late. Try Locanda Galileo, Via Santa Maria 12 (Tel. 40621), down Via San Lorenzo, or the campsite at Viale delle Cascine 86 (Tel. 501512). The Mensa's on Via Martiri and there are several other cheap places round the university. If you're stuck, ask at tourist information.

Florence–Rome

It's about six hours from Florence to Rome and there are two alternative routes: one runs straight down through Arezzo, Chiusi and Orte; the other veers off and takes in the attractive towns of Perugia and Assisi. If you choose the latter route and decide to stop off for a few hours at each place, here is some basic information on these two places:

PERUGIA: This beautiful medieval hill town is about 2½ hours from Florence. Although the centre and university are quite modern, a walk up the side streets will take you back to the days of Perugino – Raphael's teacher. The tourist office is at Corso Vannucci 96 (Tel. 23327), the main street. It's open 8.30 a.m.–1 p.m., 4 p.m.–7 p.m. See the PALAZZO DEI PRIORI, CATHEDRAL, NATIONAL GALLERY OF UNITORIA, NATIONAL ARCHAEOLOGICAL MUSEUM and the ARCH OF AUGUSTUS.

ASSISI: The BASILICA OF ST FRANCIS is a noteworthy building housing medieval and early Renaissance art. Opposite the Roman columns of the TEMPLE OF MINERVA (now a church) is the tourist office (Piazza del Comuna), which is open 9 a.m.–1 p.m., 4 p.m.–7 p.m. Climb up the ROCCA MAGGIORE for a view over the town and the valley.

Rome (Roma)

Rome, the 'eternal city', is so called because it is a place of great beauty, contrast and life. There are really three Romes: the religious world centre of the Catholic Church, the incredible ruins of the centre of the Roman Empire, and modern, dirty, bustling Rome. All three seem incongruous, yet they live inside and beside each other with great ease. You'll soon realize Rome was built to rule and dominate the world. Everything is on a massive scale, solid and 'eternal'. You'll get ripped off by the shopkeepers and find the Romans proud, arrogant and conceited; unless you're very careful, you'll meet with some nasty fate in the station if you dare camp out there; but you'll look back on the overwhelming beauty and dimensions of St Peter's, the atmosphere in the Colosseum at dusk, and the Trevi Fountain when it's floodlit at night and buzzing with young people, and remember it affectionately.

STATION FACILITIES

	ROMA TERMINI
Train information	7 a.m.–11 p.m. (Tel. 4775)
Reservations	7 a.m.–10 p.m.
Tourist information	8 a.m.–10 p.m. (with siesta)
Foreign exchange	Mon.–Fri.: 8.30 a.m.–1.30 p.m. in bank. Other times, window 28
Left-luggage store	All hours
Bar, Buffet	6 a.m.–11.25 p.m. and 7.20 a.m.–8.40 p.m.
Cafeteria	10.30 a.m.–11 p.m.
Bath, Shower	7.20 a.m.–8.40 p.m.
Waiting room	Closed 4 a.m.–6 a.m.
Shops	7 a.m.–9 p.m.
Post office	Mon.–Fri.: 8.15 a.m.–8 p.m., Sat.: 8 a.m.–12 noon
Station shuts	1 a.m.–4 a.m.

Daily trains to: Pisa, Genoa, Nice, Milan, Innsbruck, Venice, Florence, Bologna, Ancona, Naples, Brindisi, Sicily.

TOURIST INFORMATION

Before leaving the station, go along to the EPT tourist office and pick up a map of the city, plus two booklets, 'Qui Roma' ('Here's Rome', current events, etc.) and 'Roma Giovane' ('Young Rome') as these are a great help in getting to know your way around.

Apart from the office at the station, there's one at Via Parigi 5 (Tel. 463748) (open 8.30 a.m.–1.30 p.m., 2.30 p.m.–7.30 p.m.) and the one at Via Marghera 2, which deals with the rest of Italy (9 a.m.–2 p.m.). Pick up 'Qui Roma' here and, rather than leave yourself open to their accommodation suggestions (all over 10,000 L), hand them some of our telephone numbers and ask them to phone for a reservation for you.

Generally, shops and churches are open 9 a.m.–1 p.m., 4.30 p.m.–7 p.m. Museums generally close about 1 p.m. or 2 p.m. and all day Monday, though the Campidoglio museums open late on Tuesdays and Saturdays. In August, Romans take their holidays and you'll find many restaurants shut.

● **Addresses:**
POST OFFICE: Piazza San Silvestro, open 8 a.m.–9 p.m. for poste restante, telephones 8 a.m.–12 midnight.
AMEX: Piazza di Spagna 38, open Mon.–Fri.: 8.30 a.m.–6 p.m., Sat.: 9 a.m.–12.30 p.m.
UK EMBASSY: Via XX Settembre 80 (Tel. 475 5441).
US EMBASSY: Via Vittorio Veneto 119a (Tel. 4674).
CANADIAN EMBASSY: Via G.B. Rossi (Tel. 855341).
CTS (YOUTH TRAVEL SERVICE): Via Genova 16 (Tel. 479931). They help out on accommodation, issue ISICs, etc.
TRANSALPINO: 8a Piazza Esquilino (Tel. 475 1075) and in the station.
24-HOUR CHEMIST: In station.

● **Getting about:** The buses are cheap, and the underground continues to expand yearly, but it's difficult as they keep finding new archaeological sites where they want to lay tracks. Buy tickets from Tabac shops or the stations. Buses run from 5.45 a.m.–12 midnight.

SEEING

Though the three sides of Rome (ancient, religious and modern) are virtually inseparable, we've tried to separate the sights into the three categories. If you give yourself a day for each you'll make it, but by the end you'll need to head for a beach to soothe your blisters in the sea. Ideally, give yourself 4–5 days here, and unless you're really flattened, use the afternoon siestas to get round the sights which are otherwise mobbed. A final word: be on your guard constantly for pickpockets, and particularly the motorized ones who cruise about on mopeds and whip handbags off shoulders and wallets from pockets, then make off at great speed.

• **Ancient Rome:** The sites of ancient Rome are clustered round the Piazza Venezia, the modern city centre, and lie on the PALATINE, CAPITOLINE and AVENTINE hills.

The COLOSSEUM is the biggest site of ancient Rome. This huge arena sat 55,000 Romans who passed many an afternoon watching the local Christians being eaten for dinner by lions, etc., or gladiators fighting it out to the bitter end. The Palatine Hill is where Nero, Mark Antony, Cicero and co. were based. The VILLA FARNESE incorporated many ancient structures into it when it was built in the sixteenth century, and the BOTANICAL GARDENS here were the world's first. See the frescoes on the HOUSE OF AUGUSTUS and the remains of the PALACE OF THE FLAVIANS and the PALACE OF SEPTIMIUS SEVERUS.

The ROMAN FORUM, adjoining the Palatine Hill, was the commercial, religious and civic centre of ancient Rome. Look out for the three TRIUMPHAL ARCHES, HOUSE OF THE VESTAL VIRGINS and the half-dozen temples. Enter by Via dei Fori Imperiali (closed Tuesdays). Opposite is the IMPERIAL FORUM; Caesar started this annexe of the Roman Forum when the expanding empire's paperwork was getting too much for the one place. See TRAJAN'S FORUM with its famous column, and the BASILICA OF ST MAXENTIUS, the ancient law court and exchange (closed Mondays). the MAMERTINE PRISON, just off Via dei Fori Imperiali, is where Nero kept St Peter, and many others were tortured here.

The PANTHEON is the best preserved of all the sites of ancient Rome. It was started in 27 BC, rebuilt in AD 125 and, having been a temple to the gods for over 700 years, became a Christian church in the seventh century. The kings of Italy and the artist Raphael are buried here. It's at Piazza della Rotonda, near the Tiber.

On the APPIAN WAY, the 2,300-year-old Roman road stretching as far south as Brindisi, you'll find the third-century BATHS OF CARACALLA (near Piazzale Numa Pompilio), and the CATACOMBS OF ST CALIXTUS. There are five tiers of burial chambers, and many Christian saints and martyrs here, at 110 Via Appia Antica (closed Wednesdays). The NATIONAL MUSEUM OF ROME has the world's best collection of artefacts from the Roman Empire (Via delle Terme di Diocleziano, closed Mondays). CASTEL SANT' ANGELO, built by Hadrian in AD 139, was the Pope's fortress to flee to in times of danger. Now it's a museum of weapons, art and relics (Lungotevere Castello, closed Mondays). That leaves only the THEATRE OF MARCELLUS (13 BC), the PYRAMID OF CAIUS CESTIUS on Piazza San Paolo, and the remains of four ancient ROMAN TEMPLES in Largo Argentina. All the Roman remains that don't close on Mondays tend to close on Tuesdays.

• **Papal Rome:** The independent state of the VATICAN CITY is the spiritual centre for 146 million Roman Catholics. The Vatican has its own post office with stamps, printing press, currency, radio station, newspaper and railway, all within one square mile. The Pope's in charge here and the Swiss Guards keep order. ST PETER'S SQUARE is a seventeenth-century baroque masterpiece, designed by Bernini, which leads up to ST PETER'S BASILICA, the church whose incredible dome can be seen all over Rome. Inside the huge interior are works by Raphael, Michelangelo (his famous Pietà), Bernini and Bramante. (Don't wear shorts if you want to get in.) For the full emotion of this church to hit you – even if you're an atheist – come when it's just opened at 9 a.m. The VATICAN MUSEUMS which include such treasures as Michelangelo's SISTINE CHAPEL, the RAPHAEL ROOMS, the GRAECO-ROMAN MUSEUMS, and the VATICAN LIBRARY are located north of St Peter's on Viale Vaticano. It costs about 3,000 L on ISIC, more without, but it's well worth it. There are four alternative routes to follow through the museums; we suggest you take C or D, and skip through the bits you're not interested in (closed Sundays). The two churches that must be included here, though they're not located in or near the Vatican, are ST JOHN LATERAN with the HOLY STAIRS and SANTA MARIA MAGGIORE. The former is the church of the popes, founded in the fourth century.

The stairs are believed to be those from the palace of Pontius Pilate which Christ ascended during his Passion. You can only climb them, however, if you're officially worshipping, and then you have to do it on your knees. The church is south-east of the Colosseum at Piazza San Giovanni in Laterno. The latter is another fourth-century church, though rebuilt in the thirteenth and with an eighteenth-century façade. The campanile is the tallest in Rome and there are some interesting fifth-century mosaics (Via Liberiana 27).

• **Modern Rome:** The squares of Rome are worth seeing as sights in themselves. The PIAZZA DEL CAMPIDOGLIO, designed by Michelangelo, is flanked by palaces and is considered to be the political city centre. Of the three palaces one is the senatorial office, one is the CAPITOLINE MUSEUM of antique sculptures, and the other is the CONSERVATORIO which has large chunks of hands, toes and heads from Roman statues.

The PIAZZA NAVONA is another Bernini work, as is PIAZZA BARBERINI. The SPANISH STEPS (Piazza di Spagna) are eighteenth-century and the Barcaccia fountain at the bottom attracts a young crowd of manwatchers, but *the* fountain of Rome has got to be the TREVI. This baroque work was finished in 1762. If you're looking for your Latin lover, come here after dark. The fountain's floodlit and the atmosphere typically Roman, including the pickpockets. It's at Piazza di Trevi.

The MONUMENT TO VICTOR EMMANUEL II, in the Piazza Venezia, is the huge white marble 'wedding cake' at the end of Via del Corso. It was built in 1911 to celebrate Italy's unification. The VILLA BORGHESE, in the north of Rome, is the most splendid of Rome's parks. The zoo and two art galleries are out here, and though this seems like the best place to sleep out in Rome, it's actually one of the worst – more than half who risk it seem to end up mugged.

SLEEPING

Though Rome gets packed in July and August, beds are never really a problem as there are literally hundreds of pensions, locande and alloggi. There are plenty of cheap places beside the station and, though this isn't right in the centre, it's not so far out you can't walk to the sights, and the prices are the cheapest in town. To help you find a place, use either CTS (see addresses), the Student Help Office or the tourist offices; but remember to get them to phone only your own suggested places, as theirs are all over the top.

• **Student hostels:** The youth hostel is at Viale delle Olimpiadi 61 (Tel. 3964709), quite far out and reports on it vary dramatically. Centro d'Accoglienza 'Pax Christi', Via di Santa Maura 2 (Tel. 350988), has large dorms for 8,000 L; and Locanda del Conservatorio, Via del Conservatorio 62 (Tel. 659612) has clean central rooms for 9,000 L single, 16,000 L double, but reserve ahead. The Casa dello Studente, Città Universitaria on Via Cesare de Lollis 24 (Tel. 490 243), does dormitory beds from June to September. Near the station there's the Centro dei Giovani at Via degli Apuli 40 (Tel. 4953151); it's cheap and convenient but tends to fill up quickly, so get there early.

• **Pensions near the station:** As you leave the station you can turn either right or left to begin your search. On the right are: Pensione Cervia, Via Palestro 55 (Tel. 491056) with singles around 12,000 L and doubles for 20,000 L. This is one of the better ones, clean and friendly. At No. 15 of the same street Pensione Bolognese (Tel. 485 848) is on a similar price scale, and at No. 35 is Pensione Michele (Tel. 4743383), with Pensione Katty (Tel. 4751385) on the third floor at the same address. Pensione Cristallo, Via Montebello 114 (Tel. 4759810), has doubles and triples for 14,000 L each; Pensione Blanela, Via Castelfidardo 31 (Tel. 464756) asks similar prices, as does Pensione Asmara downstairs.

On the left of the station you'll find another spate of pensions, and also several cheap eating-places. This is a very Roman working-class neighbourhood, full of colour and life. Via Principe Amedeo has a collection of very good bed bargains; all ask about 12,000–16,000 L a person. The pensions include Cotorillo, Govoni and di Rienzi, which are all very acceptable. Next door at No. 79 is Pensione Pezzotti with free showers and doubles for 22,000 L; and at 79d on the sixth floor is Pensione Tony (Tel. 736994). His rooms are clean and have their own shower.

If you want to be nearer the centre, try: Locanda Sud America, Via Cavour 116 (Tel. 464507), or Locanda Chic at No. 266 (Tel. 4758614). Both are near ancient Rome and in the 20,000–30,000 L per double range. On Via Nazionale there's Pensione Casa Christiana (Tel. 460014) at No. 13, with doubles for 24,000 L; and' the St Moritz at No. 51 (Tel. 4743068).

If things are desperate and you're sleeping out, no matter how desperate you are avoid flaking out in the park outside the station. Each summer the muggings seem to get more numerous and vicious, and the gypsies that hang out there should be watched like hawks. The park at Calle Oppio, near the Colosseum, is your best bet, but even that is to be avoided. One final piece of advice. Roman pensione owners are notorious for attempting the great tourist rip-off. Always check the prices with those posted in the room, and argue for the difference.

EATING AND NIGHTLIFE

For about 12,000 L you can eat a good, filling meal in Rome. Almost every neighbourhood has its own collection of cheap trattorie and rosticcerie, as the Romans eat out a lot themselves. Go for the menu turistico and spoil yourself on the delicious pasta and pizza dishes which fill you up for very little money. There's little point buying food for picnics (though if you do, bar owners will let you eat it inside if you buy a drink from them) as good supermarkets are few and far between. Don't trail across town to follow our few suggestions; just eat at the nearest likely spot wherever you happen to find yourself. The Mensa Universitaria on Via Cesare de Lollis 20 is closed all August. Aureli, Via Quattro Fontane 38, is particularly good and also serves vegetarian dishes; and for really authentic Roman cooking try Il Falchetto, Via Montecatini 12/14, off the Corso. Palmerie, Via Cimarra 415, is where some of the trendy Roman crowd hang out. The fixed-price menus are reasonable. The area on the right-hand side of the station as you leave is good for tourist menus. Especially good value is Osteria de Salvatore at Via Castelfidardo 39c.

The Romans are big manwatchers, so when in Rome . . . Sit out and scrutinize the passers-by in Piazza Navona or Piazza del Popolo, or go and revisit some of the sights when they're floodlit: the Trevi, the Colosseum, St Peter's, etc. You're likely to encounter young Romans in a trattoria, disco or bar. If opera is your cup of tea, try and make it along to the outdoor performances in the

Roman Baths of Caracalla. Buy tickets from the Teatro dell'Opera. Giolitti's are reputed to have the best ice-cream in Rome. They're near the Pantheon at Via Ufficio del Vicario 40.

● **Excursions:** Nineteen miles east of Rome is the sixteenth-century Renaissance cardinals' palace, VILLA D'ESTE at Tivoli. The gardens with their 500 fountains are the main attraction here, and your ISIC will get you in free in daytime, though the floodlit fountains do make a colourful nocturnal visit. Take a train from Rome station, or bus RT from Via Gaeta if you don't have a rail pass. If you bus it, you could also take in HADRIAN'S VILLA (closed Mondays).

Mussolini's 1940s quarter of Rome – the EUR – has an amusement park (LUNA PARK) and the MUSEUM OF ROMAN CIVILIZATION which reconstructs ancient Rome as it was under Constantine in the early fourth century. Should you have hit a heatwave, the nearest beach is OSTIA–LIDO. It's not one of Italy's best but it's only eighteen miles away (two trains an hour).

Southern Italy

Using the old geographical 'boot' analogy of Italy, CAMPANIA is the ankle, BASILICATA the arch, PUGLIA the heel, and CALABRIA the toe.

There's a lot to take in in Campania. Apart from the colourful chaos of Naples, there's the smouldering volcano of Vesuvius, the archaeological remains of Pompeii, Herculaneum and Paestum, the romantic towns of Sorrento, Amalfi and Positano and the islands off the coast of Naples: Capri, Ischia and Procida.

Naples (Napoli)

Naples is overcrowded, dirty, crime-ridden and chaotic. It's also a real experience. If you've come down from Florence or Venice, you'll feel you're in a different country: the people, the climate, and the colours and smells round the busy port all strengthen your belief that now you're really in southern Europe. More than anywhere else in Italy, watch your belongings here – over a third of Neapolitans are unemployed and the police officially put the number of smugglers at 40,000. Don't expect northern standards of hygiene either: until 1973 (when a cholera epidemic broke out), Naples had no sewers; but things are much better now.

STATION FACILITIES

Trains from Rome, and those going on to Sicily, invariably use the central station. The Rome–Bari trains stop at both stations, PG or Centrale. There's a connecting elevator between the two. Trains to Sorrento on the Circumvesuviana railway leave from Napoli PG. Space permits details of Napoli Centrale only as the most used by eurorailers.

	NAPOLI CENTRALE
Train information	7 a.m.–11 p.m.
Reservations	7 a.m.–10 p.m.
Tourist information	Mon.–Sat.: 8 a.m.–8 p.m.
	Sun.: 8 a.m.–1 p.m.
Foreign exchange	7 a.m.–11 p.m.
Left-luggage store	All hours
Bar, Buffet and Restaurant	6 a.m.–midnight
	(meals 11 a.m.–4 p.m.)
Bath, Shower	Tue.–Sat.: 8 a.m.–8 p.m.
	Sun.–Mon.: 8 a.m.–2 p.m.
Waiting room	All hours
Shops	6 a.m.–12 midnight
Post office	Mon.–Fri.: 8.15 a.m.–7.30 p.m.
	Sat.: 8.15 a.m.–1 p.m.

Daily trains to: Rome, Florence, Bologna, Genoa, Milan, Sicily,Venice, Brindisi.

TOURIST INFORMATION AND ADDRESSES

Apart from the one at the station, there's an office at Via Partenope 10/A (Tel. 406 289).
POST OFFICE: Via Matteotti, open Mon.–Sat.: 8.30 a.m.–8 p.m., Sun.: 8.30 a.m.–noon.
AMEX: c/o Airontour, Via S. Brigida 68.
UK CONSULATE: Via Francesco Crispi 122 (Tel. 209 227).
US CONSULATE: Piazza della Repubblica (Tel. 660 966). Open Mon.–Fri.: 9 a.m.–12.30 p.m.
24-HOUR CHEMIST: Mattera, Via Carbonara 43.

SEEING

If you visited Pompeii or Herculaneum and were disappointed to find none of the artefacts – or bodies – there, then visit the NATIONAL ARCHAEOLOGICAL MUSEUM on Piazza del Museo. In this sixteenth-century palace you'll find one of the best Graeco-Roman collections in the world, as well as the Borgia collection of Etruscan art. It's open mornings, except Wednesdays. The CAPODIMONTE MUSEUM overlooks the city from its highest hill and has collections of fine art from the fourteenth century on. The Royal Apartments on the first floor of this former royal estate include a parlour completely built from Capodimonte ceramics. Bus 24 takes you there and it's closed on Mondays. Near Corso Vittorio Emanuele III is the Vomero Hill where you find the CARTHUSIAN MONASTERY. The NATIONAL MUSEUM is housed here, and it was the view from the belvedere of Room 25 that inspired the saying 'See Naples and die'. The CASTEL NUOVO was built in the late thirteenth century for Charles I of Anjou, then rebuilt for the fifteenth-century Aragons. Open daily at Piazza Municipio. The Neapolitans overdo everything and their over-ornate churches are a perfect example of overkill. Look in SAN GENNARO CATHEDRAL (tours of its catacombs at 9.30 a.m. and 12 noon), where every year St. Gennaro's blood apparently turns to liquid, SAN DOMENICO MAGGIORE and SAN GREGORIO ARMENO.

SLEEPING

Round the station is seedy but cheap. Try Albergo Vittorio Veneto, Via Milano 96 (Tel. 201 539), or Albergo Columbia at No. 103 (Tel. 201 548).

The youth hostel's at Salita della Grotta 23, Mergellina (Tel. 685 346), on the funicular, which is so old it's surprising that it's not being pulled up the hill by horses. You can camp on Viale Giochi del Mediterraneo 75 (Tel. 517 969) on bus route 152.

EATING AND NIGHTLIFE

Pizza was born in Naples, so this is the place to find out just how far from the original the Pizzaland restaurant-chain really is. There are hundreds of cheap pizza places, and none charge more than 6,000 L for a plateful big enough for two. If you're flush, try one of the seafood restaurants down by the port in the Santa Lucia district. Renzo e Lucia on Via Tito Angelini 31/33 do good baked fish, and Caffe Osteria at Via Miroballo 14 gives good value for money.

There are plenty of shady bars and rip-off joints down by the port. Shaker on Via Nazario Sauro is meant to be one of the best nightclubs, but the competition isn't fierce. You'll find your evening strolls being interrupted by people trying to sell you anything from cabbage-leaf Marlboros (which pass off as the real thing till you light them) to watches made from bottle lids – some of these are worth buying for the craftsmanship involved. Also the 'genuine Scotch' is more often than not cold tea. Be warned!

• **Excursions:** The PHLEGREAN FIELDS, in the peninsula north of Naples, still has some active volcanoes you can visit. MOUNT VESUVIUS hasn't erupted since 1944, but they reckon it's due for another blow-out soon, so take the chairlift up to the crater at your peril. The Circumvesuviana line, from Stazione Vesuviana near Central Station, serves this area. It'll also take you to HERCULANEUM and POMPEII. These two towns fell foul of a Vesuvian outburst in AD 79. The latter was covered in ashes, the former with mud. Both offer unique insight into first-century Roman imperial life. From Naples it's possible to ferry over to the islands. CAPRI is the most touristy, while the Italians favour ISCHIA.

If you're heading south for Sicily, you can stop off at Salerno and head for PAESTUM where you'll find three Greek temples better than many in Greece.

Sicily

From Naples to Sicily takes about ten hours. Sicily is an interesting place to visit, and comes as a complete contrast to Italy, which is not surprising really as parts of it are nearer North Africa than mainland Italy. It's the largest island in the Mediterranean and because of its strategic position has been in the hands of just about every empire there ever was.

● **Getting there:** The standard ferry crossing is from VILLA SAN GIOVANNI to MESSINA on the train-ferry. In summer, the Rome–Sicily run gets crowded, so reserve ahead if you can. Once you're there you'll have to use the railway as your main sightseeing medium. The services are slow and pretty inefficient. Ignore the ferries from Naples to Catania, Syracuse and Palermo. They're expensive and if you're on Inter Rail you'd have to pay to get over.

Sicily: the east coast

The port town of MESSINA, founded by the Greeks in the eighth century BC, has been rebuilt twice this century: once after the 1908 earthquake, and again after the bombing of the Second World War; consequently, there's not *that* much to see, but if you've time to kill waiting on a ferry, take in the following sights: the largest ASTRONOMICAL MECHANICAL CLOCK in the world in the thirteenth-century Norman cathedral, the church of ANNUNZIATA DEI CATALANI, and the NATIONAL MUSEUM. The tourist office is on Via Calabria Isolato, and there's another at the station. Half an hour from Messina is TAORMINA, a historical resort popular with middle-aged Italians. The GREEK THEATRE is overlooked by the smoking live volcano of MOUNT ETNA which makes this setting for Greek drama suitably dramatic. The PALAZZO CORVAIA, the Sicilian parliament house dating from the fourteenth century, is in Piazza Vittorio Emanuele, and the beach of MAZZARO can be reached by funicular.

CATANIA hasn't been swamped by Mount Etna since 1693, so the old town dates from the seventeenth century. At Piazza del Duomo is the CHIERICI PALACE. From Catania you can visit Mount Etna, but dress properly. SIRACUSA is a strange mixture of ancient Greece and Rome. This was once as important a centre as Rome or Athens and there are plenty of archaeological sites to back this up. The ARCHAEOLOGICAL MUSEUM is at Piazza del Duomo and the remains are behind the present city. The GREEK THEATRE here is considered the best of its kind in the world. Opposite the theatre is the altar used for public sacrifices; a short walk takes you to the ROMAN AMPHITHEATRE from the fourth century BC. Tourist information is at Corso Gelone 92, and the youth hostel's at 45 Via Epipoli (Tel. 711118). For pensions, try Centrale (Tel. 60258) at the station, or Gran Bretagna, Via Savoia 21 (Tel. 68765).

Palermo

The capital of Sicily has a modern north side and historic south side. The mixture of Arabic and Western is noticeable here, as can be seen in the PALACE OF THE NORMANS (see especially the PALATINE CHAPEL mosaics in the palace). Five miles away in MONREALE is the Norman CATHEDRAL with its unique biblical mosaics, and just next door the BENEDICTINE CLOISTER has a garden with medieval columns. Tourist information at Piazza Castelnuovo 34 is generally helpful. Try round the harbour for cheap rooms, or near the station. Albergo Pretoria, Via Maqueda 124 (Tel. 331 068), or Albergo Rosalia Conca d'Oro on Via Santa Rosalia 7 (Tel. 233 543) are good places.

3½ hours from Palermo on the southern coast is AGRIGENTO. This hillside town is the site of the VALLEY OF TEMPLES, a collection of columns and temples dating from the sixth and fifth centuries BC.

Sardinia (Sardegna)

The mountainous and untamed island of Sardinia is about halfway between Italy and Africa's northern coast. The 1.5 million Sardinians do not consider themselves to be Italians; the region has been granted its own autonomous status. The west of the island is hilly but mainly cultivated; the east is wild and almost completely untouched. There are about half a dozen towns in all, and only a few real roads, so be prepared to rough it a bit if you're camping – but camp all the same, as this is by far the best means of accommodation on the island, and the scenery and climate are beautiful.

• **Getting there:** From Italy there are ferries to Cagliari (the capital), Olbia (on the east coast), Porto Torres (the northern tip) and Golfo Aranci (on the Costa Smeralda). The best overnight crossing is with the Tirrenia Line from Civitavecchia (one hour north of Rome) to Olbia. It costs about 16,000 L and reservations in summer are advisable. The Tirrenia office in Rome is at Via Bissolati 41.

For a daytime crossing, the state railways one from Civitavecchia to Golfo Aranci is the cheapest. A second-class reclining seat will cost 10,000 L plus. The crossing takes about nine hours, and there are five crossings a day. At the other end, there's a train waiting to take you on to Olbia or Sassari.

• **General information:** Once you're there, the rail network connects up the northern and western coasts, but that's about it. Services are slow and a bit unpredictable, but it's a lot better than hitching it round.

As far as accommodation goes, the tourist office will help you out. Good cheap pensions are thin on the ground and hotels, where they exist, expensive. In the north, youth hostels are your best bet. They're cheap (6,000 L) and usually on the beach. Generally, though, you can't beat camping. There are several official sites, but the true joy comes only with setting up on your own.

Avoid the restaurants – they're aimed at the wealthy tourists. Go for pizzerie, tavole calde or rosticcerie. Fish and seafood are cheap on the coast (cook them yourself), and the markets provide ample picnic food. The local wine is Vernaccia.

Sardinia: the east coast

South from Olbia is the most unspoiled region of Sardinia. There are miles of beautiful quiet beaches, and in these parts the women still wear the national costume. NUORO and ARBATAZ are particularly beautiful and are the sites of archaeological remains. To get to this area, you'll need to take the train from Macomer or Cagliari. The coast around SANTA MARIA NAVARRESE is good for beaches.

Going north from Olbia you enter COSTA SMERALDA, the 'millionaires' playground'. This is the most commercialized part, though it's not yet spoilt. If you have enough time, take a trip to Porto Cervia and see some of the most expensive real estate in Italy. Don't attempt to stay the night, however, unless you don't mind paying Aga Khan prices. Golfo Aranci is in this region, and from here you really have to bus it. ARZACHENA is worth heading for, and has some very good beaches. Again not on the rail line but worth seeing is SANTA TERESA DI GALLURA on the northernmost tip of Sardinia with a view of Corsica. This little fishing village is currently becoming 'touristy', so get there before it finally succumbs.

Sardinia: the west coast

SASSARI, Sardinia's second city, has an interesting old medieval town which centres on the CATHEDRAL. There are a couple of churches and the SARDINIAN NATIONAL MUSEUM to see here, and tourist information is at Piazza Italia 19 in the Banco di Napoli building. This is your best base for exploring north-west Sardinia and you'll find cheap rooms and meals along Corso Vittorio Emanuele. An hour from here is one of the prettiest towns on the island, ALGHERO. It's more Spanish than Italian as for many years this was a Catalan colony. The churches are the main sites of the town, and from here you can take a boat out to CAPO CACCIA and the Neptune Grotto: a series of underground caves, some of which are still unexplored.

Cagliari

The capital city of Sardinia. Ignore the new town and concentrate on the medieval centre, the CASTELLO, behind the harbour. The thirteenth-century CATHEDRAL is here and not far away is the ROMAN AMPHITHEATRE. The NATIONAL ARCHAEOLOGICAL MUSEUM (closed Mondays, open 9 a.m.–2 p.m.) is famous for its collection of 'Nuraghic bronzes', and its Punic-Roman section. Tourist information is at Piazza Deffenu 9, and for cheap beds and meals try the streets between Corso Vittorio Emanuele and Via Roma.

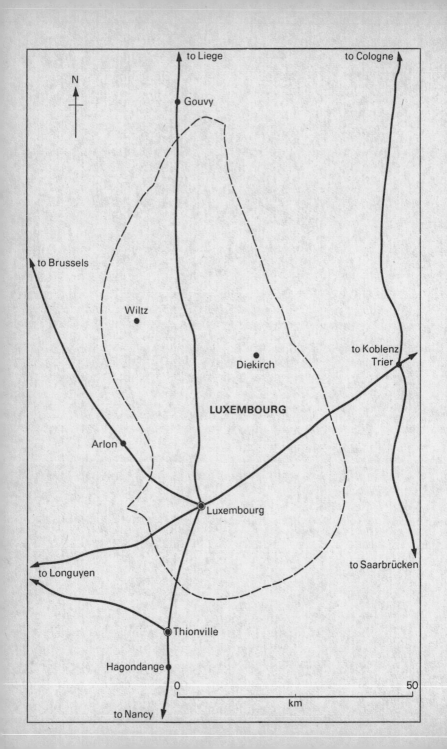

LUXEMBOURG

Entry requirements	Passport
Population	360,000
Capital	Luxembourg City (pop.: 100,000)
Currency	Luxembourg Franc (interchangeable with the Belgian)
	£1 = approx. 63 fr.
Political system	Constitutional Monarchy
Religion	Roman Catholic
Languages	Officially French and German though Letzeburgesch (the people's language) is spoken by everyone
Public holidays	1 Jan.; 14 Feb.; Easter Sunday and Monday; 1 May; Ascension Day; Whit Monday; 23 June; Assumption Day; All Saints Day; 25, 26 Dec.

Luxembourg provides a welcome break from any train. The greater part of its 999 square miles is heavily wooded and makes ideal camping and hiking country. During the medieval period it was four times the size, and its royal house was so important that four of its members were elected as emperors of the Holy Roman Empire. All this changed in 1443 when Philip the Good of Burgundy bought the lot and added it to his other investment, the Netherlands. It subsequently passed into the hands of the Spanish and Austrian Habsburgs, and finally the French. Independence came in 1815, and despite being overrun by Germany in both World Wars, it has managed to survive intact. Today its low unemployment and declining birthrate make Luxembourg a very prosperous country with a remarkably high GNP for its size.

LUXEMBOURG NATIONAL RAILWAYS
(Société Nationale des Chemins de Fer Luxembourgeois, CFL)

With only 210 miles of track, this is the smallest national rail network in the world – it takes only two hours to cross the whole country. There are, however, sixty-four stations, so the train really can take you to even the most obscure corners, and there are no supplements to worry about.

TRAIN INFORMATION

For information on international trains, go to the Rail Tour Office where English is spoken. If there's a queue, or it's a simple question, look for the information officers wearing yellow cap-bands. The luggage lockers take two 10 fr. pieces.

● **Reservations:** It's not possible to reserve on internal trains, and on internationals it's optional, but must be done twenty-four hours in advance. Luxembourg is connected to the German and French railways' computer, so it's possible to reserve sleepers and couchettes in these countries.

TOURIST INFORMATION

Apart from the National Tourist Office to the right of the main station in Luxembourg there are local offices (Syndicats d'Initiative) scattered throughout the country. Most open at 8 a.m. and shut at 6 p.m. with a two-hour lunch break.

● **ISIC bonuses:** Some museums and galleries half price.

● **Money matters:** 1 Luxembourg franc (fr.) = 100 centimes.
Banking hours are Mon.–Fri.: 9 a.m.–12 noon and 1.30 p.m.–4.30 p.m. The Luxembourg franc is interchangeable with the Belgian franc, but you're best to change them before leaving the country.

● **Post offices:** Open Mon.–Fri.: 9 a.m.–5 p.m. Permanent service in post office opposite station.

● **Shops and museums:** Vary in their times of opening. Tue.–Fri.: 9 a.m.–12 noon and 2 p.m.–6 p.m. seems to be the general rule. Some museums and shops shut on Mondays.

SLEEPING

Pick up the tourist board's excellent free guide on accommodation at the main office next to the station. This lists prices and facilities for all Luxembourg's hotels and pensions. If you're thinking about camping, ask for the free folder giving all the campsites and prices. There are eleven youth hostels for which you need IYHF membership, charging about 130 fr. per night.

EATING AND NIGHTLIFE

Dishes have a strong French flavour and specialities include Ardennes ham which you can pick up at supermarkets. Check up with the tourist offices for what's happening in the week ahead.

Luxembourg City

The old part of this 1,000-year-old city is on a high plateau overlooking cliffs, and the valleys of the Alzette River. Around the edge of the plateau is the PROMENADE DE LA CORNICHE which offers spectacular views over the city. Just below the promenade are the CASEMATES, thirteen miles of connecting underground passages from the times when this area was a fortress. You can explore these tunnels: enter from Place de la Constitution or from 'Bock' – fortress reconstruction. Also in the old town is the Renaissance GRAND DUCAL PALACE, the seventeenth-century CATHEDRAL OF NOTRE DAME and the NATIONAL MUSEUM on Fish Market Place (closed Mondays).

STATION FACILITIES

	GARE DE LUXEMBOURG
Train information	7 a.m.–8 p.m.
	(Tel. 492424)
Reservations	7 a.m.–8p.m.
Tourist information	Mon.–Fri.: 9 a.m.–12 noon,
	2 p.m.–6.30 p.m.
	Sat.: 9 a.m.–12 noon
	(in Luxair building)
Foreign exchange	Mon.–Sat.: 8.30 a.m.–9 p.m.
	Sun.: 9 a.m.–9 p.m.
Left-luggage lockers	No access 1.30 a.m.–4 a.m.
Left-luggage store	All hours
Bar, Buffet	8 a.m.–7 p.m.

	GARE DE LUXEMBOURG
Restaurant	Mon.–Fri.: 12 noon–3 p.m.
	(Relais Gastronomique)
	5 a.m.–12 midnight (Le Transit)
Shops	6.30 a.m.–8 p.m.
Bath, Shower	6 a.m.–9.30 p.m.
Waiting room	All hours
Post office	Across from station
Station shuts	1.30 a.m.–4 a.m.

Daily trains to: Brussels, Strasbourg, Basel, Zürich, Milan, Bologna, Paris.

TOURIST INFORMATION AND ADDRESSES

Next to the station is the Luxair Terminal building. In summer it opens 9 a.m.–7.30 p.m., and hands out free information on all Luxembourg, as well as handling accommodation inquiries.
POST OFFICE: 1 Place de la Gare. Twenty-four-hour service. Post restante at 8 Avenue Monterey. Mon.–Fri.: 7.30 a.m.–7 p.m., Sat.: 8.30 a.m.–12 noon.
LUXEMBOURG STUDENT TRAVEL (TEJ): 21 rue Aldringen (upstairs) (Tel. 22673), open Mon.–Fri.: 9.30 a.m.–12 noon, 1.30 p.m.–6 p.m., Sat.: 9.30 a.m.–12 noon.
24-HOUR CHEMIST: Tel. 012.
UK EMBASSY: 28 Boulevard Royal (Tel. 29864).
US EMBASSY: 22 E. Servais (Tel. 40123).
TRANSALPINO: 15 rue Notre Dame (Tel. 22931)

SLEEPING

Stay close to the station for cheap hotels. Rue Joseph Junck is a safe bet, as is rue de la Liberté. Doubles average about 800 fr., but Atlas, 30 rue de Fort Niepperg (Tel. 487255), has rooms for less. The youth hostel's good but is far out and full of adolescent groups; moreover it has an 11 p.m. curfew and a 9 a.m. eviction, and the fare out there's 20 fr. If you fancy it, it's on bus route 9 and is at 2 rue Fort Olisy (Tel. 26889). Camping's at Kockelscheuer (Tel. 471815). Free showers and reasonable rates. Open Apr.–Oct. Buses 13 and 14 and a twenty-minute walk.

EATING AND NIGHTLIFE

Food isn't terribly cheap, so use the supermarkets and bakeries near the station. Try the tourist menu at Le Papillon, 9 rue Origer. Place d'Armes is where to head in the evenings. People generally congregate here and often there are free concerts in the square. 'La Semaine à Luxembourg' is the 'what's on' and is available from tourist information.

The Countryside/Provincial Luxembourg

On the banks of the River Sauer lies the medieval village of ECHTERNACH. Though badly damaged in the Second World War (that's Germany just across the river) it has been well restored now, and the 1328 TOWN HALL is as good as ever. The BENEDICTINE ABBEY has some impressive frescoes and stained-glass windows. There's a youth hostel at 9 rue André Duchscher (Tel. 72158). Just a few minutes north of Echternach is a small wedge of a hiker's paradise: LITTLE SWITZERLAND. This is the Moellerdall section of the Ardennes, and a walk through the steep gorges and forest makes an exhilarating hour or so. In the northernmost part of the Ardennes is TROISVIERGES, the heart of hiking country. The Clerve Valley leads to CLERVAUX, about an hour on the line from Luxembourg City. The castles of BOURSCHEID and CLERVAUX, both eleventh-century and in good repair, are here in fairytale settings. There are permanent exhibitions in Clervaux Castle, including Steichen's 'Family of Man' collection. The tourist office at Clervaux is at 27 Grande Rue. They'll help you find a bed. Not on the railway, but definitely worth a visit, is VIANDEN, with its cobbled streets and its magnificent castle (the biggest west of the Rhine). This was the cradle of the Grand-Ducal dynasty and dates back to the ninth century. Try the chairlift, and also the open-air swimming pool with impressive views over the castle. The youth hostel is at 3 Montée du Château (Tel. 84177), and the tourist office is in the Victor Hugo House, close by the bridge (closed 12 noon–2 p.m.).

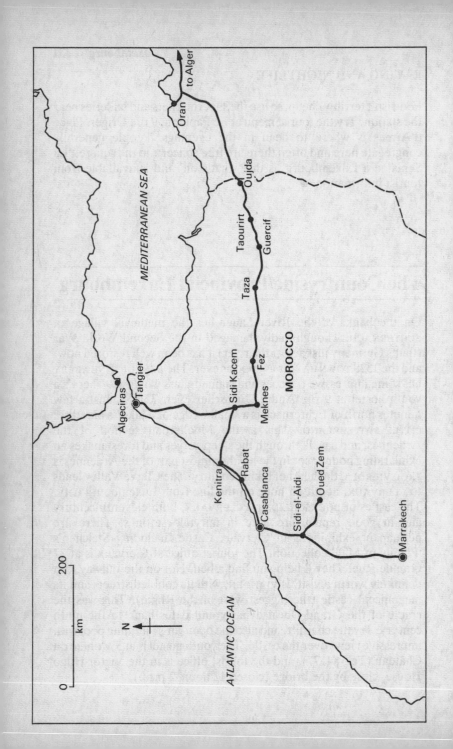

MOROCCO

Entry requirements	Passport
Population	20,000,000
Capital	Rabat (pop.: 700,000)
Currency	Dirham
	£1 = approx. 11.35 dh.
Political system	Constitutional Monarchy
Religion	Muslim
Languages	Arabic (French and Spanish also official languages) (English spoken in tourist towns)
Public holidays	1 Jan.; 1st of Moharrem (moveable); 3 March; Moulid El Nabi (moveable); 1 May; Aid Es Seghir; 6 Nov.; 18 Nov.; Aid El Kehir (moveable).

Nothing in Europe can prepare you for the cultural differences you're likely to encounter in Morocco. If you accept at the outset that Western standards of punctuality, hygiene and sexual equality simply don't apply here, your path will be that much smoother. Girls in particular will have a rough time avoiding harassment, so think twice about travelling alone. Fortunately, things have been changing in recent years and stories of being held up at knife-point are becoming less frequent, but always be on your guard as in nearly every medina (old city) there's a thief just waiting to get his hands on your wallet. Most of Morocco was a French protectorate between 1912 and 1956, except for the north which was Spanish. The lowland areas, where the trains run, are the richest and most populous parts of Morocco. Avoid going further south than Tan Tan as there are still sporadic skirmishes between the Moroccans and Mauritanians over the former Spanish Sahara.

• **Getting there:** There are various ferries from Spain to Tangier and Ceuta in Morocco, with the Algeciras–Ceuta being the shortest and cheapest crossing, but as it's not on the railway you'll do best to use the Algeciras–Tangier crossing. It costs about 1,500 pesetas and unless you've an Inter Rail there are no reductions. (It's included with a Transalpino ticket.) Don't rely on the information posted in Algeciras Ferry Terminal; ask. And don't count on punctual sailings. Sometimes there are hassles at the border with the customs men – try to look as clean and wholesome as possible (which is a bit of a contradiction, considering where you're entering), but don't get smart with the officials.

MOROCCAN RAILWAYS
(Office National des Chemins de Fer, ONCF)

It probably won't knock you out to learn that Moroccan trains are among the dirtiest, slowest and least reliable around. Still, the Inter Rail card's valid here and the railway does run to the main tourist towns and regions. There are three classes on the trains: first, second and 'Economique'. Your Inter Rail or BIJ ticket entitles you to use the second-class facilities and if you're prepared to pay the 10–15 dh. supplement, you can travel in an air-conditioned carriage. The rail network runs east from Marrakesh to Casablanca and Rabat, then splits at Sidi Kacem, one line going north to Tangier, the other to Oujda and over the border to Algeria.

• **Inter Rail bonuses:** The Algeciras–Tangier crossing is half price on Inter Rail.

TRAIN INFORMATION

You'll find the odd official who speaks pidgin English, but in smaller places you'll have to resort to French.

• **Reservations:** Not compulsory, but not a bad idea if you're on a long haul in peak season.

• **Night travel:** Sleeping cars are first class only and come in singles or doubles. They're fairly expensive so unless you're feeling particularly delicate, try and schedule your travelling for daytime.

TOURIST INFORMATION

Most towns have both a tourist office and a Syndicat d'Initiative. The tourist office should be your first port of call as they have information on all of Morocco, and will also help find a bed if necessary. When you're organized, make your way back to the Syndicat d'Initiative which has leaflets on local sights, etc.

A word of warning: unofficial guides (mostly young boys) will pester you with their dubious services. A good impersonation of Finnish usually puts them off your track. Hustlers are another problem: they'll approach you in the medina and kasbah (old fortress), be incredibly friendly, and be conversant in a dozen languages. Ignore and avoid them. Finally, when you're at the sights don't feel obliged to accept the custodian's offer of a guided tour or feel it necessary to give him a tip, as he is already paid by the government and does very well from other tourists.

• **Money matters:** 1 dirham (dh.) = 100 francs.
Banking hours are Mon.–Fri.: 8.30 a.m.–11.30 a.m., 3 p.m.–5.30 p.m. Banks charge no commission and have the same rate of exchange everywhere. Keep your receipts to change dirhams back at the border.

• **Post offices:** Open Mon.–Sat.: 8.30 a.m.–12 noon, 2.30 p.m.–6 p.m. (Closed Sat. p.m.)

• **Shops:** Open Mon.–Sat.: 8.30 a.m.–12 noon, 2 p.m.–6.30 p.m. Bargain like mad wherever you go in the markets (souks), even when you see the 'prix fixe' sign. Haggling is a way of life here and, unless you manage to get the price down by at least 50 per cent, consider yourself a failure. Remember: you can never start low enough. Check with the Syndicats for opening times of museums and other sights.

SLEEPING

Morocco is a country where it pays dividends to be tough. You can live off next to nothing if you don't mind roughing it a bit. Camping and youth hostelling are very cheap, as little as 8 dh. a night under canvas or 18 dh. in a hostel dormitory, but you're not guaranteed central locations or cleanliness. The medina hotels/pensions offer the most central and colourful locations and are usually cheaper than the places in the new areas of town. Hotels are graded from one to five stars and there are fixed maximum prices for each category. You pay by the room, so doubling up with friends can bring the unit cost of a room down. If you find the water is hot at any time of day, seize the chance for a shower while you can (these usually cost 5–8 dh.) as the plumbing here is decidedly erratic. As far as public toilets go, always carry your own loo paper or you'll have to resort to the traditional local methods . . .

EATING AND NIGHTLIFE

If you've an iron stomach, take full advantage of it in Morocco by eating in the kasbahs and from shishkebab stands. But don't look too closely. Most decent restaurants offer a good selection of Moroccan dishes. Try harina, a rich soup of chicken and spices, followed by touojen (lamb or chicken stew) or couscous, Morocco's most famous dish (made from semolina, with lamb, fish or chicken). If you like something sweet to finish the meal, ask for kab el ghzal (almond pastries) and some mint tea. If you're unsure of your capabilities, drink only mineral water and take no chances. Often it is difficult in the more remote places to find meals during the day, so eat well at night; and don't expect alcohol to be widely available. The local Syndicat will let you know where the nearest belly-dancer performs and what's happening on the disco scene.

Tangier

This isn't the best Morocco has to offer, but if you're on a day trip from Spain, it'll show you some of the exotic and colourful differences between Europe and North Africa. As Tangier receives more than its fair share of tourists, be particularly on your guard for hustlers.

The GRAND SOCCO connects the medina and the new town. Tourist information is at Boulevard Pasteur (open Mon.–Sat.: 8 a.m.–2 p.m.; closed Sundays), as is the post office. In the medina, the rue des Postes is where to look for cheap hotels and restaurants. The Pensione Palace (Tel. 33468) is at No. 2 and has doubles for under 50 dh. The beaches and nightlife are both good, though single girls on the beach are in for a hard time.

Rabat

From Tangier to the capital of Morocco – Rabat – is about five hours on the main line. This is a surprisingly clean, organized and structured city. It has numerous parks and gardens, and most of the town is new and affluent by Moroccan standards. There is a kasbah in the old town but the medina lacks atmosphere, and you feel you're back in Europe a lot of the time.

TOURIST INFORMATION AND ADDRESSES

TOURIST INFORMATION: 22 Charia Al-Jazair or rue Patrice Lumumba, open Mon.–Fri.: 8 a.m.–2 p.m. Closed Saturday p.m. and Sunday.
POST OFFICE: Avenue Mohammed V. Open Mon.–Fri.: 8 a.m.–2 p.m., Sat.: 8.30 a.m.–12 noon.
AMEX: In Rabat Hilton (Tel. 72151). Take bus for Agdal.
UK EMBASSY: 17 Boulevard Tour Hassan (Tel. 20905).
US EMBASSY: 2 Avenue de Marrakesh (Tel. 30361).
CANADIAN EMBASSY: 13 Zankat Joafar Essodik, Agdal (Tel. 71375).

SEEING

The TOUR HASSAN minaret in the twelfth-century mosque and the MAUSOLEUM OF MOHAMMED V are close to each other, and about a mile's walk away is the CHELLAH, an Arab necropolis built in the old Roman section of Rabat called SALA COLONIA. There are gardens here that are ideal for a picnic. The OUDAIAS KASBAH fortress has another beautiful garden, a Moorish café, and the MUSEUM OF MOROCCAN HANDICRAFTS: carpets, musical instruments, furniture, etc. (open 8 a.m.–12 noon, 2 p.m.–6 p.m., closed Tuesday and Saturday p.m.). The ROYAL PALACE is also located here in the capital, though it dates only from the 1950s.

SLEEPING, EATING AND NIGHTLIFE

The youth hostel on 66 Boulevard de la Résistance is cheap but terrible. For camping, take bus 6 or 24 to Salé terminal and follow the signs for Camping Municipal. For cheap hotels, try Central Hotel, 2 rue Al Basra (Tel. 22131), with singles around 28 dh. and doubles 38 dh. Alternatively, in the medina, try Hotel Marrakesh, rue Sbahi (Tel. 27703). Enter the medina on Avenue Mohammed V and turn right three blocks later: singles 18 dh. – good value. The medina is also the place for cheap eats. There are plenty of stalls and restaurants, with the Restaurant El Bahia on Avenue Hassan II offering good food at budget prices. It's located to your right as you approach the medina from Avenue Mohammed V. For an evening stroll, walk round the Oudaias Kasbah as the sun is sinking.

Casablanca

This is the largest, and in many ways the least attractive, of Morocco's towns. With over two million inhabitants and a busy port, Casablanca is a crowded, modern and somewhat squalid city, and the only thing romantic about it is its name and Play-it-again-Sam image. Take the train to the Port Station for the medina, beaches etc. Casablanca has got some character and among its sights are the GREAT MOSQUE, neo-Moorish public buildings round the PLACE DES NATIONS UNIES and the MAHAKMA (regional courts). The journey south to Casablanca from Tangier is no problem as it involves the best trains in Morocco; however, if you're going further south make sure you have supplies with you as the buffets are awful. Also, if you can afford it, pay the supplement from second to first class (if you're travelling in peak season). Still, you shouldn't judge Morocco by Casablanca. Travel through to Fez or Marrakesh for a more representative image.

Marrakesh

This red-ochre city on the edge of the Sahara desert is what you expect Morocco to be like: vibrant markets with snake-charmers, fortune-tellers and acrobats; palm trees; remains from ancient dynasties, and incredible midday temperatures of around 105°F.

On arrival get hold of a 'petit taxi' (not a regular one – they cost double) and haggle to fix a price for a ride to the Djemma el Fna. You'll be dropped off in the city's main square, and from there it's no problem finding a cheap hotel bed.

TOURIST INFORMATION AND ADDRESSES

TOURIST OFFICE: Place Abdel Moumen ben Ali on Avenue Mohammed V. English spoken. Ask for a map and a list of accommodation (though it doesn't list the real cheapies). Open 8.30 a.m.–12 noon, 3 p.m.–6 p.m.
POST OFFICE: Place du 16 Novembre, off Avenue Mohammed V. Open 8 a.m.–2 p.m.
AMEX: c/o Voyages Schwartz, rue Mauritania, 2nd floor. Open Mon.–Fri.: 9 a.m.–11.15 a.m., 3 p.m.–4.30 p.m.
CHEMIST: Near Hotel Marrakesh, Place de la Liberté. Open till 10 p.m.

SEEING

The DJEMMA EL FNA (Assembly of the Dead) is the showpiece of Marrakesh. This square is the hub of life of the city. In daytime it's a busy colourful market, and at night the street artists arrive. (Be particularly careful of your valuables here.) The medina is particularly lively and there are various photogenic markets like the ones for musical instruments or wool dyers. The old theological school, BEN YOUSSEF MEDERSA, has some fine marbles, mosaics and wood-carvings, and the pale green twelfth-century minaret of the KOUTOUBIA MOSQUE is Morocco's best example. the BAHIA PALACE is nineteenth-century and the PALACE EL BEDI is eighteenth-century. The SAADI MAUSOLEUM contains the remains of various sultans and is free, though the guide expects a tip. The bus station is at Bab Doukkala. Buses to the beach leave from here, but they travel at a relaxed pace.

SLEEPING, EATING AND NIGHTLIFE

Head for the Djemma el Fna area for cheap hotels and restaurants. Hôtel de France, Hôtel Cecil or Hôtel des Amis have doubles for under 45 dh. The youth hostel's good by Moroccan standards. It's near the station on rue el Jahid (Tel. 32831); it closes 9 a.m.–2 p.m. and after 10 p.m. Further along the same street is the campsite – Camping Caravanning – not too good. Café-Restaurant Oriental at 33 rue Bab Abnaou (off the Djemma el Fna) do good menus at reasonable prices.

Meknes

On the eastern line to Fez and the Algerian border, and 6½ hours from Tangier, lies the imperial city of Meknes. From the station, turn left for the medina, hotels and the old town. Tourist information is at Place Administrative and is open Mon.–Fri.: 8 a.m.–2 p.m.; Sat.: 8.30 a.m.–12 noon, 3 p.m.–6 p.m. English is spoken, and some literature is available. MANSOUR, the pavilion where the seventeenth-century Sultan Moulay Ismail received ambassadors, is up here. There are UNDERGROUND CAVES where the Sultan's slaves were kept which can be viewed if you ask the guards nicely. The elaborate TOMB of Moulay Ismail is further up on the right. The DAR JAMAI PALACE is now a museum. The theological school BOU INANIA is the elaborate fourteenth-century building in the medina.

SLEEPING, EATING AND NIGHTLIFE

Around Place el Hédime there are quite a few cheap hotels, but if you don't fancy these the best alternative is camping. The best site is Camping Esplanade near the Heri, on the other side of the medina from the tomb of Moulay Ismail. The youth hostel's a dead loss, but if you're desperate it's at Avenue Okba Ibn Nafii (Tel. 24698) (near Hôtel Transatlantique). For food, rue Dar Smen and Avenue de Rouamzine are the best ideas. Moroccan-style nightlife is not hard to find in Meknes.

Fez (Fes)

The oldest imperial city in Morocco is today considered her cultural and intellectual centre. The huge medina here is unmatched elsewhere in North Africa. You could easily spend days in it; the colours, smells, filth and constant arguments are as endless as the train journey that gets you there.

TOURIST INFORMATION AND ADDRESSES

TOURIST OFFICE: Avenue Hassan II. Open Mon.–Sat.: 8 a.m.–2 p.m.
POST OFFICE: On Avenue Hassan II there are three. Open 8 a.m.–2 p.m. Closed Saturday p.m. and Sunday.
BUS STATION: CTM, Boulevard Mohammed V, or from Bab Boujeloud.

SEEING

Expect to get lost in Fez. The MEDINA is so sprawling and unstructured it's inevitable, and there's no map to help you out. Refuse the offer of a guide unless you can get him down to 15 dh. or so (we've still to meet anyone who found their guide was good value or didn't try to pull a fast one about his fee). There are countless souks in the medina to look at, but only ferret out the tannery one if you've an iron stomach. The medina is the location of the tenth-century minaret of the KAROUIYNE MOSQUE, whose university claims to be the oldest in the world, and the theological schools of ATTARINE and BOU INANIA.

SLEEPING, EATING AND NIGHTLIFE

Round Bab Boujeloud you'll find a few cheap (and fairly nasty) hotels with doubles for 45–50 dh. The youth hostel on 18 rue Compardon (Tel. 24085) is good value and, by Fez standards, very clean and comfortable. Reach it by turning left off rue Mohammed

V, take rue 3 and it's the street behind the mosque. The campsite – Camping Moulay Slimani – is OK, but watch the cleanliness of the swimming pools and the food from the restaurant (Tel. 24438). Follow the arrows from Place Mohammed V.

Bab Boujeloud and the medina are the cheap eating districts. The youth hostel has a kitchen, so you could buy food there and cook it yourself (watch the meat). Avoid the local delicacy, bisteeya (which is pigeon, vegetables and nuts, covered in sweet pastry – ugh!). An evening stroll in the old Jewish quarter is more rewarding than the formal entertainments you'll find.

Off-the-track places

Many of Morocco's best places are not on the railway, so buses are the only answer. TETUAN, 1½ hours away from Tangier (cost about 20 dh.), is a relatively unspoilt town with a fascinating medina – eat there and try round Place Hassan II for rooms. ASNI is thirty miles from Marrakesh and buses leave hourly from the station. This is in the HIGH ATLAS mountain region in the Sahara. IMLIL, accessible by 'taxi' (communal truck), is even more spectacular. This is surrounded by the mountains and you can start a climb of MOUNT TOUBKAL (13,671 feet) from here. The town's refuge is your best bet for a bed, and it has cooking facilities. Don't attempt the mountain unless you're experienced and well equipped. Before heading into the deep south of Morocco, check on the current situation in the Moroccan-Mauritanian war over the Sahara, which has been going on sporadically since 1975. Don't venture beyond Goulimine, not that you easily could, as the roads are blocked for tourists.

ESSAOUIRA is a Berber town on the south coast. If you're tired out with travelling and need a break before the long haul back home, sleep here free on the beaches and take advantage of this opportunity to share in a very un-European culture and lifestyle. Take a leisurely walk up to the eighteenth-century Moorish fortress (the SKALA) at sunset. The tourist office is on Porte Portugaise. Watch out for the drug pushers, and don't be tempted into private houses which individuals claim are restaurants. Some of the locals are very experienced in conning European tourists.

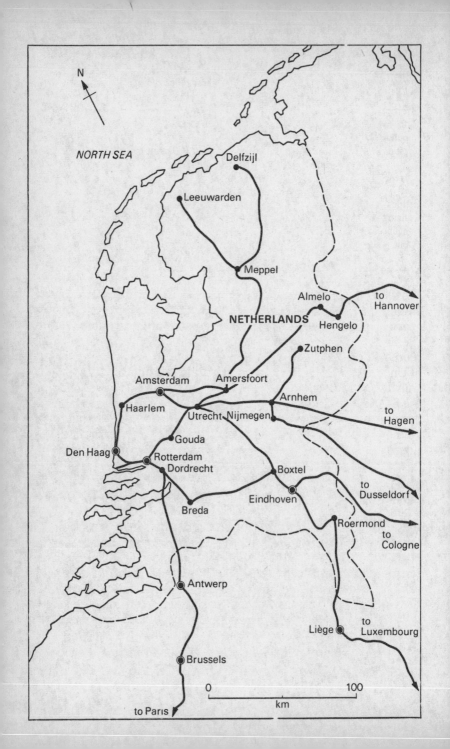

NETHERLANDS

Entry requirements	Passport
Population	14,000,000 +
Capital	Amsterdam (pop.: 1,000,000), though The Hague is the political capital
Currency	Guilder (Florin) £1 = approx. f. 4.22
Political system	Constitutional Monarchy
Religions	Protestant and Roman Catholic
Language	Dutch (English widely spoken in cities)
Public holidays	1 Jan.; Good Friday; Easter Monday; 30 Apr.; Ascension Day; Whit Monday; 25, 26 Dec.

Most of Holland's major cities are concentrated in the flat Protestant west where one has visions of windmills, tulips and clogs. However, not all of Holland is like this; the south is very different: the land is not all flat, and many of the people are Catholic and much more like the French in many respects.

Under the Burgundians and the Habsburgs, Holland was politically linked to Belgium to form the Netherlands (lowlands). Then the Spanish King Philip II started to levy heavy taxes to pay for his army, fighting for the Catholic cause in Europe. As the northern Netherlands had mostly become Protestant by this time, you can imagine this didn't go down too well. Philip tried to smooth things over by sending in Spanish governors. This was the last straw for the Dutch who, under William of Orange, fought the Eighty Years War against the Spanish, emerging as an independent country in 1648.

After this, the Dutch really got it together for the remainder of the seventeenth century and showed the rest of Europe a thing or two about seafaring and commerce. At the same time, Rembrandt et al. were hard at work creating the Dutch golden age of arts and science. Symbolically, Holland's eclipse by Britain in the eighteenth century was begun by William III moving across to England to share the throne with Mary. After the Napoleonic Wars and French domination, life for the Dutch gradually developed into parliamentary democracy.

NETHERLANDS RAILWAYS
(Nederlandse Spoorwegen, NS)

Dutch Railways are as trouble-free and efficient as you're likely to find anywhere in Europe. There are frequent intercity services between all parts of Holland, at least once an hour. The short distances involved mean you can see most of Holland while based at one city. Be careful not to end up on the 'stop-treins' which do just that, before connecting up to the main intercity network. Supplements are only necessary on TEEs and international express trains marked D or IC. Electric trains often consist of portions for two different destinations.

• **Inter Rail bonuses:** 50 per cent reduction on all regional buses.

• **Eurail bonuses:** Free passage on ships of BV Rederji NACO between Enkhuisen and Staveren or vice versa.

TRAIN INFORMATION

There should be no problem with language as nearly everyone speaks English. Ask at the information desk for the booklet called 'Holland by Rail' which has a useful map with frequency times.

• **Reservations:** It's not possible to reserve seats on inland trains. Also it's not necessary to reserve seats on the international trains, despite what they might tell you at Amsterdam Train Information Office. Trains are often very full, so if the queues are small, go ahead and reserve one. If they are not, you could literally be waiting for hours in the summer to make your reservation.

• **Night travel:** There are couchettes and sleepers on international routes only.

• **Eating on trains:** All intercities have the usual mini-bars while only international trains have diners.

• **Scenic tips:** If you're fortunate enough to be travelling at any time from March to May through the bulb fields (Bollenvelden) region (on any runs between Amsterdam, Rotterdam, Delft, Leiden and Utrecht) you will be amply rewarded.

• **Bikes:** Holland is ideal for cycling – it's flat and there are cycle tracks everywhere. Most stations hire out bikes and give reduced rates if you show your ticket.

TOURIST INFORMATION (VVV)

The local offices are run by individual towns and can be found in every town and village in Holland. They find you accommodation if required and supply you with all the information about the area. If you plan to cycle, ask for a cycle map. Unfortunately it's not always free, so inquire first.

• **ISIC bonuses:** Up to 50 per cent reduction on museums. You can get into all state museums free once you've bought your museum card (it costs f. 5) from any state museum. For further information, contact NBBS, Dom 17, Amsterdam. In the States you can buy a Culture Card from the Netherlands National Tourist Office which for around $8 gives you free museum entrances and many other bonuses.

• **Money matters:** 1 guilder (florin) (f.) = 100 cents (c.).
Banking hours are Mon.–Fri.: 9 a.m.–4 p.m.; there are also exchange offices in twenty-seven railway stations, some of which are open in the evenings and at weekends. Some VVV tourist offices also exchange money.

• **Post offices:** Open Mon.–Fri.: 8.30 a.m.–5 p.m. and, in major towns, 8.30 a.m.–12 noon on Sat.

• **Shops:** In general, Mon.–Fri.: 8.30/9 a.m.–5.30/6 p.m. and on Sat.: 8.30/9 a.m.–4 p.m.

• **Museums:** Most state museums are free on Wednesday afternoon. Anyone can buy a museum card which is essential for anyone taking sightseeing at all seriously.

SLEEPING

If you're spending a lot of time in Holland, it's a good idea to ask for the tourist board's publications on camping and hotels. If you're in luck, they will also have a photocopy of all the youth hostels in Holland. No special documents are necessary on any of Holland's 2,000 or so campsites. Expect to pay about f. 15 per night. For the fifty-two youth hostels, you have to be an IYHF member; charges vary from f. 20 to f. 30, depending on whether breakfast and an evening meal are included. Student hostels are open in summer and are fairly lax as long as you look like a student. Hotels are graded on a star basis with breakfast usually included in the price. Expect to pay f. 45 minimum for a one-star single room. Fortunately, Holland has plenty of boarding houses and private houses, most of which are very relaxed; these are your best bet. The local tourist offices keep a list and will find you a place for a small commission. Things get busy in July and August in Amsterdam and other tourist centres, so try and get along early.

EATING AND NIGHTLIFE

Most of the Dutch go in for a koffietafel (sandwich lunch and coffee) which is just as well, as evening meals have a tendency to be very high in carbohydrates. The best advice is: follow their example at lunchtime. There are over twenty-six types of cheese, so there's no excuse for sticking to just Edam and Gouda. There are numerous regional specialities to sample; one of the best is groene haring (new herring) – this is salted herring roe and is surprisingly tender and savoury. Follow the example of the Dutch and eat it from the street stalls. It's at its best during the first few weeks in May and makes a welcome change from hamburgers. For your main meal in the evening, keep your eyes skinned for one of the 600 restaurants which serve the tourist menu. This is filling and cheap and is the same price everywhere, so if you like what's on it, don't waste your time looking elsewhere. If you prefer something a little more exotic, try 'rijsttafel' from one of the numerous Indonesian restaurants in most cities. The VVV offices will keep you informed as to what's going on locally. In the larger cities there are plenty of nightclubs and discos, but expect to pay out quite a bit. Cinemas always show films in the original language with Dutch subtitles. Prices usually start at about f. 15 and performances begin at about 8 p.m.

The Northern Netherlands

Much of this area has been reclaimed from the sea and so is characteristically flat. FRIESLAND is a wildlife and bird sanctuary, and this area is more like a separate country (with its own language and separate history) than a part of Holland. The best places to make for are ZAANDAM, the 'living museum': a reconstructed village of mills and old houses; ALKMAAR (fifty minutes from Amsterdam) with its cheese market on Fridays at 10 a.m.; HOORN, which puts on a crafts and folklore market; and the capital of Friesland, LEEUWARDEN. Apart from being the birthplace of Mata Hari (her house is now the Museum of Frisian Literature), the town is also a birdwatchers' paradise; you can wade out to the islands on organized treks. See the FRIES MUSEUM, OLDEHOVE TOWER and PRINCESSEHOF MUSEUM of unique ceramics.

Amsterdam

There are two distinct faces to Amsterdam: one, the quiet graceful old town of endless canals, narrow houses and tiny winding streets; the other, the harsh reality of twentieth-century capitalist consumerism: fast food, fast sex, loud music and drug pushing. The two sides live incongruously together and have made Amsterdammers famed for their tolerance of different standards and others' opinions. There are so many things to experience in this city that it is pretty well essential to see it during any comprehensive European tour. The best time to visit Amsterdam is early June, for the Festival of Fools; you can also buy bulbs and herrings.

STATION FACILITIES

AMSTERDAM CENTRAAL STATION

Train information	Mon.–Fri.: 8 a.m.–10 p.m., Sat. and Sun.: 9 a.m.–6 p.m. (Tel. 238 383)
Reservations	Mon.–Fri.: 8 a.m.–8 p.m., Sat. and Sun.: 9 a.m.–5 p.m.
Tourist information	April–Sept.: daily, 9 a.m.–11 p.m. Oct.–Mar.: Mon.–Fri.: 1 p.m.–9 p.m.
Foreign exchange	Mon.–Sat.: 7 a.m.–10.50 p.m., Sun.: 9 a.m.–10.45 p.m.
Left-luggage lockers	No access Mon.–Fri.: 1.25 a.m.–4.25 a.m. Sat.: 1.25 a.m.–5.15 a.m., Sun.: 1.25 a.m.–5.55 p.m.
Left-luggage store	Mon.–Sat.: 5 a.m.–1 a.m., Sun.: 6 a.m.–1 a.m.
Restaurant	7 a.m.–11 p.m.
Bar, Buffet	7 a.m.–7 p.m. 'Snell Buffet' 6 a.m.–11 p.m. on platform 10a
Waiting room	All hours on platforms 7a, 10a, 13a
Shopping	6 a.m.–11 p.m. in central tunnel
Station shuts	Mon.–Fri.: 1.25 a.m.–4.25 a.m. Sat.: 1.25 a.m.–5.15 a.m., Sun.: 1.25 a.m.–5.55 a.m.

Daily trains to: Hamburg (6 hours), Hanover (5 hours), Düsseldorf (2½ hours), Cologne (3 hours), Liège (4½ hours), The Hague (¾ hour), Rotterdam (1 hour), Antwerp (2¼ hours), Brussels (2¾ hours), Paris (6 hours), Copenhagen, Munich and Zürich.

TOURIST INFORMATION

The VVV office is just outside the station. Another is at Leidseplein 10, open daily: 9 a.m.–9 p.m. Change money elsewhere if you can; the rate here is poor. Ask for the publication 'Use It', a student-orientated magazine on what's where and how much. 'Amsterdam This Week' lists current events.

● **Addresses:**

POST OFFICE: Nieuwezijds Voorburgwal 182, Mon.–Fri.: 8.30 a.m.–6 p.m., Thurs. till 8.30 p.m., Sat.: 9 a.m.–12 noon. Good currency exchange here.

AMEX: Damrak 66, Mon.–Fri.: 9 a.m.–5 p.m., Sat.: 9 a.m.–12 noon.

UK CONSULATE: Vermeerstraat 7 (Tel. 764343).

US CONSULATE: Museumplein 19 (Tel. 790321), open 9 a.m.–12 noon, 2 p.m.–4 p.m.
MEDICAL HELP: Tel. 64 21 11 for doctor or dentist.
CRISIS CENTRE: JAC, Amstel 30 (Tel. 242949).
TRANSALPINO: Rokin 44 (Tel. 239921), Mon.–Fri.: 9 a.m.–5 p.m., Sat.: 10 a.m.–2 p.m. 19, Waterlandplein, 53 Leidestraat.

• **Getting about:** Information and a map of the city's buses, trams and underground can be had from the GVB pavilion in front of the station. If you're going to make more than three journeys, invest in a twenty-four-hour pass. If you're there for a while, consider the two- or three-day pass or the multi-ride ticket. The fifteen-strip ticket (sold on buses and trams) is good value.

• **Drugs scene:** There are nearly as many pushers as eurorailers in Amsterdam station. It's up to you whether you get involved with them, but the best advice is not to. Each year, hundreds of eurorailers get on the wrong side of the drugs scene around here, and though the Dutch police had a reputation for being lax about drugs, things have changed recently.

SEEING

The four main canals (the Singel, Herengracht, Keizergracht and Prinsengracht) wind their way past the main sights, so in many ways the canal boats give you the best introduction to the city. They may really make you feel like a tourist but they're cheap. HERENGRACHT passes the rich seventeenth-century merchants' houses; at MUNT on the SINGEL is a colourful flower market.

DAM SQUARE is the heart of the city. It lies at the end of the main shopping thoroughfare, the DAMRAK, but its attraction is often clouded by the litter and the numbers of undesirables who hang around there. Still, it's always lively, and you can often find buskers and street artists performing. To the east of the Dam lies the old city centre, beautifully preserved in its seventeenth-century splendour. This area is known as WALLETJES, and you'll do best exploring it in daytime as parts of it (Oudezijds, Achterburgwal, Oude Zijds Voorburgwal and their surroundings) have a totally different character at night when they turn into the sex streets of Europe. JORDAAN is another district worth a wander. This is the Bohemian and working-class quarter bordered by Prinsengracht, Brouwers-gracht, Marnixstraat and Elandsgracht. There's a good Saturday market on Lindemarkt.

Just west of the Dam, round the back of the Westerkerk, is ANNE FRANK'S HOUSE where she wrote her famous diary while in hiding with her family from the Nazis for two years. See the Anti-Semitic Exhibition downstairs. It's at Prinsengracht 263, open Monday to Saturday: 9 a.m.–5 p.m. and Sunday: 10 a.m.–5 p.m.

The RIJKSMUSEUM at Stadhouderskade 42 is one of the world's great art museums and comes top of the list of Amsterdam's forty museums. It's really big on Rembrandts (his 'Night Watch' is there) and the Dutch masters. Open Tues.–Sat.: 10 a.m.–5 p.m., Sun.: 1 p.m.–5 p.m. The ROYAL PALACE on Dam Square is held up by 13,659 bits of wood; this led it to be known as the 'Eighth Wonder of the World'. Also there is the NIEUWE KERK, though there's nothing new about this late Gothic church which dates from around 1500. Just behind it is a 'tasting house', THE THREE BOTTLES (De Drie Fleschjes), which dates from 1650. Try the Bols and Hoppe liqueurs.

As far as museums are concerned, the favourites are the AMSTELKRING (Our Lord in the Attic) at Oude Zijds Voorburgwal 40, a preserved seventeenth-century house where repressed Catholics used to hide. REMBRANDT'S HOUSE is at Jodenbreestraat 2–6; the STEDELIJK MUSEUM, modern art, Paulus Potterstraat 13; and the VAN GOGH MUSEUM, just along the street at No. 7.

SLEEPING

As Amsterdam is the fourth most popular European city (after London, Paris and Rome), it's busy in summer, and often all the hotels are full. Still, you'll always find a bed in one of the hostels or the Sleep-In: check 'Use It' for current location. The VVV will find you a room for a small fee.

• **Hotels:** Van Onna, Bloemgracht 102 (Tel. 26 58 01).
Pax, Raadhuisstraat 376 (Tel. 24 97 35).
Hotel De Beurs, Beursstraat 7 (Tel. 22 23 08/22 07 41).
Hotel Fantasia, 16 Nieuwe Keizergracht (Tel. 23 82 59).
A walk down Raadhuisstraat, Beursstraat, Bloemgracht or Stad-

houderskade will produce something, unless the city's bursting at the seams.

• **Private accommodation:** The average is f. 40 per person; VVV will fix you up.

• **Hostels:**
Vondelpark IYHF hostel, Zandpad 5 (Tel. 83 17 44). You'll need membership. Around f. 18 in dorms. Tram 1 or 2 from station to Leidseplein, then a five-minute walk.
Stadsdoelen IYHF hostel, Kloveniersburgwal 97 (Tel. 24 68 32). Mar.–Oct. f. 18. This is more central. Take tram 4, 5 or 9 to Muntplein.
Hotel My Home, Haarlemmerstraat 82 (Tel. 24 23 20). Minimum stay of three nights. Good and friendly. Near station.
Hotel Kabul (Student Hostel), Warmoesstraat 42 (Tel. 23 71 58). Dormitory, single or double accommodation. Near station (and red- light district).
Hotel Acro, Jan Luykenstraat 42–44 (Tel. 72 05 26). Co-ed dormitories, singles or doubles. Good value.

The Sleep-In at Rozengracht is open late June–early September and at Easter. Tends to be a bit sleazy and promiscuous – not really the best place for a good night's sleep! Check address as it changes location annually. The two Christian hostels in Amsterdam are highly recommended.

For camping, try Vliegenbos at Meeuwenlaan 138 (Tel. 36 88 55).

To sleep out, try Julianapark, Beatrixpark or Vondelpark.

EATING AND NIGHTLIFE

There's a glut of cafés and restaurants near Dam Square, round the red-light district and Leidseplein: Dutch, Chinese, Italian and Indonesian. Go for the dag's menu and fill the gap with deep-fried poffertjes (mini-doughnuts) or ontbijtkoek from street stalls. Also try a rijsttafel from one of the Indonesian restaurants.

For free food and beer, hit the Heineken Brewery at Van der Helstraat 30. Go at 10 a.m. Mon.–Fri. Sometimes they take a small collection at the end which goes to UNICEF. There are several good street markets to buy picnic supplies from, and if you want to go out for a drink, head for the Leidseplein, Rembrandtsplein or Thorbeckeplein.

If you want to see 'sin city' and wander through the notorious red-light district of Zeedijk, go east of the Damrak to the area bordered by Warmoesstraat, Zeedijk and Damstraat.

Recommendations for restaurants are: H88 at Herengracht 88 (also a student hostel); Buddha's Belly at Rozenstraat 145; and Egg Cream at Sint Jacobsstraat 19, open 11 a.m.–7.30 p.m. For dancing, etc., try Melkweg at Lijnbaansgracht 243a or Bistrothèque at Korte, Leidsewarsstraat 26. The nicest old cafés are off Jordaan. Good for a gas (and it can literally be a 'gas' if you're on the wrong end of it) is the café Chris at Bloemstraat 42, whose toilet can be flushed only from the bar!

Outside Amsterdam

LEIDEN is half an hour south-west of Amsterdam and makes a pleasant day trip. This is where Descartes first published his *Discourse on Method*, and the University is still considered Holland's finest. Tourist information is at Stationsplein. See the OLD TOWN, BOTANICAL MUSEUM, the RIJKSMUSEUM VAN OUDHEDEN (National Antiquities). Both these are on Rapenburg. To clamber in a windmill and nose about, go to the MOLEN MUSEUM DE VALK, Tweede Binnenvestgracht 1. Try sleeping at Witte, Witte Singel 80, and eating at Repelsteetje on Breestraat 19 (closed Mon. and weekends).

The Hague (Den Haag)

As a major world political centre, The Hague has more than its fair share of smart elegant buildings and beautiful people. There are three royal palaces, over twenty excellent museums and two government bodies based in Den Haag: Holland's government located in the attractive BINNENHOF, and the International Court of Justice housed in the PEACE PALACE.

STATION FACILITIES

There are two stations in The Hague: Holland Spoor handles all international trains and Amsterdam trains, while Centraal Station handles trains to the east (Utrecht), south (Rotterdam) and short intercity and suburban lines.

	HOLLAND SPOOR	CENTRAAL STATION
Train information	7.30 a.m.–11 p.m. (Tel. 824 141)	7.30 a.m.–11 p.m. (Tel. 824 141)
Reservations	Mon.–Fri.: 8 a.m.–8 p.m. Sat.: 9 a.m.–5 p.m.	Mon.–Fri.: 8 a.m.–8 p.m. Sat.: 9 a.m.–5 p.m. Sun.: 10 a.m.–5 p.m.
Tourist information	–	*Summer*: Mon.–Sat.: 8.30 a.m.–9 p.m. Sun.: 10 a.m.–7 p.m. *Winter*: Mon.–Sat.: 8.30 a.m.–8 p.m. Across street: Sun.: 10 a.m.–5 p.m.
Foreign exchange	Mon.–Sat.: 8 a.m.–9 p.m. Sun.: 10 a.m.–6 p.m.	Mon.–Sat.: 8 a.m.–9 p.m. Sun.: 10 a.m.–6 p.m.
Left-luggage lockers	No access 1.30 a.m.–4.30 a.m.	No access 1.30 a.m.–4 a.m.
Left-luggage store	6 a.m.–10 p.m.	Mon.–Sat.: 6 a.m.–10 p.m. Sun.: 6.30 a.m.–10.30 p.m.
Cafeteria	6.30 a.m.–10.30 p.m.	6.30 a.m.–11.30 p.m.
Restaurant	Mon.–Sat.: 7 a.m.–9 p.m. Sun.: 8 a.m.–9 p.m.	Mon.–Fri.: 11 a.m.–8 p.m. (upstairs) Mon.–Fri.: 10 a.m.–8 p.m. ('Pub')
Post office	–	Mon.–Fri.: 8 a.m.–6 p.m.
Waiting room	All hours	In self-service
Station shuts	1.30 a.m.–4.30 a.m.	1.30 a.m.–4 a.m.

Tram 12 connects the two stations.

Daily trains to: Amsterdam (¾ hour), Rotterdam (20 minutes), Antwerp (1½ hours), Brussels (2 hours), Paris (5½ hours) and Cologne (4 hours).

TOURIST INFORMATION

Is outside Centraal Station at Koningin Julianaplein 8. Open Mon.–Sat.: 8.30 a.m.–9 p.m., Sun.: 9 a.m.–6 p.m.; there are also offices at Groenmarkt 7, Mon.: 12.30 p.m.–5 p.m., Tue.–Fri.: 10

a.m.–5 p.m., Sat.: 11 a.m.–4 p.m., and Swolsestraat, in Scheven-ingen, next to the Europe Hotel – open Mon.–Sat.: 9 a.m.–9 p.m., Sun.: 9 a.m.–6 p.m. (April–September). They'll all hand you free maps and an accommodation list or find a room for you.

● **Addresses:**
POST OFFICE: Nobelstraat, open Mon.–Fri.: 8.30 a.m.–7 p.m., Thur.: till 8.30 p.m., Sat.: 9.30 a.m.–12.30 p.m.
AMEX: Venestraat 20, open Mon.–Fri.: 9 a.m.–5 p.m., Sat.: 9.30 a.m.–12.30 p.m.
UK EMBASSY: Lange Voorhout 10 (Tel. 645800).
US EMBASSY: Lange Voorhout 102 (Tel. 624911).
CANADIAN EMBASSY: Sophialaan 7 (Tel. 614111).
AUSTRALIAN EMBASSY: Koninginnegracht 23–24 (Tel. 630983).
MEDICAL HELP: Tel. 455300.
TRANSALPINO: Plein 19a (Tel. 631550).

SEEING

The BINNENHOF – Holland's Westminster – is a complex of buildings with the thirteenth-century KNIGHT'S HALL at its centre. This is open to the public and is worth a look. There are carillon concerts at noon on Mondays, Wednesdays and Fridays in summer at the CHURCH OF ST JACOB, and on Thursday afternoons the imposing Lange Voor-hout (where the Embassy is) turns into an open-air antique market. The museums not to miss are: the MAURITSHUIS MUSEUM, Plein 29, with its superb collection of Dutch art; the GEMEENTE MUSEUM, Stadhouderslaan 41, the city museum with a collection of musical instruments and Mondrian's major works; and the GEVANGEN-POORT (Prison Gate) MUSEUM, Buitenhof 33, a morbid torture-chamber stuffed with medieval instruments to set your nerves on edge.

The main attraction of The Hague, however, is its miniature city, MADURODAM, open April–September till late at night. Tram 9 or bus 22 will take you out to Holland's Disneyland. This city, built to a 1/25th scale, has everything from trains to houses and street lamps – and everything works.

As Holland's 'greenest city', there are plenty of picnic and unofficial camping places to be had. Try the Haagse Bos, Westbroekpark or Clingendael Park. If you fancy beach-bumming it, SCHEVENINGEN is your nearest place (it's also good to sleep out on). Ten minutes from The Hague is the town of DELFT, famous for its pottery. You can see it being made at the Porceleyne Fles, Rotterdamseweg 196.

SLEEPING

Hotels aren't cheap, so try the alternatives. The VVV have a nasty habit of not using private accommodation (f. 30) till they've filled all the hotels. Beds come cheaper in Scheveningen. Try Pension Mem, Anna Paulovnastraat 8 (Tel. 637571), or Pension Centrale, Haagestraat 61 (Tel. 540955). There are campsites at Wijndaelerweg 25 (Tel. 252364) near the beach (bus 53 from the station) and Duinrell, Wassenaar (Tel. 01751/19314). The youth hostel at Monsterseweg 4 (Tel. 070/25 06 00) is very good (bus 26, 51 or 53 from station).

EATING AND NIGHTLIFE

Scheveningen is lively at night and your best bet for cheap eats and bars, though some can be fairly rough, so shop around. For groceries, try the market at Markthof, near Binnenhof, or on Grote Markt Straat.

Rotterdam

The largest port in Europe and second largest in the world, Rotterdam is Holland's second city after Amsterdam and, were it not for a Nazi air raid in 1940, would still be her rival in architectural terms. The rebuilt Rotterdam is an attractive, very modern city, best seen from the 600-foot-high Euromast.

ROTTERDAM CENTRAAL STATION	
Train information	Mon.–Fri.: 8 a.m.–10 p.m., Sat., Sun.: 9 a.m.–10 p.m. (Tel. 117 100)
Reservations	Mon.–Fri.: 8 a.m.–8 p.m., Sat., Sun.: 9 a.m.–5 p.m.
Tourist information	9 a.m.–12 midnight
Foreign exchange	8 a.m.–9 p.m.
Left-luggage lockers	No access 1 a.m.–5 a.m.
Left-luggage store	6 a.m.–10 p.m.
Restaurant	6 a.m.–11 p.m.
Waiting room	All hours
Station shuts	1 a.m.–5 a.m.

Daily trains to: Amsterdam (1 hour), The Hague (20 minutes), Antwerp (1¼ hours), Brussels (1¾ hours), Paris (5 hours), Düsseldorf (3 hours), Cologne (3½ hours), Munich, Innsbruck, Basel, London via Hook of Holland.

TOURIST INFORMATION

MAIN OFFICE: VVV Stadhuisplein 19.
DOCTOR AND 24-HOUR CHEMIST: Tel. 362244.
TRANSALPINO: Lijnbaan 26 (Tel. 132525).

SEEING

You can tour round the massive port by boat if you've spare cash, or else wander round some of its thirty miles yourself. The BOYMANS-VAN-BEUNINGEN MUSEUM on Mathenesserlaan is a superb modern-art museum. Close to the station is the GROOTHANDELSGEBOUW (the nearest post office to the station is in here), a huge complex of offices, restaurants, entertainments, etc. One part of Rotterdam which wasn't wiped out was DELFSHAVEN from where the Pilgrim Fathers left in 1620 en route to discover America. In Delfshaven they are restoring the 110 buildings left and turning the area into a craft centre.

Not far from Rotterdam is the only remaining area with lots of windmills: Kinderdijk. Go on Saturday afternoons in summer and see all nineteen at work. The cheese town of GOUDA is 25 minutes by train from Rotterdam. See its colourful cheese market in the central market on Thursday mornings (9 a.m.–10 a.m.) in summer.

The youth hostel's at Rochussenstraat 107 (Tel. 365763), and there are plenty of cheap eating places all over town.

The Southern and Eastern Netherlands

The southern part of Holland, bordered by Belgium, has as its main stopping-off places the beautifully situated, historic town of BREDA, and the reconstructed medieval town of MIDDELBURG, with its miniature town on a 1/20th scale, 'Walcheren'.

When in LIMBURG, the south-eastern province between Germany and Holland, look in on MAASTRICHT with its nine castles and 120-mile network of man-made tunnels. UTRECHT is the main town of the east. It has a medieval city centre and a thirteenth-century cathedral. For real train buffs, there's a railway museum in the old station here, housing old steam locomotives. See also the CENTRAAL MUSEUM with its Viking ship, and the MUSIC BOX MUSEUM.

ARNHEM was badly bombed in 1944 and mementoes of the battle (of *A Bridge Too Far* fame) can be seen in the twelfth-century DOORWERTH CASTLE outside the town. The main reason to stay in Arnhem is for its proximity to the fascinating OPEN-AIR MUSEUM just north of the city. There are working farms, mills and houses here to give you a fully rounded picture of traditional Dutch rural life. There's also a zoo and safari park with a mini-train running through it, and a costume museum.

Haarlem

Fifteen minutes from Amsterdam is Haarlem, one of Holland's most historic and well-preserved towns. Tourist information is at Stationsplein 1, and after your call in here go to the GROTE MARKT where ST BAVO'S CHURCH, the RENAISSANCE MEAT MARKET and the fourteenth-century TOWN HALL are located. Also see the FRANZ HALS MUSEUM, especially when they're holding candlelight concerts in it.

Try the youth hostel at Jan Gijzen (Tel. 373793). Take bus 6 from the station.

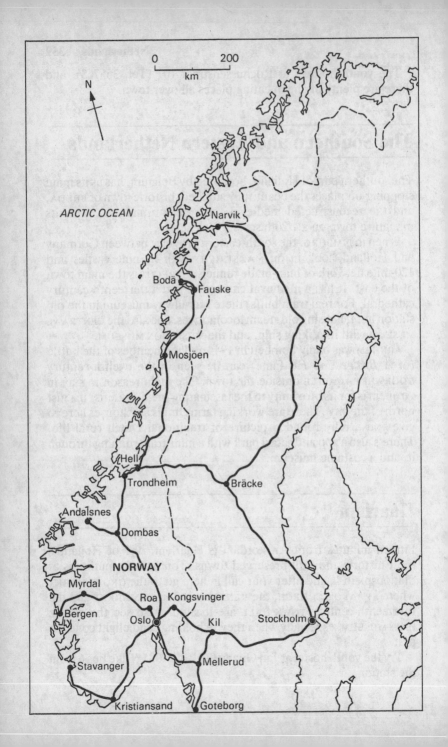

NORWAY

Entry requirements	Passport
Population	4,000,000
Capital	Oslo (pop.: 465,000)
Currency	Kroner
	£1 = approx. 16.97 kr.
Political system	Constitutional Monarchy
Religion	Lutheran
Language	Norwegian (English widely spoken)
Public holidays	1 Jan.; Maundy Thursday; Good Friday;
	Easter Monday; 1, 17 May; Ascension Day;
	Whit Monday; 25, 26 Dec.

Norway has the lowest population density in Europe – even her cities are small by Western standards (Bergen 213,000, Stavanger 87,500) – a fact which is not surprising when one realizes that about a quarter of Norway's land is above the Arctic Circle. If you're lucky and it's not raining, one of Europe's most spectacular countries awaits you; 80 per cent of her land is taken up by forests and mountains. The Sognefjord, one of Norway's best-known fjords, runs for over 100 miles inland with 4,000-foot walls in places. It was from fjords like this that Harald Fairhair's longboats sailed westward, after his unification of Norway in 885, a process which continued until the death of Harald Hardrada, at Stamford Bridge in 1066, while trying to conquer England. During the medieval period, the plague knocked off most of the Norwegian population and left the German Hansa merchants in control of the country's trade. This was followed by 400 years of Danish rule, to be succeeded by rule by Sweden after the Napoleonic Wars. Independence came in 1905 when Haakon VII was elected king, and was succeeded by his son Olav in 1957. Today, Norway has one of the highest standards of living in Europe, thanks to cheap hydro-electric power and the discovery of oil. 'Afjordable Norway', however, is one of the biggest jokes any tourist board has ever thought up, as visiting eurorailers will soon discover. Still, Norway's well worth the inconvenience of getting there – even if you can only 'afjord' a quick train through.

NORWEGIAN STATE RAILWAYS
(Norges Statsbaner, NSB)

The Norwegians have one of the cleanest and most efficient railways in Europe and it passes through some of the most spectacular scenery. There are no supplements in Norway so Inter Rails are valid on all trains. The fastest and most comfortable trains are the Ekspresstog (Et, expresses). They run between all the major cities and stop only at main stations. The regular day-trains are the Hurtigtog (Ht, fast) but they're only slightly better than the locals (Persontog, Pt), which stop at every station.

• **Eurail bonuses:** 30 per cent reduction on normal fares of the steamship company KDS between Kristiansand and Hirtshals.

TRAIN INFORMATION

No problems here as everyone speaks good English. NSB also publish an excellent free series of leaflets giving maps and descriptions of their main tourist routes.

• **Reservations:** Domestic reservations aren't cheap but are compulsory on expresses (Et), optional on all other trains. They should be made in advance, but if you don't have the time you can still do this on the train, though this won't guarantee you a seat, and you'll still have to pay. If you're travelling to Copenhagen you're advised to reserve thirty-six hours in advance and forty-eight hours at weekends.

• **Night travel:** Second-class sleepers cost about 90 kr. but are available only on runs to Sweden and Denmark.

• **Eating on trains:** Expresses have dining cars, and if you have a bit of money to blow the food is excellent, as is the scenery. All other trains have buffets which serve hot meals as well as snacks.

• **Scenic tips:** There are more scenic routes in Norway than anywhere else in Scandinavia, and possibly even Europe. The jewel of them all is the Bergen–Oslo run. Be sure to get hold of the free NSB leaflets which give good descriptions of the various lines.

TOURIST INFORMATION

There's a tourist office at every major town in Norway. They help to find accommodation if necessary and have a good supply of local information leaflets. Norway's one of the most health-conscious of all European countries, and at weekends you'll find, depending on the season, the ski slopes, forest tracks and waterways well used by the 'great outdoors' fanatics. For detailed information on hiking and mountaineering, contact DNT, Stortingsgata 28, Oslo.

• **ISIC bonuses:** 50 per cent discounts on museums, theatres and some coastal steamers. Also 30 per cent reductions on some bus services. For further information, contact UR Universiterssentret, Blindern, Oslo (Tel. 466880).

• **Money matters:** 1 Norwegian kroner (kr.) = 100 øre.
Banking hours are Mon.–Fri.: 9 a.m.–3 p.m. Some stay open till 5 p.m. on Thursdays.

• **Post offices and shops:** Mon.–Fri.: 8.30/9 a.m.–5 p.m., late-night opening Thursdays till 7 p.m.; closed Saturday p.m.

• **Museums:** Vary throughout Norway, but the general pattern is 10 a.m. opening and early closing at 3 p.m. or 4 p.m.

EATING AND NIGHTLIFE

Norway is one country you're bound to lose weight in; it's not that the food is bad, or that you'll be press-ganged into spending all day out hiking in the fjords – it's just that food is so expensive here that you'll rarely be able to afford the luxury of a full stomach. This is *the* problem in Norway: it's quite easy to spend the equivalent of 100 kr. a day just feeding yourself with average-quality meals. Avoid expensive meat dishes and turn instead to fish, and try and copy the locals: eat a full breakfast of smørgåsbord, have a snack at lunch (bought from a market/shop) and aim for a koldtbord (cold table) meal in the evening where you can eat as much as you like, or a fixed-price menu. If you're planning on self-catering a lot in Norway (and you should), bring some basic supplies with you from home.

The Norwegians have a reputation for being quite a serious lot, and to an extent that's fair comment – though catch them after a few drinks at night and you'd never believe it. They're very culture-conscious, and much effort is made to preserve the folk songs and dances of their forebears – the displays of these you may encounter are not put on purely as commercial stunts for the tourists.

Stavanger

If you've arrived in Norway at Stavanger, it'll take you about eight hours to get to Oslo. There's not that much to keep you here but if you've time to spare, the OLD TOWN gives you an idea what Norway was once like. The medieval CATHEDRAL is a good example, and is located in the colourful MARKETPLACE. If you've three or four hours to kill, the Stavanger–Sand ferry takes you through some fjords which will whet your appetite for what's to come. The 'Stavanger Guide' from the tourist pavilion has a map and all the information you'll need if you decide to stay longer.

Oslo

On Norway's south-eastern coast at the head of a 60-mile fjord lies Oslo, the oldest of the Scandinavian capitals. Outside the city limits are acres of forests, hills and unspoilt countryside which the Oslo-ites use at every opportunity to pursue their many outdoor activities. The town itself has no distinctive style, and you have to look below the surface for its real attractions: the museums and parks.

STATION FACILITIES

There are two main stations in Oslo: Central and West. Chances are you'll arrive at the Central, which serves all international trains, Bergen and Trondheim. The West operates to Kristiansand and Stavanger. Space does not permit us to give information on the West Station, especially as it is not much used by Inter Railers.

	OSLO (CENTRAL)
Train information	7 a.m.–11 p.m.
	(Tel. 209550)
Reservations	8 a.m.–4 p.m. (8 p.m. for a.m. trains)
Tourist information	Maps from train information
	Accommodation: Mon.–Sat.: 8.30 a.m.–11 a.m.,
	6 p.m.–11 p.m., Sun.: 8.30 a.m.–11 p.m.
Foreign exchange	7 a.m.–11 p.m.
Left-luggage lockers	No access at night
Bar/Café	12.30 p.m.–10.15 p.m.
Restaurant	7 a.m.–10.15 p.m. (v. good)
Waiting room	All hours

Daily trains to: Gothenburg, Stockholm, Trondheim, Bergen, Copenhagen.

TOURIST INFORMATION

Pick up maps and booklets from train information in Central Station, and use the Innkvartering (room-finding service) who ask an 8 kr. commission, but it's worth it. The Oslo Tourist Information Centre is at the Town Hall. They are extremely helpful and will give you maps, the 'Oslo Guide', 'Oslo This Week' and ferry and bus timetables. They're open Mon.–Fri.: 8 a.m.–5 p.m., Sat.: 8.30 a.m.–2 p.m., Sun.: 9 a.m.–1 p.m.

● **Addresses:**
POST OFFICE: Dronningensgate 15, open Mon.–Fri.: 8 a.m.–8 p.m., Sat.: 8 a.m.–5 p.m. Kongensgate 21 for twenty-four-hour telephones.
AMEX: c/o Winge Travel, Karl Johansgate 33, open Mon.–Fri.: 8.30 a.m.–4 p.m., Sat.: 8.30 a.m.–1 p.m.
STUDENT TRAVEL: Dronningensgate 27, open Mon.–Fri.: 8.15 a.m.–3.15 p.m.
NUH (Norwegian Youth Hostel headquarters): Dronningensgate 26. Pick up list of hostels here.
DEN NORSKE TURISTFORENING (Norwegian Mountain Touring Association): Stortingsgata 28 (Tel. 334290). If you've come to Norway to climb or camp, call in for leaflets on mountain huts, etc. Open weekdays: 8.20 a.m.–4 p.m., Thursday till 6 p.m.

UK EMBASSY: Thomas Heftyesgate 8 (Tel. 563890).
US EMBASSY: Drammensveien 18 (Tel. 566880).
CANADIAN EMBASSY: Oscargate 29 (Tel. 466955).
AUSTRALIAN EMBASSY: Jernbanstorget 2 (Tel. 414433).
24-HOUR CHEMIST: Jernbanstorget Apotek. In front of Central Station.

• **Getting about:** City transport is good and you can use your ticket to transfer to any form of transport within an hour. These include buses, trams, undergrounds, ferries and local trains (free on Inter Rail). Pick up the transit map at the station or tourist information.

SEEING

The Rådhus (Town Hall) is down by the harbour. This avant-garde 1950s structure was decorated by contemporary Norwegian artists and can be visited free. From the Rådhus Gate you can enter AKERSHUS CASTLE, built by King Haakon V around 1300, then rebuilt in Renaissance style by Christian IV. It's open weekdays 12.30 p.m.–4 p.m. (May to September); and in the grounds of the castle is the NORWEGIAN RESISTANCE MUSEUM describing the Nazi occupation of Norway. The ferry from the Rådhus over to the peninsula of BYGDOY takes you to five very interesting places:

1. The incredible NORSK FOLKEMUSEUM with 150 wooden buildings filled with material artefacts recreating Norway's past. These include Ibsen's study, houses from Lapland and museums of domestic furniture, clothes and implements.
2. THE VIKING SHIP HOUSE: Three preserved Viking longboats from AD 800–900.
3. KON-TIKI MUSEUM: The rafts used by the explorer Thor Heyerdahl on his voyages.
4. The NORWEGIAN MARITIME MUSEUM.
5. The FRAM MUSEUM: The ship used in the Polar expeditions of the nineteenth and early twentieth centuries.

All these museums are within walking distance of one another and are open 10 a.m.–6 p.m.

The VIGELAND SCULPTURE PARK and VIGELAND MUSEUM show the work and the background of the Norwegian artist Gustav Vigeland. This park is one of Norway's finest and 1,750 sculptures dotted round it have been termed everything from 'obscene' to 'serene'. The other famous Norwegian artist, EDVARD MUNCH, has his MUSEUM in the east of the city. It's a particularly fine gallery, housing literally thousands of his Expressionist works. Both these museums are closed Mondays. The NATIONAL GALLERY is at Universitetsgata 13, and has Norway's principal art collection.

SLEEPING

Oslo's not easy on eurorailers. Forget hotels completely and concentrate on the few hostels and campsites, or settle for private accommodation. You can get a room in a private house for 80 kr. single, 130 kr. double, and you must stay at least two nights. Both youth hostels are very good, clean, efficient, and with plenty of facilities, but they could hardly be called central. Bjerke Studentheim is at Trondheimsveien 271 (Tel. 579933) and charges around 50 kr. Reception opens 5 p.m. though you can phone in your booking earlier (a good idea). It's open June–August and is on bus routes 30 and 31.

Haraldsheim is at Haraldsheimveien 4 (Tel. 213990). It charges around 70 kr., including breakfast. It's open all year and is reached by the train to Grefsen from Central Station. The Seamen's Hostel, Oslo Sjømannshjemmet on Fred Olsengate (Tel. 412005), have fair rooms and serve reasonably priced meals. Reception is open twenty-four hours.

If you don't mind an institutional atmosphere, Holtekilen Summer Hotel at Micheletsvei 55 (Tel. 533853) is good value. You can choose between the ten-bed classroom accommodation (it's a school except in summer) or if you're keen to escape the classroom, the hotel side does doubles for a bit more.

The campsites are Bogstad Camping at Ankerveien 117 (Tel. 247619) (bus 41 from Central Station) and the Ekeberg site at Ekebergveien 65 (Tel. 198568) which is more central (tram 9 from in front of Central Station).

EATING AND NIGHTLIFE

Here more than anywhere else in Europe, you'll find prices sky-high. Don't attempt restaurants or stopping off for a coffee and cake (20 kr.). Eat like the Norwegians: a hearty breakfast and big dinner and expect to average 55 kr. for a full meal. There are fast-food chains – Wimpy and Kaffistovas – which can help eke out the finances, and Kveldsmat on Universitetgata, off Karl Johansgate, is cheap. Friskporten on Grensen 18 do superb vegetarian meals for about 40 kr.

● **Excursions:** Skiers should find the world's oldest SKI MUSEUM interesting. It's located inside the take-off point of the huge Holmenkollen ski jump. Exhibits here trace the history of the sport and produce evidence that it dates as far back as about 500 BC. Take the Holmenkollen railway from its underground station and walk about ten minutes from the station. EKEBERG PARK gives a great view over Oslo from its hills where Stone Age carvings from 1,000 BC have been found. If you're a group of four and have cash to spare, why not take a torch-lit sleigh ride through the woods here? (Contact Ekeberg Rideskole through tourist information.)

Oslo–Bergen: the Sognefjord

The rail run from Oslo to Bergen is one you should go out of your way to take. The scenery is incredible and during the course of this six-hour journey, you'll pass through fjords, glaciers, tundra, mountains, lakes, plateaux and gorges. Should you choose to break this journey and savour its delights slowly, stop off at MYRDAL and take the other line for the twelve-mile and 3,000-foot journey down to FLÅM. Should you decide to stay at Flåm, the Solhammer Pension, across the river from the station, is reasonable, and there's camping next door (though if you don't camp freelance here you never will). From Flåm you can tackle the fjords. A favourite trip of ours (and it won't take you out of your way from Bergen) is to take the ferry to GUDVANGEN from Flåm. This two-hour trip takes you past the spectacular scenery of the Nerøfjord, and calls at some isolated settlements en route whose sole means of communication is the ferry. From Gudvangen take the bus to Voss where you're back on the Bergen line again.

Bergen

The colourful harbour, red-roofed houses and spruce trees nestling under imposing Mount Fløyen give Bergen the reputation of being Norway's most attractive city. This was the northernmost city in the Hanseatic League and the HANSEATIC MUSEUM – a reconstruction of a sixteenth-century merchant's house – makes an interesting visit. This is in the quarter called BRYGGEN, and in the old timber houses today weavers and craftsmen carry on their trade. ROSENKRANTZ TOWER and KING HAAKON'S HALL aren't terribly interesting, so don't bother unless you're really bored. Do, however, take the funicular up Mount Fløyen and see the view. The RASMUS MEYER collection is an art gallery on the edge of the LILLE LUNGENGARDSVATNET park, and the GAMLE BERGEN (old town) with its traditional timbered buildings makes a pleasant walk. The Romanesque church of ST MARY'S is considered Norway's most beautiful church. Tourist information have details on the May–June INTERNATIONAL FESTIVAL held here, and also about the trips to the fjords that start from Bergen.

TOURIST INFORMATION AND ADDRESSES

Tourist information pavilion at Torgalmenning: walk for ten minutes up Kaigaten from the station. Open Mon.–Sat.: 8.30 a.m.–10 p.m. in summer. They change money, book you into private houses and supply maps and 'The Bergen Guide'.
POST OFFICE: Småstrandgate. Open 8 a.m.–5 p.m., Thur.: till 7 p.m., Sat.: 9 a.m.–1 p.m.
24-HOUR CHEMIST: Accident Clinic, Lars Millesgate (Tel. 210185).
STUDENT TRAVEL: Parkveien 1. 25 per cent reductions on steamer fare to Newcastle.

SLEEPING, EATING AND NIGHTLIFE

Use the tourist pavilion who charge 8 kr. commission. Private homes ask about 90 kr. single, 130 kr. double.

The youth hostel is nearly always full, so call first. It's in a good position, halfway up Mount Ulriken. It costs 65 kr. for B&B. Open May–Sept. On bus route 4 at Ravneberget (Tel. 222900), but apply at IYHA office at Strandgaten 4.

Lone is Bergen's main campsite (Tel. 240820), but it's quite far out and not that cheap. Better to walk a bit up Mount Fløyen and camp free. (Leave your pack in left luggage if it helps.)

The food and nightlife news is not too good. All you'll be able to afford are picnics and some of the fairly boring café-type places. The restaurant in the Fantoft Sommerhotel is decent and offers a 20 per cent students' discount (bus 14 or 15) and Hulen is a club run by the town's university students in an old air-raid shelter beneath Nygaardsparken. If you're over 20 (and can prove it) you can go to the disco and drink there.

Trondheim to the North Cape

The rail line runs to Bodø, capital of the Nordland province and land of the midnight sun. This is the northernmost region of Europe and its beauty is beyond the scope of any guidebook's description, so we won't start coming out with the standard string of superlatives, as you'd probably find it corny. Just take it from us you won't regret your trip up there. From Bodø you'll have to take a ferry and bus up to NARVIK, passing through the LOFOTEN ISLANDS, then on to FINNMARK and LAPLAND.

Trondheim

Trondheim is a university town whose main purpose is to produce and export timber, fish, farm products and ships. Pick up a map and the 'Trondheim Guide' at the station. The tourist office is over the bridge and right for a few blocks up Munkegata (open Mon.–Sat.: 9

a.m.–6 p.m.; Sun.: 1 p.m.–5 p.m. in season). The sights of the city are the medieval NIDAROS CATHEDRAL, the twelfth-century ARCHBISHOP'S PALACE and the interesting RINGVE MUSEUM OF MUSIC HISTORY.

Bodø

It's 11½ hours from Trondheim to Bodø, but the scenery and the comfortable trains make it feel a lot less. From 1 June–12 July, the sun never sets here. If you hit a particularly good spell of weather, walk up Mount Ronvik, taking your camera with you. The 1956 CATHEDRAL is about the only noteworthy building in the town, but you don't come here for the towns. Head instead for SALISTRAUMEN where every six hours millions of gallons of water squeeze through a tiny passage between two fjords, making a spectacular sight. Buses run to coincide with the tides – ask for the timetable at tourist information.

TOURIST INFORMATION AND ADDRESSES

Tourist office is at Storgata 46, open Mon.–Fri.: 9 a.m.–8 p.m.; Sat.: 9 a.m. to 2 p.m., and 5 p.m.–8 p.m. in season. Books private accommodation for you. Flatvoll Youth Hostel is at Rønvikkrysset (Tel. 25666). A spanking new, very good hostel with all facilities, ¾ mile from station. Open 20 June–20 Aug. Central Turiststasjon, Professor Schyttes Gate 46, for good and filling food.

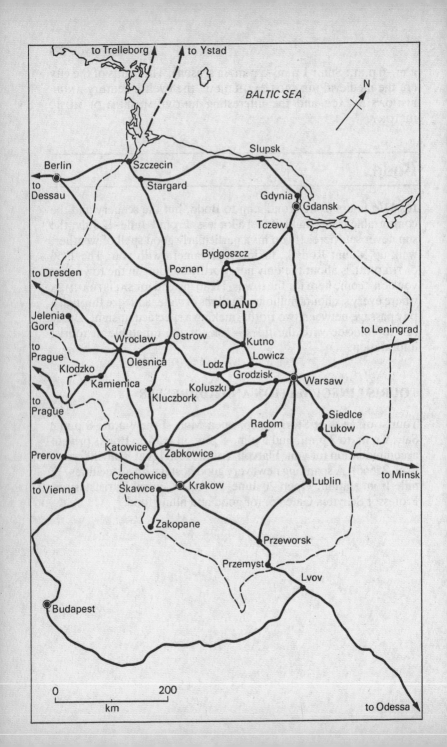

POLAND

Entry requirements	Passport and visa
Population	35,000,000
Capital	Warsaw (pop.: 1,550,000)
Currency	Zloty
	£1 = approx. 154.8 zl.
Political system	Independent People's Republic (Communist)
Religion	Roman Catholic
Language	Polish (a little German and English spoken)
Public holidays	1 Jan.; Good Friday; Easter Monday; 1 May; Corpus Christi; 22 July; 1 Nov.; 25, 26 Dec.

As a result of recent events within Poland it's been extremely difficult to get a visa unless you had a good reason for going, though restrictions are easing now. This latest set of troubles is not surprising in a country full of paradoxes, the greatest being that Poland is 90 per cent Catholic, yet Communist in government. Anti-Soviet riots also occurred in 1956 and in 1970. Solidarity and the call for free trade unions reflect the independent spirit of the Poles who resent outside pressure from the Soviet Union or wherever. This fact becomes understandable when one looks at the history of Poland, a country which has had more than its fair share of invasion and occupation. This process began in the tenth century with the eastward expansion of Germanic tribes, and continued long after the area came under the protection of the Holy Roman Empire. As an independent kingdom, Poland came into being in 1025; since then the country has been conquered and boundaries changed many times. In 1795 and 1939 Poland disappeared off the map altogether as it looked like doing again for a time in 1982.

POLISH STATE RAILWAYS
(Polski Koleje Państwowe, PKP)

Polish trains are among the slowest and busiest in Europe. Tickets are sold according to the type of train you want to travel on. Avoid the Osobowy and Pośpieszny categories and go for the Ekspresowy expresses whenever possible. All the large cities have their own commuter trains called Pociągi Elektryczne which are even more crowded than normal. Don't be talked into buying a Polrailpass from any Orbis office unless you plan on spending a lot of time going around in circles. There's no way you can avoid queueing for seat reservations, so you might just as well get a standard one-way ticket at the same time, as prices are very cheap.

TRAIN INFORMATION

Few officials speak English, so if you want to make a reservation write down the name of your destination and the time your train leaves. Speaking German is best in the south, French in the north. If you get stuck, try: 'Z którego peronu odjezda pociąg do . . . ?' (From which platform does the train to . . . leave?)

• **Reservations:** If you want a seat, you'll have to make a reservation as trains are always crowded to capacity. Go to the station at least one day in advance (several days for the Warsaw–Kraków–Zakopane run). For international trains you'll have to use Orbis and face the even longer queues. Look out for windows marked 'Polres': they deal with seat reservations (miejscówka) which are compulsory on express and international trains.

• **Night travel:** Don't expect high standards unless you're willing to travel first class. Reserve well ahead of time at Orbis, particularly for couchettes.

• **Eating on trains:** There's either a restaurant or buffet car on all long hauls.

TOURIST INFORMATION

There are local Informacja Turystyczna (IT) offices in every major town as well as at many stations. If you plan to stay for a while, it's worth buying 'A Guide for Young Tourists' from any Ruch kiosks in Poland.

• **ISIC bonuses:** For an IUS card you have to go to Almatur in Warsaw; this gives you 25 per cent reductions on international trains within the Eastern Bloc.

• **Money matters:** 1 zloty (zl.) = 100 groszy (g.).
Banking hours are Mon.–Fri.: 8 a.m.–12 noon, Sat.: 8 a.m.–10.45 a.m. It's also possible to exchange money at Orbis and at travel agents.

On entering Poland you have to change about £5 ($8) a day, either to zloty or Almatur youth vouchers. When you leave you have to show your receipts at the border. It's certainly not worth playing the black market unless you're exchanging with friends, or paying for accommodation in private homes. If you plan on doing this, don't declare all your hard currency when you arrive so the authorities won't want to know where it's all gone.

• **Post offices:** Open Mon.–Fri.: 8 a.m.–8 p.m. Getting mail sent on is more trouble than it's worth (allow at least three weeks). Most embassies will keep your letters for at least two weeks.

• **Shops:** For food, 8 a.m.–7 p.m., others 11 a.m.–7 p.m. For opening times of museums, etc., check with the local IT office.

SLEEPING

The Polish authorities don't encourage 'off-the-cuff' visits, and as a result it's almost impossible to find a room in Poland without having fixed it up beforehand. To do this contact Polorbis (see p. 51 for address). They will issue you with student accommodation vouchers. These vouchers allow you to stay at any of the ISHs (international student hostels) (open July, Aug. and Sept.) in Poland for about 260 zl. a night if you're a student or under 25. If you haven't already done this, then your best plan is to arrive as early as possible in the day – and even this does not ensure you a bed at an ISH. Vouchers are a prerequisite in Warsaw, so don't waste time going along unless you have them. If you've no luck with the ISHs, try the Polish Youth Hostel Federation (PTSM). Most require an IYHF card, but it's not always essential. The good news is that they're very cheap, the bad news is that they're like overcrowded prisons. There are over 1,000 hostels ('schroniska mlodziezowe') in Poland all of which are spartan even by Western YH standards.

The more money you have, the less your problems are likely to be. PTTK is an organization which runs cheap hotels called 'Domy

Turysty'; you can find out about these from the local IT office, but don't build your hopes up as they are nearly always full. Another organization called 'Biuro Zakwaterowania' arranges for you to stay with private families, but at a prohibitive cost. Be careful about accepting offers of private rooms on the street as, apart from being illegal, the room in question might well be a long way out of town. Finally, if you're really desperate, try the long queue at the Orbis office; they might have a spare bed in one of their hotels, if you're prepared to pay the high prices asked.

EATING AND NIGHTLIFE

Since the recent troubles, queueing for food has affected tourists as well as the Poles. Things are not as bad as the media make out, however, for it's still possible to eat very well if you know where to look. Don't worry about the meat shortages as it's not very good anyway; you're best to stick to fish or poultry with which the Poles have had plenty of experience.

Not surprisingly, nightlife was somewhat dampened by martial law. Kawiarnie (cafés) and winiarnie (wine bars) remain about the only places you're likely to encounter any form of nightlife.

Warsaw (Warszawa)

The beautiful city of Warsaw could have looked very different today had the patriotic Poles decided to replace the bombed buildings of 1944 with concrete blocks, instead of rebuilding replicas of the original nineteenth-century structures. Ignore the few Stalinesque buildings that have crept in, and judge the city instead on her elegant palaces and parks. Her past is bloody and tragic, and you only have to look back to 1943 when Hitler ordered that no stone of Warsaw should be left standing, for evidence of this. The HIS-TORICAL MUSEUM OF THE CITY, on the Old Town Market Square, has film captured from the Nazis which shows the systematic destruction of this city, and there are reminders of the holocaust dotted all round the centre.

TOURIST INFORMATION

The Warsaw information office is located in the main Orbis office at ul Bracka 16, open Mon.–Fri.: 8 a.m.–7 p.m.,Sat.: 8 a.m.–5 p.m. The Orbis branch at Marszal- kowska 142 sells international train tickets.

● **Addresses:**

POST OFFICE: Świętokrzyska.

AMEX: Al Ujazdowskie 29/31, open Mon.–Fri.: 8.30 a.m.–5 p.m.

ALMATUR (Polish Student Travel): At the university on ul Koper- nika 25 (Tel. 262356). Open Mon.–Fri.: 8.30 a.m.–8 p.m.

UK EMBASSY: Aleja Róz 1 (Tel. 281001).

US EMBASSY: Al Ujazdowskie 29/31 (Tel. 283041).

CANADIAN EMBASSY: ul Piekna 2/4 (Tel. 298051).

FIRST AID: Hoza 56 (Tel. 999).

STATIONS: There are three stations in Warsaw, but the only one you're likely to use consistently is the new Centralna.

● **Getting about:** Buy your tram and bus tickets at the kiosks marked Ruch (tramwajowe and bilety autobusowe). Buy as many as you think you'll use in one go (at the station) to avoid queues. Buses marked with letters are expresses and cost twice as much as normal buses. After 11 p.m. all fares are doubled.

SEEING

Between the STARE MIASTO (old town) and the LAZIENKI PARK lie the main sights of Warsaw. The centre of the old town is the beautiful RYNEK (market square). Rebuilt baroque houses line the square and a block to the south lies ST JOHN'S CATHEDRAL, the main church for Warsaw's deeply religious Catholics. In Zamkowy Square stands Warsaw's oldest monument, the Sigismund III column (1644), and this adjoins the ROYAL CASTLE which dates back to the fourteenth century and is still being worked on to repair its 1940s damage. The tin-roofed baroque PALACE is close by.

The Jewish population of Warsaw were literally decimated under Nazism and the PAWIAK PRISON where 35,000 were executed and 65,000 detained is now a museum. The JEWISH HISTORICAL INSTITUTE at Al Świerczewskiego 79 looks at what happened in the famous Warsaw Ghetto, and the MAUSOLEUM TO STRUGGLE AND MARTYRDOM, across the river in Praga, is housed in the former Gestapo HQ and prison.

LAZIENKI PALACE AND PARK were built for the last Polish king in the eighteenth century. The palace has been restored and there are many other buildings and monuments in this graceful park. On the southern edge of the park is the monument to Chopin, and on Sunday afternoons there are often Chopin recitals. The WILANÓW PALACE AND PARK was one of the seventeenth-century kings' summer houses. The restored palace can be visited, and while you're out here you can visit the MUSEUM OF THE POLISH POSTER in the palace grounds. The palace is closed Tuesdays, the museum shuts Mondays and you reach them by bus B from ul Marszalkowska.

SLEEPING

Finding a bed in Warsaw can be a depressing and soul-destroying experience. Your best course of action is to go to the Almatur office (see above) and ask them for the addresses of their current ISHs (they change locations annually). These are open July–August and range in price from 260–1200 zl., depending on whether you've an ISIC. Almatur also have lists of the campsites. If you're an IYHF member, go along to PTSM at ul Chocimska 28 for a list of Polish hostels. The two in Warsaw are cheap, rule-ridden and fairly depressing. They're at Karolkowa 53a (Tel. 328829) and Smolna 30 (Tel. 278952), but you must arrive before 9 a.m. to be in with a chance. PTTK at ul Marszalkowska 124 will give you a list of their Domy Turysty. The best campsite is Gromada on ul Zwirki i Wigury (Tel. 254391). There are bungalows here as well as tent sites, and they offer one of the best deals going: about 300 zl. per person in a four-person bungalow (bus 128, 136 or 175 from Centralna, direction airport). The two-tier price structure (one price for Eastern Bloc residents, one for Western tourists) puts hotels right out of the picture, so don't even contemplate them.

EATING AND NIGHTLIFE

Make up for all the hardships you've had to endure by eating out in style. Food here is cheap enough to let you eat in all the best restaurants and still think you got a bargain. If you're cutting back on food too, eat in the milk bars or at the university cafeteria on campus at ul Krakowskie Przedmieście. Cristal-Budapest, ul Marszalkowska 21–25 does good Hungarian dishes, or try the Krokodyl, Starego Miasta 21, on the old town market square.

The kawiarnie and winiarnie are the hub of social life in Warsaw, as elsewhere in Poland. It's not difficult to find good ones, but Fukier, Rynek Starego Miasta, is Poland's best and dates back to the seventeenth century. For dancing, Hybrydy, ul Kniewskiego 7/9, is a lively student disco. The cinema is cheap, and Baja, ul Marszalkowska 136/138, shows Polish films with English or French subtitles. For opera, concert or theatre tickets, go to the Orbis office.

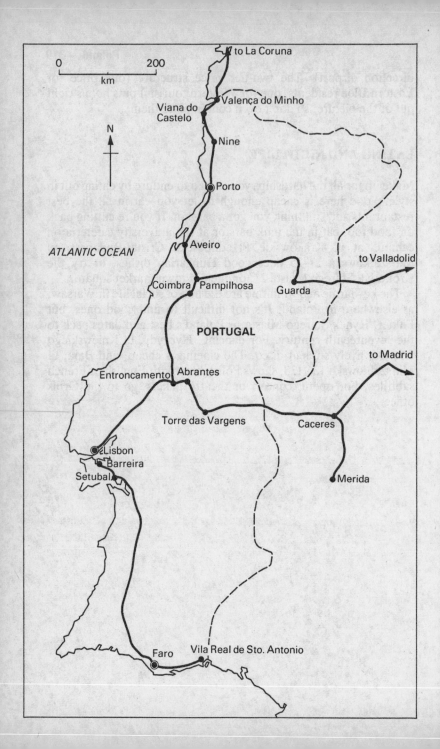

PORTUGAL

Entry requirements	Passport
Population	10,000,000
Capital	Lisbon (pop.: 1,500,000 +)
Currency	Escudo
	£1 = approx. 204 $
Political system	Republic
Religion	Roman Catholic
Language	Portuguese (some English spoken in cities)
Public holidays	1 Jan.; Shrove Tuesday; Good Friday;
	25 Apr.; 1 May; Corpus Christi; 10 June;
	15 Aug.; 5 Oct.; 1 Nov.; 1, 8, 25 Dec.

There's a lot of rubbish talked about Portugal, not least about the beautiful unspoilt Algarve where, according to most guidebooks, inviting a girl out can still be misinterpreted as a proposal. Today, certainly in the main tourist areas, attitudes of the young people are likely to be the same as their contemporaries in any other European country.

Portugal's early history is shared with the rest of the Iberian peninsula, with the Phoenicians, Greeks and Romans all leaving their mark. Portugal was recognized as a separate nation in 1385 after the Moors had been pushed from her frontiers. Throughout the fifteenth century, explorer-traders like Vasco da Gama helped Portugal's overseas empire to grow quickly through the discovery and exploration of the African coast, India, China and finally Brazil. Before long, Portugal had the world's largest empire, but her glory was to be short-lived, as conflict with Spain and rivalry with other European powers gradually brought about her decline. Eventually, even the royal family packed their bags and set off to Brazil during the Napoleonic Wars. Recently, the 1974 revolution has brought about a more liberal constitution, but the economy is still in a bad way with high inflation and unemployment. Yet Portugal remains one of Europe's most affordable countries, where it's possible to cultivate a good tan and eat well while doing it.

PORTUGUESE RAILWAYS
(Caminhos de Ferro Portugueses, CP)

The British originally built the Portuguese network with a wide gauge for extra comfort. If those early pioneers saw how crowded and uncomfortable the trains are today, they would wonder why they bothered. The fastest of the non-supplement trains are the expresses (directo). Next down the list are the semi directos, which stop nearly as often as the slow regionals. Away from the Lisbon area, services can be very frustrating, so you might feel justified in paying the extra supplements for the intercity rápidos; this works out at about 25 per cent above the normal tariff.

TRAIN INFORMATION

English is spoken by most information staff.

• **Reservations:** Are optional on inland trains and are quite cheap. For international and express trains, reservations are free of charge providing they are made the day before departure. In general, trains are crowded so it's best to reserve seats in advance.

• **Night travel:** There are no couchettes, but the sleepers are cheap.

• **Eating on trains:** All trains except the regionals have mini-bars, but only the rápidos can be relied upon to have dining cars.

• **Scenic tips:** As with Spain, there are enough problems getting where you want to go without worrying about scenic routes; however, the run from Valença in the north down to Lisbon is one of the best Portugal has to offer. Also try the run from Fuentes (Spain)–Douro Valley–Porto, alongside the River Douro.

TOURIST INFORMATION

Is provided by the government-run Postos do Turismo. They have offices all over the country and stalls at major stations.

• **ISIC bonuses:** The main perk here is admission to the cheap student restaurants on your ISIC. For further information contact Turismo Social e Juvenil, Turicoop (1st floor), Rua Pascual do Melo, Lisbon.

• **Money matters:** 1 escudo ($) = 100 centavos.
Banking hours are Mon.–Fri.: 8.30 a.m.–11.45 a.m., 1 p.m.–2.45 p.m. There are late-night exchange facilities at major tourist resorts.

• **Post offices and shops:** Open Mon.–Sat.: 9 a.m.–1 p.m., 3 p.m.–7 p.m. (closed Saturday p.m.).

• **Museums:** Open 10 a.m.–5 p.m.

SLEEPING

The government-run tourist board controls all the accommodation within Portugal and will book you a room if required. Hotels are graded from one star to five, boarding houses (estalagem, albergaria, pensão), one to four. By law, prices should be shown at reception and behind the door of each room. A double room in a three-star hotel costs about 2,500 $ a night. Student hostels tend to be more expensive than the cheap penãoes. There are twelve youth hostels (Pousadas de Juventude) in Portugal, all requiring IYHF cards, and most with an 11 p.m. curfew. Camping is another possibility, but don't expect too many facilities except in the Algarve, where you have to have a Camping Carnet. We recommend cheap hotels and boarding houses. They're normally near the stations, and as prices are unaffected by location it's not really worth shopping around.

EATING AND NIGHTLIFE

Food is cheap in Portugal and eating out is an inexpensive affair (350 $ to 600 $), except in the Algarve where prices are marked up for the tourists.

Go for fish dishes, especially chowders if you get the chance: they're invariably cheaper and tastier than meat dishes. National specialities include 'linguado delícia' (sole cooked with banana). If you don't like fish, pork represents the best value among the meat dishes. A bottle of wine is often thrown in for the price of the meal; if not ask for the local plonk (vinho da casa). The port is excellent but, rather surprisingly, it's not drunk a lot in Portugal.

If you're living on the beaches and need a meat 'booster', keep your eyes skinned for the mobile shops which serve cheap steak sandwiches (pregos).

Taverns tend to be very basic, but go down well with the local lads.

Bullfighting in Portugal is not as gory as it is in Spain – they're not allowed to kill the bull – but it's still a national obsession. Of the two types of Portuguese bullfights, the 'tourada à antiga' is perhaps the more spectacular. Here the bullfighter is dressed in thirteenth-century costume and fights from a horse.

Discos and bars are at their best in Lisbon, though by northern European standards many of the discos are pretty tame, and you'll do better heading for a bar which has 'fados' (melancholy Portuguese ballads) on the bill. There are no licensing hours in Portugal, so things can often drag right through the night till dawn.

Lisbon (Lisboa)

This westernmost capital of Europe escaped many of the influences that shaped the rest of the continent: among them the Reformation, the Industrial Revolution and the Second World War. It has developed out on a limb at a different pace and in a different way, and if any one force can be said to have affected its development, it was – and is – the sea. Lisbon was rebuilt after the 1755 earthquake; only the old Moorish quarter of Alfama escaped destruction. Essentially, it's a pleasant city to visit: beds and meals are cheap and plentiful, the nightlife's lively and there are several places of great interest to visit.

STATION FACILITIES

International trains and northern and eastern trains use Santa Apolónia Station. Trains to the south and south-east leave from Barreiro Station; trains to Sintra and the west use Rossio (on bus routes 9, 39–59 from Santa Apolónia), and trains for Estoril and Cascais use Cais do Sodré Station (bus 35).

	SANTA APOLÓNIA
Train information	8 a.m.–10 p.m.
	(Tel. 326226)
Reservations	9 a.m.–8 p.m. Window 11
Tourist information	9 a.m.–2 p.m., 4 p.m.–7 p.m.
Foreign exchange	9 a.m.–8 p.m.
Left-luggage lockers	No access 2 a.m.–5 a.m.
Left-luggage store	7 a.m.–1 a.m.
Bar, Buffet	7 a.m.–11 p.m.
Shops	Mon.–Sat.: 7 a.m.–12 midnight
Waiting room	All hours
Post office	Mon.–Fri.: 9 a.m.–7 p.m.
Station shuts	2 a.m.–5 a.m.

Daily trains to: Porto, Madrid, Irún, Paris.

TOURIST INFORMATION

The Portuguese National Tourist Office is in Palácio Foz on Praça dos Restauradores, open Mon.–Sat.: 9 a.m.–8 p.m., Sun.: 10 a.m.–6 p.m. The Municipal Tourist Office is at Rua Jardim do Regedor; and the national tourist office headquarters is at Avenida Augusto de Aguiar 86, open Mon.–Fri.: 9.30 a.m.–5.30 p.m. (by Rossio Station).

• **Addresses:**
POST OFFICE ('Correio'): Praça do Comércio, open Mon.–Fri.: 9 a.m.–7 p.m.
AMEX: Star Travel Service, Avenida Sidónio Pais 4A, open Mon.–Fri.: 9.15 a.m.–12.30 p.m., 2 p.m.–6 p.m.
UK EMBASSY: Rua S. Domingos à Lapa 35–39 (Tel. 661691).
US EMBASSY: Avenida Duque de Loulé 39 (Tel. 570102).

CANADIAN EMBASSY: Rua Rosa Aranjo 2, 6th floor (Tel. 562547).
AUSTRALIAN EMBASSY: Avenida da Liberdade 244 (Tel. 539108).
STUDENT TRAVEL OFFICE: Praça de Londres 9B (Tel. 884957), open
Mon.–Fri.: 10 a.m.–1 p.m., 2 p.m.–6 p.m.
24-HOUR CHEMIST: British Hospital, Rua Saraiva de Carvalho 49
(Tel. 602020).
TRANSALPINO: Avenida Guerra Junqueiro 28c (Tel. 8075721)

• **Getting about:** It's best to buy your tram or bus ticket from a
Carris kiosk. A 'tourist ticket' is a weekly pass for buses and trams
and costs around 750 $. Buy this from the Carris booths in the
stations. If you're in a group, taxis work out cheap with the average
fare costing 200 $. The city also has an underground system.

SEEING

It's pointless us suggesting a route round the ALFAMA district as it's
so sprawling you're bound to get lost, so just wander through at
your own pace, and if you happen to pass the church of SÃO MIGUEL
or LARGO DO SALVADOR 22 (sixteenth-century mansion house), look
in. This is one of Europe's most colourful districts, especially in the
morning when the fish market's on, or on Fridays (washday) when
the narrow streets are hung with locals' shirts and undies. The area
is enclosed roughly by the banks of the Tagus, the castle, the church
of St Vincent-outside-the-walls, and the cathedral. ST GEORGE'S
CASTLE, the fortress on the hill, has dominated Lisbon in one form
or another for 1,500 years. Its gardens of peacocks and flamingos
make a good vantage point to look over the city. Near the centre is
the SÉ (cathedral), worth a look for its ambulatory and burial
chapel.

On the outskirts of the city are quite a few sights worth visiting.
Go to the BELÉM quarter (tram 15, 16 or 17 from Praça do
Comércio), get off at the Museu Nacional dos Coches, and head for
the HIERONYMITE MONASTERY (Mosteiro dos Jerónimos). Here
Vasco da Gama is buried, as are various Portuguese kings. The
affluent merchants in the spice trade put up most of the money for
this beautiful place which was built in the early sixteenth century.
Also in this district is the TOWER OF BELÉM, one of Lisbon's
landmarks.

As far as museums go, the GULBENKIAN arts and culture centre, Av. de Berna 45 (closed Mondays), the MUSEU NACIONAL DE ARTE ANTIGA, Rua das Janelas Verdes 95, and the FOLK ART MUSEUM, Av. Marginal, Belém, are the best.

• **Excursions:** SINTRA, twenty miles north-west of Lisbon, is one of Portugal's oldest towns. The summer residence of the royal family was here and PENA PALACE AND PARK are well worth the detour. The park has more than 400 kinds of trees and many rare plants. Also out here is the sixteenth-century Capuchin monastery and Monserrate Park (closed Tuesdays). If you want a day on the beach, head for ESTORIL, a jet-set resort sixteen miles west of the city, or CASCAIS, two miles further on. Both these places are full of the beautiful people and it's possible to sleep out on the beaches. From Cascais you can catch a bus to CABO DA ROCA, the most westerly point in Europe, with a memorable view from the lighthouse. Another idea is to visit QUELUZ, the town eight miles north-west of Lisbon, where the rococo palace used to entertain VIPs of the Portuguese government. It's stuffed full of antiques and can be reached by train from Rossio Station (closed Tuesdays).

SLEEPING

An average double in a pension is about 1,000 $, a single 800 $. There are plenty of cheap places in Lisbon – not everywhere is clean and quiet, but the ones listed are about as close as you'll get. If these don't come up lucky, try yourself round Rua da Alegria, Rua dos Correiros and Praça da Figueira. The youth hostel, at Rua Andrade Corvo 46, is cheap and central. As far as camping goes, there are plenty of sites – and free beach camping close by – but the best site is the Parque Nacional de Turismo e Campismo (Tel. 708384) (bus to Parque Florestal, Monsanto). Residencial Mansarde, Avenida da Liberdade 141, 5th floor (Tel. 372963), charges 800 $ for doubles, and there are two other places on this stair. Also at No. 53 of this street, Pensão do Sul (Tel. 365647) has rooms for 700 $. Pensão Ninho de Águias, Costa do Castelo 74 (Tel. 860391), is of very high quality. Doubles start at 1,400 $ including breakfast. Pensão São João da Praça on São João da Praça 97

(Tel. 862591) is near the Alfama district and asks from 900 $ per double.

EATING AND NIGHTLIFE

Between the port and the Praça da Figueira is the best district, but there are cheap places in most areas. Use the Mercado da Ribeira outside the Cais do Sodré for picnic food, and watch out you don't get stuck on Sundays, especially in July, when many places close. Fish is generally good value, but don't eat the bread and savouries put out on the tables unless you're prepared to pay the extortionate prices that are often asked for them in tourist centres. Restaurante Trevo da Madalena and Restaurante Central on Rua da Madalena both do meals around 500 $.

Nightlife starts late and can get pretty lively. The authentic Portuguese folk music, the fado, is performed in several restaurants and cafés. Don't go till around midnight, unless you're happy to share your evenings with coach parties from package tours. Sr Vinho, Rua Praças 18, and the Patio das Cantigas, Rua São Caetano 27, offer authentic fados, but not for under 600 $. Port, the national drink, can be sampled at the Port Wine Institute, Rua S. Pedro de Alcantara, from 10 a.m.–12 midnight. From May–Sept. the Lisbon Amusement Park gives you somewhere to spend time before heading for the bars or cafés later on. The fair goes on till 1 a.m. and can be reached by the underground (station Entre-Campos).

Northern Portugal

If you're approaching Portugal from the north, the places worth stopping for are Viana do Castelo, Óbidos on the Costa de Prata, and Coimbra. PORTO is an industrial town, very much a mixture of old and new. Much of this region is unspoilt, as most eurorailers head for either Lisbon or the overrated Algarve; but stick to the remote rural areas as the towns that are being 'developed' have little charm.

VIANA DO CASTELO: this pretty little fishing resort, 1½ hours from Porto, has a vantage point for views over the whole region: the BASÍLICA OF SANTA LUZIA. You can take the funicular up or, better still, walk up the twisting road past the pine and eucalyptus trees till you reach the top. Back down in the town, look out for the reminders of the Renaissance in the buildings of the PRAÇA DA REPÚBLICA and the church of SÃO DOMINGOS. If you're here in the third week of August, you'll catch the festival: bullfights, processions, fireworks, dancing, etc. The MUNICIPAL MUSEUM has a collection of the ceramics Portugal is famous for. Rooms aren't a problem: try the streets off Avenida dos Combatentes, or camp at CABEDELO BEACH.

ÓBIDOS is a little medieval village, seven miles from the sea, and is worth seeing for its preserved CASTLE, old TOWN WALLS and the two churches of SANTA MARIA and the MISERICÓRDIA. Tourist information is on Rua Direita.

COIMBRA: this university town is second only to Lisbon in terms of historical and cultural importance. It is set among the beautiful forests and woods of the Beira Litoral region, and is about 2½ hours from the capital. Get off at Coimbra 'A' station, walk two blocks east for the turismo in Largo da Portagem. It's open Mon.–Sat.: 9 a.m.–8 p.m., Sun.: 10 a.m.–5 p.m., and operates a currency exchange desk.

The UNIVERSITY is the best sight of the town. The OLD LIBRARY (Biblioteca), the CHAPEL and the MUSEUM are all impressive and the CEREMONIAL HALL is decorated with some fine 'azulejos' (ceramic tiles). The MACHADO MUSEUM nearby was a former episcopal palace, and today houses many of Portugal's artistic treasures. The town's CATHEDRAL is twelfth-century, as is the Cistercian convent, MOSTEIRO DE CELAS. Not far out is a reconstructed village of all the famous buildings in Portugal, miniature-size: PORTUGAL DOS PEQUENINOS.

For cheap beds, look out for 'dormidas' round the station: Rua da Sota and the streets around should produce something. For eats, try 'Zé Manel', Beco do Forno 12, just off Rua da Sota. Apart from good cheap food, this place has character. Open 12 noon–3 p.m., 5 p.m.–10 p.m. and closed Mondays.

The Algarve

Here we differ from other guidebooks. We're not going to sing the praises of this region, or tell you it's the best-kept secret in Europe with mile after mile or white sand, interspersed with picturesque fishing villages and friendly locals – it's not . . . not any more. Vast areas of the Algarve (the southern coastal region on the Atlantic) are ugly cement heaps. Hotels have been thrown up and many resorts are just small facsimiles of Spain's Costa del Sol, only more expensive and with fewer facilities. You'll really have to look hard now to find an unspoilt and economical base and, should you travel after September, you lay yourself open to the gusty winds that do such a good job of cooling things down considerably. The good news is that English is the second language of this province (thanks to the colony of English people who've settled here), and the local cuisine is very tasty – plenty of fish chowders and seafood delicacies. For cheap rooms, you'll have to use the 'casas particulares' (private accommodation) or camp out on the beaches. The Algarve is a sportsman's paradise (assuming he's not short of a quid or two), and there are several very exclusive golf and sports clubs tagged on to hotels. Some of them let you swim in their pool (for a price) or use the sports facilities, but you must look and sound respectable – hotel receptionists are great classists. The train runs from Lagos in the west through Tunes to Faro, the Algarve capital (and on to Vila Real de Santo António from where the ferry to Ayamonte in Spain leaves).

LAGOS is the most attractive of the port towns in the Algarve though, apart from its centre which the English have done up, it's nothing to write home about. The things to look out for are the church of SANTO ANTÓNIO with its riot of gilt and gold, and the REGIONAL MUSEUM next door. The beaches here are good, but usually packed out with package deals. Turismo is on Largo Marquez de Pombal.

FARO: Don't go out of your way to get here. Apart from the old MOORISH DEFENCE WALLS, CATHEDRAL and ETHNOLOGICAL MUSEUM, it's just another dusty jumbled town on the coast. Its beach, however, is good, though you have to go by bus to it as it's out of town. The park down by the docks, JARDIM MANUEL BIVAR, is the high spot of Faro. Turismo's at Rua da Misericórdia, open 9 a.m.–8 p.m.

To get to the places that have given the Algarve such a glowing reputation, you'll really have to abandon the railway and take to the buses. Generally, the west looks less like a builder's yard than the east, so head for places like SAGRES and ALBUFEIRA.

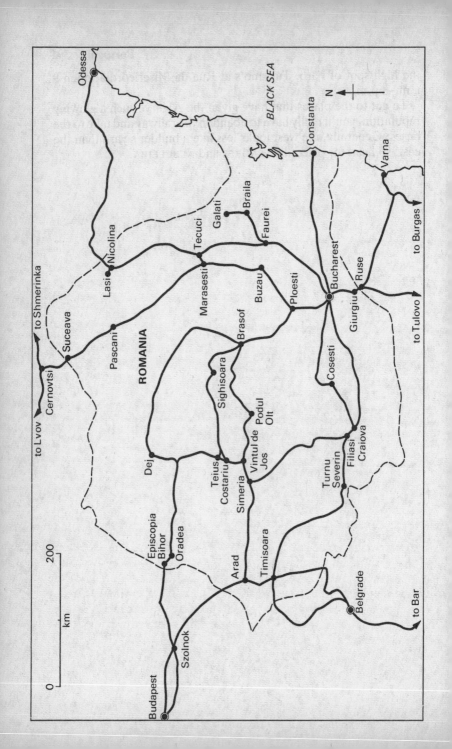

ROMANIA

Entry requirements	Passport and visa (available at border)
Population	21,500,000
Capital	Bucharest (pop.: 1,800,000)
Currency	Leu
	£1 = approx. 19 lei
Political system	Socialist People's Republic
Religion	Romanian Orthodox
Language	Romanian (some French and German spoken)
Public holidays	1, 2 Jan.; 1, 2 May; 23, 24 Aug.

Romania is keen on encouraging tourism, but this with an eye on filling her Black Sea hotels rather than on individual eurorailers. Still, as a direct result of this policy, things are becoming easier all round.

Once a Roman province, the area was overrun by Asian, Slavonic and Turkish tribes giving a real mixture of peoples. Moldavia in the north and Wallachia in the south were united to form Romania in 1859. Transylvania, the area in between, is full of forests and fortified towns and was once a good place for blood donors, but the demand has fallen away with the death of Count Dracula. During the 1960s, Romania began to break away from Moscow's sphere of influence. This trend has continued, making Romania one of the most pro-Western countries in Eastern Europe.

ROMANIAN RAILWAYS
(Caile Ferate Romane, CFR)

In recent years Romania has improved its services considerably in response to increased demand. Most trains are still dirty and overcrowded by Western standards, so imagine what they were like before. To travel at reasonable speed and comfort on any of the Rapide (fast) and Accelerate (semi-fast) trains you will have to pay a supplement. To avoid this, you have to travel on the local Personal trains – a fate worse than death. In other words, pay the supplement.

• **Inter Rail bonsues:** Free entry to the railway museum at Gare du Nord, Bucharest.

TRAIN INFORMATION

English is not widely spoken, so be prepared with a French back-up. (French is Romania's second language.) If all else fails, try: 'De la ce peron pleacă trenul spre . . . ?' (From which platform does the train to . . . leave?)

• **Reservations:** To be sure of a seat on any of the fast trains, it's best to reserve at least a week to ten days in advance from CFR booking offices.

• **Night travel:** Couchettes and sleepers hardly come up to Western standards and need to be booked well in advance, particularly on the Bucharest–Budapest run. Rates vary according to distance.

• **Eating on trains:** There are restaurants on all long-distance fast trains, and buffets on shorter-distance fast trains.

TOURIST INFORMATION

ONT is the national tourist organization. They have offices in all large towns which give out information and help in finding a room.

• **ISIC bonuses:** Reductions for all international rail travel in the Eastern Bloc. Also museum entrances reduced with an IUŞ card. For further information, contact BTT, Str. Onesti 4–6, Bucharest 1.

• **Money matters:** 1 leu (plural, lei) = 100 bani (b).
Banking hours are Mon.–Sat.: 9 a.m.–12 noon, 1 p.m.–3 p.m. (closed Saturday p.m.). You have to cash about £7 ($9) for every day you stay in Romania.

• **Post offices, shops and museums:** All vary their times of opening, depending on the district. Most keep to the 9–5 routine six days a week. In Bucharest, some shops open on Sunday mornings.

SLEEPING

One's choices are limited in Romania by the absence of cheap class-three hotels and the fact that it's illegal to stay in private homes. Hostels (caminul de studenti) are run by the student travel service, BTT, and give preference to large groups when they open during July and August. If you're lucky and make the effort to get to the hostel direct, you might get a bed there for about 100 lei. Most eurorailers camp and accept the poor facilities, or pay for a class-two hotel which can be anything up to 350 lei for a double room.

EATING AND NIGHTLIFE

As elsewhere in Eastern Europe, eating is inexpensive, so you can afford to eat well. Local dishes are normally good value, particularly soup and fish dishes. Mititei (small spicy sausages) make filling snacks and are easy on your pocket. Romania's nightlife is not up to Hungary's standards, but after a few glasses of tzuica, the local plum spirit, you'll never know the difference.

Bucharest (Bucureşti)

The journey here on the dismal trains is not one of Europe's best and you'll probably wish you hadn't bothered halfway through the night, but take heart: Bucharest is known as the 'Paris of Eastern Europe', though considering the lack of nightlife and scarcity of actual 'sights', this is a bit over the top.

STATION FACILITIES

	GARE DU NORD
Train information	24 hours
Reservations	24 hours
Tourist information	See below
Foreign exchange	8 a.m.–6 p.m.
Left-luggage lockers/store	24 hours
Café, Restaurant	6 a.m.–12 midnight
Waiting room	24 hours
Post office	24 hours

Daily trains to: Athens, Cluj, Belgrade, Berlin, Basel, Budapest, Munich, Paris, London, Prague, Sofia, Warsaw, Vienna, Zürich.

TOURIST INFORMATION

The station office is open 7 a.m.–9 p.m. weekdays, 7 a.m.–3 p.m. weekends. The main tourist office is at Blvd Magheru 7, open Mon.–Sat.: 7.30 a.m.–9.30 p.m., Sun.: 7.30 a.m.–2.30 p.m. Take bus 87 from the station to Piata Romana. You can change money at all offices. BTT, the youth tourist service that deals with groups (the whole of Romanian tourism centres on groups), is at Strada Onesti 4–6, and opens 25 May–15 Sept., 8 a.m.–5 p.m., Sat.: 8 a.m.–1.30 p.m.

● **Addresses:**
POST OFFICE: Str. Matei Millo 10, off Calea Victoriei, open 7 a.m.–midnight daily.
UK EMBASSY: Str. Jules Michelet 24 (Tel. 111635).
US EMBASSY: Tudor Arghezi 7–9 (Tel. 124040).
CANADIAN EMBASSY: Nicolae Lorga 36 (Tel. 506140).
24-HOUR CHEMIST: Blvd Magheru 18. Also at Gare du Nord.

● **Getting about:** Buses, trolley-buses and trams are incredibly cheap, and tickets can be bought from all kiosks. Taxis too are a bargain at about 12 lei a mile.

SEEING

Modern Bucharest is hard on the eye, so ignore the new and concentrate on the old. The name Bucharest was given to this town in 1459 by none other than Dracula, a local lad, known here as Vlad the Impaler. By far the most pleasant day's sightseeing is spent out on the HERĂSTRĂU PARK where the VILLAGE MUSEUM is. This collection of peasant houses gathered from all over the country is open 9 a.m.–6 p.m. every day but Monday. Parks and museums are Bucharest's main assets. LIBERTY PARK, the STUDENT PARK on Lacul Tei, or the central CISMIGIU PARK are great meeting places and the places to head for to meet young Romanians. As far as museums go, out of the forty or so to choose from, we'd recommend the HISTORY MUSEUM; the former royal palace, today the NATIONAL ART MUSEUM; and the GEORGES ENESCO MUSEUM.

SLEEPING

For a bed in a student hostel, go to ONT or BTT (see above) and ask them for addresses as these change yearly. Camping is out at Camping Baneasa (Tel. 794525). It's not central and lacks hygienic facilities, but is cheap. Grade-two hotels are your best bet here. Get a list from ONT and if you're told they're all full, ignore it and go along to the hotels regardless and ask at reception. There are quite a few near the Gare du Nord, charging 190–220 lei single, and 300–380 lei for a double. Try Hotel Dunarea, Calea Grivitei 140 (Tel. 173220); Hotel Bucegi, Strada Witing 2 (Tel. 495120); Hotel Cerna, Blvd D. Golescu (Tel. 493250).

EATING AND NIGHTLIFE

The twenty-four-hour stand-up Buffet Expres are the cheapest form of eats, but a lot of the food is fairly revolting and high in stodge content. La Doi Cocqsi, Soseaua, Străuleşti is well worth finding for good food and authentic gypsy music, and next to the History Museum at Stavropoleos 5 is Carcul cu Bere, which does some particularly fine snacks.

As far as nightlife goes, don't build your hopes up as it's a bit of a non-event. ONT will tell you what's on in town, but usually the choice is between the Circus at Aleea Circului, the cinema, or the theatre. The University Student Club is an alternative where you can meet young Romanians, a surprising number of whom speak English. It's on Calea Plevnei 61, and you need your ISIC.

Transylvania

This picturesque region, home of the notorious Count Dracula, is Romania's most scenic. The Transylvanian Alps and the small peasant villages with their rich, active folklore make travelling here interesting and rewarding. The best towns to base yourself in are Braşov or Sighisoara.

BRAŞOV, about 2½ hours from Bucharest, is on the edge of the Carpathian Mountains and set among the Transylvanian Alps. In its old town are the BLACK CHURCH and the TOWN HALL – both fourteenth-century, but the main attractions are outside the town. The CASTLE OF BRAN, Dracula's summer house, is reached by bus 12 to the bus station, then bus 23 to the castle, and is open from 9 a.m.–6 p.m. (closed Monday). ONT, in Hotel Carpati, 9 Ch. Gheorghiu-Dej Blvd (open 7.30 a.m.–10 p.m. daily), will give you details of the best excursions. BTT in Hotel Carpati will hand you this year's list of student hostels.

SIGHISOARA, 2¼ hours away from Braşov, is a beautiful medieval town, as yet unspoilt by tourism. This is an ideal spot to break the long haul from Bucharest to Budapest (nearly 14 hours), and it offers more in the way of sights than Braşov. The OLD WALLED TOWN is well preserved and among its sights are the CLOCK TOWER, the TOWN MUSEUM (closed Monday), the GUILD TOWERS, and the BERGKIRCHE, a church with good views over the town. The CHURCH OF THE MONASTERY off Clock Tower Square is the town's oldest building and not far from here is Dracula's father's house. ONT is across from the main thoroughfare of Str. Ch. Gheorghiu-Dej. It's open Mon.–Sat.: 8 a.m.–1 p.m., 2 p.m.–8 p.m., Sun.: 8 a.m.–11 a.m. Get your map here. You've a choice of camping at Campground Hula Danes (bus direction 'Mhedias') or paying up for Hotel Steaua (Tel. 71594), who do singles for 140 lei, doubles 250 lei. To meet the locals and have a drink, try the beer hall at 34 Piata Leni.

Moldavia

This region of Europe is known for beautiful mountain monasteries, small rural villages and its completely unspoilt lifestyle, where locals still wear national costume and not a word of English seems to be spoken. The trains are pitifully slow and you can't afford to be in a rush. Ask at Bucharest for times and routes – mostly you have to change to the smaller lines at Cluj.

SUCEAVA is the capital of Moldavia and the best starting point for a tour of the monasteries. The FOLK ART MUSEUM is a worthwhile visit. It's in the 'Princely Inn' and in only an hour or two fills you in on the culture of the people that surround you. The ONT office is at Nicolae Balcescu 2 (open Mon.–Sat.: 8 a.m.–8 p.m., Sun.: 9 a.m.–12 noon), and they'll supply you with bus schedules and details on the monasteries.

THE MONASTERIES: VORONET is the most famous and ancient of the monasteries, dating back to 1488. It's known as the 'Sistine Chapel of the East', owing to its amazing frescoes and unique shade of blue. HUMOR, a nearby village, has a monastery obviously built by misogynists (the devil is portrayed as a woman in the frescoes), and from here you can set off for SUCEVITA MONASTERY. This one is absolutely covered in fascinating frescoes from portraits of Plato to the 'Arabian Nights', and the actual village of Sucevita has got to be the most charming in Romania.

The Black Sea Coast

Romania's coastline starts at the Danube Delta on the Russian frontier and stretches south for about 150 miles to the Bulgarian border. The resorts are largely unspoilt, and the main town on the coast is the ancient port of CONSTANŢA. The city is a curious mixture of Roman, Greek and Eastern Byzantine (there's even a mosque and minaret here). Part of the beach is sheltered by a tree-and-hedge wind-break; however, you may find that Constanţa gets busier than the other resorts in summer, so use your rail ticket to the full and head off for somewhere smaller down the line.

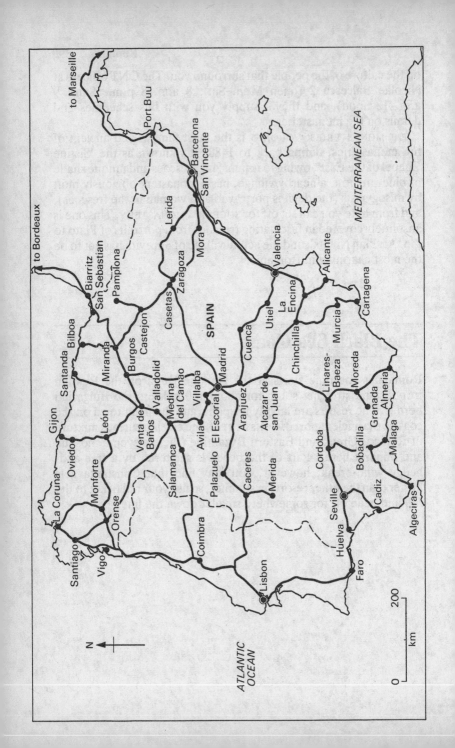

SPAIN (España)

Entry requirements	Passport
Population	38,500,000
Capital	Madrid (pop.: 3,250,000)
Currency	Peseta
	£1 = approx. 209 ptas.
Political system	Constitutional Monarchy
Religion	Roman Catholic
Language	Spanish (some English spoken)
Public holidays	1, 6 Jan.; 19 Mar.;
	Maundy Thursday; Good Friday;
	Easter Monday; 1 May; Corpus Christi;
	29 July; 15 Aug.; 12 Oct.;
	1 Nov.; 8, 25 Dec.

Spain is the third largest country in Europe and culturally one of the most diverse. The Phoenicians, Greeks, Celts, Carthaginians, Romans, Visigoths and Moors were all here. Throughout the Christian reconquest, Spain consisted of several independent kingdoms united in 1479 by the marriage of Isabella of Castile to Ferdinand of Aragon. Shortly after this unification, the new king, Charles I, landed well and truly on his feet by inheriting the Netherlands and becoming Holy Roman Emperor in 1519. At the same time his 'conquistadores' were bringing enough gold and silver back from South America to make Spain a major world power. The defeat of the Spanish Armada in 1588 began a slow period of decline which ended in the loss of her colonies after the Napoleonic Wars. More recently, the abdication of the king was followed by a left-wing republic which gave rise to the Civil War of 1936–9. Since the death of the fascist dictator Franco in 1975, King Juan Carlos has steered Spain towards democracy.

SPANISH NATIONAL RAILWAYS
(Red Nacional de los Ferrocarriles Españoles, RENFE)

Easily the worst in Western Europe unless you're prepared to pay the heavy supplements required on all fast trains: Talgos, TERs and ELTs, or the less steep Rápido supplement. For starters, you'll have to change trains at the Spanish border, so don't go for a sleeper from France unless you're travelling on a Talgo which adjusts its wheels to the broader gauge. It's safe to say that all non-supplement trains are slow, crowded and dirty, but they'll get you there in the end. The Tranvias and Correos (locals) crawl along at a walking pace and are only for the stalwart.

● **Inter Rail bonuses:**

	FROM	TO	REDUCTION %
Cia de Navegación Transmediterránea	Algeciras	Tangier	50
	Barcelona	Palma de Mallorca	30
	Valencia	Palma de Mallorca	20

● **Eurail bonuses:** 20 per cent reduction on normal fares of the Transmediterránea Company between Barcelona or Valencia and Palma de Mallorca and between Algeciras and Tangier (Morocco).

TRAIN INFORMATION

English is not always spoken, so always have a Spanish back-up prepared. Expect long queues.

● **Reservations:** If you can face the queues it's advisable to reserve a seat in Spain. Unfortunately, if you decide not to reserve there's often no way of telling if someone else has, as reserved seats are not always indicated. On many occasions you settle down in an apparently empty compartment, only to be thrown out just when you thought you were safe. Reservations are obligatory on all expresses.

● **Night travel:** Spanish couchettes sleep six and are very old and dirty – more often than not you are better off on the floor. Sleepers are cheap, however, so all's not lost. For a journey under 550 km, a berth in a tourist-class sleeper will cost about 1,500 ptas.

• **Scenic tips:** In Spain, it's normally effort enough to get from A to B without thinking about scenic routes. Entering from France, the most scenic route is from Toulouse over the Pyrenees, arriving at Barcelona. The main line from here on to Madrid takes in much that is typically Spanish without you having to go out of your way. If it's mountains you're after, then it's best to head towards the north-west (León-Túy) or the south (Córdoba–Málaga, Granada–Almería).

TOURIST INFORMATION

The government-run tourist office has branches in all major towns and at many stations. They have an excellent collection of free handouts on all the regions of Spain. In addition, there are local city tourist offices which supply maps and more detailed information.

• **ISIC bonuses:** Reduced entrance to the Prado and Bellas Artes museums. For further information, contact Viajes TIVE, Fernando el Católico 88, Madrid.

• **Money matters:** 1 peseta (pta.) = 100 centimos (c).
Banking hours are Mon.–Fri.: 9 a.m.–1.30/2 p.m. Shop about, as there's no set rate of exchange, and exchange rates are high.

• **Post offices:** Open Mon.–Sat.: 9 a.m.–2 p.m. and often later in larger cities. 'Lista de Correos' = poste restante.

• **Shops:** Open Mon.–Sat.: 9 a.m.–1.30 p.m., 5 p.m.–7.30/8 p.m. (closed Saturday p.m.).

• **Museums:** Vary considerably; most open 10 a.m. and shut again for lunch 12.30/1 p.m., opening again at 4 p.m. till 7 p.m.

SLEEPING

Every large town in Spain has a Brujula office to help find rooms for a small fee. In addition the tourist information office issues lists to help freelancers. You shouldn't have any problems as there's always plenty of cheap accommodation around the stations, all of which is inspected and graded by the government. By law, prices should be shown behind the door of each room. During the summer it's legal for prices to be increased by about 15 per cent, so don't get too excited until you've worked it out. Hotels start at about 1,000 ptas. for a single and prices are nearly always charged by the room, not per person. Pensiones and Hostales are officially graded (Hs = hostal, HsR = hostal residencia, P = pensión, CH = casa de huéspedes and, cheapest of all, F = fonda). For the bare necessities, expect to pay about 750 ptas. per person. Always check to see if breakfast is included in the price; don't assume the management will tell you. Hot showers are another extra which can cost up to 150 ptas. If you think you're being done, the mere mention of 'libro de reclamaciones' (complaints book) should sort out your problems. To use any of Spain's seventy youth hostels, you'll need a IYHF card. At 350–900 ptas. a night, they are easily the cheapest accommodation you're likely to find. If you are thinking about camping, go to ANCE, Medinaceli 2, Madrid 14; they will give you a map and a rundown on official campsites. Prices start at about 200 ptas. per person per night. Sleeping on the beaches is another alternative, but don't make it too obvious or you'll attract trouble from the police or worse.

EATING AND NIGHTLIFE

As two victims of the 1981 olive oil calamity, we feel inclined to say that, if you eat in Spain, you can forget about the nightlife – but this is unfair, as Spain offers some of the most affordable restaurants in Europe. Give your stomach a chance to adapt to the excess of olive oil, and don't have too much seafood to start with. Once you've adapted to local conditions, there's an endless variety of regional specialities to sample, all at reasonable prices. Go for the tourist or house menu where possible, as it's usually a safe bet and works out a lot cheaper than ordering individual dishes. Expect to pay anything from 500 to 1,200 ptas. for your evening meal and remember that the Spaniards don't eat until at least 9 p.m.–10 p.m. If there's no fixed tourist menu, ask if they do combinados – an all-in feast on one plate which often includes something to drink as well. For those low in funds, try tapas – delicious and varied titbits that are sometimes free – available at most bars. Local wine is cheap at about 150 ptas. a bottle, and is a much better buy than beer, though it's often rough and tastes like weak sherry. Wine cellars and bars are cheaper and have more local colour than the discos which make their living by fleecing tourists at the resorts.

The bullfighting season runs from March to October and is recommended only for the bloodthirsty.

Madrid

Madrid is not one of Europe's most attractive capitals. The old town has charm, the nightlife is amongst the hottest in Europe and the Prado is definitely one of the world's great art galleries, but the sprawling concrete districts and lack of major sights entice one to leave Madrid in favour of Toledo or Seville. Still, sleeping and eating aren't a problem and many argue that Madrid is worth the trip for the tapas and fandangos alone.

STATION FACILITIES

Madrid has three stations: Chamartín, serving the north-east, France and eastern Spain; Atocha, serving Portugal and the south of Spain; and Norte, handling what's left. Some trains, e.g. the Paris–Algeciras Express, pass through more than one of them. There are interconnecting trains every 20 minutes, and also an underground service. Due to bomb scares, the left-luggage lockers are not in use. This is tough luck at Chamartín, but at Atocha head for some of the bars behind the station (round Calle de Rafael de Riego), and deposit your rucksack for around 100 ptas. There is tourist information at Chamartín. (We give no information on the Norte Station as it is little used by eurorailers.)

	CHAMARTÍN	ATOCHA
Train information	7 a.m.–10 p.m. (Tel. 247 7400)	7 a.m.–10 p.m.
Reservations	8 a.m.–9 p.m.	9 a.m.–9 p.m.
Hotel reservations	9 a.m.–11 p.m.	–
Foreign exchange	7 a.m.–10 p.m.	8.30 a.m.–9.30 p.m.
Left-luggage store	7 a.m.–12 midnight	7 a.m.–12 midnight
Restaurant, Cafeteria	12 noon–4 p.m. 7 p.m.–12 midnight	7 a.m.–12 midnight
Shops	7 a.m.–11 p.m.	–
Waiting room	All hours	All hours
Post office	Mon.–Fri.: 9 a.m.– 2 p.m., 5 p.m.–10 p.m. Sat.: 9 a.m.–2 p.m.	Mon.–Sat.: 9 a.m.–2 p.m. 7 p.m.–10.30 p.m.
Station shuts	12 midnight–5 a.m.	12 midnight–5 a.m.

Daily trains to: Bilbao, Paris, Zaragoza, Barcelona, Valencia, Alicante, Granada, Córdoba, Seville, Lisbon.

TOURIST INFORMATION

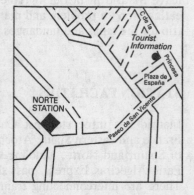

The main national office is at Maria de Molina 50, and there's another one at Plaza de España. Both are open 9 a.m.–7 p.m., Mon.–Fri., Sat. 9 a.m.–1.30 p.m. The municipal office is at Plaza Mayor 3, open 10 a.m.–1.30 p.m., 4 p.m.–7 p.m., Saturday 10 a.m.–1.30 p.m., closed Sunday; and the provincial office is at Duque de Medinaceli 2. Pick up a free map and information leaflets here.

● **Addresses:**

POST OFFICE: Palácio de Comunicaciones, Plaza de Cibeles. Open 9 a.m.–10 p.m. Poste restante and telegraphs here.

AMEX: Plaza de las Cortes 2. Open Mon.–Fri.: 9 a.m.–5.30 p.m., Sat.: 9 a.m.–12 noon.

UK EMBASSY: Fernando el Católico 16 (Tel. 4191528).
US EMBASSY: Serrano 75 (Tel. 2763400).
CANADIAN EMBASSY: Núñez de Balboa 35 (Tel. 4314300).
AUSTRALIAN EMBASSY: Paseo de la Castellana 143 (Tel. 2798501).
TRANSALPINO: 9 Plaza de España (Tel. 413478).
BRITISH-AMERICAN HOSPITAL: Paseo de Juan XXIII (Tel. 234 6700).

• **Getting about:** For price and speed, the metro is the best means of getting about. It runs till 1.30 a.m. and has eight lines. Buy tickets from machines or kiosks and hang on to your ticket till you've finished the journey. Buses are pretty efficient, and microbuses are the more luxurious versions of the same theme.

SEEING

The PRADO MUSEUM is the reason why thousands of art-lovers descend on this city each summer. There are over 3,000 master-pieces here, mainly collected by the Spanish royal family in the seventeenth and eighteenth centuries. The old Spanish masters (El Greco, Goya, etc.) are well represented, and there's a fair number of Flemish works collected by the Habsburg kings of the sixteenth century. There's such a glut of genius here, you'll need to pay two or three visits at least. The entrance is reasonable, but ISIC holders are no longer free. Near the exit is a shop selling very reasonably priced reproductions, postcards and books. The Prado is open daily, except Mondays, May–October, 10 a.m.–6 p.m., 2 p.m. on Sundays and till 5 p.m. out of season. The ROYAL PALACE is the only other 'must' in Madrid. A 2½-hour guided tour will take you through the various apartments and the Royal Armoury, which is considered one of the world's best collections of medieval weapons. The palace gardens, especially the CAMPO DEL MORO, are particularly fine and make good venues for regal picnic lunches.

Parks are, in fact, Madrid's speciality. The RETIRO PARK in the city centre is huge and, apart from its rowing lake, theatre, fountains and statues, the CRYSTAL PALACE of the Bourbon kings is here. North-west of the palace is another park on ten times the scale of the Retiro, which the young Spaniards tend to patronize at weekends: the CASA DE CAMPO has among its attractions a zoo, amusement park, swimming pool and outdoor theatre.

OLD MADRID lies between PUERTA DEL SOL (known as the centre of Spain) and the Crystal Palace; notice the descriptive pictures above the street signs to help the illiterate seventeenth-century locals. These narrow winding streets are the most colourful in Madrid, and the taverns in the alleys off the PLAZA MAYOR are good starting places for your evening's pub crawl, Madrid-style. On Sunday mornings there's a flea market (the Rastro) off the southern corner of the square where gypsies often congregate and put on street shows.

SLEEPING

Cheap beds aren't a problem here, even in summer. The tourist offices will advise you on accommodation, but won't arrange it for you; Brujula, a private placing agency, will do this for a small fee. They have kiosks at the stations, but you shouldn't even need them as there are hundreds of suitable places, many near the centrally located Atocha Station, in streets like Calle Toledo. If you're really cutting corners and don't mind other people's nocturnal 'goings-on', or the odd bed-bug, the area south of Puerta del Sol will produce some very cheap (550–850 ptas.) casas de huéspedes. The university let out rooms to those wanting to stay five or more days, and there are two youth hostels which aren't too far away from the centre. One's at Calle Santa Cruz de Marcenado 28 (Tel. 247 4532) and the other's at Casa de Campo (Tel. 463 5699) in the park there. You need IYHF membership, and a bed will cost about 350 ptas. Ask at Turismo for the camping leaflet, and don't risk the parks unless you're desperate.

The street with more cheap beds than anywhere else is Gran Vía in central Madrid. Hostal Alcázar-Regis, on the 5th floor of No. 61 (Tel. 247 9317), is good value for what you get; La Costa Verde (9th floor) is cheaper, and Buenos Aires (Tel. 247 8800) on the 2nd floor have singles for around 700 ptas. and doubles for 1,200 ptas. Hostal Amayo (Tel. 222 2151) on the 1st floor of No. 12 and at No. 38, Hostal California (Tel. 222 4703) and Don José (Tel. 232 1385) have good rooms averaging 3,500 ptas. a double.

EATING AND NIGHTLIFE

Tapas (the tasty snacks served in infinite varieties to accompany your drink) are at their best in Madrid. Most Madrileños spend between 6 p.m. and 10 p.m. on the tapas circuit in either Pasage de Matheu or the area round Plaza Mayor. Mussels, mushrooms, omelettes and filled rolls are some of the savouries with which to bridge the gap till dinner, washed down with sangría or wine. The main meal of the day is eaten at lunchtime (2 p.m.–4 p.m.) and dinner, around 10 p.m., is quite a light affair. Argüelles, on the metro, is the city's main student quarter. Make for this area to eat cheaply and meet the university students. The bars along Calle de la Princesa are a safe bet to make friends, and back in the centre Calle Echegaray and Ventura de la Vega, off Calle San Jerónimo, also have cheap restaurants. Restaurant Copatisan, Calle del Barco 16–18, is very cheap and very good. Closed Aug. For a good paella try Restaurant El Parque, Fernando el Católico 78.

The nightlife starts with the pub crawl and continues in the salas de fiesta (nightclubs), winding up around 3 a.m.–4 a.m. At weekends, things are twice as lively and the discotecas (which are on the expensive side) hold afternoon as well as evening sessions to cope with the insatiable demand ('afternoon' in Spain seems to mean 7 p.m.–10 p.m.). The salas de fiesta shows range from awful cabarets to sex shows.

This list of current events in the 'Guía del Ocio' is all you need. Avoid the heavily advertised flamenco shows, as they're incredibly commercial and plastic, and ask about for the best discos, etc., in the bars along the Aurrera in the Argüelles quarter.

• **Excursions:** Thirty miles from the Norte Station is the huge granite palace of EL ESCORIAL. This was King Philip II's country house and though it took over twenty years to complete, it still looks more like a high-security prison than a palace. The guided tours take you round the museums, library, church, art gallery and royal apartments (open 10 a.m.–1 p.m., 3 p.m.–7 p.m.). A few miles further on is the VALLE DE LOS CAÍDOS – a memorial to those who died in the Civil War, and where Franco is buried. Or if you just want to cool off, stay in the train to Cercedilla and take the branch line up into the Sierra de Guadarrama Mountains.

ARANJUEZ, en route south to Córdoba or Seville, is worth a stop-off to see the ROYAL PALACE, the SAILOR'S HOUSE, the PRINCE'S GARDEN and the FARMER'S HOUSE. The campsite here, Soto del Castillo, will entice you to stay a night or two as it's about the best one in Spain.

Northern Spain and the Basque Country

This region runs from the foot of the Pyrenees to close to Portugal. It is one of Spain's least touristy areas, and the lush forests, good beaches and historic towns make it worth exploration. The Basques – possibly the oldest ethnic group in Europe – have their own very separate history, culture and language. Since Franco's death, the ETA (Basque Liberation Front) have been increasingly active in their terrorist acts of bombings and murder, and the issue is still anything but settled.

San Sebastián

This was, until recent terrorist attacks, one of Spain's major holiday resorts for the rich and famous. Now its position as one of the main Basque cities makes it a slightly less safe bet for a family holiday, but the choice is yours; the odds of anything nasty happening are weighted heavily in your favour. It's an interesting and attractive place; the beaches are good and it will break up a run from Paris to Madrid nicely.

TOURIST INFORMATION AND ADDRESSES

TOURIST OFFICES: Andia 13, and Reina Regente (ground floor, Victoria Eugenia Theatre), open Mon.–Sat.: 9 a.m.–2 p.m., 3.30 p.m.–7 p.m.
POST OFFICE: Calle Urdaneta 9.
FIRST AID: Cruz Roja, Calle Matia 7 (Tel. 214600).

SEEING

The SAN TELMO MUSEUM, in a sixteenth-century Renaissance monastery on Calle Coro, will fill you in on the differences between the Basques and the Spanish or French; or visit the AQUARIUM down on the port to see the collection of sea creatures. From the beach you can rent out a boat and go over to the island of SANTA CLARA, or else just laze about on the beaches of LA CONCHA and ONDARRETA.

SLEEPING

During the summer, cheap beds are hard to find. Try the campsite on the Carretera de Monte Igueldo or the youth hostel at Ciudad Deportiva Anoeta (Tel. 452970). The best pension deals are at Pensión La Perla, Loyola 10 (Tel. 428123), and Hostal Gran Bahía, Embeltran (Tel. 423838).

EATING AND NIGHTLIFE

It's not easy to cut corners in San Sebastián for two reasons: first, there are hardly any places with tourist menus in the eurorailer's budget range; and secondly, the food is so good you won't feel like living off bread, cheese and fruit. This is one Spanish town where the food is consistently good and, of course, the fish dishes are excellent. The city actually has a Gastronomic Academy, and the exclusive and chauvinistic male-only dining clubs frequently sponsor eating contests. There are several bars and restaurants in the central square, Plaza del 18 de Julio, but watch the prices here.

For pre-dinner 'tapas', try the bars along Calle Fermin Calberton and, for dancing, Zorongo, San Martín 66, is meant to be pretty hot. There are festivals all summer, the most interesting being the Basque folklore one. Ask tourist information for details. If you're there 7–14 July and enjoy the blood and gore of bullfighting, take a bus a few miles to PAMPLONA where you can join in the 'Running of the Bulls' festival. There are twenty-four-hour celebrations and, from all the stories, the bulls aren't the only wild animals in town.

Santander

The port town of Santander is wedged between the Basque and Galician regions in the province of Cantabria. This part of northern Spain is mountainous with a rugged coastline, and contains some of the world's best prehistoric cave art in the ALTAMIRA CAVES.

The beaches at Santander are the main reason to stop off, particularly the ones at EL SARDINERO, COMILLAS and LIENCRES. The area by the harbour is the 'new town' and this is where the restaurants and bars are located. Tourist information is at Jardina de Pereda, open Mon.–Fri.: 9 a.m.–1.30 p.m., 4.30 p.m.–7.30 p.m.; Sat.: 9 a.m.–12 noon. There are plenty of cheap hostales, or campsites outside the town.

Santiago de Compostela

This is the main town in the beautiful province of Galicia, though if you really wanted to explore the dramatic Atlantic coastline you'd be better staying at La Coruña, on the main line to Madrid. Santiago was a popular place of pilgrimage in the Middle Ages for up to two million Christians a year who made the journey here to see where the Apostle St James is buried. The CATHEDRAL dominates the town, but it's difficult to isolate other main sights as the whole inner town is a national monument, and deserving of it. The cathedral was started in the eleventh century but encompasses many architectural styles. The student quarter lies between the cathedral and the university and this is the best area to head for at night. The tourist office is at Rúa del Villar 43 (closed Saturday p.m., all day Sunday and 2 p.m.–4.30 p.m. daily), and they have a list of the pensions with their prices posted up, but once you're at Turismo you're already in Santiago's main hostel street. Try Hospedaje Santa Cruz at No. 42, or Pensión Lens at No. 73. You may have trouble during the annual festival (25 July) or around religious feast days when pilgrims still flock into the town.

Barcelona

Situated across the Pyrenees from France and on the Mediterranean south of the Costa Brava, Barcelona seems to have as many links with France as with Spain. It's proud of its position as capital of Catalonia, and the language you'll hear in the streets, Catalan, is derived not from Spanish but from the French langue d'oc.

The old quarter of BARRIO GÓTICO with its medieval streets is particularly lively, though the whole city is bustling and vivacious. Regarded as the literary capital of Spain, and with an important university, Barcelona has the added attraction of its proximity to the Mediterranean and good beaches.

STATION FACILITIES

Barcelona has three main stations: Término, Sants and Paseo de Gracia. By and large, international trains use Término; rápidos to Valencia stop at Paseo de Gracia, some inland trains to the west and south originate at Término and most make stops at both Paseo de Gracia and Sants. Trains for the north-west leave from Sants. There are interconnecting trains between the stations every twenty minutes. Space permits information on only Término and Sants as the two stations most used by eurorailers.

	SANTS	TÉRMINO
Train information	6.30 a.m.–10.30 p.m. (Tel. 310 7200)	6.30 a.m.–10.30 p.m.
Reservations	7 a.m.–8 p.m.	7 a.m.–7 p.m.
Tourist information	Mon.–Fri.: 8 a.m.–8 p.m. Sat.: 8 a.m.–1 p.m.	Mon.–Fri.: 8 a.m.–8 p.m. Sat.: 8 a.m.–1 p.m.
Foreign exchange	–	8 a.m.–10 p.m.
Left-luggage store	5 a.m.–11 p.m.	4 a.m.–11 p.m.
Bar, Buffet	7 a.m.–11 p.m.	7 a.m.–11 p.m.
Restaurant	12 noon–3 p.m.	12 noon–3 p.m.
Shops	7 a.m.–10.30 p.m.	–
Post office	–	Mon.–Fri.: 9.30 a.m.–2 p.m.
Station shuts	12 midnight–4 a.m.	12 midnight–4 a.m.

Daily trains to: Paris, Geneva, Valencia, Zaragoza, Madrid, Irún.

TOURIST INFORMATION AND ADDRESSES

TOURIST OFFICE: Gran Vía de Les Corts Catalanes 658, open Mon.–Fri.: 9 a.m.–1.30 p.m., 4 p.m.–7 p.m., closed Saturday p.m. and Sundays. Ask them for their list of budget accommodation, along with your map and leaflets.
POST OFFICE: Plaza di Antoni López.
AMEX: Paseo de Gracia 101, open Mon.–Fri.: 9.30 a.m.–6 p.m., Sat.: 10 a.m.–12 noon.
UK CONSULATE: Avenida Generalísimo Franco 477 (Tel. 322 2151).
US CONSULATE: Vía Laietana 33 (Tel. 319 9550).

SEEING

Head for the BARRIO GÓTICO and look out for the GREAT ROYAL PALACE in Plaza del Rey, the CATEDRAL DE SANTA EULALIA and go inside the DIPUTACIÓN PROVINCIAL (council buildings). The hub of the city, however, is LAS RAMBLAS. This collection of streets starts at the port and runs to the city centre at Plaza de Catuluña. For sheer entertainment value you can't beat Las Ramblas. It's the Piccadilly Circus of Barcelona, so popular that you pay for a folding chair to spectate, come nightfall. The incredible cathedral of TEMPLO EXPIA-TORIO DE LA SAGRADA FAMILIA is the work of the Catalan architect Gaudí; however, his death before construction was completed put a spanner in the works as he didn't leave any plans. South of Barrio Gótico is MONTJUICH PARK. The buildings erected here for the 1929 International Exhibition are of varying interest, but the model town in PUEBLO ESPAÑOL is well worth seeing as it shows all the different regional styles of architecture in Spain. Take the funicular up, and admire the view over the port and city or for even more dramatic views, take the tram and the funicular up to TIBIDABO.

The PICASSO MUSEUM is at Calle de Montacada 15: lots of his works from the early sketches to his final masterpieces.

SLEEPING

The new youth hostel on Pas Pujadas 29 (Tel. 300 3104) charges 350 ptas. and is very good. The owners are friendly and supply cheap, reasonable meals for around 350 ptas. No IYHF card needed. For

camping, there are quite a few sites; the nearest one is four miles out
on the Espluges bus route: Camping Barcino. The University at
Calle Mestre Nicolau 14 (Tel. 250 1419) offers both sexes bed and
breakfast for 800 ptas. Your best bet for cheap casas and hostels is in
Las Ramblas. Pensión Fernando, Calle Ferran 31 (Tel. 301 7993),
is cheap and friendly; Hostal Alicante, Ronda Universidad 4 (Tel.
318 3470), is a good splurge. Hostal Noya, Ramblas 133 (Tel. 301
4831), and Hostal Canaletas on the 3rd floor (Tel. 301 5660) start
around 700 ptas. for singles and are situated right in the city centre.
If all else fails, there's a Brujula (accommodation-finding kiosk) at
Término Station.

EATING AND NIGHTLIFE

The Catalans eat late. Dinner time averages 9 p.m.–11 p.m. There
are plenty of places offering menu del día in Barrio Gótico, and if
you get a chance to sample the regional speciality, Catalan stew,
escudella i carne d'olla, do so. Casa José, Pl. San José Oriol 10, is
the cheapest, though not friendliest, feed in Barcelona. For a
splurge, go to Barceloneta, the area of colourful winding streets
down by the port, and savour the fresh seafood concoctions in Casa
Costa on Juicio.

If you've money to blow, go to the nightclubs and discos like
Georgia, Pelayo 58, or El Cordobés on Ramblas Capuchinos, but
for our money strolling through the Ramblas, stopping at a few
cafés en route, is better value. It gets quite lively at the top of the
Montjuich on summer evenings, but if that's too sedate for you,
head down to El Barrio Chino (near the docks). By Spanish
standards some of the shows down there are pretty hot stuff.

• **Excursions:** The town of MONTSERRAT is thirty-eight miles from
Barcelona, reached by Catalan Railways (from Plaza de España).
Set among the mountain peaks, there is a Benedictine monastery
and a Gothic basilica. It's a nice day trip if you're sick of crowds.

If the oppressive heat of the city is getting you down, you've not
far to go to get to the good but crowded beaches of the COSTA BRAVA
and the COSTA DORADA. LLORET DE MAR is infested with package
tourists but pretty, while S' AGARÓ is the St Trop of the Costa

Brava. Stay at SAN FELÍU DE GUIXOLS and travel in the two miles to S' Agaró to save yourself a fortune. Buses run to these and other, closer resorts from Vergara 5, Barcelona.

Valencia

If you're taking a detour off the railway to visit the Balearic islands of Majorca, Minorca or Ibiza, Valencia is logically en route, so you may feel like stopping off here. There's nothing very exciting here, but it is the point of departure for steamers to the islands, as are Alicante and Barcelona.

STATION FACILITIES

	VALENCIA TÉRMINO
Train information	7.30 a.m.–10 p.m. (Tel. 3214561)
Reservations	8 a.m.–8 p.m.
Tourist information	At town hall
Foreign exchange	8 a.m.–9 p.m.
Left-luggage store	All hours
Bar, Buffet	6 a.m.–1.30 a.m.
Cafeteria	7.30 a.m.–11.30 p.m.
Waiting room	All hours
Station shuts	3 a.m.–5 a.m.

Daily trains to: Barcelona, Alicante, Córdoba, Madrid.

TOURIST INFORMATION AND ADDRESSES

TOURIST OFFICE: Calle de la Paz, open Mon.–Fri.: 9.30 a.m.–2 p.m., 4 p.m.–7 p.m., closed Saturday p.m. and all day Sunday.
POST OFFICE: Plaza del Pais, Valenciano 24.
AMEX: c/o Viajes Melia, Calle de la Paz 41, open Mon.–Fri.: 9.30 a.m.–1.30 p.m., 4.30 p.m.–8 p.m., Sat.: 9.30 a.m.–1 p.m.

US CONSULATE: Calle de Ribera 3 (Tel. 3216973). Mon.–Fri.: 10 a.m.–1.30 p.m.
FERRIES TO THE ISLANDS: Transmediterránea, Avenida Manuel Soto Ingeniero 15.

SEEING

The PALACE OF THE MARQUÉS DE DOS AGUAS is about the most interesting building around. It's eighteenth-century rococo and contains about the best collection of Spanish pottery in Spain (2 p.m.–4 p.m., siesta, closed Sunday p.m. and all day Monday). The GOTHIC CATHEDRAL is also worth a look: climb its tower for a view over the city. Apart from these, the MUSEO PROVINCIAL DE BELLAS ARTES is the only other place really worth visiting. The best beaches are further south at BENIDORM and ALICANTE, but there are closer ones on the Costa del Azahar accessible by bus.

SLEEPING, EATING AND NIGHTLIFE

Round the Plaza del Mercado are plenty of grotty casas and fondas with beds around 800 ptas. Behind the Silk Exchange, the Lonja, are a few reasonable habitaciones. The Barrio del Carmen is the area both for cheap eating and for nightlife. Rice dishes are the Valencian speciality, but you often have to watch the prices. There are lots of spit'n'sawdust bars in this area which vary from colourful and 'ethnic' to grimy and revolting.

Castile: Central Spain

About two hours from Madrid lie two towns which should ideally be included on any Spanish itinerary: ÁVILA and SEGOVIA. Ávila (famous because of Saint Teresa) has some of Europe's best-preserved medieval battlements, dating from the eleventh century, and there are other buildings in the town from this same period. Tourist information is at Pl. de la Catedral (Tel. 21 13 87) and there's no problem finding cheap rooms. Segovia has a ROMAN AQUEDUCT antedating Christ, a fourteenth-century ALCÁZAR (palace) (rebuilt in the nineteenth century), and dozens of churches in different architectural styles. The tourist office is at Plaza Mayor 10 and there's plenty of cheap rooms nearby. Try Fonda Cubo, third floor at 4 Pl. de Franco. Whilst both these towns are interesting enough to make the effort to get to them, you'd be absolutely crazy not to make it to the town of Toledo.

Toledo

This is the town which can show you the past four centuries of Spanish history and culture in one or two days. From the Moorish and Visigothic mosques and synagogues to the Renaissance buildings of the Spanish Inquisition, every architectural style is represented and wonderfully preserved. It's interesting to note that Toledo was one of the world's few centres of Arab, Jewish and Christian co-existence. It's possible to make Toledo a day trip from Madrid (it takes 1½ hours) but you'll kill yourself trying to see all the sights in just one afternoon. Perched up on the high town are buildings such as the MOSQUE OF THE CHRIST OF LIGHT (tenth century), the SYNAGOGUE OF SANTA MARÍA LA BLANCA, the incredible medieval CATHEDRAL; and dominating the violet-coloured sky is the ALCÁZAR which once housed El Cid. EL GRECO lived in Toledo, and his HOUSE AND MUSEUM can be seen (closed Saturday p.m. and Mondays). There are many more things to see: go along to Turismo, just outside the Puerta de Bisagra (closed Saturday p.m. and Sundays), and pick up your glossy leaflets and map. This office, like many of the sights, takes a long siesta and doesn't re-open till 4 p.m. From the station (at the foot of the hill) take the bus marked Santa Barbara to the centre.

For accommodation, there are two campsites: Camping El Greco (Tel. 220090) and Circo Roman (Tel. 220442). Tourist information will suggest pensions. Fonda Lumbreros, Calle Juan Labrador 7 (Tel. 221571), or Fonda Escobar, Cuesta de Santa Leocadia 4 (Tel. 229465), are good bets. Shop around for your meals and eat at the fixed-price menu places near the central Plaza de Zocodover if possible.

Salamanca

Further down the line from Ávila is Spain's oldest university town, Salamanca. The main reason for going there is to see Spain's most beautiful square, the PLAZA MAYOR, built by Philip V in the eighteenth century. From the station take bus 1 to the centre of the town where tourist information is at the Plaza Mayor (Tel. 21 83 42). An afternoon should be long enough to take in the main sights: the square, university, OLD AND NEW CATHEDRALS, and HOUSE OF SHELLS, but if you come in term-time you might want to stay a night for the active student nightlife. Look for a room round the Plaza Mayor and call in at Calle Meléndez for a cheap meal.

Burgos

Most Madrid–Paris runs go through this old tenth-century capital of Castile. Franco was declared military commander here in 1936 and none other than El Cid is buried in the CATHEDRAL that you should head for, as the rest of the town has nothing spectacular in it. Tourist information is at 7 Pl. de Alonso Martínez (Tel. 20 18 46).

Valladolid

Just over an hour from Burgos is the university city of Valladolid. If you take a break here, visit the sixteenth-century house of MIGUEL DE CERVANTES, who wrote *Don Quixote*, off the Calle Miguel Iscar, the CATHEDRAL, the cloisters of the sixteenth-century S. GREGORIO COLLEGE, and the UNIVERSITY. Tourist information is at 3 Pl. de Zorrilla.

Cuenca

If you're heading for Valencia and the Costa del Azahar, and fancy a short break in the 5-hour journey from Madrid, take an hour or two off at Cuenca, about halfway up the line. Walk round the old town, starting at the PLAZA MAYOR, and take in the CITY HALL, the CATHEDRAL and the incredible fourteenth-century HANGING HOUSES on the banks of the Huécar River. Turismo is at Calle Colon 34.

Costa del Sol

This exploited cement-heap of coastline, best reached via Málaga, is all that you'd expect. It's difficult to know you're in Spain, the food and nightlife are plastic and often vulgar, and you'll begin to understand the background to the jokes about package deals to Torremolinos. Don't come here to look for quiet fishing villages, deserted beaches or friendly locals. However, if you're low on cash, keen to rough it on the beach, meet Europeans and pick up a tan, then you'd be hard pressed to find a better deal in Europe. If you avoid July and August and the main package-holiday resorts, you'd be amazed how different a picture can emerge.

Málaga

Don't stay in Málaga too long: not just because you run a higher risk of getting mugged here than anywhere else in Spain, but because the resorts are often crowded, and it's advisable to make for one and get established first, then head back for a day trip to see this city's sights.

Tourist information in Málaga is at Calle de Larios 5 (closes for 1.30 p.m.–4 p.m. siesta). If you feel you're being followed from the station, turn round and take a good look, then stick to major streets. The instances of eurorailers being followed from station to tourist information and being mugged en route are amazing. Whatever happens, don't even think about sleeping out at Málaga Station. We realize you'll probably know plenty of people who have and have come out unscathed, but we also know scores who've had their rucksacks actually cut off their backs and been threatened at knife-point to hand over their valuables. Honestly, it's not worth the risk. The British Consulate is at Edificio Duquesa, Duquesa de Parcent 8 (Tel. 217571), in case anything nasty happens. The US one is at Avenida Fuengirola (Tel. 461865). Tourist information will give you a leaflet on Málaga's sights. Take in the ALCAZABA Moorish palace and GIBRALFARO CASTLE if you can. 'El Corte Inglés', the big department store, is useful to stock up in. Usually its toiletries, etc., are cheaper than at the resorts, and its cafeterias are worth a visit too.

The Resorts

The resorts to the east of Málaga are less exploited, but the beaches aren't so good. In places like CASTELL DE FERRO and TORRENUEVA you'll avoid the package tourists, but will find the facilities basic. It's easier coming down from Granada to get to the eastern resorts and using the bus for the last lap.

West of Málaga, the electric train runs as far as FUENGIROLA, stopping at Torremolinos, Benalmadena, and Los Boliches en route. This train is free on Inter Rail, but to get on to Marbella or further west, you have to resort to buses.

TORREMOLINOS is the most commercialized centre. Look for rooms in hostels leading down to the beach and, as far as eating and nightlife goes, you'd have a job actually to miss the tourist menus, bars and discos, so there's no problem there. Tourist information is on Avenida Miguel Cano (1 p.m.–4.30 p.m. siesta). If this doesn't appeal, move on to other resorts till you find a suitable one. MARBELLA is slightly more 'up market', so prices can be higher here. There's a good youth hostel here on Trapiche (Tel. 771491), and for pensions, try round Aduar or Germán Porras. FUENGIROLA'S a good compromise between the two and, with its four miles of beaches and many cheap beds and restaurants, an attractive proposition to the footsore eurorailer.

Andalusia (Andalucía)

This is stereotyped Spain: flamencos, bullfights, Moorish palaces and hilltop villages. This province is bordered by the Mediterranean, the Straits of Gibraltar and the Gulf of Cádiz, and the principal centres are Seville, Granada and Córdoba.

Seville (Sevilla)

If Madrid disappointed you, head for Seville. It's a great city to visit: typically Spanish and colourful, and as alive at night as in the day. There are plenty of sights and cheap beds and it seems impossible to hit a day in summer when the heat doesn't drive you into the nearest shady park for a siesta, no matter how dedicated a sun-worshipper you might be.

STATION FACILITIES

There are two stations in Seville: San Bernardo and Plaza de Armas.

TOURIST INFORMATION AND ADDRESSES

TOURIST OFFICE: Avenida de la Constitución 21B, open 8 a.m.–3 p.m., closed Saturday p.m. and Sundays.
POST OFFICE: Avenida de la Constitución 20, open Mon.–Fri.: 9 a.m.–8 p.m., Sat.: 9 a.m.–1 p.m.
AMEX: c/o Viajes Alhambra, Teniente Coronel Segui 3, open Mon.–Fri.: 9.30 a.m.–1.30 p.m., 4.30 p.m.–8 p.m., Sat.: 9.30 a.m.–1 p.m.
UK CONSULATE: Plaza Neuva 8 (Tel. 228875).
US CONSULATE: PEU Paseo de las Delicias 7 (Tel. 231885), open 9 a.m.–1 p.m., 2 p.m.–4.30 p.m., closed Wednesday p.m., Saturdays and Sundays.
FIRST AID: Jesús del Gran Poder 34 (Tel. 224760).

SEEING

The CATHEDRAL and ALCÁZAR complex should be your first stops. The cathedral, the third largest in the world, is built on the site of a former mosque, and the Moorish tower, LA GIRALDA, is a leftover from this period. Leave the cathedral at Puerta de los Naranjos, cross the plaza to Puerta Oriente and you'll come to the fourteenth-century Alcázar palace with its combination of Moorish and Gothic architecture.

PLAZA DE ESPAÑA and the nearby parks offer romantic settings for the evening stroll, and you can hire out boats at reasonable rates and row round the Spanish Square taking it all in.

Behind the cathedral is the picturesque old Jewish quarter of SANTA CRUZ. There are guided tours, but you're better off wandering round yourself.

SLEEPING

Concentrate your efforts on finding a cheap pension (there's no convenient campsite or central youth hostel). Down from the Plaza de Armas Station or in the Santa Cruz area are your best bets. Rooms start about 800 ptas. single. Try to get fixed up early as Seville's popular with eurorailers and Spaniards alike. The hostels on Archeros are among the best in town. Try Pérez Montilla at No. 14 (Tel. 361740) or Casa de Huéspedes Orellana (Tel. 362259) at No. 19. Another good street to try is Calle San Eloy with the Hostal La Gloria at No. 58 (Tel. 222673) among the best. Sleeping rough in the parks is a dicey proposition as you have not only the police to contend with, but also the local rats. The youth hostel is at Calle Issac Peral 2 (Tel. 613150), bus 19.

EATING AND NIGHTLIFE

Prices in Seville tend to be over the top, but there are plenty of central places with fixed tourist menus, and there are even a few fast-food places creeping in now. Again, the area round the Plaza de Armas Station isn't bad, and you can eat for about 800 ptas., but some of these places aren't too fussy about hygiene.

The Barrio Triana is a good place to make for to try the local tapas, though some bars seem a bit hostile to women coming in on their own. Casa Manola at San Jorge 16 in the Barrio Triana is cheap and lively. But best value is El Diamante, Constitucion 10, where an all-you-can-eat buffet costs under 500 ptas.

Going to a flamenco is *the* thing to do in Seville. There is no shortage of venues, and by and large they're good value. Avoid the heavily advertised ones and try and make your drinks last as long as possible, as they're (surprise, surprise) overpriced. Los Gallos at Plaza Santa Cruz 11 charge about 1,000 ptas. for entrance, including your first drink. This is about average, but the entertainment here is above average.

• **Excursions from Seville:** The sherry capital of JEREZ DE LA FRONTERA is about 2 hours from Seville. If you're in this region in the second week of September go down for the fiesta. There are free guided tours and liberal samplings at the bodegas of Sandeman, Gonzalez Byass, etc. CÁDIZ, another 50 minutes away, hasn't much to commend it unless you're after a heavy nightlife scene.

Granada

Bus 4, 5, 9 or 11 will take you from the station to the centre of Granada, and once you've found your bed and left off your things, you should walk up to the incredible ALHAMBRA, *the* sight of the city.

TOURIST INFORMATION AND ADDRESSES

TOURIST OFFICE: Casa de los Tiros, Calle de Pavaneras 19, open 9.30 a.m.–2 p.m., 5 p.m.–7.30 p.m., closed Saturday p.m. and Sunday.
TRAIN INFORMATION: Tel. 271272.
POST OFFICE: Puerta Real, open 9 a.m.–2 p.m., 4 p.m.–6 p.m., closed Saturday p.m. and Sunday.
AMEX: c/o Viajes Bonal, Avenida Calvo Sotelo 19, open Mon.–Fri.: 9.30 a.m.–1.30 p.m., 4.30 p.m.–8 p.m., Sat.: 9.30 a.m.–1 p.m.

SEEING

The huge Arabic fortress on the hill dominating the city – the ALHAMBRA – is one of the world's best-preserved Moorish palaces. The ALCAZABA and WATCH TOWER go back to the ninth century, and for your 100 ptas. (ISIC; 200 ptas. without) you can take in the GENERALIFE, the summer house of the sultans, the fourteenth-century palace, and see the incredible mosaics and examples of Muslim art. Go early in the day to get its full atmosphere.

Opposite the Alhambra is ALBAICÍN, the hilltop Arab quarter with its crowded, winding streets; and on the other hilltop is the gypsy quarter of SACROMONTE. Down in the town take in the Renaissance CATHEDRAL and ROYAL CHAPEL.

SLEEPING

Though the youth hostel's a bit out of town, it's still the best deal in Granada. It's in the Colegio Emperador Carlos at Camino de Ronda (Tel. 231600). For pensions, try round the station on Avenida Andaluces, or the road up to the Alhambra, Cuesta de Gomérez. Hostal Residencia San Joaquin, Mano de Mierra 14 (Tel. 282879), is excellent, and the Sierra Nevada campsite at Carretera Madrid (Tel. 232504) is OK, but charges almost as much as a pension.

EATING AND NIGHTLIFE

Round Cetti Meriem is the place for cheap meals. La Riviera at No. 5 starts meals around 500 ptas. Avoid the 'gypsy flamenco' at Sacromonte come what may, and instead head for the bars in the centre. As far as nightlife's concerned, save your pesetas and go for a nocturnal stroll up by the Alhambra instead.

Córdoba

The Roman and Moorish remains are the reasons to include Córdoba in an itinerary. This was the eighth-century capital of Moorish Spain, though in many ways today's Córdoba looks as if it's had its heyday.

TOURIST INFORMATION AND ADDRESSES

TOURIST OFFICE: Calle Hermanos Gonzales Murga, open Mon.–Fri.: 8.30 a.m.–3 p.m., Sat.: 9 a.m.–2 p.m. Also at Pl. Tereriad in the Jewish quarter.
POST OFFICE: Cruz Conde 21, open 9 a.m.–1.30 p.m., 5 p.m.–6 p.m., closed Saturday p.m. and Sunday.

SEEING

LA MEZQUITA was a mosque before the Christians made it into a cathedral in the eighth century. The structure has an incredible array of decorated arches and pillars, and if you climb the tower you'll see how big the mosque must have been, as the cathedral fits into its original centre. The fourteenth-century SYNAGOGUE isn't exactly riveting, and the MUSEO MUNICIPAL could be missed out too. The ALCÁZAR is at its best floodlit at night. It's on the banks of the Río Guadalquivir and the Moorish gardens, towers and fountains make it an interesting place to take in.

SLEEPING, EATING AND NIGHTLIFE

Cheap pensions are on Calle Rey Heredia, at La Milagrosa, No. 12 (Tel. 223312); 1,000 ptas. doubles. There's camping about a mile out at Carretera Córdoba–Villaviciosa (Tel. 275048). Tourist menus are found most easily in the old quarter and, for tapas and bar crawls, try the Jewish quarter (round the Mezquita).

Ronda

The main line from Córdoba to Algeciras passes through this delightful town impressively perched on a gorge. See the CASA DEL REY MORO and the RENAISSANCE PALACE. For a room try around the tourist information office at Pl. de España. Open Mon.–Fri.: 9.30 a.m.–2 p.m., 5 p.m.–7 p.m., closed Saturday afternoon and Sunday.

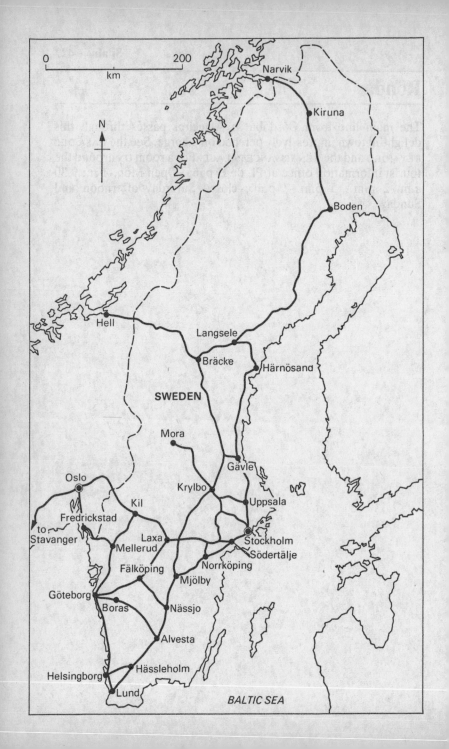

SWEDEN (Sverige)

Entry requirements	Passport
Population	8,300,000
Capital	Stockholm (pop.: 1,500,000)
Currency	Krona
	£1 = approx. 10.75 kr.
Political system	Constitutional Monarchy
Religion	Lutheran
Languages	Swedish, English
Public holidays	1, 6 Jan.; Good Friday; Easter Monday; 1 May; Ascension Day; Whit Monday; Midsummer's Day; All Saints' Day; 25, 26 Dec.

Over half of Sweden's land surface is covered by forests and lakes, an area larger than the whole of the British Isles.

Geographically isolated in the ninth and tenth centuries, the Swedish Vikings pushed eastwards down the Russian rivers to trade their furs. This trade eventually caught the attention of the Hanseatic League who were always keen to capitalize on others' labour. By the fourteenth century, all Scandinavia had had enough of these German merchants who controlled so much. The Swedes hoped that the Union of Kalmar between Sweden, Norway and Denmark (1397) would change all this; instead, all that happened was that Denmark came out on top.

In 1523 Gustavus Vasa was elected king for successfully defeating the Danes, and from then on the Swedes never looked back.

Sweden reached her zenith in the seventeenth century under Gustavus Adolphus who procured a Baltic empire for her. Defending this new position meant constant warfare until the early nineteenth century; it was therefore widely welcomed when Sweden declared herself neutral at the end of the century.

Today Sweden enjoys one of the highest standards of living in the world and a quality of life to go with it, thanks to the highly developed social welfare system.

• **Getting there:** The alternative routes are London–Dover–Ostend and up through Germany, or from Harwich to the Hook of Holland, then up. This takes about 22–25 hours to reach Stockholm. By sea there are four sailings a week from Harwich to Gothenburg and twice a week from Newcastle to Gothenburg in high season. Also there's another ferry to Esbjerg in Denmark which connects up to a through-train to Copenhagen, and a line operates from Newcastle to Esbjerg.

SWEDISH STATE RAILWAYS
(Statens Järnvågar, SJ)

Swedish trains are efficient, clean and comfortable. They are very rarely late and run frequent services (every hour or so) to most of the major cities. The journey from Stockholm to Malmö takes only six hours, and to Narvik in the far north of Norway twenty hours. The long-distance rapids (Expresståg, X) are the fastest trains, followed by the expresses (Snälltåg, S) which are used on regular routes. The local trains (Persontåg) are not as slow as in some countries, but still stop at every station. There are no supplements on any trains, but see Reservations.

● **Inter Rail bonuses:**

	FROM	TO	REDUCTION %
Stena Line	Gothenburg	Frederikshavn	50
Silja Line	Stockholm (2)	Helsinki (2)	50
	Stockholm (2)	Turku (2)	50
Saga Linjen	Malmö	Travemünde	50 (third class)

● **Eurail bonsues:** Free:
—Steamer service of the Silja Line between Stockholm and Helsinki and between Stockholm and Aland Islands–Turku. (Full fare is charged for cabin space.)
—Ferry crossings operated by the Swedish and Danish State Railways between Helsingborg and Helsingør (Denmark).
—Ferry crossings operated by Stena Sessan Line between Gothenburg and Frederikshavn (Denmark).

Reduced fares:
—50 per cent reduction on the Danish Navigation Company, Oresund, on the hydrofoil between Malmö and Copenhagen.

—50 per cent reduction to Eurail Pass and Eurail Youthpass holders on the normal fares of the ferry crossings operated by TT-Saga-Line between Malmö and Lübeck–Travemünde (Federal Republic of Germany).

TRAIN INFORMATION

No problems here, as everyone speaks perfect English and queues are never too long.

● **Reservations:** (10 kr.) are compulsory on all rapid X trains. Failure to reserve means paying double on the train and does not guarantee a seat.

● **Night travel:** Is relatively cheap in Sweden at about 70 kr. for a couchette and about double that for a tourist-class sleeper.

● **Eating on trains:** All long-distance expresses have a buffet or dining car, other trains have only snack bars. Drinking water is nearly always provided at the end of each carriage.

● **Scenic tips:** Any line north of Stockholm is of interest, particularly from Östersund onwards, either to Trondheim in Norway or to Kiruna in the far north.

● **Bikes:** enquire from local tourist offices or in stations.

TOURIST INFORMATION

Every Swedish county has a tourist board in addition to the local tourist information offices called 'Turistbyrå'. They are very helpful and always have a good selection of maps and brochures.

● **ISIC bonuses:** Few reductions here; the main one is 20 per cent off tours and day trips to historic places. For further information, contact SFS–RESOR, Drottninggatan 89, Stockholm.

● **Money matters:** 1 krona (kr.) = 100 öre.
Banking hours are Mon.–Fri.: 9.30 a.m.–3 p.m. Bank charges are high for traveller's cheques (approximately 10 kr.) so it makes sense to cash large denominations.

● **Post offices and shops:** Post offices open Mon.–Fri.: 9 a.m.–6 p.m., and 9 a.m.–4 p.m. on Saturdays. Most shops are open 9 a.m.–6 p.m. The poste restante service is free in Sweden, and stamps are sold at newsagents as well as post offices.

● **Museums:** Normally open from about 10 a.m.–5 p.m.

SLEEPING

All regional and local tourist offices have free lists of hotels and campsites; many also have a room-finding service called Rumsför-medling. They charge a commission of about 10 kr., and can find you a room in a private house or in a hotel. In smaller towns and villages look for the sign Rum (the Swedish equivalent of B&B, except there's no breakfast). At about 90 kr. for a single, this represents as good value as you're likely to get. Youth hostels are clean and cost about 35–45 kr. per night; add another 10 kr. to this if you're not a member. Camping's no problem thanks to the Allmansrätt law which allows anyone to camp on unfenced land. If you prefer your comforts, most towns have campsites with excellent facilities costing about 35 kr. per tent, but these require a camping pass (10 kr.) obtainable at the site.

EATING AND NIGHTLIFE

Eating out is expensive in Sweden even at self-service restaurants and fast-food joints. Always check to see if there's a tourist menu or a cheap set meal (dagens rätt). More often than not, you'll be forced to eat from supermarkets, which is no bad thing as the quality and choice are excellent. Most of the regional specialities, such as smoked reindeer meat from Lapland, are expensive and confined to the best restaurants. Smörgåsbord is cheaper here than in Norway, so if you feel like a Scandinavian splash-out do it here.

Nightlife is what you make it in Sweden, and there's no shortage of options in the larger towns. Alcohol and tobacco are expensive and controlled by the government, but there's not much the government can do during the midsummer festival when everyone lets rip with non-stop dancing and drinking, particularly in the north.

Stockholm

All the qualities one associates with the Swedes are reflected in their capital. It's tidy and well laid-out, socially minded and efficiently run, and the high level of money floating around has permitted them to improve their environment with schemes like making the city's waterway safe for swimming and erecting new buildings with more of an eye towards appearance than to economy. The 'porn capital of Europe' is in many ways more discreet about it than Amsterdam or Copenhagen. It's very much an 'it's there if you want it' attitude; by the way, guys will be in for a disappointment if they go there believing all the stories they've heard about Swedish girls.

It's difficult to make out on a tight budget here, as even supermarket food is expensive, but you'll get by if you follow our suggestions and use your common sense.

STATION FACILITIES

	STOCKHOLM CENTRAL
Train information	Mon.–Fri.: 7 a.m.–10 p.m., Sat. and holidays: 7 a.m.–7 p.m. (Tel. 225060)
Reservations	Mon.–Fri.: 8 a.m.–10 p.m., Sat.: 9 a.m.–1 p.m. (Tel. 248040)
Tourist information	*Summer*: 8 a.m.–11.30 p.m. (not Sun.) *Winter*: Mon.–Fri.: 8.30 a.m.–5 p.m. Downstairs
Foreign exchange	8 a.m.–9 p.m.
Left-luggage lockers	No access 1.10 a.m.–4.50 a.m.
Left-luggage store	9 a.m.–4.30 p.m.
Café, Bar	6.30 a.m.–10.30 p.m.
Restaurant	6.30 a.m.–12 midnight
Provisions	9 a.m.–10 p.m. (Mon. opens at 7 a.m., Sat. 8 a.m.)
Post office	Mon.–Fri.: 7 a.m.–9 p.m., Sat.: 8 a.m.–4 p.m.
Station shuts	1.10 a.m.–4.50 a.m.

Daily trains to: Malmö, Copenhagen, Gothenburg, Oslo, and all Sweden.

TOURIST INFORMATION

Apart from the station, there's an office in the centre at Sweden House (Sverigehuset), Hamnagatan 27. Pick up maps, 'This Month in Stockholm' and take a look at the 'Alternative Guide'. The Swedish Institute on the ground floor gives out free fact-sheets on Sweden, and everyone involved seems incredibly helpful.

• **Addresses:**
POST OFFICE: Vasagatan 28–34, open 8 a.m.–8 p.m., Sat.: 9 a.m.–3 p.m., Sun.: 9 a.m.–11 a.m.
AMEX: Sturegatan 8. Open Mon.–Fri.: 9 a.m.–5 p.m.
UK EMBASSY: Skarpögatan 6 (Tel. 670140).
US EMBASSY: Strandvägen 101 (Tel. 630520).
CANADIAN EMBASSY: Tegelbacken 4, 7th floor (Tel. 237920).
AUSTRALIAN EMBASSY: Sergelstorg 12 (Tel. 244660).
24-HOUR CHEMIST: Apoteke Scheele, Klarabergsgatan 64 (Tel. 248280).
TRANSALPINO: Birger Jarlsgatan 13.
SVENSKA TURISTFÖRENINGEN: Vasagatan 48. Call in for information if you're camping or hostelling in Sweden.
INTERNATIONAL YOUTH CENTRE: Valhallavägen 142. A helpful lot who offer cheap bus excursions, free cooking facilities, games rooms, etc. Great place to meet students.

• **Getting about:** The underground and buses are good and charge by the zone. Three-day transit passes cost 50 kr. (including free entry to some museums and ferries); twenty-four-hour passes cost 14/24 kr., depending on the areas covered. Buy these at tourist information or stalls in the underground. The 'Stockholmcard', valid for 24, 48 or 72 hours, gives free buses, trains, boats, museum entrances, some gifts in the big stores and free coffee at certain places; its cost is from 50 kr. upwards.

SEEING

South of the centre lie the islands of GAMLA STAN, SKEPPSHOLMEN and DJURGÅRDEN where the vast majority of sights are located. Gamla Stan, or the Old Town, dates back to the mid-thirteenth century. The narrow medieval streets are full of trendy shops and restaurants, nightclubs and studios. The eighteenth-century ROYAL PALACE is on the border of the Gamla Stan, and parts of it are open to the public till about 3 p.m. daily, except Mondays. The NATIONAL MUSEUM and MODERN ART GALLERY are located east of the Old Town in Skeppsholmen, and east of this again is the Djurgården, an island almost entirely devoted to recreation. Take the ferry over from Slussen or Nybroplan, or walk from Strandvägen. This is where the seventeenth-century warship *Wasa* is on view. This flagship of the Swedish navy only lasted ten minutes on her maiden voyage before sinking into oblivion, till she was rediscovered in 1956 and brought up. She's in a remarkable state of preservation and is well worth the 10 kr. fee.

Sweden's open-air museum, SKANSEN, is definitely one of Europe's best. It's called 'Sweden in Miniature' with good reason, as an afternoon spent there will fill you in more on Swedish folklore, architecture and history than will a week touring the country. There are over 150 buildings of authentic Swedish design, demonstrations of folk dancing, craftsmen at work, a zoo and lots more. Open Apr.–Sept.: 8 a.m.–11.30 p.m.; Oct.–Mar.: 8 a.m.–9 p.m.

GRÖNA LUND, or Tivoli, is the amusement park on Djurgården. It's better than Copenhagen's and averages 4 kr. on most rides.

The Swedish 'House of Culture' (KULTURHUSET) at Sergelstorg is a good example of the country's social-mindedness. Exhibitions of crafts and art are always on and there are free 'creative activities' for anyone who wants to participate so, if you're feeling inspired, jog along and model or paint your masterpiece. There's also a library and access to foreign newspapers and records. It's open in summer, Mon.–Thur.: 9 a.m.–9.30 p.m., Fri.–Sat.: 9 a.m.–6 p.m. and Sun.: 11 a.m.–6 p.m. (July: closed Saturday p.m. and Sundays).

SLEEPING

Hotellcentralen at Central Station will give you a map and list of hostels and hotels or find you a hostel space for 5 kr. or a hotel bed for 10 kr. The International Youth Centre will also help out if you're really stuck. You'd do well to make use of these services, especially in peak season, as beds (especially cheap ones) are thin on the ground. Theoretically they can arrange private accommodation at the station if you're staying more than a few days, but in general in summer there are never enough to go around. If it's at all feasible to call ahead and reserve, do so; and this goes for hostels, campsites or hotels.

The most memorable place to stay in Stockholm is definitely on board the AF *Chapman*. This youth hostel is a nineteenth-century sailing ship, fully rigged and decked out, and harboured opposite the Gamla Stan; it costs 45 kr. for a 'berth' in a 4–8-bed cabin. Arrive early to stand a chance; to reserve, call 205705. The other central youth hostel is also popular and good: Frescati Hostel at Professorsslingan (Tel. 157996) is part of Hotel Frescati and offers great doubles for 90 kr.

For hotels try one of the following: Hotel Domus, Körsbärsvägen 1 (Tel. 160195), Pensionat Oden, Odengatan 38 (Tel. 306349), or Gustavsvikshemmet at Vastmannagatan (Tel. 214450). All are within the 160–220 kr. per double range.

Out of the four city campsites, the nearest ones are Ängby Camping on Lake Mälaren (Tel. 370420) on underground 17 or 18, and Bredäng Camping (Tel. 977071) on subway 13 or 15 to Bredäng Station. For a list of Swedish youth hostels contact STF at Vasagatan 48, and for student hostels contact SFS at Drottninggatan 89 (Tel. 340180).

EATING AND NIGHTLIFE

Face the fact, you're going to have to spend twice as much as you would in southern Europe to eat out here. Picnics are the answer, in conjunction with bar meals ('Bars' are self-service restaurants here). Buy in supplies at Östermalms Saluhall or Hötorgshallen, the two big indoor markets. The central supermarkets also do a good line in groceries. There are some old cellar restaurants offering dagens rätt (today's special) in the Gamla Stan. While smörgåsbord are filling and tasty, they also tend to be pricey; however, if you arrive in Stockholm Central after a long train journey, treat yourself to the excellent stora frukost (eat-as-much-as-you-like breakfast). It's about 26 kr. and will keep you going all day. Annorlunda at Malmskillnadsgatan 50 does good healthy meals for around 28 kr. and Gässlingen, Brännkyrkagatan 93, is another homely and reasonable place. If you're cutting all corners and don't mind plastic atmospheres and fast food, there are several outlets to choose from. In the evening Gamla Stan tends to be the best area to head for. There are plenty of pubs and clubs with bands for around 35 kr. For cheaper entertainment, go over to Skansen or Gröna Lund where there's usually dancing, etc. Check with 'This Month in Stockholm' for current events and, unless you're rolling in cash or desperate, steer clear of the notorious sex clubs – not that they'll short-change you in what they offer, but the admission fee's about half the price of your train ticket.

• **Excursions:** The old university town of UPPSALA is 45 minutes away by train. On a day trip here you can see the medieval CATHEDRAL, seventeenth-century CASTLE, the oldest UNIVERSITY in Sweden, VIKING BURIAL MOUNDS, and the UPPLANDS MUSEUM which details the city's history and customs. Turn right on leaving the station for tourist information at Kungsgatan 44. An alternative excursion is to DROTTNINGHOLM PALACE, built in the seventeenth century, five miles west of the capital on the island of Lovön. It's all very pretty: Chinese pavilion, rococo summerhouse, etc. To get there, either head for Klara Mälarstrand (near City Hall) and take the steamer, or take the underground to Brommaplan and then change to Mälaröbuses.

Gotland

Sweden's largest island of Gotland was the strategic centre of the Vikings and their remains are still dotted around the island, along with those of the plethora of medieval churches. You'll find fewer Europeans here, more Swedes, and fewer still eurorailers, since to get here you need a ferry from Oskarshamn or Nynäshamn over to VISBY, the major town on Gotland. Ask tourist information for connection times and details. In Visby, tourist information is at Skeppsbron 20 at the harbour. Before heading off to the unspoilt countryside of Gotland (preferably on a bike), wander through Visby and take a look at the OLD CITY WALLS, the Viking remains in the GOTLANDS FORNSAL MUSEUM and the ST MARIA CATHEDRAL.

Gothenburg (Göteborg)

Sweden's second city is about four hours from Stockholm, and the detour to the west coast provides an interesting alternative route to get down to Copenhagen, as the direct line running straight down to Malmö is not that interesting. Gothenburg's big on parks, museums and canals – in fact there's a bit of Dutch influence left over from its origins as a seventeenth-century Dutch colony, and its harbour is the largest in Scandinavia.

STATION FACILITIES

	GÖTEBORG CENTRAL
Train information	Mon.–Sat.: 8 a.m.–10 p.m.
	Sun.: 8 a.m.–7 p.m.
	(Tel. 175000)
Reservations	Mon.–Fri.: 5 a.m.–11.55 p.m., Sat. and Sun.:
	6.30 a.m.–11.55 p.m. (Tel. 175500)
Tourist information	In 'Östra Nordstan' (2 minutes away)
	Mon.–Fri.: 9 a.m.–6 p.m., Sat.: 9 a.m.–3 p.m.
Foreign exchange	Mon.–Fri.: 9.30 a.m.–6 p.m. (In tourist information)
Left-luggage lockers	Access 12 midnight–5 a.m. with ticket
Left-luggage store	Mon.–Fri.: 6.30 a.m.–10 p.m.
	Sat.: 6.30 a.m.–8 p.m.
Cafeteria	Sun.:–Fri.: 6.30 a.m.–8 p.m.
	Sat.: 7 a.m.–8 p.m.
Bar	5 p.m.–12 midnight
Restaurant	Sun.–Fri.: 6.30 a.m.–8 p.m.
	Sat.: 7 a.m.–8 p.m.
Shops	In 'Östra Nordstan' (2 minutes away)
Post office	Mon.–Fri.: 8 a.m.–7 p.m., Sat.: 8 a.m.–1 p.m.
Station shuts	12 midnight–5 a.m.

Daily trains to: Oslo, Stockholm, Malmö, Copenhagen, Frederikshavn.

TOURIST INFORMATION AND SLEEPING

Apart from Östra Nordstan, the main tourist office is at Kungsportsplatsen 2, open daily 10 a.m.–8 p.m. Both offer an accommodation service including private accommodation lodgings for 55 kr. each. Their hotels start at 75 kr. single, 120 kr. double, and they take 10 kr. commission. The youth hostel is good and not too far out. Ostkupan (Tel. 401050) at Mejerigatan is about two miles from the centre on bus 64.

Kärralund (Tel. 252761) is the most central campsite and is reached by tram 5 to Welandergatan.

SEEING

The centre of Gothenburg is very modern but if you head off to HAGA, the old district of wooden houses and local bars, you'll see a different side of the city. Of the many parks worth visiting try to take in the BOTANICAL GARDENS, SLOTTSKOGEN with its zoo, lakes and birds, and LISEBERG LEISURE PARK which has everything from discos to fun fairs. The INDUSTRIAL MUSEUM and ART CENTRE on Götaplatsen are interesting places, and for the nautically minded the MARITIME MUSEUM (Sjöfartsmuseet) has ships from Viking times to the present day. The KRONHUSET is the oldest building in the city and its museum, telling Gothenburg's history, includes such exhibits as reconstructed shops of the last century. Next to the fish market in the harbour is the FESKEKÖRKA, a nineteenth-century church filled with fish stalls and vendors. The 7 a.m. auction is worth getting up for.

EATING AND NIGHTLIFE

Along Kungsportsavenyn (the main boulevard) are restaurants of all kinds and descriptions (from Chinese to Scottish), and alongside them are the increasingly popular fast-food chains. Fish and seafood are naturally in abundance in Gothenburg and often the dagens rätt will include a local fish dish. La Gondola at Kungsportsavenyn 4 does good large meals for under 35 kr., and they have outside table service. For picnic food, the markets on Kungstorget are best.

At night, a lot of the young locals seem to gather round the Poseidon fountain at Götaplatsen to cast an eye over the visiting talent; otherwise, you're most likely to meet the resident students in

the bar at the Students' Union, Puboteque, which is near Götaplatsen. Behind the market on Kungstorget is Ölhallen, an authentic
Swedish pub, and there are quite a few disco and jazz clubs, though
their entrance fees put most of them safely out of the average
eurorailer's reach.

Lapland

If you were put off going up to Lapland in Norway, let yourself be
persuaded now you're in Sweden. It's easier here: the trains run
right up to RIKSGRÄNSEN, just before the border and NARVIK in
Norway. From Stockholm to the border is a straight 24 hours,
though the conditions on the trains don't make this seem as much of
an ordeal as it sounds, and the scenery once you're around
GÄLLIVARE or KIRUNA is breathtaking. Once you're up there,
there's an inland line from Gällivare down through JOKKMOKK and
ARVIDSJAUR to ÖSTERSUND. It's legal to camp where you want
(except on fenced-in land) so you can go it alone in a big way,
especially out of season. Unless you've skin like leather, take with
you mosquito repellent of some sort as they're out in force up there.
The Svenska Turistföreningen, Box 7615, Stockholm, are the
people to write to for information on mountain tourist stations and
huts, and suggested hiking routes. To get the most out of a trip to
Lapland, plan and book ahead as much as possible. Don't just
wander aimlessly on to the train in Stockholm with no food or
proper walking boots and expect to pick up relevant supplies once
you're there, and don't go with fantasies in your head of great
wilderness adventures with Lapps, reindeer and huskies. It's a bit
like that, but in reality the towns are a bit grey and morose, and the
Lapps are pretty sick of wide-eyed tourists pointing and gawping at
them from June to September.

Gällivare

This strategic mining town is at the junction of the main line to
Narvik and inland line to Jokkmokk. If you've time to kill here

waiting for connections, go to the nearby iron mines at MALMBER-GET and take the tour round (check first with tourist information, as they seem to be closing them in summer now), or go to the museum at VASARA where there are skis dating back before the time of Christ. Apart from the ETTORE CHURCH and the largest log cabin in the world, that's about it here. The tourist office is near the station at Lasarettsgatan 8, and is open 8 a.m.–8 p.m. in summer, 12 noon–4 p.m., 5 p.m.–9 p.m. Sun. They'll give you details on how to get up to the Stora Sjöfallet National Park and the surrounding mountains. If you're staying, ask about the private accommodation here.

Kiruna

As the city's fairly unattractive, use Kiruna as a base for the surrounding countryside. Tourist information is at Mangigatan 12, open 9 a.m.–8 p.m. weekdays, 3 p.m.–8 p.m. Sun. There's a youth hostel called Strandstigen 10 minutes from the station, open June–Sept. (Tel. 17195), or tourist information will get you into private houses. There are mine tours at Kiruna for 30 kr.

Jokkmokk

The JOKKMOKKS MUSEUM will fill in a lot of gaps on the Lapps (their history and culture) and is well worth the 3 kr. entrance fee. You'll find tourist information at Porjusbagen 4, open Mon.–Fri.: 8 a.m.–9 p.m.; Sat. and Sun.: 9 a.m.–9 p.m. The tourist office give out (or did recently) 'Polar Certificates' to prove you've made it to, and crossed, the Arctic Circle (well, your Mum'll like it). The GAMLA KYRKA (Old Church) is the other main sight. There's a youth hostel at Borgargatan 2 (Tel. 10214) and an official campsite, Notuddens, a couple of miles from the centre.

Arvidsjaur

The LAPP VILLAGE in the town of Arvidsjaur is still used today by Lapps visiting the town for festivals and gatherings. Tourist information is at Storagatan 12, open 9 a.m.–7 p.m. daily, and they'll arrange private accommodation for you. The campsite at Storagatan 26 (Tel. 10139) does huts as well as tent sites, and opposite the station is the Central Hotel at Järnvägsgatan with rooms at 80 kr. single, 120 kr. double.

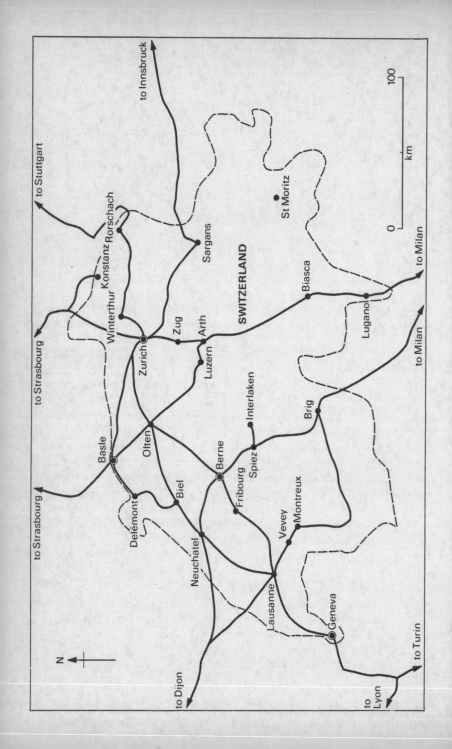

SWITZERLAND

Entry requirements	Passport
Population	6,300,000
Capital	Bern (pop.: 145,000)
Currency	Swiss franc
	£1 = approx. 3.09 F
Political system	Federal Republic
Religions	Roman Catholic and Protestant
Languages	German, French, Italian, Romansh
	(some English spoken in cities)
Public holidays	1, 2 Jan.; Good Friday; Easter Monday;
	Ascension Day; Whit Monday; 1 Aug.; 9 Sept.;
	25, 26, 31 Dec.

Cross the border from France or Italy to Switzerland and almost immediately you'll notice even the wood-piles are neater. Where the Swiss obsession for punctuality and cleanliness comes from is open to debate, but we suspect it's an ongoing process started when the Romans cleaned up after the Celts. Then along came the Germanic tribes who brought with them the obsessive work ethic we still see in their Swiss descendants, only now it's in the form of high finance and flashy watches. By the end of the thirteenth century, William Tell and his friends were demanding independence from the Habsburgs. This sparked off a proud tradition of self-government among the cantons which continues to this day. One of the reasons why the Swiss are so prosperous is the country's neutrality since Napoleon's invasion of 1815. Physically, Switzerland is one of the most beautiful countries in Europe and yet despite this apparent good fortune, many Swiss seem a bit tight-lipped and lacking in the vitality of their Italian neighbours.

SWISS FEDERAL RAILWAYS
(Schweizerische Bundesbahnen, SBB)
(Chemins de fer fédéraux suisses, CFF)
(Ferrovie federali svizzere, FFS)

Swiss federal railways and various private railway companies combine to give one of the most extensive and efficient services in

Europe. The private outfits tend to serve the resort areas, except for the two largest. Most notable is the Bern–Lötschberg–Simplon line (BLS), Europe's largest private operation, which runs in friendly rivalry with the federal railway. International and intercity trains are federal-run, and intercity or express trains run hourly between all the main centres, while inland expresses run at least every other hour. There are no supplements on any of the inland trains. A useful spin-off are the free maps and leaflets given out to lure custom.

● **Inter Rail bonuses:** Free entrance to Swiss Transport and Communications Museum, Lidostrasse, Lucerne.

On many private railways of Switzerland, Inter Rail will bring you a 50 per cent reduction, so always ask first. Those that don't are Jungfrau, Furka Oberalp, Gornergrat and Bernese Oberland.

● **Eurail bonuses:** Free:
—Regular steamer services on the lakes of Geneva, Lucerne, Thun, Brienz, Zürich, Neuchâtel, Biel, Murten, on the Rhine from Schaffhausen to Kreuzlingen and on the Aare from Biel/Bienne to Solothurn. Seasonal services – please consult timetables.

Reduced fares:
—50 per cent reduction on steamer services on Lake Constance between Romanshorn and Friedrichshafen and between Rorschach and Lindau.

● **Europabus:**
A 10 per cent reduction is granted by Europabus on transportation costs only and by local offices in Europe on:
200 St Moritz–Munich.

TRAIN INFORMATION

English is widely spoken throughout Switzerland and most Swiss timetables have an English section. If you have no luck finding anywhere to stay, look out for the travel-aid men with red, white and yellow armbands.

● **Reservations:** Can only be made on international routes, but as they are expensive it's not really worth it.

• **Night travel:** Wagons-Lits run couchettes and sleepers on all international routes at their standard rates. SBB have no services on any inland runs.

• **Eating on trains:** Most stations are fairly well provided for, which is just as well as even the mini-bars are very expensive. If you've money to burn, the self-service buffet is much better value than the dining cars.

• **Scenic tips:** To get to grips with Switzerland's many scenic rail routes would take at least a month and involve paying out vast amounts for private lines. Swiss Holiday Card holders get round this problem, but most Eurorailers have to be content with mainline runs. The possibilities are endless, without even leaving the main lines. All the main centres make excellent bases for touring the Alps. From Zürich the main line to Chur–St Moritz–Tirano is Europe's highest at 7,400 feet as well as one of the most spectacular. At Chur an alternative is to head towards Zermatt. This line passes over the Oberalp (6,700 feet) and through the Furka tunnel but it gives no reduction to Inter Railers.

Lucerne offers the greatest possibilities; foremost among them is the main line to Milan through the nine-mile-long Gotthard tunnel which took 2,500 men over seven years to construct in the 1880s. If this isn't spectacular enough, take the branch line to Locarno where you change trains for Domodossola in Italy. This line is a real favourite, passing through some incredible gorges. Also from Lucerne, the line to Interlaken is equally awe-inspiring. If you haven't already seen enough and don't mind paying out, take the private line up to Kleine Scheidegg where, after you change trains, the line goes under the Eiger and on to the Jungfraujoch, Europe's highest station at 11,300 feet. Private lines also take you up to Mounts Rigi, Pilatus and Titlis from Lucerne, so good luck if you've got the money. Bern makes an alternative base for any of these trips, but if, like most Eurorailers, you're in a hurry the main line to Milan via Brig will not be a disappointment. At Brig, if you've spare cash why not head for Zermatt, and take the cogwheel train up to Gornergrat and see the Matterhorn from close to. Approaching from the west, the train follows Lake Geneva as far as Lausanne where the line splits to enter Bern or Brig – either route is beautiful. The Martigny to Le Châtelard (and on to Chamonix) route is another classic.

• **Bikes:** Can be hired out at most SBB stations and some private ones; cost approximately 10 F a day.

TOURIST INFORMATION

Every town has its own well-organized tourist office near the station. They keep a good selection of maps and leaflets, as well as running a room-finding service. Ask for the Swiss Holiday Card map: this shows the rail network of the country.

• **ISIC bonuses:** There's a variety of reductions on internal fares and in some museums. For further information, contact SSR Leonhardstrasse 10, Zürich, or SSTE, 3 rue Vignier, Geneva.

• **Money matters:** 1 franc (F) = 100 centimes (c.).
Banking hours are Mon.–Fri.: 8 a.m.–12 noon., 2 p.m.–4.30 p.m. Many stations have exchanges which stay open seven days a week. Post offices open Mon.–Fri.: 7.30 a.m.–6 p.m., Sat.: 7.30 a.m.–11 a.m. Shops open Tues.–Fri.: 8.30 a.m.–6.30 p.m. Many shops shut for lunch 12 noon–2 p.m., particularly in small towns.

SLEEPING

Availability and price are the two main problems you're likely to face in Switzerland. During the summer, the tourist resorts are packed and then there's always that unexpected conference in town. To avoid paying through the nose for somewhere to stay, arrive as early in the day as possible and start looking right away. Tourist offices keep lists of hotels and hostels in the area, and will find you a room if required for a small charge. Hotels tend to be expensive with singles costing around 40 F, so think twice before committing yourself. Even a dormitory bed in a student hostel will set you back 25 F or more. Youth hostels often provide the only answer; there are over 100 of them in Switzerland, most of which are very clean and have excellent facilities. IYHF cards are required and you can expect to pay 15–20 F for a bed. Swiss campsites are among the best in Europe, and at only 4 or 5 F per person you can't go wrong. If you're forced to the hills to sleep out, remember it can get bitterly cold in Switzerland at night even during the summer.

EATING AND NIGHTLIFE

Eating out is expensive and not particularly spectacular for what you get. Fortunately, a lot of the regional specialities can be bought from supermarkets. Alpine areas have a good selection of cheeses and cold meats ideal for picnics. The cheapest restaurants (Gemeindestube) don't serve alcohol, so if you want a glass of wine with your meal you'll have to check out the fixed-price menus. Look out for rösti (a filling potato dish from the German area) or berner platte (a mixture of ham, bacon, and sausage with potatoes and pickled cabbage thrown in). If you can get a group together it's worth going for a fondue. The Swiss don't exactly specialize in budget entertainment; as a result, most young people take to the bars which serve excellent beer. During the spring there are plenty of local folk festivals going on in the mountains, and on 1 August the sky is set alight by fireworks commemorating the founding of the Swiss Confederation.

Zürich

The largest city of Switzerland and home of the 'gnomes' (as Harold Wilson so aptly put it) of the international money market. Walking on the average Zürich pavement, you're literally on top of gold: vaults containing much of the world's gold reserves lie buried beneath them. Zürich is one of Europe's most expensive cities, and in our estimation doesn't merit more than a couple of days of a tight timetable, though there's no denying the Old Town is picturesque. Situated in northern Switzerland, not far from the West German border, Zürich handles trains to an impressive number of destinations in Switzerland, France, Germany, Belgium, Holland, Hungary, Austria, Yugoslavia and Italy.

STATION FACILITIES

	ZÜRICH HAUPTBAHNHOF
Train information	Mon.–Fri.: 7 a.m.–9 p.m., weekends: 6.30 a.m.–8.45 p.m. (Tel. 2115010)
Reservations	7 a.m.–7.30 p.m.
Tourist information	8 a.m.–10 p.m.
Foreign exchange	6.30 a.m.–11.30 p.m.
Left-luggage lockers	No access 12 midnight–4 a.m.
Left-luggage store	All hours
Self-service buffet	6 a.m.–1 a.m.
Restaurant	6 a.m.–11.40 p.m.
Bath, Shower and Shops	In complex under Bahnhofplatz
Post office	Mon.–Fri.: 7.30 a.m.–6.30 p.m. Sat.: 7.30 a.m.–11 a.m.
Station shuts	12 midnight–4 a.m.

TOURIST INFORMATION

The main office is on Bahnhofplatz 15, just outside the station. It's open Mon.–Fri.: 9 a.m.–10 p.m., weekends: 8 a.m.–8.30 p.m. There are leaflets on everything here and an accommodation service for 2 F.

Though the Swiss Student Reception Service is mainly a travel agent, it does also have information on Switzerland. It's at Leonhardstrasse 10 (Tel. 473000).

• **Addresses:**
AMEX: Bahnhofstrasse 20, open Mon.–Fri.: 8.30 a.m.–12.30 p.m., 1.30 p.m.–5.30 p.m.
UK CONSULATE: Bellerivestrasse 5 (Tel. 471520).
US CONSULATE: Zollikerstrasse 141 (Tel. 552566).

SEEING

To the right of the Limmat River is OLD ZÜRICH with its sixteenth- and seventeenth-century guild houses, now restaurants and trendy shops, and close by the town's two medieval churches: FRAUMÜN-

STER on the left bank and GROSSMÜNSTER, the austere Protestant cathedral, on the right. For a view over the old town, climb to LINDENHOF just up from the Fraumünster. BAHNHOFSTRASSE is said to be 'the most beautiful shopping street in the world' – we don't know about that, but it's certainly one of the most expensive; it runs down from the station to the lake where you can indulge in a boat trip if the weather's up to it. The ZOO in the Zürichberg woods and BOTANICS at Zollikerstrasse are wonderful picnic spots on good days, and on bad the SWISS NATIONAL MUSEUM behind the station and the RIETBERG MUSEUM in the Wessendonck villa at Gablerstrasse are excellent. The latter has one of the best collections of non-European art in Europe. There are all sorts of boat trips on Lake Zürich lasting 1½–4 hours which Inter Railers get concessions on, or there's the trip down the River Limmat which takes you through old Zürich. Inquire at Selnau Station about the private mountain trains (Inter Railers: always check in case you don't get half price on the line you've chosen) and strongly consider the chance to get up to an Alpine village, away from the bourgeois bustle of Zürich. From the Hauptbahnhof, take the train for about an hour to SCHAFFHAUSEN, then a further 20 minutes to STEIN AM RHEIN. This beautiful little place with its half-timbered houses and wonderful location can also be reached by boat from Schaffhausen quay. Inter Railers get concessions and you can take the boat as far as Konstanz.

SLEEPING

Forget hotels and keep it as basic as you can. The campsite on the Zürichsee is very good (train to Wollishofen, then 10-minute walk) and works out as your cheapest option. It's on Seestrasse (Tel. 451612).

The youth hostel's big and strictly run. It's at Mutschellenstrasse 114 (Tel. 453544) and is reached by tram 7 to Morgental (10 p.m. curfew; reception closes 9 a.m.–2 p.m.). For cheap pensions, try the following: Foyer Hottingen, Hottingerstrasse 31 (Tel. 479315); Josephsheim, Hirschengraben 64 (Tel. 2512757); Justinusheim, Freudenberg Strasse 146 (Tel. 3613806); or Schaefli, Badergasse 6 (Tel. 2514144). These range from 30–40 F singles, 60–70 F doubles.

EATING AND NIGHTLIFE

Round the station's as good as anywhere for cheap places, or use one of the many central Migros cafeterias. Jelmoli, the department store on Bahnhofstrasse, do good meals, but their best value is the all-you-can-eat breakfast for 12 F. There's enough there to keep you sustained till dinner. The Mensa at Rämistrasse 71 does cheap meals for students, and there are a few beer halls where you can pick up Würst snacks for not a lot. The bars, discos and clubs are all around Niederdorfstrasse, but don't get too excited if you're a night owl, as most places close at midnight. Underneath their pin stripes, it seems as if a lot of Swiss bankers must be gay, as there are more than enough gay bars for your average city of less than a million.

Lucerne (Luzern)

If you can only stop once in Switzerland, make it at Lucerne. It's Switzerland's prettiest, and most touristy, town, and in this country that's saying something on both scores. Set on Lake Lucerne with the Alps in the background, it's beautifully preserved and has everything you always associated with Switzerland. It's 1½ hours from Bern and only ½ hour from Zürich.

TOURIST INFORMATION AND ADDRESSES

The tourist office is a 5-minute walk from the station at Pilatus-strasse 14, open Mon.–Fri.: 8 a.m.–12 noon, 2 p.m.–6 p.m.; Sat.: 9 a.m.–12 noon; closed Sun. When closed use room-finding service at the station. If you're staying a while, consider the Lucerne season ticket, which admits you to monuments, the beach and trips on cable railways and steamers.

POST OFFICE: Bahnhofstrasse, open Mon.–Fri.: 7.30 a.m.–6.30 p.m., Sat.: 7.30 a.m.–11 a.m.

AMEX: Schweizerhofquai 4, open Mon.–Fri.: 8 a.m.–12 noon, 2 p.m.–6 p.m.

SEEING

The fourteenth-century covered wooden bridge, KAPELLBRÜCKE, spanning the River Reuss, is the symbol of the town. Walk over it to see the 120 paintings dating from the sixteenth to the eighteenth century which tell the town's history. The adjoining WATER TOWER served as a lookout tower, prison, and archive store. On Kornmarkt is the beautiful old TOWN HALL, and on WEINMARKT are old painted houses. The SPREUERBRÜCKE is another covered bridge, this time with paintings on the 'Dance of Death'.

The SWISS TRANSPORT MUSEUM sounds boring as hell, but is actually quite interesting, and free to Inter Railers. It's at the end of the park en route to the campsite. The WAGNER MUSEUM in the suburb of TRIBSCHEN shows the house where he worked and lived, and some of his possessions. You can get here by bus 6/7 or by the boat from in front of the station (Inter Rail concession).

SLEEPING

If you're intent on a pension or hotel (you must be mad), use the station's accommodation service (open 2.30 p.m.–10 p.m.) and clearly state your price range – the cheapest rooms available in July 1984 were 27 F per person per night. The campsite is excellent: its situation couldn't be improved – near the beach and the lake – and to get to it you can walk through the park. It's at Lidostrasse (Tel. 312146) and on bus route 2. The youth hostel Am Rotsee on Sedelstrasse 12 (Tel. 368800) has over 200 beds and is very reasonable (13.5 F). It's not central and closes 10 a.m.–5 p.m. Bus 1 to Schlossberg, then a 10-minute walk will get you there. Try to arrive early, as we've had reports of 1½ hours queueing, even at 5 p.m. Hotel Weisses Kreuz at Furrengasse 19 (Tel. 516023) is an old city hotel within the 30–35 F bracket, and is as good as you can expect. Hotel Jlge, Pfistergasse 17 (Tel. 220917), is in the Old Town and one of the best buys in Lucerne. Dormitory beds are cheap, and include use of the pool and breakfast.

EATING AND NIGHTLIFE

Both tend to cater for monied European tourists, but if you walk the length of Hertensteinstrasse, you should come up with some suitable pub or restaurant, even if it's just Migros at No. 46, or a fast- food place.

Apart from the International Music Festival (mid-August–early September), Lucerne is exceptionally sedate. A pub with a collection of eurorailers determined to make merry will probably be your high spot, unless your budget is elastic.

● **Excursions:** The steamer cruises down the VIERWALDSTÄTTERSEE are well worth it. Inter Railers go half price, and you leave from the quay near the station (ask tourist information for details of the alternatives).

The huge towering mountain dominating Lucerne is MOUNT PILA-TUS (7,000 feet). To get up there, you'd do best to take the boat from Lucerne to ALPNACHSTAD (half price Inter Rail) and then travel up on the steepest cogwheel railway in the world. Return by cable car to KRIENS then bus 1 back to Lucerne. It's well worth the effort, and really is an experience you won't forget, assuming you manage to avoid the mid-afternoon crowds and can afford the 40 F fare.

Bern

There's nothing to keep you in Bern for much more than a day if you're a restless type. It's pretty but not spectacular, and once you've seen the CLOCK TOWER, BEAR PIT (complete with bears), GOTHIC CATHEDRAL and BERNESE HISTORICAL MUSEUM you've more or less done the rounds unless you collect Swiss stamps and want to visit the POSTAL MUSEUM.

STATION FACILITIES

	BERN BAHNHOF
Train information	7.30 a.m.–8.30 p.m.
	(Tel. 222404)
Reservations	7.30 a.m.–7.45 p.m.
Tourist information	Mon.–Sat.: 8 a.m.–6.30 p.m.
	Sun.: 10 a.m.–5 p.m.
Foreign exchange	6.10 a.m.–10 p.m.
Left-luggage lockers	No access 12 midnight–4 a.m.
Left-luggage store	6 a.m.–12 midnight
Bar, Buffet	4 a.m.–11.30 p.m.
Shops	Tue.–Fri.: 6.30 a.m.–6.30 p.m.
	Sat.: 6.30 a.m.–5 p.m.
	Mon.: 2 p.m.–6.30 p.m.
Bath, Shower	6.30 a.m.–8 p.m.
Station shuts	12 midnight–4 a.m.

Daily trains to: Brussels, Basel, Milan, Zürich, Lausanne, Geneva.

TOURIST INFORMATION AND ADDRESSES

The main tourist office is the one at the station upstairs. When they close, they leave information on accommodation posted up outside, and there's a free phone to make reservations.

POST OFFICE: Schanzenpost 1, open Mon.–Fri.: 7.30 a.m.–6.30 p.m., Sat.: 7.30 a.m.–11 a.m.

AMEX: Marktgasse 37, open Mon.–Fri.: 8.15 a.m.–12.30 p.m., 1.30 p.m.–5.30 p.m., Sat.: 8.15 a.m.–12 noon.

UK EMBASSY: Thunstrasse 50 (Tel. 445021).

US EMBASSY: Jubiläumstrasse 93 (Tel. 437011).

CANADIAN EMBASSY: Kirchenfelderstrasse 88 (Tel. 446381).

AUSTRALIAN EMBASSY: Alpenstrasse 29 (Tel. 430143).

SLEEPING

Definitely avoid hotels here and stick to the youth hostel or campsite. The hostel is at Weihergasse 4 (Tel. 226316) near the Houses of Parliament. It closes 9.30 a.m.–5 p.m. (9 a.m.–6 p.m. on

Sun.) and is run quite strictly. Camping Eichholz is down by the river (Tel. 542602), a bit out of the city. Tram 9 to Eichholz. For a central pension, try Hotel Bahnhof-Süd, Bumplizstrasse 189 (Tel. 565111).

EATING AND NIGHTLIFE

The Mensa is at Gesellschaftstrasse 2. Their meals aren't terribly exciting, but at 3–6 F what do you expect? They close mid-July–August. For picnic food there are shops in Marktgasse and Zeughausgasse near the station, or there are always Migros for cheap meals. About the only place you can afford, or would find remotely lively, is the Kornhauskeller on Kornhausplatz. Don't eat there, but go for the local beer.

● **Excursions:** The best day trip you can take from Bern is to the ancient town of FRIBOURG, only 20 minutes away. The river that runs through it, the Sarine, is commonly regarded as the boundary line between the French- and German-speaking sections of Switzerland. Visit the ÉGLISE DES CORDELIERS with its original St Anthony altar-piece, and take in the view from the bridges that span the river. Most of the sights are on rue de Morat: the church mentioned above, the CATHEDRAL, the sixteenth-century TOWN HALL and the MUSEUM OF ART AND HISTORY.

The Bernese Oberland

The region round INTERLAKEN is stunning in its beauty, but from a eurorailer's point of view, unless you're stopping off to ski or climb, there's not that much to see apart from the scenery. Only an hour from Bern, Interlaken is a good base for heading off into the Bernese Oberland, though Inter Rails are not valid on any of the private railways that take you there. If you've decided that, now you're this far, you want to spend a bit of time here, consider buying a rail pass from this area's private railways board. It costs 92 F for five days' unlimited travel on trains and the expensive cable cars and 'gondolas' which hoist you up thousands of feet in next to no time. It also gives you the remaining ten days' travel at half price; still it is a lot of money, so make sure you'll use it to the full. Tourist information is at Höheweg, as well as at Westbahnhof; and for rooms, look at the bulletin board at Westbahnhof listing the Zimmer frei alternatives.

GRINDELWALD is *the* destination for serious climbers. What with the NORTH FACE OF THE EIGER, the JUNGFRAU and the MÖNCH, you won't know where to begin. There are hourly trains here from Interlaken, though Inter Rail's not valid. If you get this far, don't leave till you've taken the cable car to MÄNNLICHEN, WENGEN and up to PFINGSTEGG. From Pfingstegg, walk to STIEREGG. More than likely, this will be the high spot of your travels in this spectacular country. KLEINE SCHEIDEGG and JUNGFRAUJOCH are also in this area and accessible with the help of an extortionately priced mountain railway. If you're staying, try for the youth hostel Die Weid at Terrassenweg (Tel. 531009), or camp. If this has whetted your appetite, you might as well carry on to the MATTERHORN. Your best base for excursions here is ZERMATT which you reach by private railway from BRIG or VISP (Inter Railers half price). Tourist information is to the right of the station. They'll fix you up with maps, hiking suggestions and a bed. Hotel Bahnhof opposite the station is reasonable and has dormitories as well as rooms.

Lausanne

The French Alps are visible from Lausanne, home of the most spectacular Gothic building in Switzerland: its cathedral; the old medieval quarter is the most interesting (as the rest of the town is very modern) and here you'll find the HÔTEL DE VILLE, the EARLY GOTHIC CATHEDRAL and the CHÂTEAU SAINTE MAIRE, the Bishop's Palace. The funicular to OUCHY will take you down to the busy port which looks over to Lake Geneva and the Alps. Of the museums try to take in COLLECTION DE L'ART BRUT in the Château de Beaulieu where there are interesting exhibits by psychologically disturbed people, criminals and recluses.

TOURIST INFORMATION AND ADDRESSES

TOURIST OFFICE: 60 Avenue d'Ouchy, open Mon.–Fri.: 8 a.m.–7 p.m., Sat. and Sun.: 8 a.m.–12 noon, 1 p.m.–7 p.m., and at the station. They'll kit you out with maps, etc., and arrange accommodation.
POST OFFICE: Avenue de la Gare, open Mon.–Fri.: 7.30 a.m.–12 noon, 1.45 p.m.–6.30 p.m. (closed Saturday p.m.).
AMEX: 14 Avenue Mon Repos, open Mon.–Fri.: 8.15 a.m.–12.15 p.m., 1.45 p.m.–5.30 p.m., Sat.: 8 a.m.–12 noon.

SLEEPING

The youth hostel's down by the lake at Chemin du Muguet 1 (Tel. 265782). Bus 1 to Batelière (direction La Maladière), then follow the signs. The very good campsite is also by the lake: Camping de Vidy-Lausanne (Tel. 242031). For rooms or dormitories, try Foyer la Croisée, 15 Avenue Marc Dufour (Tel. 204281); or Logement des Prés-de-Vidy, Chemin Bois-de-Vaux 36 (Tel. 242479); Hôtel Pension Select, 10 rue des Terreaux (Tel. 223316).

EATING AND NIGHTLIFE

Food shouldn't be a problem. There are plenty of grocers' and bakers' shops to buy from, and no shortage of affordable restaurants, but watch out down in Ouchy – most restaurants are overpriced. There's no unique nightlife here, except in the Festival and Fête in late June, when the town offers plenty to do at night.

Basel (Basle)

Situated on the crossroads of France, Germany and Switzerland, Basel is the country's second city and is considered the cultural capital of Switzerland. From Basel you can take the train just about anywhere in Europe, from Warsaw to Stockholm.

STATION FACILITIES

As Basel is the border, the French effectively share the station with the Swiss. You'll find information for both SNCF and SBB at the station. French trains stop at the west end of the station.

	BASLE BAHNHOF
Train information	SBB 6 a.m–9.45 p.m.
	(Tel. 225011)
	SNCF 7.30 a.m.–7 p.m.
	(Tel. 225033)
Reservations	8 a.m.–7.30 p.m.
Tourist information	6 a.m.–9.45 p.m.
Foreign exchange	Mon.–Sat.: 6 a.m.–11.15 p.m.
	Sun.: 6 a.m.–10.30 p.m.
Left-luggage lockers	No access 0.30 a.m.–4 a.m.
Left-luggage store	5.30 a.m.–12 midnight
Bar, Buffet	6 a.m.–11 p.m.
Shops	Mon.–Fri.: 7 a.m.–6.30 p.m.
	Sat.: 7.30 a.m.–4 p.m.
Bath, Shower	Mon.–Sat.: 7.30 a.m.–4 p.m.
Post office	Mon.–Fri.: 7.30 a.m.–12 noon,
	1.45 p.m.–6.30p.m.
	Sat.: 7.30 a.m.–11 a.m.
Station shuts	0.30 a.m.–4 a.m.

TOURIST INFORMATION AND ADDRESSES

As well as the one at the station, there's a tourist office at Blumenrain 2.
POST OFFICE: Nauenstrasse, next to station. Open Mon.–Sat.: 6 a.m.–11 p.m., Sun.: 9 a.m.–12 noon, 3 p.m.–11 p.m.
AMEX: c/o Reisebüro Kundig, Aesdiengraben 10, open Mon.–Fri.: 8.15 a.m.–6 p.m.

SEEING

It's the museums in Basel that hog the limelight. If you're tired of trudging round museums and galleries, just take in the two bare essentials: the FINE ARTS MUSEUM and the CHERRY ORCHARD

MUSEUM, housed in an old patrician mansion at Elisabethenstrasse 27. As for the town itself, the twelfth-century MÜNSTER (Cathedral) is surrounded by medieval houses and stands in an attractive square. The TOWN HALL is on Market Square, and there are still markets held here today; THREE COUNTRIES' CORNER is the spot where the Swiss, French and German borders all meet.

SLEEPING

The large youth hostel is at St Alban-Kirchrain (Tel. 230572). As far as hotels go, try the following, but insist on their cheapest rooms: Hotel Bernerhof, Elisabethenstrasse 62 (Tel. 230955); Hotel Engel, Kasernenstrasse (Tel. 912511); or Hotel Engelhof Garni, Stiftgasse 1 (Tel. 252244). They start at 35 F single, 65 F double.

EATING AND NIGHTLIFE

You shouldn't have many problems finding shops and cafés to feed yourself from, there are plenty of alternatives. Zum Goldenen Sternen, the oldest pub in Switzerland, at St Albanrheinweg 70, is good for a drink, but watch the food prices. 'This Week in Basel' will fill you in on events, and if you're there around Ash Wednesday, you should catch some local festivities.

Geneva (Genève)

This is perhaps the most international of all European cities, home to dozens of multinational organizations and peace-negotiating bodies such as the Red Cross and United Nations. The town has a rich and well-cared-for air, and is a good place to break up a long haul like Paris–Rome.

STATION FACILITIES

	GENÈVE CORNAVIN
Train information	7.30 a.m.–9 p.m.
	(Tel. 316450)
Reservations	7.30 a.m.–8 p.m.
Tourist information	*Summer*: 9 a.m.–12 midnight
Foreign exchange	Mon.–Fri.: 5.15 a.m.–10.45 p.m.
	Sat.–Sun.: 5.15 a.m.–8.45 p.m.
Left-luggage lockers	No access 1 a.m.–4 a.m.
Left-luggage store	All hours
Snack bar	5 a.m.–12 midnight
Bath, Shower	Mon.–Sat.: 7 a.m.–7 p.m.
	Sun.: 7 a.m.–12 noon
Post office	6 a.m.–10.45 p.m. (next building)
Station shuts	1 a.m.–4 a.m.

Daily trains to: Lausanne, Basel, Bern, Zürich, Milan, Rome, Nice, Barcelona, Lyon, Paris.

TOURIST INFORMATION

The station office operates only in summer. The main office is at 2 Tour de l'Ile, open Mon.–Fri.: 8.15 a.m.–6 p.m., Sat.: 9 a.m.–5 p.m., Sun.: 10 a.m.–12 noon, 2 p.m.–5 p.m.

• **Addresses:**
POST OFFICE: Poste Gare Cornavin (next to the station).
AMEX: 7 rue du Mont Blanc, open Mon.–Fri.: 8.30 a.m.–5.30 p.m., Sat.: 9 a.m.–12 noon.
UK CONSULATE: 37–39 rue Vermont (Tel. 343800).
US CONSULATE: 11 route Pregny (Tel. 990211).
MEDICAL HELP: 'Permanence', rue Chantepoulet 21.

SEEING

Most of the things to see in Geneva can be taken in on the one main walk. Starting from the station, walk down RUE DU MONT BLANC till you're at the lake, then turn right on QUAI DES BERGUES, cross the river on the PONT DE L'ILE to the PLACE BEL-AIR, then head on to the PLACE NEUVE down RUE DE LA CORRATERIE. Once here, enter the park which contains the university and the famous statue to the Reformation. The VIEILLE VILLE is the old cobblestoned quarter round the CATHÉDRALE ST PIERRE, where Calvin preached. On RUE HÔTEL-DE-VILLE is the TOWN HALL where the Geneva Convention was signed, and some seventeenth-century houses built by Italian religious refugees. The best museums are the PETIT PALAIS (Impressionist paintings), INSTITUT ET MUSÉE VOLTAIRE, 25 rue des Délices (Voltaire's house), and the PALAIS DES NATIONS on Avenue de la Paix. Geneva is the world's top watchmaking centre, so hide your Japanese digital and wander round the WATCH MUSEUM, 15 rue de Malagnou (closed Mondays). Boat trips on Lake Geneva (Lac Léman) are pleasant, but compare prices first.

SLEEPING

Summer in Geneva makes affordable beds scarce, so arrive early and immediately aim at getting fixed up. Ask tourist information for their list of foyers, dormitories, etc., and phone around. The youth hostel is on rue des Plantaporrets (Tel. 290619), 20 minutes from the station. Reception closes 10 a.m.–4 p.m. The nearest campsite is Sylvabelle, 10 Chemin de Conches (Tel. 470603); take bus 3 to Rond Point de Rive, then bus 8 or 88. Maison des Jeunes, 5 rue du Temple (Tel. 322060), is a hostel for anyone. It's central but basic. Hôtel St Pierre, at Cour St Pierre by the Cathedral, is a great place. It takes couples or women and is deservedly popular (Tel. 283707). The Coopérative du Logement, rue H. Senger 2 (Tel. 292033), is the handling office to fill the four university dormitories. They charge around 30 F each. Alternatively, you could stay just over the border in France.

EATING AND NIGHTLIFE

Geneva definitely aims its tourism at the well-heeled, but there are some Migros and budget restaurants dotted around. A picnic down by the lake is your cheapest and most memorable option, but if it's wet, try the restaurant opposite the station on 17 Place Montbrillant, or Le Zofage, the university's place at rue des Voisins, with cheap filling plats du jour.

Tourist information will tell you what's on. Geneva actually has the most swinging nightlife in Switzerland, but then that's not hard. Before you get excited, I'm afraid there's nothing much you can afford, so content yourself manwatching in Place Molard or head for a lively bar like Mr Pickwick's Pub, 80 rue Lausanne.

The Grisons (Graubünden)

From the source of the Rhine east to the River Inn and on to Austria is the canton of Grisons. Here you'll still hear Romansh spoken along with Swiss-German. CHUR is the cultural and administrative centre, and such flashy resorts as St Moritz are in this region. The trains are narrow-gauge, but Inter Rails are valid. Take the CHUR-ST MORITZ line (2½ hours), even if you don't get off at the other end, as the scenery is quite beautiful.

Chur

Walk through the old-town streets with their medieval houses and pass through the old gate to the CATHEDRAL, with its pre-Christian sacrificial stone. The HOF (Bishop's Palace) next door is still in use, so don't nose about too much. The pub in there (the Hofkellerei) is a good watering-hole, but a bit touristy in summer. Tourist information is at Ottostrasse 8, Bahnhofplatz, and there's a good youth hostel at Berggasse 28 (Tel. 226563).

St Moritz

The actual town's nothing special, and apart from the ENGADINE MUSEUM en route to the famed healing waters of the MAURITIUS SPRINGS which reconstructs life of days long ago, there's not much else to see. But people don't come here to sightsee, they come to ski or climb. The general information centre is Kur-und-Verkehrsverein on Place Mauritius, open Mon.–Sat.: 9 a.m.–12 noon, 2 p.m.–6 p.m.

If your time's short, do just two things: take the cable car up the 8,000-foot MUOTTAS MURAGL and walk the path along the SILS LAKE. If your're staying, try your best to get into the youth hostel at Via Serpunt (Tel. 33969). It's beautiful, and cheap by Swiss standards. There's camping at Olympiaschanze (Tel. 34090) about 30 minutes from the station. Forget hotels; you're outclassed here, I'm afraid.

If you're heading for Italy, take the train in the direction of TIRANO on the Italian border (1½ hours) as the scenery around here and on the Passo del Bernina is incredible. Get off at every station and make a day of it, if you've time, as this is the highest line in Europe without cogs or cables.

Ticino

This region, next to Italy and known as the 'Swiss Riviera', has the best of both countries: the scenery, tidiness and efficiency of Switzerland, and the sun, language and ambience of Italy. Lugano and Locarno are the main centres and the area round the lakes of Lugano and Maggiore makes wonderful camping, swimming and walking, away from the crowds.

Lugano

This is a particularly pretty town of sunny piazzas, palm trees and the dominating Monte San Salvatore. It's on LAKE LUGANO, and lies on the Zürich–Milan main line. Stroll through the little winding streets on the hill at SAN LORENZO for a view over the town, stopping off at SANTA MARIA DEGLI ANGIOLI to admire the sixteenth-century frescoes. Walk down to the lake and Riva Albertolli 5 where the tourist office is. They're open Mon.–Fri.: 8 a.m.–12 noon, 2 p.m.–6 p.m., Sat.: 9 a.m.–12 noon, 2 p.m.–5 p.m., Sun.: 10 a.m.–12 noon, and they'll give you maps, lists of the local mountain huts, and arrange accommodation.

The VILLA FAVORITA CASTAGNOLA houses one of Europe's finest private art collections: Rembrandts, Dürers, Rubens, etc. It's open Fri. and Sat.: 10 a.m.–12 noon, 2 p.m.–5 p.m., Sun.: 2 p.m.–5 p.m., 7 F. From the Paradiso quarter, it's a 10-minute ride on the funicular up MONTE SAN SALVATORE, with a great view over the Alps and lakes. The funicular from Via Cassarate up to MONTE BRÉ on the other side of the town is another scenic excursion.

There's a youth hostel in Lugano-Crocifisso (at the terminus of bus 5) of an exceptionally high standard (Tel. 562728). Aris Pensioni, Via Guidan 15 (Tel. 541478), in nearby Paradiso is a good place to stay or eat, with rooms averaging 25 F per person and meals 15 F. There are plenty of markets and food shops offering Swiss-quality Italian food. Commercios on Via Lodovico Ariosto do great pizzas. In the evening there are often concerts down by the lake, but nightlife here is fairly sedate in general.

Locarno

From Lugano it's about half an hour to Ticino's capital BELLINZONA, and from there another half-hour will take you into Locarno, the best place to base yourself for trips round LAKE MAGGIORE. To explore this region you'll need to resort to buses. One of the buses from Locarno station goes through Ascona, Brissago and crosses the Italian border at Madonna di Ponte. Get off at Brissago and make for the island where there's a beautiful botanical garden.

Back in Locarno itself there's a MUSEUM OF MODERN ART in Castello Visconti, and funiculars to take you up to see the town's landmark, the MADONNA OF THE ROCK. Try the Gottardo (Tel. 334454) above the station for a bed. The private Centrovalli railway from Locarno to Domodossola on the Milan–Brig line is well worth re-routing for.

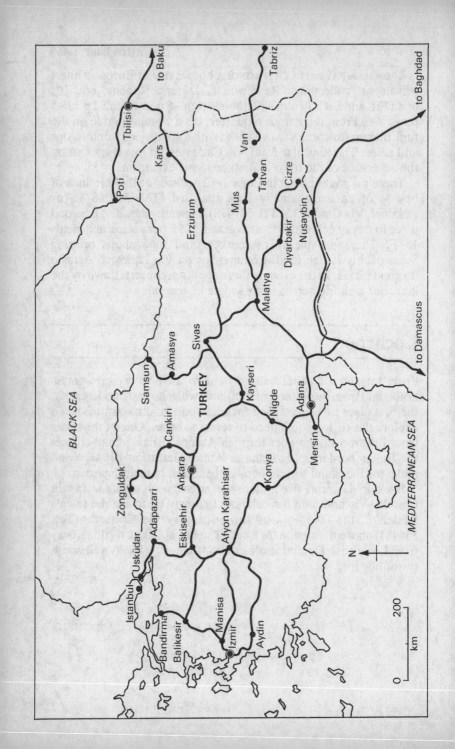

TURKEY

Entry requirements	Passport
Population	50,000,000
Capital	Ankara (pop.: 3,000,000)
Currency	Lira
	£1 = approx. 525 TL
Political system	Republic
Religion	Muslim
Language	Turkish (some English and French spoken in cities)
Public holidays	1 Jan.; 19 May; 30 Jun.–2 Jul. 3-day Muslim lunar holiday; 30 Aug.; 6 Sep.–9 Sep. 4-day Muslim lunar holiday; 29 Oct.

Only 3 per cent of Turkey is in Europe, the rest lies firmly in Asia. The Islamic and European blend of culture makes Turkey a fascinating experience and quite different from a jaunt through Europe. Of its previous civilizations, the best-preserved remains are to be found on the west and south coasts, the Aegean and Mediterranean. Until 1453 the European area of Turkey was under the umbrella of the Christian Byzantine Empire, but the Ottoman conquest put a stop to this. From then on there was no looking back, and under Süleiman the Magnificent (1520–63) the Ottoman Empire reached its zenith; it was largely thanks to him that the Christianity-versus-Islam wars of the sixteenth century were staged. It wasn't till the eighteenth and nineteenth centuries that this powerful empire went into decline; however, once it did the gradual process of westernization began. After the First World War Turkey was divided into British, French and Italian spheres of influence. The result was the War of Independence 1919–23. No one did more for the modernization of Turkey in the twentieth century than their national hero Atatürk, but though he made tremendous progress, travelling in Turkey for women alone today can be a very risky business and their attitude towards drugs is still extremely harsh, so avoid getting involved. Don't, however, get the idea the Turks are a hostile and unfriendly lot as, if you're befriended over there by a local, the hospitality they'll show you will leave any European pleasantries standing.

TURKISH STATE RAILWAYS
(Turkiye Cumhuriyeti Devlet Demiryollari Isletmesi, TCDD)

Even the tourist board officially describes expresses as being relatively slow. Think twice about travelling via northern Greece as the authorities feel obliged to make the train wait as long as possible at the border before moving on at a snail's pace to Istanbul (12 hours). Unfortunately, your problems don't end there, as most trains are crowded, dirty and unreliable. This is worst in Asia where trains are liable to be cancelled or altered without notice. From 1985 'European Turkey' is included in the Inter Rail scheme.

TRAIN INFORMATION

English is spoken by the information staff in big cities, while German and French are more useful elsewhere.

• **Reservations:** It's always advisable to reserve between Istanbul and Ankara, particularly if you want a couchette or to travel first class.

• **Night travel:** Generally, this is the best way of travelling in Turkey. There are first- and second-class couchettes to choose from.

• **Eating on trains:** Always be prepared with your own drinks. All expresses have a mini-bar or buffet.

TOURIST INFORMATION

There are tourist offices in all the major cities and tourist centres.

• **ISIC bonuses:** 50 per cent off museums, cinemas, concerts, and 20 per cent off rail tickets within Turkey. For further information, contact the nearest Turkish tourism and information office.

• **Money matters:** 1 Turkish lira (TL) = 100 kurus.
Banking hours are Mon.–Fri.: 8.30 a.m.–12 noon, 1.30 p.m.–5 p.m. Bear the following points in mind: Turkish banks give really lousy rates for Greek drachmas; it's definitely not worth the risk changing

money on the black market; twenty-four-hour exchange facilities are thin on the ground and there are none at stations; inflation has been running at about 40 per cent for several years, so bear this in mind when looking at our prices, which were collected in 1984.

• **Post offices:** Open Mon.–Fri.: 8.30 a.m.–12 noon, 1 p.m.–5.30 p.m. Major post offices stay open till 12 midnight, Mon.–Sat. and 9 a.m.–7 p.m., Sun.

• **Shops:** Open Mon.–Sat.: 9 a.m.–1 p.m., 2 p.m.–7 p.m., Sun.: 9 a.m.–5 p.m.

• **Museums:** All museums shut on Mondays, except for the Topkapi Palace which shuts on Tuesdays. Most offer half price at weekends.

SLEEPING

There's no problem finding cheap accommodation in Turkey, but we can't guarantee you'll be happy with the standards of cleanliness. Tourist information help out here and will find you a room in your price bracket. Basically, the hotels registered with the tourist board are called 'touristic' and are graded deluxe, 1, 2, 3 and 4. Also there are plenty with no grades at all, many of which are dirty but safe enough. In general, though, discretion is the better part of valour when it comes to a shady set-up. Expect to pay from 900 TL upwards for a half-decent double. Always check the room first and be prepared to bargain if the price seems too high. This tends to be the norm along the Bosphorus, but there's normally a 25 per cent reduction off season. There are very few pensions in Turkey and private accommodation is not formally recognized. Student dormitories are another option during July and August, as are youth hostels of which there are about 45 in Turkey; most of them allow you to stay if you have a student card, but it's best to have an IYHC to be on the safe side. Campsites are growing in number but are still a bit primitive in their facilities.

EATING AND NIGHTLIFE

Turkish cuisine is among the best in Europe for sheer good value. The variety of dishes is staggering and, as often as not, you're invited into the kitchen to choose your own. (If you don't like the look of things while you're in, now's your chance to skip out with a suitable excuse.) Turkish specialities include dolmas (just about anything stuffed with rice) and anything called 'sis' (like siskebabh) is done on a spit. Kadin budu is a concoction of fried rice and meatballs and, literally translated, means 'woman's thigh' (we don't quite see the analogy). Then how about kadin gobegi ('woman's navel') for dessert? The wine's not bad and the grape brandy, raki, is hot stuff. Expect to pay around 1,000 TL for a full meal including wine, though you *can* eat for a lot less.

The Turks are big folk-dancers and you should be able to catch each region's favourite without too many problems. The Turkish coffee houses (Kahve) are great meeting places and, of course, there's always the Turkish bath. Go and see a belly dancer if there's one advertised, even though they're terribly commercialized these days, but avoid the poor Western imitations of discos and clubs.

Istanbul

Incredible mosques share the spotlight with bazaars and the largest Roman building in the world in this fascinating city, and the blend of Asia and Europe makes it quite unique. If you're thinking of a trip to Turkey, make this your destination. It's dirty and pretty rough in some parts, and the intensive train travel will give you ulcers, but there's so much here to catch the eye and imagination that it's all worthwhile.

STATION FACILITIES

Sirkeci is the main station of Istanbul; from here leave the trains bound for Sofia, Belgrade, Athens and the West. Haydarpasa is the city's other station, on the opposite shore of the Bosphorus; services to Asia, Ankara, Anatolia, Iran, Syria and Baghdad leave from here.

Facilities at both stations tend to close down at night and there is no bath/shower at either station.

TOURIST INFORMATION AND ADDRESSES

TOURIST OFFICES: 57B Meşrutiyet Caddesi, Galatasaray; Divanyolu Caddesi, Sultanahmet; entrance of Hilton Hotel; Karaköy Harbour Terminal; Yeşilköy Airport.

POST OFFICE: 25 Yeni Postane Çokak (two blocks from Sirkeci Station).

AMEX: Hilton Hotel. Will sell, but not cash, traveller's cheques.

TOURIST POLICE: Across from St Sophia at beginning of Yerebetan Caddesi, open 9 a.m.–8 p.m. (Tel. 285369).

UK CONSULATE: 34 Meşrutiyet Caddesi, Tepebasi (Tel. 1447540).

US CONSULATE: 104 Meşrutiyet Caddesi, Tepebasi (Tel. 1453220).

STUDENT TRAVEL: Gencturs, 15/3 Yerebatan Caddesi (Tel. 280734); open Mon.–Sat.: 8.30 a.m.–6.30 p.m. Free maps, poste restante, student cards, etc.

MEDICAL HELP: 100 Siracevizler Caddesi (Tel. 1435500).

• **Getting about:** There are cheap buses which leave from Taksim Square. The communal taxis are also a good buy. They have routes between the main quarters, though if you specify you should get dropped off where you ask. Don't take the official taxis unless you agree a price beforehand or are sure it has a meter.

SEEING

Basically, Istanbul divides into two main areas which are further subdivided into several small districts. The European part of the city is divided by the GOLDEN HORN, and the European and Asian parts are separated by the BOSPHORUS STRAIT. The vast majority of sights are on the southern bank of the Golden Horn.

OLD STAMBOUL is the old walled city across the Golden Horn and it looks like something out of the 'Fry's Turkish Delight' advert. The mosques and palaces are wonderful examples, as good as you'll find anywhere, especially ST SOPHIA, built in AD 347 by Constantine, then rebuilt in the sixth century after a fire. Today it's a museum, though some of the original mosaics can still be seen. The BLUE MOSQUE dating from the seventeenth century is an amazing feat of engineering, built, as it was, to bend with the force in times of earthquakes – a performance it has done twenty times already. You can go into any mosque in Istanbul as long as you take off your shoes and keep quiet. Not far from the Blue Mosque is the ornate FOUNTAIN OF SULTAN AHMED. The Roman HIPPODROME was the venue for chariot racing, and today there's a MOSAIC MUSEUM.

The GRAND BAZAAR (or Kapaliçarşi) is colourful and entertaining, but barter like mad before buying anything. The palace of the Ottoman Sultans, TOPKAPI SARAY, is today a complex of museums: have a look in the HAREM and TREASURY. There's enough here to interest you for hours (open 9 a.m.–5 p.m., closed Tuesdays and half price at weekends). The other notable museums are: the ARCHAEOLOGICAL MUSEUM, and the MUSEUM OF THE ANCIENT ORIENT, both of which are self-explanatory. Another couple of mosques worth taking in on your itinerary are the BEYAZIT, near the university, and the sixteenth-century SULEYMANIYE. As a break from the hot dirty city, take a cruise down the Bosphorus. Boats leave Galata Bridge on three-hour round cruises between Europe and Asia. They are dirt cheap, great fun and highly recommended.

SLEEPING

As long as you're not expecting Scandinavian-style cleanliness, you'll cope fine in Istanbul. Beds are cheap and plentiful, and as prices vary little between districts aim for the most central or convenient. Round the station is OK, but a bit on the noisy side. The central Sultanahmet quarter is near the sights and about the best place to head for.

Istanbul Youth Hostel, 63 Cerrahpaşa Cad, Aksaray (Tel. 212455), is OK, but hardly central. There are several campsites, but Yeşilyurt (Tel. 738408) or Ataköy (Tel. 720802) are two of the nicest. The Sultan Tourist Hotel on Yerebatan Cad (Tel. 5207676) is good, with doubles around 1,200 TL, or try the Güngör on Divan Yolu Cad (Tel. 262319), or the Yörük at 35 Inçiliçavuş Sok (Tel. 276476).

Don't try sleeping rough in Istanbul, it's not worth the risk; there are too many stories of muggings and rape. Don't bother with the black market here either, as police informers are out in abundance, especially in summer, and manage to make a good living out of turning in mugs who accept their offers. The same goes for drugs.

EATING AND NIGHTLIFE

You'll be pleasantly surprised on both scores here. It's possible to eat exceptionally well for next to nothing, whether you eat from the street stalls or at top restaurants. Fish and seafood are particularly good: go down to the Galata Bridge where there are dozens of seafood restaurants, or eat from the pavement fish-grilling stalls. If you've saved sufficient by getting into cheap accommodation, treat yourself to a proper Bosphorus meal (about 1,000 TL) of meze (mixed starters) and fresh fish. You'll have no trouble finding plenty of suitable places to patronize. The area behind the station (Eminonu) is a good area. Our only particular recommendation is the Murat Restaurant on Ordu Cad, Aksaray. Reasonable menus at good prices, next to the Hacibozan Ógullari Baklavaci.

Don't bother with the fabricated westernized nightlife of discos and nightclubs. To get a taste of real Istanbul, eat late and wander along Meşrutiyet Cad and sample the music in the little cafés. Sultanahmet Square will also be lively but can get pretty seedy late-on. There are a few pubs in the area, however, where you'll meet up with other eurorailers and hitchers. The Istanbul Festival is on from mid-June to mid-July but it's fairly classically minded (opera, concerts, etc.). Ask at tourist information for details. If you're after belly dancing, head for the Galatasaray district and Istiklâl St; or if you've promised yourself an authentic Turkish bath, ask at tourist information for their recommendations. Cağaloglu Hamami at Yerebatan Cad in Cağaloglu is excellent – the full works for 650 TL.

Izmir and Ankara

Transalpino also sells tickets to the port town of Izmir, which has nothing much to recommend it, and Ankara, the capital city. If you've time to kill in Izmir, take a look at the remains. In Ankara the tourist office is at 33 Gazi Kemal, open daily 8 a.m.–7 p.m. Get maps, etc., here. The US Embassy in Ankara is at Atatürk Bulvari 110 (Tel. 265470), the UK Embassy is at 46A Sehit Ersan Caddesi

(Tel. 274310), and the Canadian Embassy, 75 Nenehatun Caddesi (Tel. 275803). As far as sightseeing goes, head for ULUS, the old town where the CITADEL and MUSEUM OF ANATOLIAN CIVILIZATIONS are. This museum is exceptionally interesting and opens 9 a.m.– 12.30 p.m., 1.30 p.m.–6 p.m. (closed Mondays). The other main sight of Ankara is the tomb of their national hero, Atatürk. The museum and mausoleum have the same opening times as the museum mentioned above. Ask tourist information about accommodation, or stay in Ulus where there are plenty of cheap (and grotty) hotels.

UNITED KINGDOM

Entry requirements	Passport
Population	56,429,000
Capital	London (pop.: 7,550,000)
Currency	Sterling
	$1 = approx. 77p
Political system	Constitutional Monarchy
Religion	Protestant
Language	English
Public holidays	1, (2, 3 Scotland) Jan.; Good Friday; Easter Monday; 1st Monday in May; Spring Bank Holiday; (Early August Bank Holiday, Scotland), Late August Bank Holiday; 25, 26 Dec.

Even the British get confused about their nationhood, so it's not uncommon to hear 'England', 'Great Britain' and the 'United Kingdom' used incorrectly in conversation. The island of Great Britain isn't just England; it comprises Wales and Scotland too. Add to this Northern Ireland, and you have the United Kingdom of Great Britain and Northern Ireland, more commonly known as the UK.

England, the largest of the four countries, has always attracted the majority of immigrants from pre-Celtic times to the present day. With the Normans in 1066 came feudalism and a power struggle among the nobles. Pretty soon the barons were in a position to lay down the law and force King John to recognize their rights by getting him to sign the Magna Carta in 1215. By the end of the Tudor era, Henry VIII had been through six wives, and England was a prosperous nation. The seventeenth century saw a Civil War between the Parliamentarians and Cromwell, and the royalist supporters of Charles I. The eighteenth century began with the union of Scotland and England and continued with the development of the British Empire in North America and India. Britain was the world's leader in the Industrial Revolution, and became known as the 'workshop of the world'.

The economic strain of being heavily involved in two World Wars, and increased rivalry in the marketplace has led to her decline as a world power. From a eurorailer's point of view, the United Kingdom offers a diversity of not just geography but of history and culture too – all you'd expect from a country made up of four separate nations.

BRITISH RAIL (BR)

In recent years, British Rail have streamlined their services and improved their corporate image. In terms of speed and comfort they now rank on a par with France and excel over Germany. There are four main categories of trains: (1) The extra-fare Manchester Pullman which is first class only, and of no interest to Inter Railers. (2) High-speed trains (HSTs), commonly known as 125s, as this is the speed they travel at. These excellent trains, the fastest diesels in the world, are used on the long hauls. (3) The intercities are either diesel or electric and reach 110 m.p.h. on long runs. (4) The cross-country and local trains run on the more out-of-the-way routes or in the suburbs of the large towns. There are no supplements to worry about on any of these services. For details of the new discounts on the Hoverspeed Channel crossings, ask British Rail before travelling.

TRAIN INFORMATION

All main stations have their own information counters and there are free timetables for the main-line routes.

• **Reservations:** Never compulsory but advisable on main lines in summer.

• **Night travel:** No couchettes, only sleepers at around £12 for second class (two berths) and £16 for first class (single berth). A bonus is free tea and biscuits in the morning. All sleepers are air-conditioned and manufactured within the last five years.

• **Eating on trains:** Expensive restaurant cars run on all main lines, Mon.–Sat. Buffets with average-priced snacks run daily on the major routes.

• **Scenic tips:** There's nothing in Britain to compare with Switzerland or Norway, but the Lake District and parts of North Wales are interesting enough. The really scenic routes are up in the Scottish Highlands, particularly the Fort William–Mallaig and Glasgow–Oban runs.

• **Bikes:** There are no facilities for hiring out bikes at British Rail stations, so ask at the tourist office for local suggestions.

TOURIST INFORMATION

Every major city or town has its own tourist information office, and they will fix you up with accommodation for around 75p and supply you with maps and leaflets. There are also regional and national tourist boards who supply information.

• **ISIC bonuses:** Up to 50 per cent reduction at some monuments where you have to pay, but (in the main) museums and galleries are free. For further information, contact World Wide Student Travel, 37 Store Street, London WC1 (Tel. 580 7733), or NUS Travel, 12 Dublin Street, Edinburgh.

• **Money matters:** 1 pound (£) = 100 pence (p).
Banking hours are Mon.–Fri.: 9.30 a.m.–3.30 p.m. In Scotland banks close for lunch 12.30 p.m.–1.30 p.m., and Thursday is often a late opening. There are many bureaux de change open outside banking hours.

• **Post offices:** Open 9 a.m.–5.30 p.m., with sub-post offices generally closing for lunch; Sat.: 9 a.m.–1 p.m.

• **Shops:** 9 a.m.–5.30 p.m. is average. Large stores take no lunch breaks, and in London and major cities shops are open late on Wednesdays or Thursdays.

• **Museums:** 10 a.m.–5 p.m. is the norm, and in many cases entrance is free.

SLEEPING

The wonderful institution of Bed-and-Breakfast (B&B) is the cornerstone of accommodation in Britain, and between B&Bs and youth or student hostels you should easily get by. B&Bs average £7 and this includes an English breakfast (bacon, eggs, etc.) which should keep you going all day. Always go for small B&Bs where you'll feel like one of the family and will get good value for money. Hotels in Britain are very expensive and are best avoided. Many universities let out their student flats and hostels in summer, and these average £7 a night. Youth hostels charge according to your age and the facilities on offer. The borderline for reduced rates is age 21, and hostels are either 'simple, standard or superior' grade: expect to pay between £2 and £6. If you're thinking of doing much hostelling, pick up the 'YHA Guide to England and Wales' or 'Scotland YHA Guide' which will show you the locations, etc., of the hostels. It's possible to join the IYHA at most of the large hostels for around £6. As far as camping goes, the vagaries of British weather may make this a dicey proposition, but if you're keen count on £2–4 a night, and bring mosquito repellent and warm clothes.

The English and Scottish Tourist Boards have guides called 'Where to Stay' costing around £1. These aren't bad though they're a bit sparse on cheap suggestions. You'll do better getting the lists of local campsites and accommodation from tourist information, or using their bed-booking service for about 75p.

EATING AND NIGHTLIFE

British food has a bit of a bad reputation, but during the past decade or so much has been done to overcome this, and eating out in Britain today is no longer an expensive and tasteless affair. If you've got the cash, go for the traditional dishes like roast beef and Yorkshire pudding, or Scotch salmon and beefsteak. Often you'll find these on the set-lunch menus offered by hotels, and this is your chance to cash in and sample them at a reasonable price (£4 upwards). Always check if VAT (a 15 per cent tax) is included in the price, before deciding. For your picnics, look out for the impressive variety of British cheeses, Cheddar, Cheshire, Wensleydale, Double Gloucester, Stilton, etc., and shop at stores like Marks & Spencer, British Home Stores, Safeway and Sainsbury's, where you can be sure the produce is fresh and reasonably priced. While in the UK, at least once try to partake in the age-old custom of afternoon or 'high' tea. This filling snack of scones, jam, cream and tea is often served in even the most luxurious hotels for only a pound or two, and it really gives an insight into the civilized Britain of yesteryear.

It's possible to make out in Britain on very little indeed if you know where to look. All the major centres have fast-food chains of some description, and even the smallest village has its own local fish'n'chip shop where you can fill up for just about £2. Chinese and Indian meals are also good value, as (in general) are pub lunches.

The pub is the mainstay of British social life and this is where you should make for to meet the locals. Many pubs, however, are soulless places and don't merit five minutes of your time, so be selective and choose either one with a historical connection or those that go to the effort of putting on live music. Pubs open 11 a.m.–2 p.m., 5.30 p.m.–10.30 p.m. in general. Some pubs in Scotland remain open all afternoon but are closed on Sundays. You must be over 18 to drink alcohol. The English and Welsh pride themselves on their 'real ale', the Scots on their whisky and the Irish on their Guinness.

London is the home of British theatre and cinema – but this doesn't mean other cities are dead ducks; Edinburgh's International Festival and Fringe in August–September puts London in the shade for the three or four weeks it's on. In general, the live music and dancing scene is better in Britain than in most other European countries. Pick up the tourist board's list of current happenings from whichever town you're in, and remember to try for student discounts on theatre tickets, etc.

London

London is a must in any European wanderings. There are three Londons to take into account: the CITY of London (the financial and administrative centre of Great Britain), WESTMINSTER (the political, royal and religious centre), and the WEST END (home of the

British theatre and cinema, smart shops and clubs). Each area has a different feel to it, and the combination of all three with over a thousand years of history and traditions, plenty of open green spaces and the buzz of Europe's largest city, makes a visit here unforgettable.

STATION FACILITIES

There are eight stations in London, all interconnected by the fast and efficient tube (underground railway). To ensure you're at the right station, here's a quick checklist of which station serves where:

• **Charing Cross:** Handles suburban lines and the London–Folkestone and London–Hastings trains. If you're travelling by hovercraft to France, this is also where you depart for Dover Priory.

• **Euston:** Central England and the north-west, Birmingham, Coventry, Liverpool, Manchester, Glasgow and on to Dublin.

• **King's Cross:** The north-east, Leeds, York, Hull, Newcastle and on to Edinburgh and Aberdeen. From Newcastle you sail to Norway, Denmark and Sweden.

• **Liverpool Street:** The area north-east of London, Cambridge, Harwich, Norwich. From Harwich you can sail to Holland, Germany, Sweden and Denmark.

• **Paddington:** The south-west of England, Exeter, Plymouth, Penzance, Bristol, Swansea, Oxford, Gloucester.

• **St Pancras:** Trains bound due north, Nottingham, Derby, Leicester, Sheffield.

• **Victoria:** South-east England, Newhaven, Brighton, Eastbourne, Hastings and Dover, the main gateway to France, Belgium, Spain, Italy, etc. The 40-minute train journey to Gatwick Airport leaves from here too.

• **Waterloo:** Trains to the south of England, Bournemouth, Portsmouth, Southampton and Weymouth.

We are reliably informed by British Rail that the stations detailed below are the ones you are most likely to use.

	KING'S CROSS	VICTORIA
Train information	24 hours (Tel. 278 2477)	7.30 a.m.–9.30 p.m. (Tel. 928 5100)
Reservations	Mon.–Sat.: 7.15 a.m.–8 p.m. Sun.: 8 a.m.–8 p.m.	7.30 a.m.–9.30 p.m.
Tourist information	–	9 a.m.–9 p.m.
Foreign exchange	Sun.–Thur.: 8 a.m.–8 p.m. Fri. and Sat.: 8 a.m.–9.30 p.m.	T. Cook office 8.15 a.m.–9 p.m.
Left-luggage lockers	–	Always access
Left-luggage store	Open daily	Open daily
Bar, Buffet	Mon.–Sat.: 11 a.m.–3 p.m. 4.30 p.m.–11 p.m., Sun.: 12 noon–2 p.m., 7 p.m.–10.35 p.m.	7 a.m.–10.40 p.m.
Restaurant	Mon.–Sat.: 7 a.m.–10 a.m. 11 a.m.–7 p.m.	7 a.m.–10 p.m.
Self-service	7 a.m.–9 p.m. daily	–
Showers	Ladies only. Open 24 hours	Closed temporarily
Post office	In road opposite station	None
Station shuts	Only Christmas Day and Boxing Day	Always open

	EUSTON	LIVERPOOL STREET
Train information	6.45 a.m.–10 p.m. daily (Tel. 387 7070)	7.15 a.m.–10.30 p.m. daily (Tel. 283 7171)
Reservations	6.45 a.m.–9.45 p.m.	Mon.–Sat.: 8 a.m.–6.45 p.m.
Tourist information	Mon.–Fri.: 8 a.m.–8 p.m. Sat.: 8 a.m.–6 p.m.	8 a.m.–6 p.m.
Foreign exchange	6.30 a.m.–11 p.m.	7.30 a.m.–8.30 p.m.
Left-luggage lockers	None	None
Left-luggage store	Open 24 hours	7 a.m.–10.30 p.m.
Bar, Buffet	7 a.m.–10 p.m.	7.30 a.m.–10.30 p.m.
Restaurant	7 a.m.–10 p.m.	Mon.–Fri.: 8 a.m.–9 p.m.

	EUSTON	LIVERPOOL STREET
Bath, Shower	Mon.–Fri.: 7 a.m.–10 p.m.	None
	Weekends: 11 a.m.–6 p.m.	
Shops	8 a.m.–6 p.m.	Various times, Mon.–Sat.
Post office	None	None
Station shuts	Open 24 hours	Open 24 hours

CROSS-CHANNEL FERRIES

The ferries to Calais, Dieppe, Boulogne, Dunkirk and Ostend are usually packed out in high season, so before embarking on the crossing take a look at the alternatives open to you. Sealink, SNCF and the Belgian ferries offer discounts to Inter Rail holders, and with the Britrail Pass you purchase a special coupon for a reduced fare to France. By far the most civilized form of Channel crossing is to use the Jetfoil from Dover to Ostend, or the hovercraft from Dover to Boulogne. For the £5 supplement you get a guaranteed seat, far shorter crossing, and a speedier city-to-city connection.

TOURIST INFORMATION

England, Northern Ireland, Wales and Scotland have separate Tourist Boards, all of which have offices in London. The National Tourist Information Centre at Victoria Station forecourt carries information on London and England. Leaflets, maps, guidebooks, tourist tickets for buses and the underground, and sightseeing tour and theatre tickets are available. Same-day hotel accommodation can be booked. The Centre is open seven days a week, 9 a.m.–8.30 p.m. with longer hours in July and August.

Information on Northern Ireland is available from the Northern Ireland Tourist Board, Ulster Office, 11 Berkeley Street, London W1, open Mon.–Fri.: 9.05 a.m.–5.15 p.m. The Scottish Tourist Board is at 19 Cockspur Street, London SW1, and is open

Mon.–Fri.: 9 a.m.–5 p.m., and the Wales Tourist Board is at 2–3 Maddox Street, London W1, open Mon.–Thur.: 9.15 a.m.–5.15 p.m. and Fri.: 9.15 a.m.–5 p.m.

The City of London Information Centre, with detailed information on the City as well as more general information, is directly across the road from St Paul's Cathedral. It is open Mon.–Fri.: 9.30 a.m.–5 p.m., Sat.: 9.30 a.m.–1 p.m. during April–September and 9.30 a.m.–12 noon October–March.

● **Addresses:**

POST OFFICE: King Edward Building, King Edward Street (tube, St Paul's), open Mon.–Fri.: 8 a.m.–7 p.m., Sat.: 9 a.m.–12.30 p.m. This is where all poste restante mail will end up. The twenty-four-hour post office is at St Martin's Place, Trafalgar Square.

AMEX: 6 Haymarket (tube, Piccadilly). Exchange open Mon.–Fri.: 9 a.m.–5 p.m., Sat.: 9 a.m.–6 p.m. (8 p.m. in season), Sun.: 10 a.m.–6 p.m.

US EMBASSY: 24 Grosvenor Square, W1 (Tel. 499 9000) (tube, Bond St).

TRANSALPINO: 71–75 Buckingham Palace Rd, SW1 (Tel. 834 9656) (tube, Victoria). Their same-day booking office is at Hudson Place, outside Victoria Station, near Platform 1.

● **Getting about:** The tube is efficient and fast, but expensive. Pick up an underground map, free at any station, and hang on to your ticket till the journey's through. Tubes run 6 a.m.–12 midnight. Like the tube, the red double-decker buses operate on a zone system, and you pay the conductor on the bus, while the single-decker Red Arrows are express buses with ticket machines on board. There are some night buses which run 12 midnight–5 a.m. on certain routes.

If you're in London for a while, pick up the leaflets on the Go-As-You-Please tourist tickets, etc., but these are expensive by other European standards. If you're taking a tube after 10 a.m. and returning to the same place the same day, buy a cheap day return which will save you up to a third. Unless you're in a desperate rush, don't bother with the expensive taxis and, though it's impossible to get round all the sights on foot, try to see as much as you can of London through walks. The 'London A–Z' (about £1.50) is the best long-term map investment you can make.

SEEING

London has swallowed many villages into its bulk in the course of its development, but even today each village (now district) has its own character and traditions. Soho, Hampstead and Chelsea are as different from each other as individual towns. It's easy to divide London into its three sections but this would neglect the areas that fall between, like trendy COVENT GARDEN, or the intellectual centre of BLOOMSBURY where the BRITISH MUSEUM and London University are located. Don't forget either the wonderful days out you can have at the maritime centre of GREENWICH, or at the Royal Botanical Gardens at KEW, or HAMPTON COURT PALACE, and many more. This rundown is just a small sample of what you can see, but once you've made your visit to tourist information, you should be in a position to work out your own best itinerary.

The City of London

The London of the eleventh century is that area known as 'the City'. In this 'square mile', the wheelings and dealings of the Stock Exchange and big business take place, and the Bank of England and Royal Exchange have their headquarters here. The sights include: the beautiful Renaissance cathedral of ST PAUL'S (the one Charles and Di chose for their wedding in 1981), where Nelson and Wellington are buried; FLEET STREET, the home of the British press; the INNS OF COURT and the OLD BAILEY – the heart of the British legal system; and the TOWER OF LONDON which dates back to William the Conqueror and has served as prison, palace and mint. The Crown Jewels, the White Tower and Tower Green where Henry VIII had Anne Boleyn and Catherine Howard executed, are among some of the sights to see here.

Westminster and the West End

Roughly, this stretches from HYDE PARK (the famous expanse with Speakers' Corner – a national venue for impromptu free speech on Sundays) to WESTMINSTER ABBEY, the incredible Gothic church so central to the country's history. WHITEHALL and the HOUSES OF PARLIAMENT, the centres of British government and administration, are along here, and so is the timekeeping landmark of London, Big Ben. To go in and listen to Parliament (a fascinating experience), line up at St Stephen's entrance opposite the Abbey. THE MALL is the boulevard leading from TRAFALGAR SQUARE, home of the NATIONAL GALLERY, to BUCKINGHAM PALACE, the home of the monarchy, which is not open to the public. The hub of the capital is PICCADILLY CIRCUS with its statue of Eros, and SOHO, the seamy cosmopolitan entertainment district that comes alive after dark. The museums to look out for in this part of London are: the TATE GALLERY at Millbank (a fine collection of modern masterpieces and sculpture); the VICTORIA AND ALBERT at Cromwell Road; the BRITISH MUSEUM, which is worth at least a day of anyone's time (everything, from the Elgin Marbles from the Acropolis to Magna Carta, is here); and MADAME TUSSAUD'S wax museum, where the famous are immortalized. The famous department store HARRODS where you can buy 'absolutely anything', is close to KNIGHTS-BRIDGE. Wander round the food hall there – they sell every type and variety of eats you'd ever imagined. Other shops worth taking in for their sheer entertainment value are LIBERTY'S (the neo-Tudor building on Regent Street) and FORTNUM AND MASON, Piccadilly.

SLEEPING

The possibilities are endless, but in the lower price-bracket (£6–8) you can't expect much in the way of comfort. London is busy all year, but in summer it's absolutely packed. Student and youth hostels average £8, halls of residence about £10, and B&B £12. Ask for leaflets on hostels, etc., at the London Tourist Board office in Victoria Station. There are five youth hostels: 36 Carter Lane (Tel. 236 4965) (tube, St Paul's), the largest in Britain; Holland House, Holland Walk, Kensington (Tel. 937 0748) (tube, Holland Park); 4 Wellgarth Rd, Hampstead (Tel. 458 9054) (tube, Golders Green, followed by bus 210 or 260); 38 Bolton Gdns (Tel. 373 7083) (tube, Earls Court); 84 Highgate West Hill (Tel. 340 1831) (tube, Archway, then bus 148, 210 or 271).

Other hostels: These range from a tent city to charity set-ups. Try some of the following: Tent City, Old Oak Common Lane (Tel. 743

5708) (tube, East Acton); Fieldcourt House, 32 Courtfield Gdns (Tel. 373 0152) (tube, Gloucester Rd); Astor Museum Hostel, 27 Montague St (Tel. 580 5360) (tube, Tottenham Court Rd); International Students House, 229 Gt Portland St (Tel. 631 3223) (tube, Great Portland St). If you're staying a while, two good ideas are to contact either the London University Students' Union (Tel. 636 2818) or Universal Aunts (Tel. 730 9834). Some of the cheaper B&Bs are really depressing, and you're invariably better in hostels, but anyway the areas to head for are Earls Court, Paddington and Bayswater. Simone House Hotel, 49 Belgrave Rd (Tel. 828 2474) (tube, Victoria); Leinster Hotel, 7–11 Leinster Square (Tel. 229 9641) (tube, Bayswater); Vicarage Hotel, 10 Vicarage Gate (Tel. 229 4030) (tube, Kensington High St). As far as camping goes, there are plenty of sites. Ask at tourist information. The best one is Pickett's Lock Centre, Pickett's Lock Lane (Tel. 803 4756) (tube, Seven Sisters, then bus 149, 259 or 279). It's a bit out of the way but very well equipped. The Tent City (see above) is probably the most central and your best bet.

With violence on the increase, it's stupid to sleep rough in London, but if you're determined to spend nothing, the embankment at Westminster Bridge, or Hyde Park are your best bets, though the police are becoming increasingly active in stamping this out.

EATING AND NIGHTLIFE

Eating for under £3 is no great problem with the spate of fast-food chains, Indian and Chinese restaurants and very good supermarkets increasing every year. Many pubs serve lunches and, of course, there's always the great British invention, fish'n'chips. Always check if VAT is included on a menu as this tax can fairly bump up the bill. You can't go too far wrong for fast food in McDonalds and Pizzaland, but branches of Wimpy vary dramatically. For the best non-European meals, head for Soho. Marks & Spencer, Safeway, Sainsbury's and British Home Stores are all reliable for high-quality groceries, and if it's a good day you can do no better than get a picnic together and head for one of the parks.

Cranks Health Foods, Covent Garden, and 196 Tottenham Court Road, are excellent but a bit pricey; in Soho, Poons, Leicester St,

Lee Ho Fook, Macclesfield St, and Chan May Mai, Lisle St, are all good value. For Indian food try around Bayswater, or for unbeatable value the Oval Tandoori Restaurant at 64A Brixton Road, SW9, which, although out of the centre, is worth the effort to get there.

Nightlife and London are inseparable from each other. London's no longer swinging the way it was in the 1960s, but there's still a lot happening. Your best source of information is the weekly magazine *Time Out*. The theatre is firmly entrenched in London's nightlife, and you really ought to try and make it along to a show. Take along your ISIC to any theatre displaying (S) in its write-up, and you will be able to get cheap standby tickets before the curtain rises. In summer there's open-air Shakespeare in Regent's Park. Expect an average theatre ticket to cost £5. There's music to suit all tastes on offer, from the 'Proms' classics in the Albert Hall to punk in The Marquee, 90 Wardour St.

There are endless lists of pubs, and these are as good a place as any to watch the locals in their habitat. Try the Sherlock Holmes, 10 Northumberland St, Dirty Dick's, 202 Bishopsgate, or Ye Olde Cheshire Cheese, just off Fleet St. Pubs open Mon.–Sat.: 11 a.m.–3 p.m., 5.30 p.m.–11 p.m., Sun.: 12 noon–2.30 p.m., 7 p.m.–10 p.m. With over 4,000 pubs in London, you're bound to find one to your liking. If you're after some 'heavy nightlife', a wander through Soho should take good care of that, or if you want to be entertained while having a drink, try the Allsop Arms, 137 Gloucester Place.

South-east England

If you're arriving in Britain from France or Belgium, chances are your first impressions will be of DOVER or FOLKESTONE. Dover, with its famous chalky white cliffs, dates back to the Romans and there are still remains to be seen from their time. If you've a bit of time to spend before making the direct two-hour journey to London, take in the NORMAN CASTLE, the PAINTED HOUSE (a Roman townhouse off New St, closed Monday), and the Roman PHAROS. Tourist information is near Dover Priory Station and at Townwall St. They'll give you help with accommodation if you're staying overnight.

Half an hour up one of the lines to London lies the ancient pilgrimage centre of CANTERBURY. The CATHEDRAL, where St Thomas à Becket was murdered in 1170, is well worth breaking your journey for, and not far from here you can see the remnants of the old city walls at DANE JOHN GARDENS. ST MARTIN'S CHURCH has evolved from fourth-century Roman villas and is one of the oldest churches in England. There are various remains of long-defunct religious orders: ST AUGUSTINE'S ABBEY outside the city's East Wall, and EASTBRIDGE HOSPITAL on St Peter's St, open Mon.–Sat.: 9.30 a.m.–5.30 p.m. Food and beds shouldn't cause you any problems, but Canterbury can easily be seen as a day trip from London.

Other noteworthy places in this area, though not on the Dover–London line, are CHICHESTER, WINCHESTER and BRIGHTON. Lying 1½ hours from the capital on the London–Portsmouth line, CHICHESTER holds a summer theatre festival worth investigation, and has a ROMAN PALACE and CATHEDRAL of note. Tourist information is at St Peter's Market, West St, open Mon.–sat.: 9.15 a.m.–5.30 p.m. WINCHESTER is a wonderful place, an archetypal English town. The CATHEDRAL is its pride, and rightly so. Walking down Cathedral Close, you'll come to WINCHESTER SCHOOL, England's first 'public' (private) school, which has nurtured the sons of the élite for six centuries. Not far from here (on bus route 214) is CHAWTON, home of the English novelist Jane Austen of *Pride and Prejudice* fame. Her house is open 11 a.m.–4.30 p.m. Winchester is on the London–Weymouth line, about 1½ hours down the line from London. Another ideal day trip from the capital is to BRIGHTON. Since the mid-eighteenth century, this has been a popular holiday resort, especially with the Victorians. In 1783 the ROYAL PAVILION was constructed when the Prince Regent came to settle here, and it's here and to the PALACE PIER you should head. Wander round the narrow streets from the Old Steine to West St. Tourist information is in Old Steine, open Mon.–Sat.: 9 a.m.–6 p.m., Sun.: 10 a.m.–6 p.m. in season.

South-west England

From the rail network point of view, we've divided the country so that we start the south-west at Salisbury and Bath, and extend down to Devon and Cornwall. This region is one of England's most picturesque and has some of the country's best weather.

Salisbury

Salisbury is dominated by its thirteenth-century CATHEDRAL, with the tallest spire in England. Take the tour round the cathedral and visit the cloisters and Chapter House. CATHEDRAL CLOSE was a religious city and you can still see some of its buildings, especially MOMPESSON HOUSE, now cared for by the National Trust.

Salisbury is on the London–Exeter and Bristol–Portsmouth lines, 1½ hours from London. This is the best place to stay if you want to visit the ancient religious site of STONEHENGE, ten miles north of Salisbury. If you know nothing of its history or aren't really interested don't bother making the trip as you won't understand what all the fuss is over. All that's there is a circle of stones they make you pay 30p to see, but they date back to 1500 BC, so that makes them rather special. It's thought they were an astronomical calendar, and later on, in 250 BC, the Druids used them for their sun-worshipping festivals. Ask at tourist information about getting there. The Salisbury office is 10 Endless St, open Mon.–Sat.: 9 a.m.–7 p.m. in season, and they'll help with accommodation. There's a youth hostel at Milford Hill (Tel. 27572) and several reasonable B&Bs.

Bath

Just 15 minutes from the city of BRISTOL, and in the south-west corner of the Cotswolds, lies the elegant Georgian spa town of BATH. This town was second only to London for style in the eighteenth century; successive generations of the aristocracy came to 'take the waters' and left behind an architectural legacy as rich as you'll find in England. Trains run hourly from London and the journey takes only 1¼ hours; if you're travelling on to Oxford you change at Didcot and Bath's proximity to Bristol means you could also use it as a jumping-off point for Devon and Cornwall.

SEEING

The heart of Georgian Bath is the CIRCUS, the circle of townhouses where the artist Gainsborough lived at No. 17, and William Pitt, the Prime Minister, at Nos. 7 and 8. Leaving the Circus at Brock St, you come to ROYAL CRESCENT, considered England's most attractive street. Visit No. 1 for an idea of elegant Georgian living. The MUSEUM OF COSTUME is particularly interesting, housed in the ASSEMBLY ROOMS on the Circus. From the Abbey Churchyard you enter the ROMAN BATHS AND MUSEUM. Take the tour, and visit the PUMP ROOM where the hot spring water is pumped. This complex is open 9 a.m.–8 p.m. daily.

SLEEPING

Tourist information at Abbey Churchyard will find you a room for a commission, or pick up a list of places from them. There's a youth hostel at Bathwick Hill (Tel. 65674), about a mile from the city (take bus 218 from Grand Parade), and another one at Broad Street Place (Tel. 60471). For B&Bs, look around the Wells Road or, for one nearer the station, try Prior House, 14 Gordon Rd (Tel. 313587), around £7 each.

EATING AND NIGHTLIFE

There are plenty of bakers, pubs and supermarkets, so meals shouldn't pose any problems. The City Market is good for fruit and vegetables, and Molehill Café, 14 George St, is about the best place in town. After 8 p.m., it becomes a club with live music. Take out a weekly membership for 50p, if you're staying for a while. The Bath Festival is on in late May, and ask at tourist information for the monthly 'What's On'.

Devon and Cornwall

The main centres to base yourself to explore these regions are Exeter, Plymouth or Penzance.

EXETER is the county town of Devon and is dominated by its impressive medieval CATHEDRAL. From the station of St David's, take the bus into the centre. Tourist information in the Civic Centre on Paris St will give you all you need on the region, including the national parks of Dartmoor and Exmoor. While in Exeter, take in the fourteenth-century GUILDHALL and go for a drink in the SHIP INN where Sir Francis Drake went for a jar. The youth hostel at 47 Countess Wear Rd, Topsham (Tel. 3329), is a short distance out, but good (bus 187 or 356 from Paris St bus station). Alternatively, try the Exeter Student Guest House, 16 New North Rd (Tel. 52493).

PLYMOUTH has been a major port since the fourteenth century. It was here Drake spotted the Spanish Armada and the *Mayflower* set sail to discover the New World. Spend an afternoon wandering round the Elizabethan BARBICAN QUAY, NEW ST with its timber merchant houses and the ruins of the fourteenth-century castle.

PENZANCE, 2½ hours further down the line, has a history of pirates and invaders, and makes an interesting day trip. Take in the MARKET HOUSE and MORRAB GARDENS where subtropical plants flourish, thanks to the exceptionally mild climate. From Penzance you can sail out to the Scilly Isles, or visit ST MICHAEL'S MOUNT, three miles east of the town – a castle and mountain where St Michael is said to have appeared.

The Midlands and East Anglia

The university towns of OXFORD and CAMBRIDGE, with their beautiful cloisters and unique building formations, are a must on a serious tour of Great Britain, and Shakespeare's home town Stratford-upon-Avon, however commercialized it is becoming, is still well worth a visit. Most of the Midlands is industrial and not worth stopping off at, while East Anglia is the flat land, taking in places like Cambridge, NORWICH, KING'S LYNN and the NORFOLK BROADS.

Oxford

Home of Britain's oldest and most prestigious university, which has dominated the town for over 700 years, Oxford lies 1¼ hours from London's Paddington Station, and can easily be taken in on a day trip from the capital.

STATION FACILITIES

Train information	Mon.–Sat.: 8.30 a.m.–7.30 p.m.,
	Sun.: 9.30 a.m.–7.30 p.m.
Reservations	Mon.–Fri.: 9 a.m.–5 p.m., Sat.: 9 a.m.–12 noon
Tourist information	8 a.m.–7 p.m.
Foreign exchange	8 a.m.–7 p.m.
Left-luggage lockers	All hours

Daily trains to: London, Reading, Birmingham, Manchester, Liverpool, Worcester.

TOURIST INFORMATION AND ADDRESSES

Tourist information is at St Aldate's, open Mon.–Sat.: 9 a.m.–5.30 p.m., Sun.: 10 a.m.–1 p.m., 1.30 p.m.–4 p.m. Pick up their 10p leaflet and their accommodation list.
STUDENT TRAVEL: 13 High Street.
LATE MONEY EXCHANGE: Lewis's Bank, in Selfridge's department store, Westgate. Open till 5 p.m. Saturday.

SEEING

Carfax Tower is at the centre, and from here most of the university colleges are only a few minutes away. CHRIST CHURCH, the sixteenth-century college with its beautiful library, housing the spoils of Henry VIII's monastic plunderings, is down St Aldate's. North of this is MERTON COLLEGE, dating from the thirteenth century and with a notably attractive chapel; and next door is ORIEL. Take Bear Lane now, then cross the High Street to reach BRASENOSE COLLEGE and ALL SOULS (probably the most prestigious collection of academics around – all specially appointed to the college). At the north end of the square is the BODLEIAN LIBRARY, built in 1602 and containing over three million books. The atmosphere in here must be sampled at first hand. MAGDALEN COLLEGE (pronounced 'maudlin') on the High Street makes a lovely walk through its fifteenth-century cloisters, and the ASHMOLEAN MUSEUM on Beaumont Street (Italian and English art) is worth seeing. Turn up Cornmarket Street at Carfax and, after the new shopping centre, you'll reach BALLIOL and ST JOHN'S colleges. Opposite Balliol, Latimer and Ridley were burned by Bloody Mary in 1555, with Bishop Cranmer following a year later.

If you want to be terribly traditional and you've managed to hit a sunny afternoon, hire out a punt at the CHERWELL BOATHOUSE for about £3 an hour. Worth a quick mention here is BLENHEIM PALACE, birthplace of Winston Churchill and ancestral home of the Dukes of Marlborough. You can visit the mansion for £2 in season (bus 420 or 423 from Cornmarket Street).

SLEEPING

If you don't use the tourist office's services, try calling in at the many B&Bs in Abingdon Road. The youth hostel is a little too like school to be comfortable; it's on bus routes 570, 582 or 583 at Jack Straw Lane (Tel. 62997). There's camping at Cassington Mill Caravan Park, five miles out (Tel. 881490). Mrs R. Old at 58 St John Street (Tel. 55454) is worth a try for B&B. Oxford does get busy in summer, but owing to its proximity to London, it's possible to take it in as a day trip.

EATING AND NIGHTLIFE

There are plenty of places ideal for eurorailers for, though an Oxford student may be a cut above the average, all students still look for the same type of things when it comes to eating and what to do at night. Brown's Restaurant and Wine Bar seems pretty popular from all appearances. It's at 7 Woodstock Road, and the food and atmosphere are very acceptable. Another place worth a mention is the local for Christ Church college, The Bear in Bear Lane. There are plenty of pubs; and if you want to meet the students, simply go to the pubs closest to the colleges. Oxford's July–August Festival is fairly classical; to find out the latest events, pick up the 'What's On' at the tourist office.

Stratford-upon-Avon

About 1½ hours from Oxford and 2½ from London (Paddington Station) lies the Elizabethan town of Stratford, birthplace of William Shakespeare. The house where he was born in HANLEY STREET in 1564 is charming, or would be if it weren't for the hundreds of tourists trying to get around it. He's buried in Holy Trinity Church. Shakespeare's wife's house ANNE HATHAWAY'S COTTAGE can be visited at Shottery. Americans might also like to visit the Elizabethan HARVARD HOUSE, where the parents of John Harvard (of University fame) lived. The Royal Shakespeare Theatre put on productions of outstanding quality, though the cheapest tickets are about £3 (Tel. 0789 292271 for information on what's playing). While you're in the area, you can pop into Shakespeare's mother's house and complete the family socializing. The HOME OF MARY ARDEN in the village of Wilmcote can be reached by local train in a matter of minutes.

TOURIST INFORMATION AND ADDRESSES

The tourist office is at 1 High St, open Mon.–Sat.: 9 a.m.–5.30 p.m., Sun.: 2 p.m.–5 p.m. in season. They'll give you a leaflet on accommodation, but the best bets are B&Bs on Evesham Place or Shipston Road.

• **Youth hostel:** Hemmingford House, Alverton (Tel. 297093). Bus 518 from the bus station.

• **Camping:** The Elms, Tiddington (Tel. 292312). Bus 518.

Cambridge

Oxford's great rival is the equally ancient market town and prestigious university of Cambridge which dates back to the thirteenth century and has names like Darwin, Newton, Byron and Milton in its old registers. Cambridge is 80 minutes from London (Liverpool Street Station), and once you arrive at the station, the bus to Market Square will take you to the centre of things.

STATION FACILITIES

Train information	Mon.–Sat.: 5.35 a.m.–10.35 p.m.
	Sun.: 7 a.m.–10.45 p.m.
	(Tel. 311999)
Reservations	Mon.–Sat.: 8 a.m.–8.30 p.m., British
	Mon.–Sat.: 9 a.m.–5.30 p.m., Continental
Left-luggage lockers	All hours
Left-luggage store	Mon.–Fri.: 7 a.m.–7 p.m., weekend: 9 a.m.–1 p.m.
Bar, Buffet	Mon.–Sat.: 7.30 a.m.–9.45 p.m., Sun.: 9.30 a.m.–
	9.30 p.m.
Station shuts	1.20 a.m.

Daily trains to: London, Birmingham, Peterborough, Norwich.

TOURIST INFORMATION AND ADDRESSES

The tourist office is at Wheeler St, open Mon.–Fri.: 9 a.m.–6 p.m., Sat.: 9 a.m.–5 p.m., Sun.: 10.30 a.m.–3.30 p.m. in season. Pick up the 10p 'Brief Guide' leaflet and ask about their walking tours.
CYCLE HIRE: Cambridge Cycle Hire, 118 Milton Road. £2 a day.
PUNT HIRE: Scudamore's Boatyards, Silver Street, or Magdalene Bridge.

SEEING

The area between Magdalene Bridge and Silver Street is the one to concentrate on. The town itself is quite substantial, and the university colleges are set apart, literally in a world of their own. THE BACKS are the meadows and fields on the other side of the Cam, and the best way to drink in this pastoral atmosphere is to hire a punt and picnic on the banks.

The main colleges to take in are: KING'S, QUEENS', CHRIST'S and TRINITY. At King's, look into the CHAPEL, and at Christ's visit the gardens which open weekdays, 2 p.m.–4 p.m.

SLEEPING

Tourist information will find you a bed for a small fee or hand you a list of local B&Bs. The best place to find a cheap B&B is near the station at Tenison Road or Jesus Lane in the town. Try any of the following in that lane: Mrs Spalding at No. 56 (Tel. 353858), Mrs Day at No. 72 (Tel. 356961), or Mrs Owen at No. 65 (Tel. 60648). The youth hostel is at 97 Tenison Road (Tel. 354601), and there's camping at Cambspeed Caravan Site, Wimpole Road, Barton. Not that good, 2½ miles west on bus routes 118, 120 or 175 from Drummer Street.

EATING AND NIGHTLIFE

There are plenty of pubs and shops, and the outdoor market in Market Square is the best source for picnic food. Try Crust's Wine Bar at 21 Northampton Street for good meals, or The King's Pantry at 9 King's Parade.

Ask tourist information for the 'What's On', as there's always a round of plays, films or debates. The best value is the Cambridge University Amateur Dramatic Club, Park Street. Their productions are good and their prices low, £1–2 (Tel. 352000 to see what's playing). Behind the Round Church is the clubhouse of the Cambridge Union who often have debates and social gatherings, though they're meant to be only for their students – still, if you can present a plausible case, go and see them.

During the last two weeks of July see the Cambridge Festival which is not all classical; some of their folk concerts are excellent. Get tickets from Central Library, Lion Yard. For live music, try Raffle's, Hill Road, or the Portland Arms, Chesterton Road.

Wales

Wales is a rugged land of 8,000 square miles and 2½ million people, about a quarter of whom still speak Welsh. It is wilder than England and less dramatic than Scotland, and for a while you'd never know you were over the English border; but travel to the SNOWDONIA NATIONAL PARK in the north-west, taking the SNOWDON MOUNTAIN RAILWAY up Mount Snowdon, or listen to the soft-spoken Welsh in the north, and you'll be glad you took in this extra country.

South Wales

The industrial south produces coal for most of Britain, and consequently much of the country is not very scenic. CARDIFF, the capital, is about 2 hours from London and an hour from Bristol. There's not too much here to merit a long stop, but the CASTLE and WELSH NATIONAL MUSEUM are worth seeing, and the WELSH OPEN-AIR FOLK MUSEUM, five miles out at St Fagans (bus 32), is fascinating.

From the eurorailer's point of view, southern Wales is not ideally planned, as most of the interesting places aren't on any line. The BRECON BEACONS NATIONAL PARK is best reached from ABER-GAVENNY, which is on the Crewe–Cardiff line. There's tourist information about the park at 2 Lower Monk Street (open Easter–October) and you're OK to camp where you like in the park, provided you check with the local farmer first. There are six youth hostels in all, and many B&Bs, and the countryside is marvellous. The other big attraction of the south is the other National Park: the PEMBROKESHIRE COAST, a similar set-up on the west coast.

ABERYSTWYTH, seat of the University of Wales and popular resort with Welsh grannies, is worth a look. Early Welsh manuscripts are in the NATIONAL LIBRARY, and visit the ABERYSTWYTH ARTS CENTRE while you're here. Tourist information at Eastgate Street is open 9 a.m.–6 p.m. in season. At the railway station, British Rail's only regular steam-powered train leaves for the waterfalls at DEVIL'S BRIDGE daily – a must for train buffs.

North Wales

The SNOWDONIA NATIONAL PARK covers half of North Wales and is one of Europe's best regions for getting away from it all. The terrain is ideal for climbing, hiking, camping or hostelling. Make your way to the town of CAERNARFON, the thirteenth-century town with its incredibly well-preserved medieval CASTLE where the investiture of Prince Charles took place. Take the train to BANGOR, on the Holyhead line, then bus it to Caernarfon, and from there bus to LLANBERIS, where the SNOWDON MOUNTAIN RAILWAY will hoist you to the mountain's summit (but it's expensive: about £8 return).

Northern England

The industrial north has a few saving graces from its heavy-industry towns in the form of the YORKSHIRE MOORS in the east, and the LAKE DISTRICT in the west. The moors are *Wuthering Heights* country: wild, untouched terrain, ideal for hiking and camping as long as you don't mind isolation. The NORTH YORK MOORS NATIONAL PARK has a tourist office at PICKERING STATION, which is as good a place as any to base yourself. The LAKE DISTRICT NATIONAL PARK is considered to be the country's best. The main centres, and also the most touristy in summer, are KESWICK, WINDERMERE and GRASMERE. There's a station at Windermere, and for Keswick use PENRITH. For tourist information, contact the office in Victoria Street, Penrith, open 10 a.m.–8.30 p.m. in season. There are thirty youth hostels (the world's highest density) and the Park Service run a series of free guided walks and courses in summer.

York

York dates back to Roman times and is considered Britain's best-preserved medieval city with the finest Gothic cathedral. It lies about halfway between London and Edinburgh on the east-coast line, and with the fast 125 intercity service, it takes only 2½ hours from the capital.

STATION FACILITIES

Train information	8 a.m.–9 p.m.
	(Tel. 25671)
Reservations	8 a.m.–9 p.m.
Left-luggage store	Open 24 hours
Bar, Buffet	24 hours (Platform 14)
Restaurant	6.30 a.m.–10 p.m.
Bookshop	6.15 a.m.–7 p.m.

Daily trains to: London, Edinburgh, Leeds, the Midlands, the West Country, South Wales, Liverpool, Manchester, Scarborough, Harrogate.

TOURIST INFORMATION AND ADDRESSES

The tourist information centre is in Exhibition Square, and is open Mon.–Sat.: 9 a.m.–8 p.m., Sun.: 2 p.m.–5 p.m. in season. They run a free two-hour walking tour from the Art Gallery at 10.15 a.m., 2.15 p.m. and 7.15 p.m.

SEEING

There are four main entrances to the city: BOOTHAM GATE, MICKLEGATE, MONKGATE and WALMGATE, and the city is surrounded by three miles of defensive walls. York MINSTER (the cathedral which had a tied school) is amazing: the Great East Window is as big as a tennis court, and all the stained glass is medieval. Once you've wandered around the cathedral, visit the CASTLE MUSEUM which is an exceptionally good folk museum with reconstructions of streets, people and implements of the last century. For evidence of the Romans, go to the MULTI-ANGULAR TOWER in the Yorkshire Museum Gardens. Real train enthusiasts will like the NATIONAL RAILWAY MUSEUM down by the station – plenty of steam locos, etc. There are many other historic and interesting places, like the TREASURER'S HOUSE, CLIFFORD'S TOWER, and the wonderful old shopping streets of medieval York like the SHAMBLES, and the site of the old whipping post, WHIP-MA-WHOP-MA-GATE. Pick up detailed leaflets from tourist information. While you're in the area, you might want to visit CASTLE HOWARD, the beautiful eighteenth-century setting of *Brideshead Revisited*. Ask tourist information for the best buses.

SLEEPING

Tourist information will give you lists of B&Bs and hostels, or find you a room for 75p commission. York can get very busy in summer, so get fixed up as soon as you arrive. The area round Bootham is not bad for B&B, and there's a youth hostel at Water End, Clifton (Tel. 53147), though it's rule-ridden and usually full. Bishophill House is a private hostel at 11–13 Bishophill Senior Road (Tel. 25904) or there's the International House, 33 Bootham (Tel. 22874). For B&B try Bishopthorpe Road in Bootham, or the Mount area down Blossom Street. Ask tourist information for the location of the new campsite opening 1984.

EATING AND NIGHTLIFE

There are bakers' shops, markets and pubs a-plenty in York. York Wholefood, 98 Micklegate, do good meals upstairs, and Kooks at 108 Fishergate (closed Mon.) is also worth a try. With over 150 pubs, you shouldn't get stuck for a watering hole. The Black Swan in Peasholme Green is a suitably olde-worlde place, but there are many more dotted around.

York–Edinburgh

Fifty minutes further up the line from York is the cathedral town of DURHAM. You should take an hour or two of even the most hurried journey off, and catch the next 125, to see the magnificent CATHEDRAL and CASTLE there. They face each other over Palace Green in a dramatic setting. The cathedral is eleventh-century and is considered one of Europe's finest Romanesque examples; and the castle dates from the same time with fourteenth-century additions. The fortified town of BERWICK-UPON-TWEED is the border between

the ancient enemies, Scotland and England. Should you break your
journey here, see the old city walls and elegant eighteenth-century
TOWN HALL. From the border it's an hour to Edinburgh, Scotland's
majestic capital.

Scotland

The scenery in the Scottish Highlands is outstanding: the glens and
mountains, lochs and islands are unique in their unspoilt beauty.
Were the weather only a bit better, Scotland would be the answer to
everyone's holiday problems; however, let's be honest – you don't
come here for a tan, you come to hike on the hills or wander through
the historic streets of Edinburgh. The rail network is a bit restricted
up north, but if you travel up the east coast to Inverness, then over
to Kyle of Lochalsh, taking the boat down to Mallaig, then back
down the west coast via Oban to Glasgow, Scotland's largest
industrial city, you'll get a good idea of the geography. Now,
without going into a detailed account, until the eighteenth century,
the English and the Scots shared nothing in common and, as far as
many Scots are concerned, they still don't. Remember this when
you're making small talk with them, and do try not to refer to the
whole of Great Britain as just 'England' – it doesn't go down too
well in these parts.

Edinburgh

The elegant city of Edinburgh can't fail to strike the visitor as
dramatic: built on extinct volcanoes with a fairytale castle dominating the city, and hills and the sea all around. It's the artistic,
commercial, academic and legal centre of Scotland and its history
goes back to the seventh century. As soon as you walk up from
Waverley Station you're in the centre of things, with the castle and
'old town' on your left, and the 'new town' from the Georgian era on
your right.

STATION FACILITIES

	WAVERLEY STATION
Train information	Mon.–Sat.: 8 a.m.–11 p.m., Sun.: 9 a.m.–11 p.m. (Tel. 556 2451)
Reservations	Mon.–Sat.: 8 a.m.–8 p.m., Sun.: 9 a.m.–8 p.m.
Tourist information	100 yards from station
Foreign exchange	3 a.m.–12 midnight
Left-luggage store	Mon.–Sat.: 6 a.m.–10.50 p.m. Sun.: 7 a.m.–10.50 p.m.
Bar	Mon.–Sat.: 9 a.m.–11 p.m. Sun.: 11 a.m.–2.30 p.m., 6 p.m.–10.30 p.m.
Restaurant	6.30 a.m.–10.30 p.m.
Bath, Shower	3 a.m.–12 midnight
Station shuts	0.30 a.m.–2.30 a.m.

Daily trains to: Aberdeen, Birmingham, Bristol, Glasgow, Inverness, Liverpool, London, Manchester, Perth, Stirling.

TOURIST INFORMATION AND ADDRESSES

The tourist office is at 5 Waverley Bridge, just up the ramp and to your left from the station, open weekdays 8.30 a.m.–9 p.m., Sun.: 11 a.m.–9 p.m. in season. Ask for 'What's On', and get details on the rest of the country from the Scottish Tourist Board desk in there.

POST OFFICE: Waterloo Place (at east end of Princes Street), open Mon.–Fri.: 8 a.m.–6 p.m., Sat.: 8 a.m.–12.30 p.m. Currency exchange.

AMEX: 139 Princes Street, open Mon.–Fri.: 9 a.m.–5 p.m., Sat.: 9 a.m.–12 noon.

US CONSULATE: 3 Regent Terrace (Tel. 556 8315).

MEDICAL HELP: University Health Service, Bristo St (Tel. 667 1011).

TRANSALPINO: 14 North Bridge (Tel. 557 3140)

SEEING

The medieval ROYAL MILE was so called because it stretches from the CASTLE to the royal palace of HOLYROOD. You can't possibly miss the castle which dates back to the seventh century. It stands on an extinct volcano and can be seen from virtually every corner of

Edinburgh. Though entrance is £1 (50p to students), if you're keen on history it's worth it. The Scottish Crown Jewels and the smallest chapel in Scotland are here, as well as several museums and a sweeping view over the city and River Forth. Walking down the Royal Mile, you'll find GLADSTONE'S LAND, a beautifully preserved medieval townhouse in the Lawnmarket, well worth a visit, and behind this is LADY STAIR'S HOUSE with Burns, Stevenson and Scott mementoes. ST GILES' CATHEDRAL, the Gothic 1385 High Church of Scotland, is on the right, as are various buildings of the Scottish parliament. Halfway down in the Canongate is JOHN KNOX'S HOUSE and the MUSEUM OF CHILDHOOD, an interesting collection of toys and games from bygone days. After a tour of the sixteenth-century palace, clear your head with a good blast of Scottish air up another of Edinburgh's extinct volcanoes, ARTHUR'S SEAT, or walk to CALTON HILL at the east end of Princes Street to look at 'Edinburgh's Disgrace': the replica of the Athens Parthenon that ran out of money and remains unfinished.

On one side of Princes Street are the city's main shops, while opposite are gardens and the two neo-classical art galleries: the NATIONAL GALLERY and the ROYAL ACADEMY, both particularly impressive. WALTER SCOTT'S MONUMENT, the huge Gothic tower in Princes Street Gardens, affords a good view from the top, and from here a walk up Hanover Street will take you down to Queen Street where, along on the right, you'll find Scotland's MUSEUM OF ANTI-QUITIES. Bus 23 or 27 from Hanover Street will take you down to the BOTANICAL GARDENS which are a glorious picnic venue and where you'll find the NATIONAL GALLERY OF MODERN ART. If you've any time left, search out the GEORGIAN HOUSE, CHARLOTTE SQUARE, THE ZOO, and take bus 41 out to CRAMOND, down by the sea. During the International Festival and its Fringe, literally hundreds of events are staged: plays, concerts, exhibitions; and every church hall in the city has some university group performing in it. Thousands of students descend on the city, as tickets start as low as £1. Running at the same time are the film and jazz festivals, and the bonanza of the MILITARY TATTOO with enough kilts and bagpipes to satisfy even the most ardent American.

SLEEPING

Aside from late August–September (Festival time), a bed's not too much of a hassle, and the tourist bureau will help you out. They're open till 9 p.m. and have a free list of suggestions. For B&Bs, take a bus out to Newington and look round there, or try the Bruntsfield area.

• **Hostels:** The youth hostels are at 17–18 Eglinton Crescent (Tel. 337 1120) and 7–8 Bruntsfield Crescent (Tel. 447 2994).

The University Halls of Residence, Pollock Halls, 18 Holyrood Park Road (Tel. 667 1971), are very good and offer 1,500 single rooms at around £7 for students, £11.50 otherwise. Take buses 14, 21 or 33 to the Commonwealth Pool.

The YMCA, 14 South St Andrew Street (just off Princes Street), is open to anyone under 26, while the YWCAs admit only women to their hostels: 4 Randolph Place (Tel. 225 1875); 2 Randolph Crescent (Tel. 226 3842); and Kinnaird Hostel, 14 Coates Crescent (Tel. 225 3771); all are central and good value. To camp, take bus 33 or 49 out to Little France, Old Dalkeith Road (Tel. 664 4742).

EATING AND NIGHTLIFE

Cheap eats are no problem in Edinburgh and it's possible to fill up for under £1.50 at either a fish'n'chip shop or a filled baked potato carry-out; Edinburgh specializes in these, and these are Spud-U-Like shops dotted around the centre. Pick up the free leaflet from tourist information on restaurants. Pubs often offer cheap lunches, and this capital has over 500 to choose from. The University Students' Union at Teviot Row (up the Mound, and George IV Bridge) do meals for about £1.50, or try Henderson's Salad Table, 94 Hanover Street, for healthy meals around £2.50.

If you're here in Festival time, the nightlife position is unmatched anywhere else in Britain. Go along to the Fringe Club (venue changes, so ask at Fringe Office, 170 High Street) where performers, the media and the public gather to socialize (£5 membership for the Festival's duration). If you're visiting at any other time, pick up 'What's On' from tourist information and combine some events with a visit to some of the city's pubs; a popular pub crawl is along the nineteen bars of Rose Street. Check out what's playing in the Film House, Calton Studios or Traverse.

Inverness

From Edinburgh it's a 4-hour journey up to Inverness, capital of the Highlands. The route is via Perth and Aviemore and, once you're up at Pitlochry, the scenery is wonderful. A quick rundown on Inverness is all that is needed, for while it's a pleasant enough place, you should really just use it as a base for the surrounding country. While there, wander round LOCH NESS where the elusive monster is said to live, and visit CAWDOR CASTLE (twelve miles east) where Shakespeare set *Macbeth*. There are plenty of B&Bs around Old Edinburgh Road, a youth hostel at Castle Street (Tel. 31771), and camping down by the river on the Craig Dunain bus route (Tel. 36920). Tourist information at 23 Church Street is open Mon.–Sat.: 9 a.m.–8 p.m., Sun.: 2 p.m.–6 p.m. in summer.

The Highlands and Islands

From Inverness, take the train west to KYLE OF LOCHALSH, a 170-minute journey of beautiful unspoilt scenery through the Wester Ross mountains. From Kyle there's a frequent five-minute ferry over to Kyleakin on the ISLE OF SKYE, Britain's most dramatic island. The peace and beauty of the Black Cuillin Hills and the haunting cloud formations are quite unmatched elsewhere. PORTREE, the island's capital, has a tourist office overlooking the harbour. Skye can also be approached from MALLAIG, and from Mallaig you're back on the main line to FORT WILLIAM and GLASGOW. If you were thinking of heading further north, there's a line for Inverness to WICK; but it's pretty desolate up there, so think twice. If it's isolation you're after, try the ORKNEY ISLANDS. These ex-Danish colonies are well worth visiting; the easiest approach is the ferry from John O'Groats. Visit the Stone Age settlement of SKARA BRAE and the Bronze Age STANDING STONES OF STENNESS and RING OF BRODGAR. The Oban–Glasgow run is another favourite for Highland scenery, 3½ hours of it. From OBAN you can visit the beautiful ISLE OF MULL, and from there go to the smaller, more isolated islands of Iona, Staffa, Coll and Tiree. Tourist information in Oban is at Argyll Square, turn right from the station; and there's a hostel on the Esplanade (Tel. 62025).

Northern Ireland

Before you completely write off the possibility of visiting Northern Ireland because of the current 'troubles', bear in mind that the media tend to inflate it out of all proportion, and that most of the province is safe to visit, particularly if you're obviously a tourist. However, you will lay yourself open to continual security-checks from the armed forces in the affected areas; and, to be honest, the scenery is *not* Britain's best.

The Northern Irish Railways Board offer a 50 per cent discount if you bought your Inter Rail from BR, NIR or CIE. As far as the rail network goes, the main line is from LONDONDERRY through COLERAINE, BALLYMENA and ANTRIM to BELFAST, meeting the line from Belfast towards Dublin at Lisburn.

Taking the capital, Belfast, as the centre, you'll find COUNTY DOWN and the MOURNE MOUNTAINS to the south, ARMAGH to the west, FERMANAGH further west and TYRONE inland. COUNTY DERRY is in the north-west corner and COUNTY ANTRIM in the north-east. At TORR HEAD you're only thirteen miles from Scotland, and in the north-west of Antrim's coast is the GIANT'S CAUSEWAY, the famous rock formation.

Belfast is a bit grim, but not as bad as you'd expect from all the reports. The main things to see are in the UNIVERSITY area and the city centre round DONEGAL SQUARE where the Renaissance City Hall is. Also worth a mention are the OPERA HOUSE and the ULSTER MUSEUM and ART GALLERY in the Botanic Gardens. The ULSTER FOLK AND TRANSPORT MUSEUM at Cultra Manor, Holywood, six miles from Belfast, is well worth the detour. There are reconstructions of nineteenth-century life from farms to craft centres. Tourist information is at 48–52 High Street and there's a youth hostel at 11 Stainfield Rd (Tel. 647865) on bus routes 83 or 84.

LONDONDERRY, 2 hours from Belfast, is one of Northern Ireland's most attractive towns. The OLD CITY WALLS have withstood invaders for over 350 years, and today they're laid out as a walk. The GUIDHALL in Shipquay Place is a modern Gothic building whose stained-glass windows tell the city's history. You'll find tourist information down here too, at Foyle Street, and the seventeenth-century Protestant cathedral. Outside the city walls is the Catholic area of Bogside.

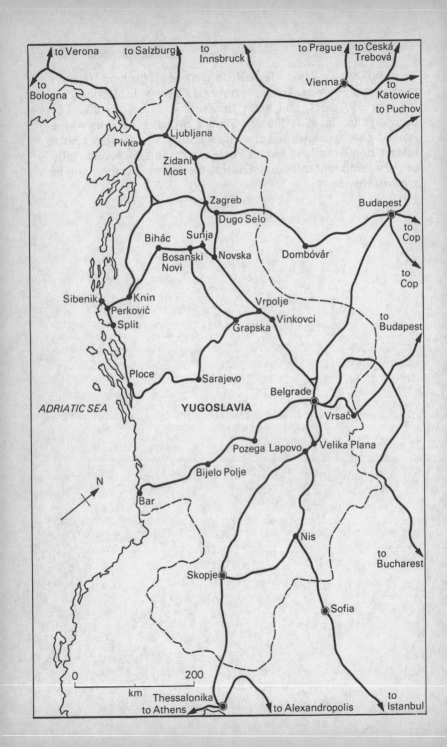

YUGOSLAVIA (Jugoslavija)

Entry requirements	Passport
Population	22,500,000
Capital	Belgrade (pop.: 1,850,000)
Currency	Dinar
	£1 = approx. 209 D
Political system	Socialist Federal Republic
Religions	Serbian Orthodox, Muslim, Catholic, Protestant
Languages	Serbo-Croat, Slovenian, Macedonian (some English, German, Italian and French understood)
Public holidays	1, 2 Jan.; 1, 2 May; 4 July; 29, 30 Nov.

Yugoslavia is one of the most complex and culturally diverse countries in Europe. There are no less than six republics (Bosnia–Hercegovina, Montenegro, Croatia, Macedonia, Slovenia and Serbia) inhabited by at least eight nationalities, speaking five different languages and using two alphabets (Cyrillic and Latin). To make matters even more complicated, they practise four separate religions. Understandably, the country is rich in folklore and the Yugoslavs are proud of their traditional differences. For several centuries Yugoslavia was dominated by the Austro-Hungarian Empire in the north and by the Turks in the south. Then, in the aftermath of the First World War, present-day Yugoslavia was created. During the Second World War about a fifth of the country's population was killed, many by fellow Yugoslavs in the civil war which developed. From this period emerged Marshal Tito who died in 1980. He managed to keep the country together and preserve a non-aligned status until his death. Today Yugoslavia is a centralized economy, where tourism is encouraged as an important source of revenue.

YUGOSLAV STATE RAILWAYS
(Jugoslovenskin Zeleznica, JZ)

Most Yugoslavian trains have got a reputation for being slow and dirty. All the major towns are linked by rail, but only a few lines go as far as the coast. Don't be misled by the impressive variety of trains operating within Yugoslavia, as only the international expresses are worth travelling on. Listed here in descending order of comfort and speed are the options open to the eurorailer: international expresses, inland expresses (Ekspresni), rapides (Poslovni), fast (Brzi) and the unspeakably slow trains (Putnicki). Unless you plan to visit Belgrade, go for a through express, as changing trains here nearly always means no seat for the second leg of your journey. To make things easier, here are the origins and destinations of the main international expresses:

Simplon: London–Paris–Milan–Belgrade
Venezia: Venice–Belgrade–(Sofia–Istanbul)–Athens
Acropolis: Munich–Ljubljana–Belgrade–Kosovo Polje–Skopje–Athens
Yugoslavia: Frankfurt–Munich–Ljubljana–Zagreb
Hellas: Dortmund–Munich–Belgrade–Skopje–Athens
Tauern: London–Ostend–Aachen–Cologne–Munich–Zagreb–Knin–Split
Istanbul: Munich–Belgrade–Sofia–Istanbul
Mostar: Stuttgart–Munich–Zagreb–Sarajevo–Kardeljevo (in winter also Zagreb–Knin–Split)

It's strongly advisable to reserve a seat on any of these expresses, all of which are valid on Inter Rail. Reservations are obligatory from stations in Germany to stations in Yugoslavia and Greece. (See also 'Getting There' under Greece.)

TRAIN INFORMATION

English is spoken by most information staff; if not, have a German back-up ready.

● **Reservations:** Aren't obligatory, but are strongly recommended. In summer, the Belgrade–Athens route is usually booked up months in advance, so try and reserve a seat on one of the through international trains. It pays to plan ahead.

● **Night travel:** Yugoslavian couchettes are very basic and difficult to get hold of (if possible, try for a couchette from Vienna). The price of sleepers will keep you awake worrying, so you may as well forget them.

- **Eating on trains:** Most expresses and fast trains have bars and diners. Other trains may have mini-bars.

- **Scenic tips:** Three-quarters of Yugoslavia is covered by mountains and one-third by forests, so there are plenty of options. The most spectacular route is the recently opened Belgrade–Bar line to the Montenegrin coast.

TOURIST INFORMATION

All major cities have a tourist office (Drušno or Turističko); they're normally near the stations. They keep maps and leaflets on their region and help find a room if required.

- **ISIC bonuses:** Discounts are given on some museums and cultural tours. For further information contact Karavan Student Travel Agency, Takovska 2, Belgrade.

- **Money matters:** 1 dinar (D) = 100 paras.
Banking hours are Mon.–Sat.: 7 a.m.–7 p.m. Away from the tourist centres, some banks shut from 12 noon to 3 p.m. It's also possible to change money at many travel agencies. Expect to pay 2 per cent commission on all transactions, and keep your exchange slips for reconversion. It's the same rate everywhere so don't bother to shop around.

- **Post offices:** Open Mon.–Sat.: 7 a.m.–7 p.m. Stamps can also be bought from tobacconists and Trafik shops. Glavna Posta = poste restante.

- **Shops:** Open Mon.–Sat.: 8 a.m.–8 p.m. with an optional 12 noon–3 p.m. siesta.

SLEEPING

Tourist offices help out a bit by supplying booklets and information on camping, private accommodation and hotels, as well as running a room-finding service. Hotels are pricey, with even the cheapest C grades charging upwards of 12,000 D per person. Private accommodation (sobe) is a much better bet at about 800 D per person. If you're approached at the station by locals offering a room in their house you could try and negotiate but it is illegal. Student hostels are another alternative in July and August, with doubles at anything between 400–500 D. Also, there are about thirty youth hostels scattered throughout the country, most of which are very basic, though the ones in the major cities are better. For camping, pick up the tourist information booklet which gives facilities and distances from the nearest town. Prices range between 150–250 D per person.

Finally, you can be sure to be moved on if you try to sleep at the stations, as the authorities don't look too kindly on this.

EATING AND NIGHTLIFE

The endless variety of regional specialities should make eating out in Yugoslavia a pleasure, but if you go for westernized restaurants you'll find prices high. Your best bets are the self-service places or take-away stalls. If you're really low on readies, try the workers' communal eating halls (large soup-kitchen-type places full of men putting away mundane meals at an incredible pace). These are very cheap but not for those of a delicate disposition, as you'll see a lot of spitting (and worse) which can lessen the appetite somewhat. As a general rule, meat dishes represent the best value, particularly from the take-aways. Try ćevapčići (grilled and spiced beef), or raznjici (grilled pork, veal or lamb, on a spit). If you're really hard up, go for a burek (a pastry with meat, cheese or vegetable filling) or just a plain pancake washed down with yoghourt, as the locals do. If you're eating out, it's best to stay with the local wines: Riesling and Smederevka are the most popular white, Zupsko and Prokupac the most popular red.

People stare at each other a lot, so why not try and outdo the locals at their own game by taking part in the korzo, a pre-dinner evening stroll where everyone eyes up their neighbours in the town to see who's with who and what they're wearing.

Slovenia

The proximity and influence of Austria over this rural region of Yugoslavia have helped make it one of the more comfortable to travel in. Hygiene and standards are generally more westernized than further south; in fact, northern Slovenia is just like an extension of Austria, and it's not till the Julian Alps that the scenery begins to flatten out and change. In southern Slovenia, there are some smallish beaches at KOPER and PIRAN; and some winter sports centres.

Ljubljana

This is the capital of the region, but it's an industrial centre and not really worth special attention. However, if you are breaking a journey here, take in the OLD TOWN with its castle, cathedral and medieval streets, or the old NATIONAL MUSEUM (a good rainy-afternoon alternative). In summer, the cultural festival means there are plenty of concerts and plays going on. Sleeping and eating shouldn't put you out: get the tourist office to fix you up with private accommodation or camp at Titova 260a (Tel. 341113) on bus route 6.

TOURIST INFORMATION AND ADDRESSES

TOURIST OFFICE: Titova Cesta 11, open Mon.–Sat.: 7 a.m.–10 p.m., Sun.: 8 a.m.–12 noon, 5 p.m.–8 p.m.
POST OFFICE: Titova Cesta 8, open Mon.–Fri.: 8 a.m.–8 p.m., Sat.: 8 a.m.–2 p.m.
AMEX: c/o Atlas, Trg. Mestni 8, open Mon.–Fri.: 7.30 a.m.–9.30 p.m.; Sat.: 7.30 a.m.–1 p.m.
STUDENT TRAVEL: Celovsuka 49. Pick up youth hostel lists here and let them help you out on accommodation, open Mon.–Fri.: 10 a.m.–2 p.m., 3 p.m.–5 p.m.

Zagreb

Zagreb is 2¾ hours from Ljubljana and is the regional capital of Croatia and cultural capital of Yugoslavia.

The city is divided into three main areas: the Upper Town, dating back to the thirteenth century; the Lower Town, which is nineteenth-century; and the modern, postwar New Zagreb. Concentrate your efforts on Upper Zagreb (north of the station) and see: ST STEPHEN'S CATHEDRAL, ST MARK'S, the CROATIAN NATIONAL THEATRE and some of the many galleries and museums. There are several festivals, and the nightlife here is the most cosmopolitan you'll get. Check out accommodation at the Studentski Centar Turist Biro, Savska Cesta 25 (Tel. 278611); or the youth hostel, Petrinjiska 77 (Tel. 441405).

Trieste–Dubrovnik

The Adriatic is fast becoming the goldmine of Yugoslavia as intensified tourism increases each year. Trains run as far south as Split. To get to Dubrovnik, you have to bus it from Kardeljevo (Ploče). The coast is Yugoslavia's main redeeming feature – in fact, it's the only part of the country where touring isn't hard work, and even here it's bad enough; but console yourself with the fact that there are over 1,000 little islands out there in the Adriatic, and that there are towns like Split and Dubrovnik, which are well worth visiting. You're bound to find somewhere to take off your shirt and relax for a day or two. If you're interested: Yugoslavia's Adriatic coast is *the* centre for 'naturism' in southern Europe. Though unofficial camping's illegal, you should get away with it in the less obvious places, though there are quite a few youth hostels on the coast.

The rail network on the coast is virtually non-existent, which is the annoying aspect of travelling here. Places to head for are ZADAR or PULA and RIJEKA in the northern Adriatic, from where you can head off to the islands. As with Greece, ask other eurorailers which islands they'd recommend. Suggestions are CRES, KRK, RAB and BRAČ.

Split

The regional capital of Dalmatia dates back to the fourth century AD and to the Romans. The magnificent PALACE built by Diocletian in the third century developed into a medieval town, and the former palatial apartments have over the years become houses, while the corridors became streets. The basement now houses several museums and galleries. Other things to look out for are the CATHEDRAL, the ARCHAEOLOGICAL MUSEUM, with many of the palace's fittings, and the BAZAAR. The city outside the walls is the new commercial centre where the hotels and nightclubs are.

Sleeping's a problem in Split as prices are high and it's a seller's market. You could try camping at Put Trstenik (Tel. 521971) on bus route 7 or 17, but it's usually pretty unsavoury; or for a dormitory bed you could try the student hostel at Ul. Spinutska (Tel. 42822). The best of the cheap hotels is the Srebrena Vrata inside the east gate at Kralja Poljana Kraljice 3 (Tel. 46869), around 550 D.

TOURIST INFORMATION AND ADDRESSES

TOURIST OFFICE: Titova Obala 12, open Mon.–Sat.: 7 a.m.–10 p.m., Sun.: 7.30 a.m.–12.30 p.m., 4 p.m.–8 p.m. in season. They handle private accommodation, but it's not cheap.

AMEX: Trg. Preporoda 7 (on the southern wall of the palace), open Mon.–Sat.: 7 a.m.–9 p.m. in season.

Dubrovnik

This is undoubtedly the most attractive city Yugoslavia has to offer. It was one of Europe's leading centres in the fifteenth century – so much so it rivalled Venice in looks and wealth, and the Renaissance palaces and churches can still be seen today.

• **Transport:** Since 1976 when the railway disappeared, the bus services to and from Dubrovnik have become the main mode of transport. Unfortunately, they're inefficient and every year the situation gets worse as the tourists increasingly flock in. The two nearest stations are Kardeljevo (Ploče) and Bar. The ferry situation isn't quite as bad. Take a deck ticket on one of the weekly ferries which stop at Bar, Dubrovnik, Split and Rijeka. To get from Split to Dubrovnik, there's no better way. (Or if you were thinking of heading down to Greece, you can leave from Dubrovnik for Corfu every Monday at 5 p.m. or Wednesday at 6 p.m.) Once you've arrived at Dubrovnik by either ferry or bus, take a bus to the Old City, and head for tourist information.

TOURIST INFORMATION AND ADDRESSES

TOURIST OFFICE: Poljana Paška Milicěviča 20, open daily: 9 a.m.–9.30 p.m. Located by the west gate, they'll arrange accommodation and hand out maps and leaflets.
AMEX: c/o Atlas, Pile 1, open daily: 8 a.m.–8 p.m.
MEDICAL HELP: Maršala Tita 61 (Tel. 94).

SEEING

A wonderful introduction to the city is to walk along on top of the old city walls – don't worry, they're thick enough to be safe. This'll give you an idea of the layout. Dubrovnik's actually tiny, so you can quite easily get round the sights on foot.

The most inspiring buildings are the DOGE'S PALACE, the baroque CHURCH OF ST VLAHO beside ONOFRIO'S FOUNTAIN, the FRANCISCAN MONASTERY and the DOMINICAN CLOISTER AND MUSEUM (closed Sundays). The beaches are always busy in summer and charge, so you're actually far better taking the ferry over to LOKRUM, the island offering a national park and bathing area. (The nudist beach here is known to get quite lively in peak season!)

SLEEPING

As with most commercial resorts, sleeping can be a problem: hotels are over the top and there aren't enough hostels to go round. Sleeping on the beaches seems the natural solution – only the police don't quite view it that way, and for the kind of fines they'll impose, you could have slept at the best hotel in town. The International Student Centre is very good, but unless you reserve, you don't stand a chance. It's at Ivanska 14 (Tel. 23841), bus 2 or 4 from the bus or ferry stations. The youth hostel, Ferijalni Dom, at Oktobarske Revolucije 25 (Tel. 23241), is open April–October and is worth a try. For hotels, try the Lapad (Tel. 23473) or Gruz, Gruška Obala 68 (Tel. 24777), but even they're in the 750–1,000 D per double range. There is a campsite one and a half miles east of the station. Three buses an hour to the old city. Expensive.

EATING AND NIGHTLIFE

Neither is a problem. To cater for the tourists there are plenty of restaurants with reasonable menus, or you could live out of the self-service Express, at Ulica c. Zuzoric. The summer festival draws top names in 'high culture' to the town, but if that leaves you cold, there's always good manwatching potential, once everyone changes at night (or gets dressed for the first time, in many cases) and parades up and down the main streets, having an occasional drink or ice-cream. There are also nightclubs, strippers, etc., in some of the flashy hotels.

Bosnia–Hercegovina

The Turkish-influenced region of Bosnia–Hercegovina, set among the central mountains, is en route to Dubrovnik from Zagreb or Belgrade. The stretch of line from Sarajevo to MOSTAR runs through this region, and a day's stop-off in either of these towns will be an interesting experience.

SARAJEVO, 8½ hours from Zagreb and 6½ hours from Belgrade, was under Turkish rule for over 500 years and there are still minarets, mosques, and culinary reminders of this all around. Tourist information is at Jugoslovenske Narodne Armije 50, open 7.30 a.m.–8 p.m., and to get fixed up with private accommodation, go to Unis Turist, Vase Miskina 16. There's a youth hostel at

Zadrugina 17 (Tel. 36163). Eat in the Turkish quarter and on your sightseeing tour look out for BEY'S MOSQUE, the COPPERSMITH'S MARKET, the bridge where Archduke Ferdinand was shot (think back to your First World War history), and the SERBIAN ORTHODOX CHURCH.

Belgrade (Beograd)

The capital of Serbia (the eastern half of Yugoslavia), and of the country as a whole, is not one of Europe's best cities. This is probably because since its founding in the third century the city has been destroyed and rebuilt thirty-six times, and little but grey, high-rise, concrete blocks stand there today.

TOURIST INFORMATION AND ADDRESSES

There's an information booth inside the station, open 7 a.m.–9 p.m., but the main office is in the subway at the Albanija Building on Terazije, and is open 8 a.m.–8 p.m. All the main hotels will hand you a free map if you ask at reception.

POST OFFICE: Takovska 2, open Mon.–Sat.: 7 a.m.–8 p.m. Poste restante and telephones also here.

AMEX: Zmaj Jovina 10, open Mon.–Sat.: 7 a.m.–8 p.m.

UK EMBASSY: Generala Zdanova 46 (Tel. 645055).

US EMBASSY: Kneza Milosa 50 (Tel. 645655).

CANADIAN EMBASSY: Proleterskih Brigada 69 (Tel. 434524).

KARAVAN STUDENT TRAVEL: Takovska 2, open Mon.–Fri.: 7 a.m.–6 p.m., Sat.: 8 a.m.–6 p.m.

SEEING

As Belgrade Station is one of the bleakest in Europe, if you've a few hours to kill between trains get out of it and head for the town – not that it's much better, but at least the KALEMEGDAN PARK provides a picnic place where you won't get too depressed waiting. If you've hit a wet day, the NATIONAL MUSEUM at the corner of TRG. REPUBLIKE (the main shopping street) is your best alternative. This is full of icons, paintings, prehistoric remains, weapons, etc., and is closed Mondays. Aside from this, there's not a lot, though the nineteenth-century quarter of the city, SKADARLIJA, is the most pleasant to stroll through.

SLEEPING

If you insist on spending the night here, go to the tourist office and ask them to help you out, as there are very few affordable beds. The youth hostel at Bulevar Jug. Narodne Armije 56a (Tel. 463846) is on tram 9 or 10. You're usually deluged with offers if you hang round the station long enough, but haggle with them to reduce prices dramatically although, strictly speaking, this is illegal. Across from the station is the Pansion Centar, at Trg. Bratstva Jedinstra 17. For a room for three or four people, you'll pay about 400 D here. The station closes from midnight till 5 a.m., and if you try hanging around the police give you a hard time, so take bus 53 from the station, walk up Nemanijina and turn left at Kneza Milosa out to its terminus, and camp out in the forest.

EATING AND NIGHTLIFE

For both activities the Skadarlija district is best. There are plenty of places to eat cheaply, but avoid stopping off for just a drink in cafés, as prices are high. There are enough stalls selling snacks dotted round Skadarlija to get a meal together as you walk, and there are street performances and music and dancing in most of the restaurants in this part.

Montenegro

South of Dubrovnik is the varied region of Montenegro. The train services are restricted, and to get to the interesting places you really have to resort to buses. However, if you want to try and see some of Montenegro, the main line to concentrate on is the one from

Belgrade to Bar, which runs via TITOGRAD. Bar itself has nothing to commend it, and the only real reason to stay on the train and endure the 8-hour journey is to see the scenery en route, especially the Moraca Canyon which you reach after Titograd. Again, Titograd isn't much of a place to stop at. In fact it's deeply depressing and the only justification for travelling there is to see the mountains.

Macedonia

This is one of the most backward regions of Europe, and the pleasure of seeing a primitive land such as this is greatly diminished by the many inconveniences you'll have to put up with: hardly any trains, and expect great problems with eating and sleeping. If you're one of the brave ones on the Belgrade–Athens run, you'll pass through SKOPJE, the capital of the region. Unless you're feeling really grotty and don't think you could make it straight down to Athens, don't break your journey in Skopje. It gets 9 out of 10 for being unattractive, unfriendly and uninteresting but, to be fair, the recent tragic earthquake has a lot to do with this. If you're staying the night, try Studentski Dom, Kuzman Josifonski (Tel. 235360).

The area to head for in Macedonia is LAKE OHRID, along the Albanian border. From Skopje take the train to Kicevo or Bitola, then the bus to Ohrid. The draw here is the unspoilt beauty of the lake and hills. Tourist information is at Partizanska (open 7 a.m.–8 p.m.), and they'll help you out with accommodation.

ACKNOWLEDGEMENTS

We would like to thank the following people for their support and cooperation throughout this project: Gerry James (the 'Inter Rail King'), Gill Edwards and Tony Stone of British Rail, Terry Williams and Ian Wiseman of Transalpino, Chris Potts and Malcolm Clark; and Dick Whitfield for his work on the Hungarian chapter. Also a special thanks to Julia Bennett and Eva Licciardello, and Syd, Katie's long-suffering husband, who helped collate our illegible manuscript right up to the eleventh hour. Last but not least, our thanks to our families for their kindness and encouragement, without which this book would not have been possible.

Each year we receive dozens and dozens of letters from you, the readers, telling us of your euroracing experiences, and how you found the book. Without your help we would find it very difficult to keep abreast of all the changes in all 26 countries, so please keep up the good work. We try to acknowledge each letter individually, but sometimes it gets hard, and between trips, meeting publishing deadlines and organizing future research trips some people may wait longer than we'd ideally like for their personal 'thank you'. This year your response has been terrific, and to those of you who wrote especially detailed letters we'd like to take this opportunity to acknowledge your contribution: J. Durrant of Chingford, London; Lars Schmitz-Eggen from Berg. Gladbach, Germany; Anne Berry of Market Harborough, Leicestershire; Chris Kyprianou of Leicester; Jane Pavitt of Merstham, Surrey; Kenneth Kennery of Blanney, County Cork; Ian Fleming of Inverness; and Asher Thompson of Cheltenham.
Please keep writing to us.